MODERN CHINESE RULES OF ORDER: PARADOX OF LAW AND ECONOMICS

Modern Chinese Rules of Order: Paradox of Law and Economics

Ulric Killion

Nova Science Publishers, Inc.
New York

For permission to use material from this book please contact us:
Telephone 631-231-7269; Fax 631-231-8175
Web Site: http://www.novapublishers.com

LIBRARY OF CONGRESS CATALOGING-IN-PUBLICATION DATA

Killion, Ulric.
Modern Chinese rules of order : paradox of law and economics / Ulric Killion.
p. cm.
Includes bibliographical references and index.
ISBN-13: 978-1-60021-837-8 (hardcover : alk. paper)
ISBN-10: 1-60021-837-7 (hardcover : alk. paper)
1. Law reform--China. 2. China--Economic policy. 3. Law and economics. 4. Justice, Administration of--China 5. China--Politics and government. I. Title.
KNQ470.K55 2007
340'.30951--dc22 2007022578

Published by Nova Science Publishers, Inc. ✦ New York

CONTENTS

PREFACE

In the new millennium, China faces many new challenges, as equally true of the "other" world as it increasingly intertwines with its burgeoning economic growth, and even in some cases grows increasingly dependent on its economic growth. For many, from some Western countries to even some ASEAN countries, and other developed and developing countries, a question of our times is whether the opening of China's economy some twenty-eight years ago is a good or bad consequence. One only needs to visit the United States and other Western countries and cultures to find that there is a distinctive Western perception regarding China's economic rise and growing geopolitical power. While the viewpoints regarding China appear varied and different, there is still the commonality of a problematic "China threat." Then there is Mainland China and the problematic "Western threat," though, admittedly, the official media never mentions this equally difficult phenomenon and consequence. All of this drives East-West relations toward tenuous rather than optimality.

While Western perceptions of China seem many and varied, they are actually limited conceptualizations, because the typical Westerner will never set foot on the shores of the mainland. Tourists, corporate executives and politicians may briefly visit, but by seeing China only so briefly one does not begin to know and understand China. The exceptional foreign diplomats; Western business persons, managers and entrepreneurs; and some foreign experts and teachers, who reside in China for a substantial period, typically enjoy a lifestyle well above the average Chinese citizen, and routinely reside in a foreign complex or a residence of foreigners. For foreign experts and teachers at various universities, the same observation is more or less true, because upon their arrival at a university many search out the safe haven of a lifestyle that parallels Western culture and society, such as upscale Xintiandi in Shanghai, while spending only one or two semesters in China. Conversely, there are the expatriates, who live in China for a substantial period, who live among the Chinese people and actually experience some aspects of "real" life in China. Someone once remarked that only by living in a different culture for a period of three to four years can one, actually, begin to know and understand a different culture.

For Westerners, there are consequences that attach to this lack of knowing and understanding. For instance, in the United States, the typical citizen shows small concern for China and issues of economic reforms, legal reforms, political liberalization, geopolitical posturing, modern military modernization and other related issues. The typical U.S. citizen when speaking of China seems spellbound by the media's weaving of a "China threat," especially in terms of the outsourcing of U.S. jobs, though politically motivated and presenting the worst of reasons to approve or disapprove of modern China. Outside of the primordial concerns of the "China threat" and outsourcing of American jobs, there is small concern for China. In this respect, though sad, the typical U.S. citizen, and even seemingly more so than his/her European counterpart, continues to live in a world that resembles a world of old such as that of early U.S. isolationists. It is an unrealistic, perhaps even selfish, view of the world. No doubt, an existentialistic reality that dares not, nor wants, to venture outside the solace of a safe haven of comfort. The latter produces the problematic proclivity of mostly confining China-concerns to the U.S. government and its foreign policy agenda, corporate heads and executives, and the halls of academia, while leaving those who stand for election primarily focusing on the "China threat" and outsourcing of U.S.-jobs.

As for Mainland China, the viewpoint of the typical Chinese citizen is, actually, no different. The generation that felt the blunt of Mao's socialism, the infamous Cultural Revolution and then the tragedy of Tiananmen Square have been relegated, like their U.S. counterparts, to an existentialistic existence with the primordial concerns of survival and simply "making life" controlling their outlooks on life, especially life outside the mainland. They, like their Western counterparts, are hardly concerned with the issues of economic reforms, law reforms, political liberalization, geopolitical posturing, modern military modernization and other related issues. There is, of course, always the exception to the rule such as those who want the U.S. to get out of Iraq, quit starting those small wars and steer clear of the Beijing-Taipei controversy. As for perceptions of the United States, many would actually like to immigrate (or emigrate) to the United States, while others, and contrary to many Western perceptions and biases, have no desire to immigrate (or emigrate) to Western countries. Most Chinese citizens, like U.S. citizens and their pride of country, are proud of being Chinese and equally proud of their country.

Otherwise, in Mainland China, there is, generally, toleration of foreigners. The toleration of foreigners is not meant to cast the typical citizen in a bad light, because the typical citizen, if one is every truly graced with the opportunity of knowing him/her, is kind, generous, honest and all of the adjectives that generally describe a good person. If one has truly lived in the now more open modern China for a substantial period, then he/she knows that they can, generally, go anywhere they please, walk down any street in any neighborhood, and not fear the same threats when walking down the "wrong" streets in urban America. Modern China, admittedly, is not without crime; rather it seems less obvious and less threatening than in many Western cultures and societies, especially the United States. However, in the United States, this same citizen enjoys the inalienable right to stand for election, and thereby contribute to peaceful transitions in government and changes in government policies such as reducing crimes on the streets via liberal democracy. Problems of modern China's image are predominantly crimes against humanity such as Tibet (1989), Tiananmen Square (1989) and, recently, selling weapons to Nepal security forces and Myanmar's military junta. The CCP's (Communist Party) use (or misuse) of the power of government may pose the greatest threat to internal or domestic peace, rather than the threat of crimes on the streets.

The issues of China and legal reforms, economic reforms, political liberalization, geopolitical posturing, modern military modernization and other related issues are presenting growing concerns for many experts and authority, which is mostly due to China's growing economic prowess. Many Western experts and authority hail China for its burgeoning economic growth and seemingly now open economy, or perhaps more accurately, now more open economy. China is still transitioning from socialist planned (or command) economy to market economy. Many also anticipate, or at least hope for, a change in modern China's social-political environment. However, it is a hope that fails to correspond with the reality of China and its socialist-political polity or Marxist-regime, or even Marxist-inspired constitutionalism and rule of law. Moreover, this book is not about praising the typical Chinese citizen, or complaining about the typical U.S. citizen and his/her primordial concerns of the "China threat" and outsourcing of U.S.-jobs. In particular, the typical Chinese citizen simply bears mentioning, because it is important to know and understand that he/she is not government, but a subject of a government that does not allow him/her to stand for election. While this typical Chinese citizen finds his/her own peace in life, after all, he/she must survive, he/she does so under the influence of a Marxist-regime, the Communist Party and its one-party rule. For China's citizenry, the influence of a Marxist-regime is more or less important; it simply depends on the circumstances. One recalls a Chinese business person or entrepreneur who joins the Communist Party for selfish or individual reasons, which are the advantages of belonging to the party such as contacts, networking, access to capital, and other opportunities or benefits. He was an individual mostly in search of business opportunities, and as he tells it, party affiliation has been the avenue to opportunities that would not exist, except for party affiliation. Consequently, the reality of life in modern China's social-political environment is, in part, reflective of the reality of Marxist rule or one-party CCP rule, which, actually, often dictates modern rules of order. This does not mean that Marxist rule or one-party CCP rule, in reality, dictates every aspect of the daily lives of China's citizenry, because what remains of a distinctive Chinese culture and society, perhaps even unconsciously, still drives and influences modern social order. In modern China, traditional culture continues to bear relevancy, because traditional culture continues to exert its influence.

Then there is the question of the inevitable result of the influence of Marxism on this distinctive culture and society. More specifically, it is a question of how continuing Marxist rule or one-party CCP rule will, ultimately, affects modern reforms, especially legal reforms. The reality of life in modern society is that one-party CCP rule is incongruent with the individual and what, in essence, makes the Chinese individual, colloquially speaking, "tick," the ontology of this individual, which is the continuing influence of an undeniable ontological base in tradition. While the individual Chinese citizen may be both proud of being Chinese and proud of his/her country, this does not necessarily manifest a pride contingent on Marxist rule or one-party CCP rule. Notwithstanding the exception to the rule, what the individual Chinese citizen shares with his expatriate friend is not a pride in the history and accomplishments of one-party CCP rule, nor the achievements manifest in building a modern *xiaokang* and harmonious socialist society and world; rather it is the cultural heritage of China; i.e. the historical sites and history of a culture and society 5,000 years old or older

The latter, admittedly, presents a seemingly innocuous paradoxical interrelationship between those governed or ruled, being China's citizenry and their ontological base in tradition, and those who govern or rule, being Marxists, communists or socialists, or, simply, one-party CCP rule. However, it is a seemingly innocuous paradoxical interrelationship deserving attention, because the paradoxical interrelationship between traditional culture and society, and Marxism, communism or socialism will, inevitably, either inhibit or enhance much-needed modern reforms, especially legal reforms. The purpose of this book is to explore this paradoxical interrelationship, and also explore the attendant paradoxical interrelationship between Western universalism and traditional culture and society; while also exploring the paradoxical interrelationship between Western universalism and Marxism. In the pursuit of knowing and understanding China, this book, actually, explores both the complementary and paradoxical interrelationships between these sources of order. Moreover, this book places emphasis on modern legal reforms because the directional development of China's legal order has national, interregional and international implications, which affect the growth and prosperity of both China and the world's economy. The paradoxical interrelationships between these sources of order, effectively, render much-needed legal reforms increasingly more difficult to implement.

This book explores these complementary and paradoxical interrelationships or interrelated sources of order by engaging the disciplines or sciences of philosophy, history, politics, law, economics, sociology, international relations and other fields of study. For proponents of the idea that Marxism and post-Marxism are only the subjects of theoretical discourses in the halls of academia, or those praising China's progress in legal reforms who are either unaware or willing to deny that Marxism is still the subject of theoretical discourses within and without the halls of both Chinese academia and Western academia, it is a hope that this books reveals or redirects attention to the pitfalls of modern Marxism in China, whether attributable to the CCP's rhetoric, ideologies or actions. In the end, and borrowing from the wisdom of Fareed Zakaria, in *The Future of Freedom: Illiberal Democracy at Home and Abroad* (2003), because, historically, the rule of law and a liberal market economy precede liberal democracy and universal suffrage, the rule of law can only be the result of an evolution of legal systems and not the starting point, as the CCP attempts to do so by, simply, enacting new legal propositions or laws.

Ulric Killion
June 23, 2007

Chapter 1

IDEOLOGIZING XIAOKANG

1.1. SOCIAL ORDER, UTOPIA AND PERPETUAL PEACE

This book addresses the issues of China, social order, and law and economics. The separable, yet inseparable, concepts of social order, legal order and economic order present a modern socio-econo-legal order fraught with complementary and paradoxical interrelationships between competing sources of order. These competing sources of order are not limited to the spatial confines of modern China's political community, rather presents unique phenomenon of contrasting economic orders and legal orders, within and without its borders or jurisdiction, widely ranging from traditional culture (primarily traditional Confucianism), Marxism, to Western universalism. The competing economic orders are traditional culture, Marxist political economy and Western economic liberalism. The competing legal orders are traditional Chinese jurisprudence, Marxist legal theory, and Western rule of law, such as Anglo-American rule of law, German *Rechtsstaat* and French *État de droit*. These competing sources of order present a phenomenom that transcends and challenges the rigid spatial confines of modern Marxist rule and renders ongoing legal and economic reforms, including greater political liberalization, increasingly more difficult to implement. For China, a persistent problem of attempting to finalize the localization of Marxism to the realities of traditional culture and society is the fundamental and exclusive causal influence of economic determinism in defining and confining the development of social, political, legal, religious, artistic and other philosophical forms. In the end, we come to discover that for modern legal and economic reforms, including greater political liberalization, and the search for optimal models of reform and moving East-West relations from tenuous toward optimality, the greater issue remains the amenability and complementarity of traditional culture to Western culture and not traditional culture to modern Marxism.

The issues of competing sources of order presents the succinct question of whether traditional culture, like Hugo Grotius's (1538-1645) proposed reduction of *Christian* dogmas to those necessary for ethics,[1] is amenable to a reduction to Western *ethos*, universalism or

[1] Timothy Samuel Shah, Making the Christian World Safe for Liberalism: From Grotius to Rawls, Vol. 71, Issue 1, 121-139 The Pol. Qtrly (2000).

liberalism. While the forces of social, legal and economic order, generally, influence the directional development of modern reforms, China's modern socio-econo-legal order still presents unique phenomenon of contrasting economic and legal orders. Notwithstanding inherent problems of modern Marxism, modern Chinese society still presents a force of influence requiring the critical acceptance of modern reforms by traditional culture, or China's ontological base in tradition, when seeking to reconcile or merge reforms with Chinese society. Complementary and paradoxical interrelationships between social, legal and economic orders, especially competing legal and economic orders, produce conflicting forces of influence. Problematic are the evolving paradoxical interrelationships, which effectively render much-needed reforms increasingly more difficult to implement. Indeed, in terms of legal and economic reforms, the greater issue remains the amenability of traditional culture to Western culture and not traditional culture to modern Marxism.

In modern China, there are competing sources of order, stemming from traditional culture, Marxism and Western universalism or liberalism, which present competing and distinctively different versions of a perfect order, utopia and perpetual peace. For traditional culture, Marxism and Western universalism, there is the shared commonality of the pursuit of a perfect order, utopia or perpetual peace as translated by scholars and philosophers from antiquity, to modernity or post-modernity. However, the measure of a perfect order, utopia or perpetual peace would differ among these sources of order, and their respective scholars and philosophers from the past, to the present, thereby continuing to demonstrate the inherent complementary and paradoxical interrelationships between these competing sources of order.

From Chinese antiquity, there is the tale of a utopia of peace and harmony, which is variously described as: *Tao huayuan* (*Land of Peach Blossom*) and *Shiwai taoyuan* (*Land of the eternal peace far from the maddening crowd*, *Place of refuge*, *Secluded valley* or *The peach land outside the world*). The legend of *Tao huayuan* (or *Shiwai taoyuan*) came to be associated with the word (or characters) for utopia. The origin of this classic poem is the poet, Tao Yuan-ming (Tao Qing, Yuan-ming or Yuan-ling, AD 365-427, from the Eastern Jin to Liu-Song of Southern Dynasty). In this poem, Tao Yuan-ming created an imagery and isolated world, which was an ideal world of peace, harmony and happiness, thus, the ideal *Tao huayuan* (or *Shiwai taoyuan*) or utopia. The poem is about a lost fisherman that comes upon a large peach grove, and after entering the peach grove, he walks until reaching the other end, when he discovers a small opening in a mountain. After entering the small opening in the mountain, the fisherman discovers a path that he walks, which eventually leads him to discover a lost world. What the fisherman discovers is a world of beautiful lakes, with a level plain that stretches far and wide, and many houses and homesteads neatly arranged. He sees fertile soil, picturesque ponds, and mulberry and bamboo grooves, crisscross paths extending in all direction, cocks crowing and dogs barking in return, and people going back and forth cultivating the land. He sees the attires of men and women are exactly as those outside and yellow-tressed old folks and youngsters with flowing hair living in self-contentment. After the surprise of seeing the fisherman, they ask from whence he came, he answers, and then they invite him to their homes, where they prepare wine, slaughter chickens and cook for him.[2] As for the inhabitants, they were descendents of ancestors that had earlier fled the

[2] The Stories Behind 100 Chinese Idioms (Beijing: Sinolingua, 1999). Tao Yuan-ming, Notes on Tao Hua Yuan or Record of Peach Blossom Fountainhead, http://www.bobhuang.com/essays/essay30.htm. Fei xiang "shi wai tao yuan" ("Waijiao guan kan shijie" Xi wai congshu/Liu xinsheng, Pan zheng xiu zhu (Cheng du sichuan renmin chubanshe, 2004).

turbulence of the Qin Dynasty (221-206 B.C.). They were isolated from the outside world in their utopia and did not desire contact with the other world. When the fisherman eventually departed from this secluded place, the inhabitants requested that he not tell the outside world about them. Upon returning home, the fisherman, despite their wishes, advised the local magistrate of his adventure. When the fisherman and others tried to find this *Tao huayuan* (or *Shiwai taoyuan*) or utopia, they could not find it.

The poem *Tao huayuan* (or *Shiwai taoyuan*) draws a picture of an ideal utopia during the reign, from AD 265 to 290, of Emperor Wu of the Jin Dynasty (AD 265-420). A consequence of Tao Yuan-ming being born during the Jin Dynasty would be the contagion influence of the then fashionable ideals of Zhuang Zi, which were primarily important as an extension of Taoism (or Daoism). It was also a period of political chaos, which presented a political economy environment diametrically opposed to the ideal of a *Tao huayuan* (or *Shiwai taoyuan*) or utopia. Tao Yuan-ming came from a family closely knitted to the world of officialdom in antiquity. During this earlier period, both his grandfather and father are feudal officials, who yielded to the influence of traditional Confucianism. During his earlier years, Tao Yuan-ming following his father and grandfather also served as a member of officialdom in antiquity. Tao Yuan-ming, a native of the district of Chai Sang in Shun Yang, serves, though for brief period, as a magistrate of Pengze County, which was east of present day Hukou County, in Jiangxi Province. His brief tenure in officialdom, as a magistrate, is actually associated with the idiom of *bu wei wu dou mi zheyao* (won't kowtow for five *dou* of rice). Tao's short tenure as magistrate is attributable to his failure to extend expected courtesies to a senior official that came to inspect Hukou County. In response to an aide prompting him to make haste and don his best dress, Tao Yuan-ming reportedly retorts, "I will not dress myself up and kowtow to this pretentious bumpkin just for five *dou* of rice (referring to his salary as an official)." The following day Tao surrenders his official seal and returns home. In later years, "won't kowtow for five *dou* of rice" came to describe persons of high ideals that will not humble themselves for material gain.

There are similarities and dissimilarities between Tao Yuan-ming's notions of an ideal place to live or *Tao huayuan* (or *Shiwai taoyuan*) or utopia, and West centric concepts of utopia, including a Marxian utopia. For instance, Sir Thomas More (1478-1535), in his classic *Utopia* (*De optimo reipublicae statu deque nova insula Utopia, Louvain* 1516)[3] or his earlier conceptualization of utopianism, essentially, described a utopia hardly distinguishable from either Tao Yuan-ming's notions of an ideal place or garden (*huayuan*) to live, or even that of Karl Marx (Karl Heinrich Marx, 1818-1883). Sir Thomas More described a utopia, which was similar to Plato's Republic (Latin: *Res publica*, public matters or the state; Greek: *Politeia* or Constitution) or Plato's ideal state and his search for what is "good," or even perhaps what is a perpetual peace. Thomas More describes a utopia where the inhabitants hold all things in common, including private property. As in Tao Yuan-ming's description of houses and homesteads all neatly arranged, Thomas More also described towns and houses on the same plane. For Thomas More, and not unlike Tao Yuan-ming, all of the streets, houses or homes were exactly alike, including one door for the street and one door for the garden, and all of the inhabitants of this garden dressed alike. However, the dissimilarities override the similarities between these models of utopia or perpetual peace.

---

[3] Thomas More, Utopia (1516) (Pat Turner, trans.) (Penguin, 2003). Plato, Republic, (G.M.A. Grube, trans.) (Hackett Pub, 1992).

Tao Yuan-ming's utopia is distinguishable from the utopia described by both Sir Thomas More and Karl Marx. While Sir Thomas More's *Utopia* (1516) dealt with issues of the then new statesmanship or Machiavellian statesmanship as reflected in Machiavelli's (Niccolό di Bernardo dei Machiavelli, 469-1527) famous classic *The Prince* (*Il Principe*, 1515), he still addressed the issues of a utopian commonwealth. Although More's utopian commonwealth focused on the economic evils of England, his utopia would be a Christian undertaken that would be "at bottom inspired by the Sermon on the Mount." Thomas More's utopia is a social structure built by man, but based on Christianity, where the inhabitants hold all goods in common, there is no money and people spend their day joyfully doing good deeds for one another. As described by J. Bronowski and Bruce Mazlish, "More, who lectured on Augustine's City of God in his youth, wanted to build a City of Man, which God might not be ashamed to inhabit for a time." Saint Augustine (Aurelius Augustinus or Augustine of Hippo, 354-430), in his ancient classic *The City of God* (*De Civitate Dei*, 426), described a conflict between the City of God and City of man, which would end with the City of God being victorious. For Saint Augustine, God's real purpose in creating the world was to build a heavenly city, thus, rendering moments of history as progress toward a grand plan. In addition, Bertrand Russell (1872-1970), in his classic *A History of Western Philosophy* (1945), critiques Thomas More's utopia as being more liberal than communist or socialist. Russell writes, "More's utopia was in many ways, astonishingly liberal. I am not thinking so much of the preaching of communism, which was in the tradition of many religious movements. I am thinking rather of what is said, about war, about religion, and religious toleration, against the wanton killing of animals..., and in favor of a mild criminal law... It must be admitted, however, that life in More's Utopia, as in most others, would be intolerably dull. Diversity is essential to happiness, and in Utopia, there is hardly any. This is a defect of all planned social systems, actual as well as imaginary."[4]

Tao Yuan-ming's utopia is also distinguishable from Karl Marx's utopia, but for different reasons. It is only during Marx's last disposition for a cosmopolitan (*cosmopoliticium*) society that his utopia resembles Sir Thomas More's utopia, by furnishing a religion hope for the future generations of Marxists. However, and limiting the religion hope for future Marxists, "the misgivings of existing socialism was tolerated for the promised solace of future utopia." A Marxian ideal utopia is problematic because it promotes a statist society, while contractorily promising via ideology a communist ideal "classless society where the state has withered away." While anarchists advocated the complete elimination of the state, Marx perceived the necessity of a transitional socialist state, such as a dictatorship of the proletariat before the emergence of an ideal society or Marxian utopia. For instance, in modern China, and according to the 2005 China White Paper on Building Political Democracy, "China's democracy is a democracy guaranteed by the people's democratic dictatorship."[5]

However, Karl Marx's ideal society or Marxian utopia, supposedly, did not have a state with oppressive authority. Marx, in *Critique of the Gotha Programme* (*Kritik des Gothaer*

[4] Nicolo Machiavelli, The Prince (1515) (Luigi Ricci trans.) (New Amer. Library of World Lit., 1952). J. Bronowski & Bruce Mazlish, The Western Intellectual Tradition from Leonardo to Hegel 44-51 (Harper & Row, 1975). Saint, Bishop of Hippo Augustine, City of God (G.R. Evans, ed. & Henry Bettenson, trans.) (Penguin, 2003). Bertrand Russell, A History of Western Philosophy 519-521 (Simon & Schuster, 1945).

[5] Sam Ghandchi, Marxist Thought and Monism, Iranscope, Dec 3, 2003. China White Paper, Building of Political Democracy in China, State Council (Government Beijing, 2005). Karl Marx, Critique of the Gotha Programme (1875), In Marx/Engels Selected Works, Vol. III, 13-30 (Moscow: Progress Pub, 1970).

Programms, 1875), observed, "In a higher phase of communist society, after the enslaving subordination of the individual to the division of labor, and therewith also the antithesis between mental and physical labor, has vanished; after labor has become not only a means of life but life's prime want; after the productive forces have also increased with the all-around development of the individual, and all the springs of co-operative wealth flow more abundantly -- only then can the narrow horizon of bourgeois right be crossed in its entirety and society inscribe on its banners: From each according to his ability, to each according to his needs!"[6] Marx still realized that the administrative function of the state should remain intact. Marx's *Critique of the Gotha Programme* presented the critical question, "what transformation will the state undergo in communist society?" The same question alternatively stated is, "what social functions will remain in existence there that are analogous to present state functions?" In criticism and in answer, Marx wrote, "Between capitalist and communist society there lies the period of the revolutionary transformation of the one into the other. Corresponding to this is also a political transition period in which the state can be nothing but *the revolutionary dictatorship of the proletariat*." Marx criticized the Gotha program for failing to deal with the latter issue and for failing to adequately address the future of the Communist Party. He wrote, "Now the program does not deal with this nor with the future state of communist society." It was tantamount to failing to protect the proletariat and Communist Party, including a future utopia that Marx and Friedrich Engels (1820-1895) envision in *The Communist Manifesto* (*Das Manifest der Kommunistischen Partei*, 1848), which Marx further develops in *Capital* (*Das Kapital, Kritik der politischen Ökonomie*, 1867).

As observed by Friedrich Engels, in *Socialism: Utopian and Scientific* (*Herrn Eugen Dühring's Umwälzung der Wissenschaft*, 1878), "Once more, only the abolition of the capitalist character of modern industry can bring us out of this new vicious circle, can resolve this contradiction in modern industry, which is constantly reproducing itself."[7] However, and despite what is hailed as scientific socialism or modern communism, which Engels deemed an essentially German product, and Marxian ideals of utopia, the greater tragedy of Marx's proposed utopia remains the resulting tragedy of the state determining the ability and needs of the people. The Marxian rhetoric excerpted from *Critique of the Gotha Programme* (1875), "from each according to his ability, to each according to his needs," still bears relevancy to modern China's social order. An example is a policy statement of the 1997 Fifteenth CPC National Congress, "that 'distribution according to work' be combined with 'distribution according to the factors of production.'"

Tao Yuan-ming's ideal life, in *Tao huayuan* (or *Shiwai taoyuan*), represents a struggle between traditional Confucianism (learn and use theory) and Taoism (return to nature). More particularly, Tao Yuan-ming presents an ideal life reflective of Taoism and its return to nature thesis. Tao Yuan-ming, essentially, constructed an exogenous Garden (*huayuan*) of Eden standing outside the "other" world and reality. It is Tao Yuan-ming's manifestation of his ideal place to live and the ideal *Tao huayuan* (or *Shiwai taoyuan*) or utopia. For this reason, in the Chinese language, etymology and content, the words (or characters) *Tao huayuan* and

---

[6] Karl Marx, Critique of the Gotha Programme, 17, 27-28 (Peking: Foreign Language Press, 1972).

[7] Friedrich Engels, Herrn Eugen Dühring's Umwälzung der Wissenschaft, Geschrieben Sept. 1876 bis Juni 1878, (Anti-Dühring Herr Eugen Dühring's Revolution in Science or Socialism: Utopian and Scientific), 1-7, 100-101(1892) (Peking: Foreign Language Press, 1975). Chi Fulin, China The New Stage of Reform 8-9 (Beijing: Foreign Language Press, 2004).

Shiwai taoyuan became snynomous with utopia. *Tao huayuan* (or *Shiwai taoyuan*) represent both traditional Confucianism (and its realism) and Taoism (and its romanticism). The latter combination of traditional Confucianism and Taoism, or realism and romanticism, went against the conventionalism of Tao Yuan-ming's era. A problem inherited from antiquity and continuing in the new millennium is traditional culture going against the conventionalism of an era.

For these competing sources of order, the search for a perfect order, utopia and even a perpetual peace is, inevitably, the pursuit of the ideal "good" or the greater good (*summum bonum*) for these respective sources of order. The history of Western civilization, especially Medieval Europe, reveals a search for the ideal "good," which directly links to Christianity and the search for "good" and happiness in Heaven. Greek civilization tried to find this ideal "good" on earth, but failed to do so, and modern Western civilization continues the pursuit for this ideal "good" and happiness on earth. Saint Augustine sought a City of God (*Civitate Dei*) and Francis Bacon (1561-1626), in the quest for a Baconian hope of creating abundance on earth or scientific utilitarian utopia, sought his *Kingdom of Man* (*The Interpretation of Nature and the Kingdom of Man*, 1620).[8] Bacon writes, "Man, being the servant and interpreter of Nature, can do and understand so much and so much only as he has observed in fact or in thought of the course of nature: beyond this he neither knows anything nor can do anything."

Then there is traditional Chinese culture, which, despite Tao Yuan-ming's notions of an ideal place to live or *Tao huayuan* (or *Shiwai taoyuan*), seems to have sought neither an ideal "good" in Heaven, nor on earth. Fung Yu-lan (Feng Youlan, 1895-1990) wrote, "China, ever since the disappearance of the 'nature' line of her national thought, has devoted all of spiritual energies to another line, that is, to find good and happiness directly in the human mind. In other words, Medieval Europe under Christianity tried to know God and prayed for His help; Greece tried, and Modern Europe is trying to know nature and to conquer, to control it; but China tried to know what is within ourselves, and to find there perpetual peace." It is perhaps the same critical essence of traditional culture that would later be espoused by Zhang Zai (Chang Tsai, 1020-1077), as an early pioneer of the philosophical movement during the Sung Dynasty (960-1279), which is variously known as the Sung Confucian Revival, Study of the Way, Philosophy of Song and Neo-Confucianism, when he "put forward the difference between the knowledge of virtue and of seeing and hearing. The knowledge of seeing and hearing is from contact with matter, but not knowledge of virtue, which does not arise from seeing and hearing." In terms of the history of Neo-Confucianism, Zhang Zai would join subjective thought (Taoist school) with moral content (traditional Confucianism).[9]

An ideal perfect order, utopia or perpetual peace in antiquity is also gravely distinguishable from the perpetual peace pursued by a Western universalizing cosmopolitanism. In terms of Western theorizations, an ideal peace or perpetual peace would be defined throughout the ages and by various sources, from Dante (Durante degli Alighieri, 1265-1321) and his *De Monarchia* (vision of a restored Roman world empire, 1313), Hugo Grotius (1538-1645) and his *On the laws of war and peace* (*De jure belli ac pacis libri tres*,

---

[8] Francis Bacon, Novum Organum: Aphorisms Concerning the Interpretation of Nature and the Kingdom of Man (1620). Alastair McIntosh, Ecofeminist Critique of Science Policy, Environmental Values, 5:1, 3-30 (1996).

[9] Fung Yu-lan, Selected Philosophical Writings of Fung Yu-lan 591-93 (Beijing: Foreign Language Press, 1998). Cheng, Weili, The Knowledge of Virtue and Moral Ontology, Chapter XV, In Philosophy and Modernization in China Chinese Philosophical Studies XIII (Liu Fangtong, Huang Songjie & George F. McLean, eds.), Cultural Heritage and Contemporary Change Series III, Asia, Vol. 13 (1997).

1625), Leibnitz (Gottfried Wilhelm Freiherr von Leibnitz, 1646-1716) and his "collection of documents of the law of peoples" (*Corpus Juris Gentium* or *Codex juris gentium diplomaticus*, 1693), to the thoughts of Immanuel Kant (1724-1804) in *Perpetual Peace: A Philosophical Sketch* (*Zum ewign Frieden: Ein philosophischer Entwurf*, 1795) and his hopes for a universal state of humankind (*jus cosmopoliticium*), and many other great thinkers and scholars from the past, to the present day.[10] All of these sources sought to create a detailed plan for the foundation of an ideal peace, lasting peace or perpetual peace.

The issues of utopianism and perpetual peace, though now couched in terms of a complete and perfect *xiaokang* society and harmonious socialist society, still bear relevancy for a modern Chinese society. Modern conceptualizations of *xiaokang* and harmonious society, consequently, present issues of genuine conventionalism and legitimacy of modern rules of order. A problem exacerbated by the inherent problems of complementary and paradoxical sources of order, such as social, legal and economic orders, and further exacerbated by the consequence of modern social order, or rules of order, manifesting a conflict, struggle or paradoxical interrelationship between Marxism and traditional culture. Modern conceptualizations borrowed from antiquity, such as *xiaokang* and harmonious society, once explored in greater depth may go against the conventionalism of the new era or new millennium, being the continuing influence of Marxism.

1.2. Culture, Marxism and Building Xiaokang

The ideal utopia in antiquity presents issues of the complementary and paradoxical interrelationship between traditional culture and Marxism. In modern China, during the past few years, there have been debates concerning the critical issues of traditional culture, and modern Marxism in practice rather than in theory. In particular, there have been two key debates concerning traditional Confucianism: First, a 2004 debate focused on *dujing*, the study of the traditional Confucius classics. Second, in 2005, the focus of the public debate shifted to *guoxue*, the study of classics by the Chinese masters. The 2005 debate is sparked by Renmin University of China (RUC, *Zhongguo Renmin Daxue*) establishing a school for *guoxue*. During the public debates on *dujing* and *guoxue*, a Chinese scholar, Jiang Qing, is subject to harsh public criticism for advocating the revival of traditional Confucianism. In 2006, an especially harsh criticism of Jiang Qing appeared in an editorial in the *China Daily*.[11] A primary focus of the public criticism is directed to Jiang Qing's idea of reviving *Rujia* (literally, Confucian school). Jiang Qing contends that traditional Confucianism is the core of Chinese civilization, including political, cultural and religious institutions of society. Jiang Qing advocates that traditional Confucianism ought to be the cultural consensus and spiritual belief for modern China. Jiang also advocates that resort to traditional Confucianism and, implicitly, its notions of humanity, and potential union of universality and particularity, could solve many of China's pressing political and social crises, including the essentialization of

---

[10] Caspian Richards, A commentary on the 'Perpetual Peace' of Immanuel Kant, Vol. 2, Paideusis-Journal for Interdisciplinary and Cross-Cultural Studies (1999). John Howard Yoder, chapter eight in Chapters in the History of Religiously Rooted NonViolence: A Series of Working Papers of the Joan B. Kroc Inst. for Int'l Peace Studies (1994).

[11] Huang Qing, Confucianism will never be embraced as religion, Jan. 6, 2006, China Daily. Samuel P. Huntington, The Clash of Civilizations and the Remaking of World Order (1996).

difference and dubious conclusion of a clash of civilizations. The editorial-critique claims, though sarcastically, “Jiang is true to his title of *daru* or “big short Confucian” because he followed traditional Confucian teachings by being non-confrontational and pursuing peaceful dialogue, and “his [Jiang Qing] idea of shaping China and the Chinese in a Confucian mold will never happen in reality.” The editorial-critique concludes there are “too many opponents not willing to see Confucian religion in the land.”

There are other debates concerning the critical role of modern Marxism in moving China toward modernity. Chinese academia witnessed a continuing influence, though periodically expanding and contracting, of Marxism in the study of traditional Chinese culture and philosophy. In the new millennium, especially since 2003, the pledge of Chinese philosophers and social scientists to take Marxism as their guide is genuinely advancing from the rhetoric of a pledge to actual practice and application, especially the pursuit of a “new” materialism or dialectical materialism. In terms of Western conventionalism, for this reason and others, proponents of the idea that Marxism and post-Marxism are only the subjects of theoretical discourses in the halls of academia are gravely mistaken.[12] For instance, one Chinese scholar, Fang Keli, hails the late eminent Chinese scholar Zhang Dainian (1909-2004) for his innovations in the field of Chinese philosophy, such as his new materialism created during the 1930s and 1940s, and its relations to Marxism. The same source, regarding the pattern of confrontation and interaction between Chinese philosophy and Western philosophy, including Marxism, writes, “The road of tripartite confluence and synthesis and innovation based on dialectic materialism created by Mr. Zhang [Zhang Dainian] about half a century ago [1930s and 1940s] still serves as a correct and realistic road for Chinese philosophy in its development for the new century. We believe his [Zhang Dainian] successors will do their best and forge ahead along this route for the final realization of the Sinicization of Marxism.”

The problems are obvious, especially the advocacy by the halls of Chinese academia of Marxism, such as the Chinese Academy of Social Sciences, and its Research Academy on Marxism (RAM), which was established in 2005 and intends, “to strengthen Marxist theoretical research, consolidate Marxism’s guiding position in the ideological realm, and uphold and develop Marxism in practice.”[13] There is also the May 2004 *Notice on Further Strengthening Marxist Atheism Research, Propaganda and Education* (*Guanyu jin yi bu jiaqiang Makesi zhuyi wushenlun yanjiu he xuanchuan jiaoyu gongzuo de tongzhi).* The May 2004 notice, which was classified as a secret document, issued jointly by the Department of Propaganda of the Central Committee of the Chinese Communist Party, the Office of the Central Steering Committee on Spiritual Civilization Construction, the Communist Party School of the Central Committee of the CPC, and Ministry of Education, as well as the Academy of Social Science. The May 2004 notice was addressed to the Department of Personnel, Department of Propaganda, and the Office of Spiritual Civilization Construction,

---

[12] Zhou Fan, The Post-Marxist Context, Hebei xuekan, no. 2, (2005). Fang Keli, Zhang Dainian and Chinese Philosophy in the 20th Century, Social Sciences in China (Zhongguo shehui kexue) 52-65 (Aug. 2005). Zhao Xingliang, Is Globalization in Favor of Socialism?, Qiushi, no. 7 (2002). Sun Hui, Marx’s Ontology and Its Significance in Our Times, 29-38 Social Sciences in China (Zhongguo shehui kexue) (spring 2003). Tong Qingbing, Cornerstones of Marxist Literary Theory, Dongjiang xuekan, No. 4 (2004).

[13] Marxist Academy Founded in China, Dec. 26, 2005, China Daily. New Learning Center to Promote Marxist Theory, Cultural Liberalization Inches Forward, China Reform Monitor No. 612, Jan. 13, 2006. Religious Freedom in China, Hearing before the CECC, 108th Congress, 2nd Sess., Nov. 18, 2004. Zhong Xuan Fa [2004] No. 13, Notice on Further Strengthening Marxist Atheism Research, Propaganda and Education, May 27, 2004.

the Communist Party School, and the Department of Education of all provinces, autonomous regions, and metropolitan areas, the Communist Party Committee of all departments, ministries, and commissions of the Communist Party and the state organs, and the general Department of Political Affairs of the People's Liberation Army, with copies also directed to members and alternate members of the Politburo of the Central Committee, Secretary of the Secretariat of the Central Committee, Premier and Vice Premier, and the State Counselors of the State Council. Party officials issue the notice for purpose of further boosting Marxist atheism research, propaganda and education.

In modern China, the paradoxical interrelationship between traditional culture and modern Marxism challenges the socio-econo-legal order. The Chinese Communist Party (CCP, *Zhongguo Gongchandang*) and its ideologies epitomize the complementary or paradoxical interrelationship between these sources of order. In the new millennium, the latter debates concerning traditional culture and Marxism demonstrate that the CCP is employing the political tool of ideology for purposes of addressing both the complementary and paradoxical interrelationship between traditional culture and modern Marxism. The continuing fervor for ideology is evident in the CCP's new ideology of building a *xiaokang* (*xiaokang shehui*, literally meaning a society of small peace or comfort) and a harmonious socialist society. On September 27, 2006, the Chinese Communist Party Central Committee announced that the headline topic for its annual session scheduled for October 2006, the Sixth Plenary Session of the 16th Central Committee of the Communist Party of China (CPC), will be the major issues regarding the building of a harmonious socialist society.[14] As observed by one Chinese academic, Zhang Qingxiong, "the Confucian society of small tranquility (*xiao kang*), namely, a social market economy with the Confucian ideal of great harmony is the future of China." Further, Zhang proclaims, "In a market economy the masses have a spontaneous tendency towards individualism. Therefore, the collective spirit should be energetically encouraged. The ideal of the great harmony is the fountainhead of the collective spirit. Perhaps the society of great harmony (the Communist society) is always a utopia, but without this utopia as a moral force we cannot successfully and peacefully construct the realistic society of Small Tranquility." The goal of building a harmonious socialist society is inseparable from the goal of building a *xiaokang*. Moreover, understanding the goals of building a *xiaokang* and building a harmonious socialist society lends understanding to the complementary and paradoxical interrelationship between traditional culture and modern Marxism or, simply, one-party CCP rule and its self-chosen rationale principle.

On November 14, 2002, China's governing polity, the CCP, during the 16th Communist Party Congress (CPC), announces a goal of building a *xiaokang* (well-off) society in an all-round way, as a major part of building socialism with Chinese characteristics.[15] An excerpt from the text of the November 14, 2002 Resolution of the 16th National Congress of the

---

[14] Party sets the agenda for key meeting, Sept. 17, 2006, China Daily. Zhang Qingxiong, Marxism and Traditional Chinese Philosophy, Chapter IX, In Economic Ethics and Chinese Culture, Chinese Philosophical Studies, XIV (Liu Fangtong, Huang Songjie & George F. McLean, eds.), Cultural Heritage and Contemporary Change Series III, Asia, Vol. 14 (1997).

[15] Antoaneta Bezlova, China: The battle against social inequality, Dec 18, 2002, Asia Times. Hu Jintao Values Role of Constitution in Progress, Dec. 5, 2002, Xinhua. Gong Li, China seeks to promote a harmonious world, Feb. 21, 2006, China Daily. Documents of the 16th National Congress of the Communist Party of China (CPC), (Beijing: Foreign Language Press, 2002) (Resolution of the 16th National Congress of the CPC on the Report of the 15th Central Committee of the CPC (Adopted by the 16th National Congress of the CPC on Nov. 14, 2002)).

Communist Party of China on the Report of the 15th Central Committee of the Communist Party of China reads, "The whole Party should hold high the banner of Deng Xiaoping Theory, fully act on the important thought of the 'Three Represents,' carry forward our cause into the future, keep pace with the times, build a well-off society in an all-around way, speed up socialist modernization, and work hard to create a new situation in building socialism with Chinese characteristics." The latter, simply, translates into building the country into a *xiaokang* or moderately well-off society. In March 2003, the National People's Congress (NPC) and the Chinese People's Political Consultative Conference (CPPCC) also address the new goal of building a *xiaokang* or *xiaokang* society. Many increasingly associate the goal of building a *xiaokang* with China's current leadership, being Hu Jintao and the fourth generation leadership. The CCP's new goal of building a *xiaokang* society, though earlier failing to specify a target date, supposedly intends to address increasingly growing domestic anxiety over increasingly growing social inequalities. Increasingly growing social crises such as poverty, unemployed, social security and other crises that threaten both the legitimacy and survivability of one-party CCP rule are primordial forces driving the new goal of building *xiaokang*.

The CCP later conjoins the goal of building *xiaokang* (well-off) society in an all-round way with the goal of building a harmonious socialist society. In 2003, the CCP, at the 3rd Plenary Session of the 16th Central Committee of the CPC, introduces the new concept of building a harmonious socialist society. In 2004, the CPC, at the 4th Plenary Session of the 16th Central Committee of the CPC, officially adopts the goal of building a harmonious socialist society. The 2002 goal of building *xiaokang*, once conjoined with this new goal, became a goal of building in tandem a *xiaokang* and harmonious socialist society. The 16th National Congress of the CPC announces two strategic goals that it intends to accomplish in two consecutive stages: a first stage occurring from 1978-2020 and a second stage from 2020-2050. During the first stage, the CCP announces that it intends to improve the socialist market economic system, promote strategic adjustment of the economic structure and focus on building a well-off society that benefits a China populous during the first twenty years of the twenty-first century. The CCP outlines the second stage as a period of modernization, prosperity, democracy and a civilized socialist China, all of which is supposedly achievable by the middle of the twenty-first century. During the first stage of the two strategic goals, and while transitioning from central planning to market system, the CCP also announces that it will address the issue of bringing an end to economic scarcity and what many deem "poor socialism" or economic growth at all costs.[16] Problematic is that China and its socialist-political polity did not smoothly enter this second stage, because of challenges and changes in its economic system and operational mechanisms, and non-synchronization or collision between the economy, policy and ideology. Responding to the problem of "poor socialism," the CCP announces a development concept of building a harmonious socialist society or, alternatively, "put people first" concept, and an intention to develop a comprehensive, coordinated and sustainable concept of development, while also promoting the overall development of economic society and people.

---

[16] Lu Wei, Settlement of Final Expenses and Performance Assessment in the Course of Transition: Evidence from China, Social Sciences in China (Zhongguo shehui kexue) 110-122 (spring 2006). 16th National Congress of the CPC: Resolution of 3rd Plenary Sess., and Resolution of 4th Plenary Sess.

What remains to be determined is the true meaning underlying the party's announced goals of building *xiaokang* and harmonious socialist society. Notwithstanding problem of creating a set of tools (or additional goals) for assessing accomplishment of these goals, which is a subject of continuing debate, building a *xiaokang*, generally, represents a goal of building a well-off society or well-off society in an all-around way. The conjoining of the two goals results in the joint goals of building a well-off society in an all-around way and harmonious socialist society. In China, many also emphasize the "all-around" phrasing of the announced goal of building a *xiaokang*, as translated and extended in the phrasing or meaning, "well-off society in an all-around way," thereby elevating the concept of "all-around" and resulting in the concept of a harmonious socialist society inheriting the concept of "all-round." Building harmonious socialist society became an important ingredient and essential dimension to building a well-off society. Adding to confusion, some sources characterize the difference between building *xiaokang* (well-off society in an all-around way) and building a harmonious socialist society, respectively, as a quantitative approach (*xiaokang* approach) and qualitative approach (harmonious socialist approach) to social development and modernization. Many even suggest that linking the goals of building *xiaokang* and harmonious socialist society to the United Nations Millennium Development Goals will aid the effort in accomplishing these goals.[17] Notwithstanding the ongoing debate, within and without academia, and the questionable substantiveness of the goal of building *xiaokang*, the goal of building *xiaokang* is more substantive than the goal of building a harmonious socialist society, mostly attributable to the CCP's rhetoric, ideologies and actions. On February 2005, the General Secretary of the CPC Hu Jintao recapitulated a harmonious socialist society as a society with democracy, rule of law, equality and justice, honesty and kindness, vigor and order, and peace and harmony. In modern China, by virtue of joining these goals, a *xiaokang* (well-off) society cannot exist without a harmonious socialist society, and building a modern *xiaokang* without building a harmonious socialist society is building an incomplete and imperfect *xiaokang* society, or perhaps an imperfect social order, utopia or perpetual peace.

1.3. Complementary and Paradoxical Ideologies

The casting of the announced goals of building a *xiaokang* or moderately well-off society and harmonious socialist society in general terms makes it difficult to find an adequate, perhaps meaningful, descriptor for these goals. These goals may be a fact, fiction, slogan, ideology, mere party political rhetoric or old tricks in new conditions. In terms of the greater relevancy of the November 2002 proceedings of the 16th CPC and the March 2003 First Session of the 10th NPC and CPPCC, the more prominent and pressing concern was the upcoming 2004 proposed amendments to the Constitution of the People's Republic of China

[17] Liu Yaoqiu, Reading and Comprehending the Concept of Social Development in China in Transition: A Research Commentary, Social Sciences in China (Zhongguo shehui kexue), 100-111 (winter 2005). Gao Shangquan, Make Efforts to Establish a Harmonious Society and Push forward the All-round Development of Both Economic Society and Huam Beings (2005), http://www.Chinareform.org.cn. Miao Shubin & Kuang Xianming, Summary of the Semina for Evaluating Government Transition and Construction of a Harmonious Society (2005), http://www.Chinareform.org.cn. UNPD, Fully Constructing A Well-off China: A State Development Plan Integrating the Millennium Goals, Project No. RR/03/M02/A/PJ/99 (Dec. 2004).

(*Zhonghua renmin gongheguo xianfa*, 1982 Constitution). As a preclude to amending the 1982 Constitution, during the party's 16th CPC of November 2002, an issue of greater prominence to both China and the international community was the public controversy concerning an amendment incorporating Jiang Zeming's theory of the "Three Represents" (*San Ge Daibiao*) into the CPC Central Constitution. On July 1, 2001, Jiang Zemin, then party general secretary (from 1989 to 2002), addressed the celebration of the eightieth anniversary of the founding of the CCP and explicated the "Theory of the Three Represents." Jiang Zemin's theory of the "Three Represents" espouses that "the party must represent China's advanced productive forces, an orientation towards advanced culture, and the fundamental interests of the overwhelming majority of the people in China."[18]

Jiang Zemin's theory of the "Three Represents" was intended to appease and persuade a growingly discontent Chinese populace. Commencing in the new millennium, China's growing population became increasingly discontent with the problems of a large and growing population, economic imbalances between rural and urban areas, and increasingly diverging levels of both income and consumption per capita. Party leadership, including Jiang Zemin, was well aware of growing domestic crises. Notwithstanding economic imbalances between rural and urban areas, there is also the stark contrast in economic imbalances between coastal regions, such as Shanghai and Guangdong Province, and inland areas, such as the middle and western regions. The western region comprises twelve provinces, autonomous regions and municipalities under the direct administration of the central government. The western region includes Shaanxi, Qinghai, Sichuan, Yunnan, Guizhou, Ningxia, Xinjiang, Inner Mongolia, Gansu, Tibet, Chongqing and Guangxi. The western region covers 5.4 million square kilometers, 57 percent of China's land area, and, based on an earlier 2000 consensus, a population of about 285 million or about 23 percent of the total population.[19] This region also includes more than half of China's natural resources.

On June 17, 1999, then China President Jiang Zeming announced guidelines for development of the western region. In 1999, the goal was to achieve a satisfactory level of economic development in the western region, in a five to ten year period. It was a goal of establishing a "new western China" by the middle of the twenty-first century, where people in the region will enjoy economic prosperity, social stability, ethnic unity, and an ecologically healthy and sustainable landscape. Nonetheless, in later years, China witnesses a continuing and growing widespread disillusionment of the Chinese citizenry with party corruption and worsening socio-economic conditions. In 2005, and according to China's Ministry of Public Security, there were 87,000 protests and riots, which is an increase of 6.6 percent from 2004. As for the 2004 official reports, there were a reported 74,000 protests or mass incidents, reflecting an increase from 10,000 in 1994, with the number of participants rising to 3.8

[18] Documents of the 16th National Congress of the CPC, Id. Jiang Zemin, Build a Well-Off Society in an All-Round Way and Create a New Situation in Building Socialism with Chinese Characteristics (Report to the 16th Congress of the CPC, Nov. 8, 2002). Jiang Zemin, On The Three Represents (Lun "San ge Daibiao") (Beijing: Foreign Language Press, 2002). Jiang's Book on Party Building Published, Nov. 11, 2001, People's Daily. Jiang Zemin, On Party Building (Lun Dang De Jianshe) (Beijing: Foreign Language Press, 2001).

[19] Xi bu diqu 10 xiang zhuyao jingli zhibiao bijiao (Western area 10 main economic indicator comparisons) Aug. 2005, Zhonghua Renmin Gongheguo Guojia Tongjiju (People's Republic of China State Statistical Bureau or Nat'l Bureau of Statistics), http://www.stats.gov.cn/tjsj/qtsj/xbdqsjbj/t20051010_402284637.htm. Michael H. Glantz, Qian Ye & Quansheng Ge, China's western region development strategy and the urgent need to address creeping environmental problems, Arid Lands Newsletter, No. 49, May/June 2001. A New Attack Against Taiwan; China's Deepening Economic Divide, China Reform Monitor No. 602, Sept. 21, 2005. China Reform Monitor No. 616, Editor's Note, Feb. 8, 2006. China Reform Monitor, no. 651, Jan. 10, 2007.

million from 730,000. As of 2006, China's agriculture economy employs about 50% of the labor force. They are members of China's lowest average income group, which constitutes about 630 million persons or half of China's population, mostly comprised of the poverty-stricken, ethic minority, rural areas and remote areas, in the central and western regions.[20] For these reasons and others, such as lagging political reforms, Jiang Zemin's theory of the "Three Represents" would meet opposition within and without the framework of the CCP, perhaps what could be termed the antithesis, or more accurately, the antitheses (plural) of the "Three Represents."

The antitheses of the "Three Represents" would stand in opposition, stem from sources without and without the party, and even from sources within and without Mainland China. Many in opposition would challenge for various reasons the "Three Represents." In 2001, at the Fifteenth CPC Central Committee, a proposed amendment incorporating the "Three Represents" into the CPC Central Constitution met opposition. There were diverging opinions regarding the meaning, intent and conceptual basis of the "Three Represents," especially Jiang's call for admitting capitalists into the CCP. In August 2001, at a Beidaihe (Hebei Province) conference of the party's inner circle, there was open rift between Jiang Zeming's forces and members of the CCP's leftist elders. In response, the leftist elders wrote, in "A Letter to the Central Committee of the Chinese Communist Party" (*Letter of the Fourteen*), that Jiang's call for admitting capitalist, "in no way constitutes a 'creative renewal' of Marxism, but rather, an outright negation of its basic principles." Although called the *Letter of the Fourteen*, sixteen party members signed the letter, and the signatories are Ma Bin, Wang Dinglie, Shi Shan, Shi Shan, Qi Yiding, Liu Zhenhua, Li Yuanru, Li Feiping, Li Zhaoji, Li Dezhong, Zhang Chen, Gao Jun, Qian Min, Huang Zhigang, Han Xiya and Wei Wei. The *Letter of the Fourteen* charges that Jiang Zemin's stand on this matter contravenes the CCP's adoption of the programs and Basic Statutes at each session, from first to the fifteenth of the CCP Congress, because the nature of the CCP is definable by the stipulation that "the CCP is the vanguard of the Chinese working class." Further, it reads, "This is by no means the same as the proposition, as put forth by Comrade Jiang Zemin, that 'the CCP has at the same time become the vanguard of the Chinese people and nation.' Anyone who is at all familiar with our Party's history and has an elementary understanding of Marxism knows that a distinction must be drawn between an individual's class origin and this person's class status."

After inviting capitalists to join the ranks of the CCP, these leftist elders or old guard communists by the *Letter of the Fourteen* accused Jiang Zemin of violating party discipline and destroying party unity in a manner that would eventually lead China into a Soviet Union-type collapse. Nonetheless, and despite the government's reaction to the *Letter of the Fourteen*, the opposition to Jiang's theory of the "Three Represents" continued to grow, while also finding new outlets and forms of protest. In October 2001, during the 15th Plenum of the CCP, Jiang Zemin's proposed constitutional amendment of the CPC Central Constitution, which would permit the recruitment of capitalists into the CCP, was not brought forward, in order to avoid making the then General Secretary Jiang Zemin publicly lose face. In 2002, Jiang Zemin also aroused additional opposition from the majority of rightist intellectuals,

[20] Angang Hu & Yizhi Xiong, The Strategy of Knowledge-based Development: China's Long-run Future, Social Sciences in China (Zhongguo shehui kexue), 24-25 (winter 2003). Statistical Abstracts of China for 2001 and 2002 World Development Indicators (World Bank, 2002). 2000 Int'l Statistical Yearbook, Table 8-3 shows 47.5% of labor force employ in agricultural section.

when he campaigned to maintain one of his posts, which could have included the party general secretary position. In the international community, many watched closely and judged the indoctrination and eventual constitutionalization of a new ideology. Outside the CCP, in 2002, Bao Tong circulates a paper attacking Jiang's theory of the "Three Represents."[21] Bao Tong, former secretary to the former party chief, Zhao Ziyang, is the most senior Chinese government official imprisoned for opposing the use of force during the 1989 Tiananmen Square tragedy. Bao Tong contends that without the promotion of democratic reforms, the party would only represent "the rich, the nobility, and the powerful," and "could never claim to represent the interests of the masses because the noblemen-cadres had refused to take care of the livelihood of millions of unemployed workers and peasants." Another critique outside the CCP describes the theory of the "Three Represents" as political theory allowing "the party to widen its traditional embrace of peasants, soldiers and workers to include private entrepreneurs," or capitalists, for purpose of keeping "the private sector from forming alternative centers of authority to the party."

Despite the many critiques of Jiang's theory of the "Three Represents," in 2002, the CCP constitutionalizes the "Three Represents" in the Constitution of the Communist Party of China (CPC Constitution), which is distinguishable from the 1982 Constitution. An excerpt from the General Program of the CPC Constitution reads, "The Communist Party of China takes Marxism-Leninism, Mao Zedong Thought, Deng Xiaoping Theory and the important thought of the "Three Represents" as its guide to action." The "Three Represents," once conjoined with other ideologies serve, "as a powerful theoretical weapon for strengthening and improving Party building, and for promoting the self-improvement and development of socialism in China; and it is the crystallization of the collective wisdom of the Communist Party of China."[22] There is an interrelationship between the "Three Represents" and other party ideologies, and the goals of building a *xiaokang* and a harmonious socialist society, and understanding the influence of party ideology becomes increasingly important. Despite the many flaws of one-party CCP rule, such as failings in human rights and political liberalization, many, including many Western transnational corporations and their corporate officers, hail the CCP for its economic growth and seeming commitment to the road to capitalism.[23] In light of the General Program of the CPC Constitution, it becomes imperative to understand that the goals of building *xiaokang* and harmonious socialist society suffer a conceptual limitation, because they are operate within the confines of dominant party ideologies, which serve as the CCP's guide to action.

The "Three Represents," depending on one's perspective or political preferences, rightist or leftist, presents a complementary or paradoxical ideology that produces the most troubling irony for both Marxists and liberals or capitalists. The first of the "Three Represents" reads, "The party must represent China's advanced productive forces." Barbara Foley writes, "Informing Jiang's speech from beginning to end is a nationalist discourse that obfuscates class distinctions and precludes class analysis…The nationalistically resonant term 'the people' dominates Jiang's discussion; class as a structural relation virtually disappears as an

---

[21] Hamish McDonald, Forget the Class Struggle; Let's Welcome the Bankers, Aug. 31, 2002, Sydney Morning Herald. Joseph Kahn, China Moves to Protect Property, but the Fine Print Has a Caveat, Dec. 22, 2003, NY Times.

[22] Documents of the 16th National Congress of the CPC, Id. Constitution of the CPC (Amended and adopted at the 16th National Congress of the CPC on Nov. 14, 2002).

[23] Robert Lawrence Kuhn, The Man Who Changed China, The Life and Legacy of Jiang Zemin (Crown, 2005).

analytical category and is supplanted by such bourgeois sociological categories as 'strata' and 'circles.' The working class *qua* working class is mentioned occasionally, but the term routinely used to describe those who engage in productive labor is 'the overwhelming majority of the people.'"[24] For Foley, Jiang's use of the "advanced productive forces" language revealed an attempt to combine historical materialism with technological determinism. In terms of Marx and Engels, Foley opines, "they *never* proposed that the development of productive forces could or would in and of itself produce world-historical changes in the nature of social ownership. Only class struggle could accomplish that end." Perhaps in terms of pure (or orthodox) Marxism, Foley observes an irony in Jiang's "Three Represents" and his approach to reforms and development. Foley writes, "As he [Jiang Zemen] puts it somewhat circuitously, the purpose of the recent reforms and opening up policies" is to "adjust and reform the part of the socialist relations of production that is incompatible with the demand of the development of the productive forces and to adjust and reform the part of socialist superstructure that is incompatible with the economic base." In other words, because they cut into profits and hold back the development of a full-fledged market economy, socialist benefits such as free medical care and free education are impediments to the fuller development of Marxism. Foley perceived Jiang Zemin as preoccupied with the need to adjust and reform.

For Marx and Engels, the principal fetter to be broken, in order to allow the productive forces full play, was that of bourgeois relations of production. Marx and Engels, in *The Communist Manifesto* (1848), were clearly addressing Marx's historical materialism. "The history of all hitherto existing society is the history of class struggles. Freeman and slave, patrician and plebeian, lord and serf, guild-master and journeyman, in a word, oppressor and oppressed, stood in constant opposition to one another, carried on an uninterrupted, now hidden, now open fight, a fight that each time ended either in a revolutionary reconstitution of society at large, or in the common ruin of the contending classes." There would be class struggle under capitalism between those owning means of production, the bourgeoisie (or ruling class), and the proletariat (or the working class). Foley, in critique of Jiang's "Three Represents," further writes, "It is residual features of *socialist* relations of production that must now be abolished in order for the productive forces to be emancipated. The irony is complete, and would be farcical indeed, were its consequences not so tragic for the Chinese working class--as well as for the hundreds of millions who at one point looked to China for leadership in their struggles to free themselves from the fetters of capitalist rule." Depending on one's political preference, rightist or leftist, Jiang Zemin's thoughts on China's advanced productive forces is either one remove from pure (or orthodox) Marxism or one remove from liberalism or capitalism.

1.4. Xiaokang in Antiquity and Modern Marxism

In the public discourse, Jiang Zemin's "Three Represents" theory and amendment of the 1982 Constitution by its incorporation were of greater prominence than the goal of building a *xiaokang* society. A lesser concern for building a *xiaokang* society may be attributable to lack

[24] Barbara Foley, From Situational Dialectics to Pseudo-Dialectics: Mao, Jiang, and Capitalist Transition, 5 Cultural Logic (2002).

of a specific target date, lack of specific goals for doing so and lack of clear definitional meaning for a modern *xiaokang*. However, official party statements regarding the building of a *xiaokang* society were eventually forthcoming, when the Chinese media explains the concepts of *xiaokang* society and harmonious socialist society as, "A sign of society's acute longing for a more quality-oriented and politically balanced, economically fair and socially progressive society." According to Hu Jintao, a harmonious socialist society includes, "democracy, the rule of law, equity and justice, sincerity, amity and vitality." These concepts, supposedly, call for an alternate plan to what many deem "poor socialism" or "the single-minded pursuit of economic achievement at all costs" and using gross domestic product (GDP) as the gauge of political achievement. These goals are a subsequent development goal or ideology intending to address growing domestic crises, such as growing corruption, a widening income gap and regional imbalance, a deteriorating environment, workplace accidents and violation of farmers' rights. In 2002, China's 16th Party Congress put forward the idea of building a well-off society in an all-round way. The announced goal of building a harmonious socialist society, supposedly, brings home what a *xiaokang* society should be like, because "at the core of the new concept lies the government's commitment to equity on the basis of the rule of law." In addition, "the government needs to make greater efforts to promote social equality by improving social security, employment, medical care, poverty reduction and education. It must especially devise policies to help rural areas develop faster to catch up with better-off urban regions."[25]

Many now suggest that a *xiaokang* society for all of China, including the poorer rural areas and affluent cities, is the goal of a moderate well-off life that is attainably by the year 2020. During the 16th CPC, former China president Jiang Zemin, in a speech before the CPC, earlier admits that the well-off life Chinese people were living was at a relatively low level when compared to other countries. As outgoing party leader, Jiang Zemin pledged to quadruple China's per capita GDP in 2000 by 2020, meaning the per capita GDP would exceed $3,000 by year 2020. The year 2020 target date for achieving a *xiaokang* society will correspond with the July 1, 2021 centennial birthday of the CCP. No doubt, it is probably intended to be a centennial birthday celebrating the continuing longevity of the CCP and continuing one-party rule rather than actually achieving or building a *xiaokang* society.

In its simplest form, a modern *xiaokang* refers to a condition of moderate prosperity. Problematic for the CCP is an unwillingness to admit the thus far failed and frustrated earlier goal of creating a Chinese middle class by the end of the twentieth century. For instance, there is the earlier failed attempt by the Chinese press to apply the Chinese Academy of Social Sciences (CAAS) criteria for professionals to the 2000 Chinese census, such as party cadres, business managers, chief executive officers in the private sector, qualified technicians and office staff, in a vain attempt to argue that 2.8% of the Chinese population constituted a middle class. There is not a middle class in China and the income gap continues to widen. As of 2006, China's agriculture economy employs about 50% of the labor force, who are members of China's lowest average income group, which constitutes about 630 million persons or half of China's population, mostly comprised of the poverty-stricken, ethic minority, rural areas and remote areas, in the central and western regions. As typical of the CCP, and its leaders, they offer ideology from antiquity to appease Chinese citizens.

[25] Henry C. K. Liu, The glorious role of Tung Chee-hwa, Mar. 23, 2005, Asian Times.

As for the etymology of the word (or characters) *xiaokang*, the concept is traceable to antiquity and traditional culture. *Xiaokang* society (*xiaokang shehui*, literally meaning a society of small peace or comfort) is a society of modest means. In modern society, it is simply a middle-class society. The *Shijing* (*Book of Song* or *The She King* (*Shih Ching*) or *Book of Odes*), which is the first record of poems collected that comprises 305 poems from the Zhou (B.C. 1122 to B.C. 256), contains one of the earliest usage of the word (or characters) *xiaokang*.[26] The *Shijing* is one the six classics, the others are: namely; *The Book of History, The Book of Rites*, *The Book of Music*, *The Book of Changes*, and *The Spring and Autumn Annals*. In terms of agricultural conditions in the Western Zhou, the poems written by the common people demonstrate a harmonious picture of hard-working farmers, while also expressing their sense of life and feelings about feudal and agrarian life. In the *Shijing*, in the section Decade of Sheng Min (*Sheng Min Zhi Shi*) of the Greater Odes of the Kingdom (*Da Ya*), one can find the word (or characters) *xiaokang* in the poem or ode of the period authored by *Min Lu*, which is poem number 253. This poem includes five stanzas, with the first line of each stanza speaking of a heavily burdened people. The ending first line of each stanza, from the first to fifth stanza, respectively, reads and addresses the need for a *xiao kang* (to be well-off, or a little ease), *xiao xiu* (a little rest), *xiao xi* (a little relief), *xiao qi* (a little repose) and *xiao an* (a little peace or tranquility).

Commencing in 2002, there is an increasing use of the word (or characters) *xiaokang*, though earlier employed in modern China or post-1949 China, which is now increasingly being associated with Hu Jintao and the fourth generation leadership. During the 16th CPC, then vice president Hu Jintao ascends to party chief or general secretary of the CPC Central Committee (*Zhongguo gongchandang zhongyang weiyuanhui zong shuji*). In March 2003, at the First Session of the 10th NPC, Hu ascends to president of China (*Zhonghua renmin gongheguo zhuxi*), and then in September 2004, at the Fourth Plenum of the 16th CPC Central Committee, Hu Jintao succeeds Jiang Zemin as chairman of the CPC Central Military Commission (*Zhongguo gongchan dang zhongyang junshi weiyuanhui zhuxi*). What follows is Hu Jintao's announced CCP goal, and perhaps subsequently modified goal, of building a *xiaokang* by the year 2020. As earlier mentioned, the announced goal is a fact, fiction, slogan, ideology, political rhetoric or, simply, old tricks in new conditions. By announcing the goal of building a *xiaokang*, the CCP intended to separate current ongoing reforms from the leadership of Jiang Zemin and the policies of the 1990s. The latter effectually associates policies of the 1990s with tremendous domestic issues or crises now confronting China. In 2007, during the 17th Party Congress, the CCP will appoint a successor to Hu Jintao and the fourth-generation leadership, because the "Interim Regulations on Terms of Office for Leading Party and Government Cadres" stipulate a limit of two five-year terms for official positions throughout most of the political order."[27] The rumors concerning the leaders that will succeed the fourth generation leadership as the fifth generation leadership, generally, name Zong Hairen, Li Keqiang, Xi Jinpain, Bo Xilai and Li Yuanchao. In terms of the future and 2007, one can only speculate whether the fifth generation leadership will continue the policies and programs of Hu Jintao and the fourth generation leadership, or attempt to separate post-2007 reforms from the leadership of Hu Jintao, as Hu and the fourth-generation

[26] Jacques Gernet, A History of Chinese Civilization 13-18 (Cambridge UP, 1996). James Legge, The Chinese Classics, Vol. IV, The She King (Taipei: SMC Pub, 1994).

[27] Alice Lyman Miller, The Problem of Hu Jintao's Successor, China Leadership Monitor, No. 19, Hoover Inst. (2006).

attempted to separate current ongoing reforms from the leadership of Jiang Zemin and policies of the 1990s.

In antiquity, in a comparison to the word (or characters) *datong* (great harmony or great unity), the word (or characters) *xiaokang* is found in the *Classic of Rites*. A modern conceptualization of *xiaokang*, as currently employed by the CCP and its leadership, reflects an announced goal of promoting an economic prosperity that will move most of the Chinese population into comfortable means, with economic advancement, supposedly, not being the sole focus of society. Problematic for the CCP's new goal of building a *xiaokang* is the hidden intent to link traditional culture with Marxism. In terms of *xiaokang* from antiquity, the CCP, and its leadership, invokes traditional culture in support of modern Marxism. During antiquity, a *xiaokang* society was the predecessor to the word (or characters) *datong*. The transitional phases from *xiaokang* to *datong* serve as an ideology link between traditional culture and modern Marxism. The latter presents a nexus between the progression in antiquity from *xiaokang* to *datong*, and an ideological and corresponding progression in Chinese Marxism between a socialist market society and world communism, or perhaps more accurately, the continuing attempt to finalize the adaptation, Sinicization or localization of Marxism (*Makesi zhuyi he Zhongguo shiji xiang jiehe*).[28] The latter also epitomizes the problem of Chinese Marxism, Sinicized Marxism or localized Marxism; because Chinese Marxism has always been a variant model of orthodox Western Marxism or one remove from orthodox Western Marxism.

From antiquity, post-Sino British Opium Wars period (1839–1842 and 1856–1860), post-Chinese Revolution (1911), to post-WTO China, the conceptualization from antiquity of *datong* enjoys a persistence, which is reflexive of the persistence of traditional culture. Sun Yat-sen (Sun Zhongshan, 1866-1925), though admiring Western models of government such as the U.S. model, is still subject to influence of traditional culture when attempting to revive nationalism following the fall of dynastic rule or Chinese Revolution (1911). For Sun Yat-sen, achieving good order and peace equates to achieving the rule of *datong*, which is the same Confucian ideal of *datong* from antiquity in the *Liji* (*Book of Rites*). The high ideal manifest in the word (or characters) *datong* depicts a Chinese society where no one is selfish and everyone is selfless, with all citizens working for the good of the collective. It is an idea in search of a perfect order for society, perhaps evens a utopia or perpetual peace. In such a society, there is no intrigue or even robbery. The *Liji* attributes Confucius as saying that a *datong* society could only exist when Tao (Dao or the "Way") prevailed. In traditional culture, Tao (or Dao) would eventually evolve philosophical meanings beyond its original significance, such as by *Zuo's Commentary*, the *Laozi* (*Canon of the Way and Virtue*), the *Great Appendix* to the *Book of Changes*, the *Guanzi*, the *Xunzi*, the *Hanfeizi*, Zhang Zai, the two Cheng brothers (Cheng Hao and Cheng Yi), the Neo-Confucianist Zhu Xi and other sources. The original meaning of the word (or character) Tao (or Dao) is the "Way," referring to a path that one can travel. According to the earliest Chinese dictionary (*Explanation of Words and Characters*, compiled in A.D. 100), Tao is "that along which one walks; once obtained one calls it the Way."[29] The later philosophical development of the meaning of Tao is demonstrated by the Neo-Confucian Zhu Xi (or *Chu His*, 1130-1200), whom would

[28] Zou Shipeng, Localization of Marxism in China and the Construction of China's Modernity, Social Sciences in China, (Zhongguo shehui kexue) 12-21 (summer 2005).

[29] Zhang Dainian, Key Concepts in Chinese Philosophy, (Edmund Ryden, trans.) (Beijing: Foreign Language Press, 2002).

eventually pursue the orthodox rather then unorthodox by following the teachings of the Cheng brothers, though Zhu Xi also had other theories of the "Way," and interpret the "Way" in terms of the principle (*li*).

According to *The Root Meaning of the Changes: Great Appendix I*, "Insofar as *yin* and *yang* reach to what is far off, they are *qi*. The principle, though, by which they do so, is what is called the Way." The hexagrams and their lines, *yin* and *yang* are all what is below form; the principle by which they are is, however, the "Way." *The Evolutions of Li* (*liyu*), in the *Book of Rites* (*liji*), epitomizes the traditional Confucian ideal of *datong* (great harmony). Confucius said: "I have never seen the practice of the great Tao, and the eminent men of the three Dynasties, though I have had a mind to do so. When the great Tao was in practice, the world was common to all; men of talents, virtue and ability were selected; sincerity was emphasized and friendship was cultivated. Therefore, men did not love only their parents, nor did they treat as children only their own sons. A competent provision was secured for the aged till their death, employment for the able-bodied, and a means of up-bringing for the young. Kindness and compassion were shown to widows, orphans, childless men, and those who were disabled by disease, so that they all had the wherewithal for support. Men had their proper work and women had their homes. They hated to see the wealth of natural resources undeveloped, but also did not hoard wealth for their own use. They hated not to exert themselves, but also did not exert themselves only for their own benefit. Thus (selfish) scheming were repressed and found no development. Robbers, filchers and rebellious traitors did not show themselves, and hence the outer doors were left open. This was the period of great harmony (*datong*)."[30] However, and returning to the *Liji*, "Now that the great Tao is hiding, everyone takes to one's own family. Everyone endears only his/her parents, loves only his/her children, treating property as his/her own. Thus intrigues and utilitarianism prevail, leading to the breakout of war." The latter society is also definable as *xiaokang*.

In modern China, the new fact, fiction, slogan, ideology, or political rhetoric of the CCP attempts to link with the same two-stage development, which is a historic transition from antiquity that progresses from a *xiaokang* to *datong*. The CCP announced a goal of achieving what is essentially the first stage of *xiaokang*, or the lifting of the majority of Chinese citizens out of poverty. However, this newly announced goal of building *xiaokang* is not a new goal of the CCP and its leadership, rather a revision of earlier party goals. In 1979, Deng Xiaoping announced the same goal of building a well-off society by the end of the twentieth century, which was not attainable for various reasons. Chinese society benefits from earlier reforms, but there is an uneven sharing of the resulting benefits. Deng Xiaoping warns that in the rush to modernize, some people would "get rich first," while most of China's population, which peaked at 1.3 billion in 2005, would get rich later. The Chinese ideology of *Facai zhifu shi guangrong de* (being rich is glorious), if not (to get rich, is glorious), is attributable to Deng Xiaoping during the year of 1992. In terms of economic development, Deng Xiaoping set a goal of a per capita income of $1,000 by the end of the twentieth century. In 1987, Deng Xiaoping predicted, "When that time comes we call it a *xiaokang* society — a *xiaokang* society in which people enjoy a universally enhanced living standard." Deng Xiaoping, admittedly, did not make a direct reference to the concept from antiquity embodied in the word (or characters) *datong*. Nonetheless, the mention of *xiaokang* demonstrates the connectedness between antiquity and modernity, and a corresponding connectedness between

[30] Zhang Qingxiong, Id.

both *xiaokang* and *datong* in modernity, as demonstrated by the pronounced historic teachings and theories stemming from as early as Confucius, Sun Yat-sen, Mao Zedong (1893-1976), to Deng Xiaoping and many other great thinkers and scholars from antiquity, to the present day.

In a pre-1949 period, Mao Zedong directly related his ideas of a new democracy to Sun Yat-sen's earlier post-1911 theory of the "Three People's Principles" (Three Principles of the People, *San-min* Doctrine, or *San min zhuyi*).[31] Sun Yat-sen's "Three People's Principles" represents the principles of *minzu* (government of the people or nationalism), *minqua* (government by the people or democracy) and *minsheng* (government for the people). Many translate the principle of *minsheng* as socialism, because *minsheng* presented issues of how government would take care of the people, such as food, clothing, shelter and other necessities. The "Three People's Principles" are considered the basic philosophical ideals underlining the Chinese Revolution (1911), founding of the *Kuomintang* (Guomindang), and are also generally described as Chinese nationalism, democracy and economic equalization. In 1919, when in Shanghai, Sun Yat-sen presumably started writing the "Three People's Principles." The actual text of the "Three People's Principles" that is available today is from his lecture notes, which are written in the vernacular style in 1924, when he reorganized the *Kuomintang* in Canton, in Guangdong Province. While a source of great influence for Sun Yat-sen is the U.S. model of government, for Mao Zedong, the ideal society would be a Marxist society, though with Chinese characteristics. In 1939, Mao wrote, "The ultimate future of Chinese revolution is not capitalism, but socialism and communism."[32] Some contend that Mao Zedong's ideas of a communist society, and one where there is no exploitation and only prosperity, conform to the ideal from antiquity of *datong*, or perhaps even a perfect order, utopia or perpetual peace.

1.5. CONCLUSION

The new indoctrinations expressed in the goals of building a *xiaokang* and harmonious socialist society, epitomize the state of modern China's socio-econo-legal order. These goals, implicitly, substantiate the conflict, struggle or paradoxical interrelationship of competing sources of orders. The concepts of *xiaokang* and harmonious society are from antiquity, or traditional culture, and stand in contrast to modern Marxism. While traditional culture remains amendable to Western universalism and liberalism, modern China's socio-econo-legal order, as a courtesy of modern Marxism, continues to, historically, grow increasingly incongruous with traditional culture. It is the consequence of the early Chinese communists,

[31] Sun Yat-sen, San-min Chu-I, http://www.folkdoc.idv.tw/classic/p02/ba/ba01/a1.htm. Leslie H. Chen, On Sun Yatsen's Three Principles of the People, Presentation - ASPAC Conf. Assn for Asian Studies Pacific Univ., June 16-18, 1995. Malcolm Cook & Craig Meer, Balancing act, Taiwan's cross-strait challenge, Lowy Inst. Paper 2006, note 44.

[32] Tan Chung, The True Meaning of Peace from the Chinese Literary Perspective, In Culture of Peace, (Baidyanath Saraswat, ed.), (Indira Gandhi Nat'l Cntr. for Arts, 1999). Wu Hsiang-hsiang, Sun Yixian xiansheng zhuan (Biography of Mr. Sun Yat-sen), Vol. 2, 1654 (Far East Book Co., 1982). Leslie H. Chen, Chen Jiongming and the Federalist Movement: Regional Leadership and Nation Building in Early Republican China, (Cntr for Chinese Studies Pubs, 2000). Deng Xiaoping wenxuan (Selected works of Deng Xiaoping) 216 (Beijing: People's Pub House, Vol. 3, 1993). Mao Zedong, Zhongguo geming he Zhongguo gongchandang (Chinese

during the 1920s and 1930s, denying the relevancy of their own heritage and traditional culture or "old" culturalism. In the late Qing, traditional culture still reigned dominant, even as China struggled to modernize or Westernize in the wake of tragedies, such as the Sino-British Opium Wars and commencement of the Unequal Treaties (*Bu pingdeng tiaoyue*). During the debate between reformist policy and revolution, the Chinese Revolution (1911) and fall of dynastic (or imperial) rule witnessed traditional culture relegated to minimum importance. Commencing in the 1920s, and following the critical May Fourth Movement (1919) and then the May 30th Movement (1925), and continuing in the new millennium, the dominant ideology would be, and continues to be, Marxism.

It is the by-product of a Chinese phenomenon of taking borrowed and transplanted foreign concepts and ideas, such as Marxism and Leninism, and imbuing them with the Chinese revolutionary spirit, such as the continuing attempt to finalize the adaptation, Sinicization or localization of Marxism to the realities of traditional culture and society (*Makesi zhuyi he Zhongguo shiji xiang jiehe*). In terms of the future of modern China's socio-econo-legal order and the revolutionary spirit, and introducing Western concepts, such as liberty and democracy into the Chinese lexicon, Sinologist Rudolf G. Wagner, "traced the notion *mouvement/undo/yundong* in the sense of 'social action' from revolutionary France through Meiji Japan to China where it arrived on the eve of May 4, 1919."[33] In terms of "the cosmological opposition between 'movement' and 'stagnation,' the protagonists of May 4 consciously styled their own actions as a legitimate and necessary 'movement' for and by the people, thus paving the way for numerous future movements or 'campaigns' that were to be initiated and carried out with equal zest."

revolution and Chinese Communist Party), 331 In Vol. 3, Selected Works of Mao Tse-tung, (Foreign Languages Press, 1967).

[33] Iwo Amelung & Joachim Kurtz, Researching Modern Chinese Technical Terminologies: Methodological Considerations and Practical Problems, Univ. of Göttingen, MCST Workshp, Oct. 1997.

Chapter 2

SOCIAL ORDER IN ANTIQUITY

2.1. TRADITIONAL CULTURE AND HUMANITY

Traditional Chinese culture (primarily traditional Confucianism) teaches people how to be human by imposing demands upon themselves, by essentially compelling people to cherish an ideal form of human life, humanity and even ascend to sagehood. One ascends to sagehood and, thus, humanity by attaining the three unities -- the unity of Heaven and man, the unity of knowledge and action, and the unity of sentiment and scenery. These three unities address the critical questions of truth, goodness and beauty. In particular, traditional Confucianism begins with Confucius (551-479 B.C.).[1] The *Analects* of Confucius are the principle source of Confucianism. In terms of the etymology of humanity, traditional Confucian ethics manifest the morality (*daode*) of pre-Qing Confucians such as Mencius and Xunzi, and the Confucian virtue (*de*) of the Confucian gentlemen (*junzi*), or the character of a sage, and birth the Confucian doctrine of humanity (*ren*), which, historically, evolves from the early Zhou rites to Confucius and the Confucian School or the traditionalist school.

The Zhou rites, generally, referred to patriarchal kinship and patriarchal clan governmental hierarchies, religious regulations and exogamic restrictions. In modern China, the concept of hierarchical relationships or society may be problematic, and even subject to abuse, misuse and political machinations by a governing polity desperately in search of legitimacy. For instance, the Confucian virtue (*de*) or ethics manifest filial piety (*xiao shun*), which stems from the concept of humanity (*ren*) and the ethical morality in all human relationships. While Mencius exalted humanity over rituals, Confucius attempted to preserve a harmony and balance between humanity and rituals. Confucius when asked by his disciple Fan Chi what is humanity, responded that humanity is "loving others." Confucius was referring his student or disciple to the ideal of being, "careful in action and truthful in speech," and displaying "an expansive care for the multitude" and seeking "to draw near to those who are humane."[2] As concerns the ideal *xiaokang*, the concept of "loving others"

---

[1] Yijie Tang, Confuciansim, Buddhism, Daoism, Christianity and Chinese Culture, (Council for Research in Values and Philosophy, 1991). Wang Guowei, On the Institutions of the Yin and Zhou Dynasties, Gongren ribao (Sept. 1917). Aristotle's Nicomachean Ethics, (WD Ross, trans.) (Clarendon Press, 1908).

[2] Wan Junren, Contrasting Confucian Virtue Ethics and MacIntyre's Aristotelian Virtue Theory, 37, Social Sciences in China (Zhongguo shehui kexue) (summer 2003). Alasdair MacIntyre, Once More on Confucian and Aristotelian Conceptions of the Virtues: A Response to Professor Junren Wan, 58, Social Sciences in China (Zhongguo shehui kexue), (summer 2003). Analects 1:6, 3.14, 4:15 and 12:22.

refers to "the Way of loyalty and devotion." Confucius emphasized, "the Way of loyalty and sympathetic understanding (*zhongshu*)." When the inherent hierarchical Confucian relationships are conjoined with the concepts of "loving others" and the "Way of loyalty and devotion," the unexpected result is the production of legitimacy for hierarchical relationships or society. In terms of modern egalitarianism, the latter concepts lend to possible misuse or even non-Confucian interpretations, especially in the quest for legitimacy for a modern government or sovereignty. A problem of traditional Confucianism is that it may be subject to interpretations, though contrary to modern egalitarianism, as simply emphasizing the hierarchical nature of relationships and society, and the absolute legitimacy of the evolved hierarchal relationships and society. The previously mentioned ethics manifesting filial piety strongly influence a resulting Confucian model for an ideal governing polity. In terms of this Confucian ideal, the virtue of filial piety, ultimately, informs the virtue of *zhong* (loyalty to the monarch), because in Confucian politics the state is conceived of as an enlarged family, which results in the monarch-subject relationship becoming a social extension of the Confucian father-son relationship.[3]

The conceptualization of ascending to sagehood, alternatively, may simply be definable as a model of humanity. Zhou Dunyi (Zhou Lianxi, 1017-1073), in *Zhou Lianxi ji* (*Zhou Dunyi's Collected Works*), defined sagehood in terms of authenticity (*cheng*). The word (or character) *cheng* is prominent in the Confucian classic *The Doctrine of the Mean* (*The Doctrine of the Mean and the Common*, *Zhongyong*, 1190). The *Doctrine of the Mean* is one of four Confucian texts, which when published together in 1190 by the Neo-Confucian Zhu Xi grew into fame as the *Sishu* (*Four Books*). During the Song Dynasty, Zhu Xi selects what will be the *Four Books* of Confucianism, which are the *Analects, Book of Mencius*, *Great Learning* and *Doctrine of the Mean*. Zhu Xi uses the title of *Zhongyong* (*Doctrine of the Mean*) because of its cosmological and metaphysical inclinations, which had already drawn the attention of both Buddhists and early Neo-Confucianists. In terms of metaphysics, the concepts of *qi* and *yin-yang* were important because, from the pre-Qin confederations to the Han Dynasty, *qi* was understood as being intimately associated with the *yinyang* conceptualization. "This *qi* of heaven and earth does not lose its order. If it goes beyond the order, the people are in confusion. *Yang* bends over and cannot go out; *yin* rushes and cannot distill away, so there is an earthquake."[4] Their relationship is also important because *qi*, constituting the psycho-physical aspect, is the substance of which all existing phenomena are constituted, which includes all phases of matter, energy, mind (*xin*) and various forms of the spirit (*shen*). Zhu Xi, in the preface to *Doctrine of the Mean*, acknowledged that authorship of the treatise (a chapter from the *Liji*, one of the five classics from antiquity) belonged to *Zisi* (Kong Ji), a grandson of Confucius. An excerpt from the James Legge translation of the *The Doctrine of the Mean* reads, "The Master said, 'There was Shun: He indeed was greatly wise! Shun loved to question others, and to study their words, though they might be shallow. He concealed what was bad in them and displayed what was good. He took hold of their two

[3] Feng Lang, The female individual and the empire: A historicist approach to Mulan and Kingston's woman warrior, Comparative Literature (summer 2003).

[4] Zhang Dainian, Id. M. Lowe, ed., Early Chinese Texts, (Society for the Study of Early China, 1993).

extremes, determined the Mean, and employed it in his government of the people. It was by this that he was Shun!'"[5]

For Zhou Dunyi, being authentic (*cheng*) meant being true to the innate goodness of one's nature, which leads to actualizing one's moral potential. Zhou Dunyi defined authenticity in cosmological terms excerpted from the appendixes to the *Yi*, or *Yi Jing*, or the *I Ching* (*Book of Changes*). The meaning and significance of the *Book of Changes* occurred after Confucius added the Ten Wings, or the ten appendixes, which contained hexagrams that were supposed to represent symbolically what had happened in the heavens, including from heaven and earth to the complexity of human affairs. By doing so, Zhou Dunyi managed to use the concept of authenticity for linking cosmology with traditional Confucian ethics. In terms of sagehood (*sheng*) or the state of mind of the sage, "That which is 'completely silent and inactive' is authenticity. That which 'penetrates when stimulated' is spirit (*shen*). That which is active but not yet formed, between existing and not existing, is incipient. Authenticity is of the essence (*jing*), and therefore clear. Spirit is responsive, and therefore mysterious. Incipience is subtle, and therefore obscure. One who is authentic, spiritual, and incipient is called a Sage." Moreover, Zhou Dunyin described the process of learning to be a Sage (*sheng xue*) as follows. "[Someone asked:] 'Can Sagehood be learned?' Reply: It can. 'Are there essentials (*yao*)?' Reply: There are. 'I beg to hear them.' Reply: To be unified (*yi*) is essential. To be unified is to have no desire. Without desire one is vacuous when still and direct in activity. Being vacuous when still, one will be clear (*ming*); being clear one will be penetrating (*tong*). Being direct in activity one will be impartial (*gong*); being impartial one will be all-embracing (*pu*). Being clear and penetrating, impartial and all-embracing, one is almost [a Sage]."[6]

Since antiquity, scholars have struggled with this higher ideal form of human life, humanity or sagehood. Beginning with Confucius, philosophers have always aspired to the creation of a harmonious society. They pursued this ideal realm of existence, despite repeated failures in bringing such societies into existence, because they were driven by an obligatory state of mind towards this seemingly impossible goal. In terms of the difficulty of achieving this higher ideal, Confucius was well aware of the difficulty of creating such a harmonious society. One source observes, he [Confucius] "knew the impossibility [of the task] and yet continued to do it." In antiquity, it was the pursuit of an ideal society characterized by the Confucian ideal of harmony. For Confucius, or traditional Confucianism, it was the pursuit of the ideal society of "great harmony" (*datong*) described in both the *Li Yün* chapter of the *Book of Rites*, and the "small country with a small population," in chapter 80 of the Daoist classic *Dao De Jing* (*Tao Te Ching*). Both of these classics from antiquity present descriptors of a community manifesting the ideal form of human life or humanity -- in a unity between man and heaven, knowledge and actions, and sentiment and scenery. The ideal human life or

---

[5] Joseph A. Adler, Varieties of Spiritual Experience: Shen in Neo-Confucian Discourse, In Tu Wei-ming & Mary Evelyn Tucker, eds., Confucian Spirituality, vol. 2 (Crossroad, 2004). James Legge, in The Chinese Classics, vol. 1 (Hong Kong UP, 1960).

[6] Analects of Confucius, 4 (Cai Xiqin, trans., 1994). Richard Rutt, The Book of Changes (Zhouyi) 83-144 (Curzon Pr., 2002). Zhou Dunyi (or Chou Tun-I) Tongshu (Penetrating the Classic of Change) (Joseph A. Adler, trans.), (1994), http://www2.kenyon.edu/depts/Religion/Fac/Adler/Reln471/TSChou.htm. Joseph A. Adler, Zhou Dunyi: The Metaphysics and Practice of Sagehood, In Wm. Theodore de Bary and Irene Bloom, eds., Sources of Chinese Tradition, 2nd ed., vol.1 (Columbia UP, 1999), ch. 20. Zhou Lianxi xiansheng quanji (Zhou Dunyi's Collected Works), comp. Zhang Boxing (1708; rpt. in Zhengyi tang quanshu [Baibu congshu jicheng ed.]).

humanity manifest in the three unities and answered the critical questions of truth, goodness and beauty.

2.2. Neo-Confucianism and Humanity

The relationship between Zhou Dunyi and Zhu Xi deserves further mention. Neo-Confucianism is distinguishable from traditional Confucianism as a modern philosophy, which is also the "Philosophy of Song." While Neo-Confucians maintain that their teachings are genuine Confucianism, it is, in fact, Confucianism with an admixture of Buddhism. As earlier observed by Hu Shi, in terms of traditional culture, China had earlier been "Indianized," because an important evolution of China in antiquity was the mass conversion of the Chinese people to the alien religion of Buddhism, "as these and many other items of un-Chinese beliefs and practices poured from India by land and by sea into China and were soon accepted and made into parts of the cultural life of the Chinese people."[7] A China in antiquity had neither "the concept of Heaven in the sense of paradise, nor that of Hell as the place of Last Day Judgment." The cosmology and metaphysics of Buddhism gave China in antiquity, "not only one Paradise, but tens of paradises; not only one Hell, but many hells, each varying in severity and horror from the others." When, during the Han Dynasty (*Han Chao*, 206 B.C.-A.D. 220), Buddhism first entered China, it attached itself to native ideologies and gradually began to influence native ideologies. During the Han Dynasty, Buddhism even enjoyed the status of being on par with the mainstream Huang-Lao tradition (Huanglao Dao or Tao) or school (based on the *Laozi* or *Lao-Tzu* and the *Zhuangzi*). Buddhism eventually integrates into Taoism, constituting an important component of the religious background to the birth of Taoism. In the later Wei-Jin period (220-420), Buddhism even identified itself with the then fashionable "Mysterious Learning."

However, there was eventually a revolt against Buddhism, with the rise of Zen (*Ch'an* or *Chan*) Buddhism, and by Taoists accepting the heavens and hells from Buddhism, giving them Chinese names and inventing Chinese Gods that would preside over them. The influence of Buddhism was limited, because Buddhism in its pure Indian form never gains critical acceptance in China. Despite the conflicts of Buddhism with traditional culture and native ideologies, in early dynastic history, during the era of Emperor Ming (68-75 C.E.), Buddhism began to trickle into dynastic China the way ideologies with staying power take hold in the minds of a people. By 200 A.D., history witnesses Chinese translations of Buddhist scriptures beginning to appear. Until the twentieth century, Buddhism reigned supreme as the only foreign religion actually assimilated into Chinese culture. Nonetheless, the advent of Buddhism, especially as a foreign import, never took away from the power and potency of traditional culture, because traditional culture (primarily traditional Confucianism

---

[7] Shi Hu, Zhongguo De Wenyi Fuxing (The Chinese Renaisssance), (Beijing: Foreign Language Teaching and Research Press, 2002). Tang, Yi-jie, China and the Importation of Buddhism, in Confucianism, Buddhism, Daoism, Christianity and Chinese Culture (Cultural Heritage and Contemporary Life Series, Asia, vol. 3, 2005).

followed by Taoism) had crystallized before and after the introduction, though trickling, of Buddhism.[8]

Despite the prominence of traditional culture, Buddhism would still leave a lasting influence on traditional culture and modern culture. Although other schools of thought evolved in antiquity, such as Legalism, the Ying Yang School, Logicism and others, the influence of Buddhism resulted in the evolution of two disciplines of Neo-Confucianism, or perhaps the orthodoxy and nonorthodoxy of traditional Confucianism with an admixture of Buddhism. One school is closer in teachings to orthodox Buddhism, and the other school is closer to the teachings of orthodox traditional Confucianism. During the Sung Dynasty (960-1279), there was a revival of traditional Confucianism, being the Sung Confucian Revival. Hu Yüan (993-1059) was a primary figure in this revival. Following the Sung Confucian Revival, there is an evolution of two Neo-Confucian schools, respectively, the School of Mind (or School of Intuition), which is associated with Wang Yang-ming and others, and the School of Principle (or School of Li) that is associated with Zhu Xi (1130-1200) and others. Neo-Confucianism came to represent two primary schools, both of which originate from the Cheng brothers, because during the period of the two Cheng Masters the significance of the differences between the schools was not recognized. Cheng Yi initiates the school that Zhu Xi completes, which is the new Cheng-Zhu school. Cheng Hao, the eldest brother, initiates a school that was led by Lu Jiuyuan (Lu Chiu-yuan, 1139-1193) and Wang Shouren (Wang Shou-jen, 1472-1528), which is the new Lu-Wang school.

The commonality of the two schools is a viewpoint that the world comprised two realms, which are the realm of principle (*li* or law) and the realm of material force (*qi*). Because principle governs material force and material force makes manifest principle, the origin of principle is "the" single principle, the Great Ultimate (*tai ji*) that emanates from Heaven. Cheng Hao (1032-1085) and the School of Mind, which would later represent the orthodox school, stressed that the human mind is completely unified and reflects perfectly in itself the principle of the universe. By virtue of the human mind being perfectly identical with the universal mind (or the ultimate principle), a philosopher is duly bound to investigate the nature of the human mind to the exclusion of all other matters, because there is an immutable principle (or law) that inheres in all things, giving them form, motion and change. The mind of humanity is essentially the same as the mind of the universe and can be subject to perfection, in order to reflect that higher mind. The principle inhering in the human mind applied to everything, therefore any inquiry into any phenomenon would reveal the principle of the human and the universal mind.

Zhou Dunyi occupies a position in traditional thought based on a role assigned to him by Zhu Xi, an architect of the Neo-Confucian school. According to one version of the Succession to the Way (*daotong*), which is the Zhu Xi version, Zhou Dunyi was the first true Confucian Sage since Mencius (4th c. BCE) and was a strong influence on both Cheng Hao (1032-1085) and Cheng Yi (1033-1085) (Zhou's nephews). Zhu Xi drew significant parts of his system of thoughts and practices from the Cheng brothers (Cheng Hao and Cheng Yi), and the combined intellectual insights of Cheng Hao, Cheng Yi and Zhu Xi, eventually, came to represent the Cheng-Zhu school of the new Neo-Confucianism. Zhou Dunyi is the founder or

---

[8] Linda Brown Holt, From India to China: Transformations in Buddhist Philosophy, Qi: The Journal of Traditional Eastern Health & Fitness (1995). Nakamura, Hajime, Ways of Thinking of Eastern Peoples: India, China, Tibet, Japan, (Univ. of Hawaii Press, 1971).

founding ancestor of the Cheng-Zhu school, which dominated traditional philosophy for over 700 years. Zhou Dunyi's *Explanation of the Diagram of the Supreme Polarity* (*Taijitu shuo*), as interpreted by Zhu Xi, would later serve as the foundation for Neo-Confucian cosmology. Along with Zhou Dunyi's other major work, *Penetrating the Classic of Change* (*Tongshu*), the *Explanation of the Diagram of the Supreme Polarity* established the appendixes to the *Yijing* as the basic textual sources of the Neo-Confucian revival of the Song Dynasty.

Fung Yu-lan (or Feng Youlan, 1895-1990) also advocated the new Neo-Confucianism and many deem him a disciple of the new Cheng-Zhu school and not the new Lu-Wang school. Fung Yu-lan observed of Neo-Confucianists that they did not totally neglect the ontological approach, such as that of Plato and his contradiction of universality and particularity, and Immanuel Kant (German idealist philosopher, 1724-1804) and the contradictions between subjectivity and objectivity. It was inescapable that Neo-Confucians had to contend with the fact of the need for an ontological approach, in order to make clear the contradiction between universality and particularity.[9] The need for an ontological approach was so obvious to Fung Yu-lan that he even went as far as to characterize Zhu Xi's approach as an ontological approach. However, Neo-Confucians did not stop with the ontological approach or the analysis of the opposites of universality and particularity. Rather, it became the self-appointed intellectual mission of Neo-Confucians to attempt to achieve a unity between the two (universality and particularity), by the methodology known as the "accumulation of moral conduct." Fung Yu-lan suggested, though the different Neo-Confucian schools do not agree on this point, the universal is inherent in the particular, but the particular is not simply an imperfect imitation of the universal rather the realization of the universal. Although the realization might be imperfect, without the particular, the universal simply could not exist. The latter has direct implications for achieving the "accumulation of moral conduct."

For Neo-Confucians, the universal nature of man, as separable from man's instincts, distinguishes man from other animals that are very low on the evolutionary scale, which is "the universal of man inherent in man as a particular." Given the nature of man as a logical concept, and not a biological concept, "it includes the biological instincts but not as these instincts." Neo-Confucians insist that human nature is good, and not evil, because it could not be otherwise. As a result, and contrary to some Western philosophies such as Plato's thoughts, even sensuous desires are not by nature bad or evil. According to Neo-Confucianism, given the body as the material foundation of human existence, what becomes bad or evil is the selfishness associated with such desires rather than the desires themselves. Fung Yu-lan writes, "The standard for judging a conduct moral or immoral is whether the conduct is 'for private' or 'for public.' If it is 'for private,' it is immoral or non-moral; if it is 'for public,' it is moral. Moral conduct means that the selfishness of man is reduced." It is simply that the "accumulation of moral conduct" is the accumulation of diminished selfishness. The Neo-Confucians predict that at a certain point in the accumulation of diminished selfishness, selfishness is overcome, thereby resulting in a unity of particularity and universality. This is the point of unity or perhaps even an epiphany referred by Zhu Xi as "thorough understanding" (*Chanism*, *Ch'an*, *Zen*, or what is also referred to as "sudden enlightenment" or philosophy of silence). According to Fung Yu-lan, *ren wei Chan jishi jing*

[9] Fung Yu-lan, Selected Philosophical Writings of Fung Yu-lan, (Beijing: Foreign Language Press, 1998), 652-657. Fung Yu-lan (speech), International Conference on Chu Hsi (Zhu Xi) (Hawaii, July 1982).

de zhexue, (*Chanism*: the philosophy of silence), *zhezhong Chanyi nan yi yanci biaoda* (impossible to express), *suoyi xuyao dun wu* (or sudden Enlightenment). In short, Fung Yu-lan also considered *Chan* to be the philosophy of silence, and the meaning of *Chan* is not expressible in words, so it needed sudden Enlightenment (*dun wu*). The influence of the admixture of both Buddhism and its seemingly notional concept of *Chanism* or *Chan* may well represent the schism between the opposing schools of Neo-Confucianism.

For Taoists, the external things of this world produced confusion in man's mind, and the greater importance lie in the Enlightenment of the self. As for Buddhism and *Chanism*, they, instead, sought Enlightenment through quiescence or silence (or its philosophy of silence), such as knowledge, that is not knowledge. Feng Yu-lan offers the follow examples of this state of the attainment of non-attainment. "In *Chanism* there is the common expression that 'the mountain is the mountain, the river is the river.' In one's state of delusion, one sees the mountains as the mountain and the river as the river. But after Enlightenment one still sees the mountains as the mountain as the river as the river." Another common expression of the Chan Masters is, "Riding an ass to search for the ass." The latter represents the search for reality outside of the phenomenal (or the Wheel of Birth and Death). If one is persistent "after attaining Enlightenment that one will still attain something else, this is to ride an ass and be unwilling to dismount." According to the Chan Master Ching-yuan (Master of Shu-chou, died 1120), "But if, having found the ass, one is unwilling to dismount, this disease is most difficult to cure. I say to you, do not ride the ass at all. You yourself are the ass. Everything is the ass. Why do you ride on it? If you ride, you cannot cure your disease. But if you do not ride, the universe is as a great expanse open to your view. With these two diseases expelled, nothing remains to affect your mind. This is spiritual cultivation. You need to do nothing more!" For Zhu Xi, despite being one of the architects of the Neo-Confucianism school, the influence of Buddhism and its *Chanism* were always present. The influence of an admixture of Buddhism, though tempered by the greater influence of traditional Confucianism, manifested in several ways and ideas. For example, according to Zhu Xi, because of "thorough understanding" or *Chanism*, the nature and function of the mind becomes illuminated. Successfully overcoming selfishness does not mean the total elimination of sensuous desire. Rather, successfully overcoming selfishness eliminates the selfishness that associates with sensuous desire. Moreover, it is this unity, which also begets the unity of subjectivity and objectivity.

In the end, Neo-Confucians are in the pursuit of "supreme happiness," a spiritual world where the Confucian benevolent man merges into a whole with the universe. Benevolence becomes humanity, and learning (learning of man) begets learning of benevolence. Fung Yu-lan described this state of "supreme happiness" as an intellectual happiness, because it is achieved by not doing anything special, such as leaving society, abandoning one's family, or worshiping and praying. For the individual, daily life becomes the "accumulation of moral conduct," because the individual achieves this "supreme happiness" by simply "accumulating moral conduct" in daily life and keeping in mind an obligation to struggle against selfishness. This is the Neo-Confucian vision for developing the human intellect and advancing human happiness. It is likewise true that societal institutions and rules of order would affect a Neo-Confucian vision for human happiness, because a moral conduct is a particular, and not a universal, and is associated with societal institutions. In terms of antiquity, this meant that in the context of feudal society, what is defined as moral is associated with feudal institutions and rules of order, which is also a contraction of universality and particularity because moral conduct is the particular, whereas, the character of "being for" public is universal. The universal is inherent in the particular. In the end, and reflective of Plato's discourse and his contradiction of universality and particularity, though there are differing viewpoints such as that of Hegel and even Plato's most gifted student, Aristotle, we supposedly come to learn or understand that the universal is inherent in the particular. Moreover, and in more simplistic terms, in terms of traditional culture and the relationship between man and heaven -- heaven (the natural world or way of heaven) and man are one. Indeed, for China, from antiquity to modernity, what would constitute Enlightenment must necessarily reflect the exigencies of China's particularism, ontological base in tradition and history as a nation.[10]

The new Neo-Confucianism in adapting traditional culture to the Song Dynasty, an early twentieth century China, late twentieth century China, and now a new millennium China left, and continue to leave, many questions unanswered. For instance, the principle (*li*) encompasses both the natural and moral orders, which is both the "is" and "ought," thus, normally leaving no clear distinction between natural and moral orders. Problematic is that while the new Neo-Confucianists give principle priority over all things, there is no attempt to discern between natural and moral norms, or between that by which x "is x" and that by which x "ought to be." In addition, the controversy concerning the differences between the two schools initiated by the thoughts of the Cheng Masters continues to the present day.

2.3. Western Culture and Humanity

In Western civilization and philosophy, generally, the universal pertains to the common nature of something. In Western culture, the question of the universal and particular has a history dating back to the Middle Ages, and is especially the subject of the discipline of logic. For instance, in modern Western civilization, the important questions of universals and moral judgments have been challenged on the grounds of being either moral issues or cultural (cultural relativistic) issues. In terms of the cultural relative, a person normally fails to consider the universal, while in fact interpreting the universal in terms of the particular, thereby actually overlooking the universal. Problematic is that the cultural relative is never a universal, nor ever rises to the level of a universal. The cultural relative always remains a compound of ideas or a theoretical construct, but presenting the ideas or ideals of the cultural relative as the product of reason or as an objection to reason threatens its relevancy. For the same reasons, universals are the product of reason or reasoning, and not the product of experience, which means they are apriori and not aposteriori. In terms of Western culture, it is reason that promotes an ordered and just society. One source wrote, "In an echo of the medieval world, the modern declaration of human rights - that people have a right to freedom from torture, tyranny and a right to express themself and exert themself in reasonable ways - aims to keep the encroaching darkness at bay and draw an ever-widening circle of light around mankind. But we have to be careful, for to adhere too strictly to reason becomes unreasonable, similarly justice can be merciless and cruel. Reason has to keep that human element if it is not to become oppressive itself, as in Kafka's *Castle* or later in reality, in East

[10] Bu Xu, Postmodern-Postcolonial Criticism and Pro-Democracy Enlightenment, Vol. 25, No. 1, Modern China 117-147 (Jan. 2001).

Germany and Mao's China."[11] In terms of universal moral beliefs and democracy, "the principle of consensus which would give us a common voice which alone (because all together) could voice universal moral beliefs is derived *from reason*. Indeed, it is one of reason's - that is humanity's - great achievements, historically speaking. It was decided long ago - by the Church Fathers principally - that if reason were not tagged to the common voice - to Everyman - it was not reasonable. This was what Nietzsche detested about Christianity, its democratic spirit."

Immanuel Kant and other proponents of utilitarianism attempted to ground a rational morality on his principle of universalisability. However, there were opposing viewpoints, such as the viewpoints of the German philosophers Hegel (Georg Wilhelm Friedrich Hegel, 1770-1831) and Nietzsche (Friedrich Wilhelm Nietzsche, 1844-1900). For instance, there are Hegel's two objections: it is merely a principle of logical consistency without any specific moral content, and worse it is as a result powerless to prevent any immoral conduct that takes our fancy. There are also the viewpoints of the *philosophes* and Enlightenment thinkers, such as Voltaire (Francois Marie Arouet, 1694-1778); Montesquieu (Charles-Louis de Sécondat, Baron de la Brède et de Montesquieu, 1689–1755); Jean-Jacques Rousseau (1712-1778); Denis Diderot (1713-1784) and his idea that "the great ordering agent was reason" (Diderot's *L'Encyclopedie* or *Encyclopedie*, 1751), and other Enlightenment thinkers from the Age of Reason (1660-1798).[12] The Enlightenment thinkers, generally, considered tolerance, reason and logic, as the road to an ideal social justice. Perhaps some would have even added Deism and its ultimate rejection of revealed religion. The Enlightenment era paved the way for liberal democracy, free markets, and faith in reason and science as means of understanding the world. However, contrary to the *philosophes* and Enlightenment thinkers, there were others such as David Hume, (Scottish philosopher, 1739-1740), whom deemed reason and logic as unable to provide an adequate grounding for morality.

Friedrich Nietzsche (German philosopher, 1844-1900) perceiving utilitarianism as inadequate for the task, also strongly objected to utilitarianism as a means of understanding the new world because, "moral sensibilities are nowadays at such cross purposes that to one man a morality is proved by its utility, while to another its utility refutes it." In detesting Christianity, Nietzsche, while perhaps under the cloak of nihilist, or even perhaps following the then intellectual fashion of the English (or British) naturalist Charles Robert Darwin (1809–1882) or Darwinism (*Origin of Species*, 1859), in the late nineteenth century announced that the Christian God was dead, and that the moral foundations of the West would soon be in ruins. In announcing to the world his famous overman, or what has euphemistically referred to as his superman, Nietzsche's "Zarathustra speaks of the death of God and proclaims the overman. Faith in God is dead as a matter of cultural fact, and any 'meaning' of life in the sense of a supernatural purpose is gone. Now it is up to man to give his life meaning by raising himself above the animals and all-to-human. What else is human nature but a euphemism for inertia, cultural conditioning, and what we are before we make something of ourselves? Our so-called human nature is precisely what we should do well to overcome; and the man who has overcome it Zarathustra called the overman." The word

[11] Bertrand Russell, Problems of Philosophy 52-54 (Oxford UP, 1997). Matthew Del Nevo, On Morals and Universals, AEJT, Issue 1, (Aug. 2003).

[12] D'Alembert (Jean Le Rond d' Alembert, 1717-1783) was a contributor and co-editor with Denis Diderot of the Encyclopédie. Jean Le Rond d' Alembert, Preliminary Discourse to the Encyclodpedia of Diderot, (R. N. Schwab, trans.) (Univ. of Chicago Press, 1995).

"under" translates into the German language as *untergehen*, which by definition means either the setting of the sun, or to perish. For Nietzche and suspected ideations of nihilism, notwithstanding the supernatural, the meaning of life for modern society would hardly be found in the Enlightenment higher ideals of tolerance, reason and logic, nor Deism.[13]

What Nietzsche and nihilism strongly detest about Christianity is its democratic spirit. Democracy, like reason, is often a difficult task and arduous journey. "The end of reason, to which therefore universal moral beliefs are ordained, is a universal: the good." In terms of the universality of reason, "it doesn't matter if you are a Slavic nationalist or a pious Muslim, the same rules apply to you as to your neighbour and your women-folk; in other words the canons of moral belief are more elementary and more human than whatever else it is that you believe, and that they *come first*." Problematic are the human rights activists claiming some are ignorant of the moral code, or perhaps universal moral beliefs, while many perceive the rhetoric of human rights as an alien imposition, a conspiracy of the West, a neo-imperialistic project, or perhaps even a neo-liberal project. As one source observed, if moral beliefs are a product of reason, then the issue of how universal are they, becomes an issue of how universal are we? There are universals that are seemingly superficial, while there are the other universals, which are universal because they, perhaps as counterpart to a Sinic "sudden Enlightenment" (*dun wu*) of *Chanism*, enlighten the understanding. In measuring this pairing of universals, it is the stalwartness of reason and logic, or borrowing from Diderot's *L'Encyclopedie* (1751), "the great ordering agent of reason," discerning between these pairings of universals and their respective importance.

Nihilism is also problematic for other reasons. Robert H. Bork, when considering the many social problems confronting modern liberalism and American society addresses such problems as pornography, abuses of the welfare system, killing for convenience and the rise of nihilism in many subjects previously though to be academic disciplines.[14] In addition, the problem of nihilism goes hand in hand with the issues of metaphysical understanding, because understanding the roots of morality in modern China necessitates understanding roots grounded in antiquity or traditional culture. In other words, the history of metaphysical thought in antiquity provides a window to understanding the roots of Chinese morality. In modern China, the issue of metaphysical understanding is difficult, because it requires ascertaining whether one should embark on a metaphysical challenge to traditional culture or Marxism. It is an issue of nihilism against what societal foundation, being tradition from antiquity or Marxism. One could intimate that traditional Chinese morality suppressed individualism, especially when compared to the individualism inherent in the Western ideal of classical liberalism and economic liberalism. Marxism is a seemingly natural admixture to morality from traditional culture, especially given its seeming lack of individualism, which also seemingly proscribed individualism. China in antiquity did not need classical liberalism. Conversely, modern China may need classical liberalism, modern liberalism or economic

[13] Charles Louis de Secondat Montesquieu, (C. J. Betts trans.), Persian Letters, (Penguin Classics, 1973). Jean Jacques Rousseau, The Social Contract (1762). (Charles Frankel ed., Hafner Press, 1947) Voltaire, Treatise on Tolerance, (1763), (Cambridge UP, 2000). Robert Darnton, L'Encyclopedie; an eighteenth-century best seller – Diderot's Encyclopedie, UNESCO Courier, July 1988. Deepak Lal, Renewing the Miracle Economics Development and Asia (1999), http://www.ipa.org.au/pubs/Currentissdocs/Clough98.pdf. Charles Darwin, The Origin of Species, by Means of Natural Selection, (1859) (Barnes & Noble, 2004). Friedrich Nietzche, Thus Spoke Zarathustra: A Book for All and None (Modern Library, 1995).

[14] Robert H. Bork, Slouching Towards Gomorrah: Modern Liberalism and American Decline, (Regan Books/Harper Collins, 1996). David Gordon, A Case not closed, The Mises Review (spring 1997).

liberalism, as a counter-force against the pitfalls of Marxism. Problematic for proponents of a Chinese liberal coterie is the idea of Chinese citizens surrendering to a higher liberal ideal of individualism. Chinese antiquity was not built on mysticism grounded upon the individual or individualism, and did not require the same individualism as that of Western culture, especially classical liberalism. In terms of the Confucian value system, the Western sense of individualism is distinguishable from Confucian core values, such as benevolence, propriety, righteousness and filial piety. All of which were oriented in hierarchical relationships or society. Early Confucian scholars seemingly set these higher ideals or values at the expense of individualism. The Confucian value system and its duty to society first precept, prioritized society first and above the individual by placing first in the continuum of values, the greater concern of benefiting the state and the kingdom, loyalty to the sovereign and devolution to country.[15]

Conflicting values systems may simply present issues of Western theorizations, especially reductionism, and resolving conflicts between universality and particularity. Eugen Ehrlich, in *Fundamental Principles of the Sociology of Law* (*Grundlegung der Soziologie des Rechts*, 1913), though addressing problems of the books of law and juristic science, observed that an inherent problem of the process of universalizing is that it leads to reduction to unity. Ehlich writes, "He who universalizes merely states that which is universally valid; but reduction to unity always imports a precept to the effect that the particular should conform to the universal." Nonetheless, the greater issue of universality and particularity is in the potential union of universality and particularity. The latter potential union may assist in addressing the tensions between the West and East. The universal-particular dichotomy is a great source of tensions in East-West relations. The dichotomy is problematic because it serves as a tool demonstrating how societies apply rules of *ethos* and morals (*boni mores*).[16]

Colloquially speaking, Western culture is, generally, a universal society, because there is an underlying foundational belief that what is good or bad, true or false, and right or wrong, is discoverable, definable and uniformly applicably in every given situation in life. For Western culture, and enhancing the divide between the East and West, in terms of a Western universalizing cosmopolitanism, this underlying foundational belief is grounded in Western mysticism and Christian cosmology. In terms of both Catholicism and Protestantism, a commonality between the two, though there are differences, is the force of religious belief that drives and influences the determination of what is good or bad, true or false, right or wrong, and even how one should live or die. Conversely, Chinese culture is, generally, a more particularistic rather than universalistic culture. The particularism of China presents a particularistic culture and society where relationships and facts of circumstances are prominent forces in the determination of what is good or bad, true or false, right or wrong, and even how one should live or die. Individuals and the facts of circumstances define China's particularism and its all-important hierarchical relationships and society. In addition, in terms of traditional culture and the relationship between man and heaven -- heaven and man are one. Finally, universal cultures and societies, such as Western cultures and societies, primarily focus on rules rather than hierarchical relationships or society. Resolving the disputes and differences between how "we" versus "they," or the East versus the West,

---

[15] Tu Keguo, On the Paradox of Social Orientation and Individual Orientation in Confucianism and its Influence, Zhexue yanjiu, no. 1 (2005).

[16] Eugen Ehrlich, Fundamental Principles of the Sociology of Law (1913), (China Social Sciences Pub. House, Chengcheng Books, Ltd.: The President and Fellows of Harvard College, 1936).

defines the rules of society or rules of order offers potential for resolving many tensions between the East and West.

The issue of universals and particulars also has great relevancy concerning international human rights, especially the divide between first-generation human rights or civil and political rights and second-generation human rights or social and economic rights. The first-generation human rights or civil and political rights constitute negative rights or negative liberty, by virtue of creating a state obligation of non-interference against right-holders. Conversely, second-generation human rights, or the evolved notion of economic rights, constitute positive rights or positive liberty, because they create a state obligation of interference for purpose of providing certain benefits to right-holders.[17] Western countries such as the United States and European Union (EU) countries, generally, exalt notions of first-generation human rights over second-generation human rights, because they hail these rights as the foundation of liberty and democracy in the "free world." In terms of the EU, there may be exceptions, such as the case of former communist countries. For instance, in 1989, Bulgaria and Romania supposedly threw off communism, applies for EU membership in 1995 and, on December 31, 2006, gains admission to the EU. Conversely, non-Western, developing, and communist or socialist countries such as China, have promoted, and continue to promote, second-generation human rights (social and economic rights) as the basis for their Marxist, Leninist, communist or socialist societies.[18] A Western conceptualization of human rights and its insistence that people are born free and equal stands in stark contrast to Chinese notions of human rights. In China, the notion of human rights applies to the collective rather than the individual. For instance, while recognizing that human rights are universal in nature, Tian Dan, executive director of the China Society for Human Rights Studies, writes, "human rights have specified connotations in different countries taking into account different levels of economic development, different social systems, varying cultural traditions and values and different religious faiths. In view of this, human rights are the unity of the universal and particular." In this respect, human rights entail rights and obligations. Tian Dan further writes, "Some countries one-sidedly emphasize the universality of human rights whilst ignoring the particular nature of human rights, advocating the introduction of a unified human rights model in the world. This means imposing Western human rights ideas on the rest of the world." In terms of Chinese human rights, each person ought to fulfill their obligation to society and other persons, which is by virtue of the union of universality and particularity.

Finally, the potential union of universality and particularity may offer a solution to the problem of resolving ongoing conflicts of a multicultural world, especially between the East and West. More particularly, though a West centric perspective, Plato contended that the only way to achieve genuine unity or peace in a multicultural world is for historical diversity to yield to universality. Contrarily, the views of many Western theorists, including postmodernist multiculturalism, essentially leave the issue of conflicts of a multicultural world unanswered, as though these conflicts would eventually resolve themselves. The latter

---

[17] Isiah Berlin, Two Concepts of Liberty: An Inaugural Lecture Delivered Before The University of Oxford, Oct. 31, 1958, 7–19 (1958). J. S. McClelland, A History of Western Political Thought 264-265 (1996). Louis Henkin, The International Bill of Rights: The Covenant on Civil and Political Rights 11 (Louis Henkin ed. 1981).

[18] Zeshan Kahn, International Economic Rights, Vol. 4, Gonzaga J. of Int'l L, 11-12 (2000-2001). Philip Alston, US Ratification of the Covenant on Economic, Social, and Cultural Rights: The Need for and Entirely New Strategy, 84 A.J.I.L. 365, 372 (1990). Tian Dan, Human rights can be manifested differently, Dec. 12, 2005, China Daily.

reminds one of the wisdom of Karl Popper, "We are not students of some subject matter, but students of problems." Nonetheless, the potential union of universality and particularity, actually, offers a viewpoint requiring that "cultural distinctiveness be effaced as far as possible and replaced with a universal culture."[19] A key to the potential union of universality and particularity may, simply, be the road to resolving the conflicts between cultural relativistic meanings of humanity, or perhaps even a modern *xiaokang*, thus, producing a greater humanity for the greater good (*summon bonum*) for a globalizing multicultural world.

2.4. Conclusion

In modern China, or post-1949 China, the studies of Chinese culture, especially antiquity and traditional Confucianism, admittedly, present a host of problems. The most obvious problem is that in Chinese academia the studies of antiquity, traditional culture and traditional Confucianism have increasingly come under the influence of modern ideology, nationalism and Marxism. Classic examples are the previously mentioned orthodox and non-orthodox schools of Neo-Confucianism, or perhaps even the new Cheng-Zhu school and the new Lu-Wang school (Lu Jiuyuan, 1139-1193 and Wang Shouren, 1472-1528). In the twentieth century, especially early twentieth century, these new variations to traditional culture appeared as both an extension of traditional culture, and modern China's need to respond to Western culture, philosophy and influence. Notwithstanding an admixture of Buddhism to traditional culture, though in degrees, the greater problem in the early twentieth century lie in the challenge to the orthodoxy of pre-1949 scholarship, by the admixture of ideology, nationalism and Marxism. From the era of pre-1949 scholarship to post-1949 scholarship, Chinese academia witnessed a continuing influence, though increasing and decreasing in periods, of Marxism in the study of traditional culture and philosophy. There are many examples of this increasingly growing phenomenon. For instance, there are the discourses of the academic Fang Keli, and his advocacy of the new materialism created by the late eminent Chinese scholar Zhang Dainian (1909-2004) during the 1930s and 1940s, "as a correct and realistic road for Chinese philosophy in its development for the new century," in forging ahead towards "the final realization of the Sinicization of Marxism." There are also the many Chinese philosophers and social scientists pledging to take Marxist philosophy as their guide. Another example is the Chinese Academy of Social Sciences, Research Academy on Marxism (RAM), which was established in 2005, and intending "to strengthen Marxist theoretical research, consolidate Marxism's guiding position in the ideological realm, and uphold and develop Marxism in practice."[20]

In the pursuit of the "other" universals from the previously mentioned pairings of universals, which are the ones that are universal because they enlighten understanding through reason and logic, Marxism, ideology and nationalism erects artificial and political

---

[19] Karl R. Popper, Conjectures and Refutations: The Growth of Scientific Knowledge, (N.Y.: Routledge & Kegan Paul, 1963). Claes G. Ryn, A Common Human Ground Universality and Particularity in a Multicultural World, (Univ. of Missouri Press, 2003).

[20] Fang Keli, Zhang Dainian and Chinese Philosophy in the 20th Century, Social Sciences in China (Zhongguo shehui kexue) 52-65 (August 2005). Marxist Academy Founded in China, Dec. 26, 2005, China Daily. New Learning Center to Promote Marxist Theory, Cultural Liberalization Inches Forward, China Reform Monitor No. 612, Jan. 13, 2006.

barriers. The latter barrier is problematic when in the pursuit of the potential union of universality and particularity, the road to resolving the conflicts of cultural relativism, the greater humanity for the greater good (*summon bonum*), the high ideal of a modern *xiaokang* borrowed from the conceptualization of a *xiaokang* in antiquity, and building a genuinely harmonious society or world. Moreover, the barriers of Marxism, and its attendant ideology, presented the task of reconciling ideology, whether true or not, with the written and unwritten rules governing China in antiquity and modernity.

Chapter 3

THE SOCIO-ECONO-LEGAL ORDER

3.1. TRADITIONAL RULES OF ORDER

In both antiquity and modernity, traditional culture (primarily traditional Confucianism) influences Chinese institutions as sources of order or rules of order. Philosophical antecedents grounded in traditional culture are representative of inseparable traditional Confucian ideals, ranging from social, economic, political, legal, to other ideals. In antiquity, a systemic and persistent traditional culture would manifest a socio-econo-legal order, constituting the separable, yet inseparable, social, economic and legal orders, in the plural and interrelated sense, based on a singular socio-econo-culture-natural history of traditional culture. Traditional culture emphasizes the humanism expressed by traditional Confucian notions of being "right" and benevolent, resulting in a sometimes-authoritarian paternalism, which is tempered by the conservative proclivities, humanity and humanism of Confucianism, and inherent humanism of Taoism and Buddhism, which engenders a greater degree of temperance and humanism.[1]

In antiquity, which is the period from about 500 B.C. – the era of Confucius – to the second century B.C. – the first century of the Empire, when the institutions and culture of antiquity experienced a kind of afterlife during what is referred to as the period of the "hundred schools," traditional Confucianism would influence these earlier schools of thought.[2] For instance, Laozi (or Lao Tzu) would incorporate the traditional Confucian ideal of benevolence into his teachings of Taoism. Another scholar, Mo Zi (Motzu, 470-390 B.C.), also did not object to the fundamental values of traditional Confucianism. Many reformers, such as Guan Zhong (730-645 B.C.) and his famous "Theory (or Doctrine) of the Settlement of the Inhabitants by the Division of the Professions," would import traditional Confucian ideas into their plans for reforming government. In antiquity, traditional Confucian ideals would equally influence politics and the art of war. The most famous example is Sun Zi (Sun Tzu) and his classic *Art of War* (*Sunzi Bingfa*, about 350 BC). The novelty of Sun Zi was

---

[1] For contra view of Confucianism in governance, see Li Ma, A Comparison of the Legitimacy of Power between Confucianist and Legalist Philosophies, Vol. 10, No. 1, Asian Philosophy, Mar. 1, 2000, (the Confucianist system is less fragile than the Legalist, but also more oppressive, since it allows fewer personal choices to individuals.).

[2] Dr. Karel L. van der Leeuw, The Study of Chinese Philosophy in the West: A Bibliographic Introduction, 6 China R. Int'l 336 (1999).

taking traditional Confucian ideals as a basic requirement for generals and strategies of war. The latter instances are not exhaustive, and there are many other instances of the influence of traditional Confucianism. In both antiquity and modernity, traditional culture affects models of polities, governance and other institutions, such as socio-economic and legal institutions. As observed by Qian Mu (Ch'ien Mu, 1895-1990), "the creation and operation of any institution can never be an isolated phenomenon, an institution must be linked with other institutions existing at the same time and must be acted upon and influenced by the other institutions."[3] Despite the continuing persistence of one-party rule by the Chinese Communist Party (CCP) in modern China or a post-1949 People's Republic of China (China), the latter remains a truism, in terms of describing and defining rules of order, including what could be described as legal order in modern China.

Chinese history, generally, is describable in terms of dynasties because Chinese historiography divided history into dynastic periods. The first dynasty is the Qin Dynasty (*Qin Chao*, 221 B.C.-207 B.C.), which was ruled by the first emperor of China, the renowned Qinshi Huangdi (or Yellow Emperor of the Qin clan, a title assumed by Ying Zheng). Prior to the founding of the Qin Dynasty or what some deem the first unification of China, the Zhou tribe having overthrown the last Shang ruler, settled in the Wei Valley in modern Shaanxi Province and located the capital at Hao, which was near modern day Xian (or Chang'an). Prior to the first historic dynasty of Qin, there were the pre-Qin confederations, which were the mythical Xia (2205–1806 B.C.) that was followed by the Shang (1600–1046 B.C.) and Zhou (B.C. 1122 to B.C. 256).[4] Prior to these pre-Qin confederations, there was also a mystical period, comprising several Neolithic cultures (5900-1700 B.C.) or mythological ancestors. In understanding traditional rules of order and law, the philosophical antecedents of traditional Confucianism, as survived from the early Zhou and perhaps earlier, and up and until the present day, are important.

The concept of what is generally describable as rule by law (i.e. written law) dates back to early dynastic history or antiquity. Chinese historians attribute one of the earliest collections of laws, *Criminal Law of Yu* (*Yu Xing*), to the pre-Qin confederation of the Xia (2205–1806 B.C.). The Shang (another pre-Qin confederation, 1600–1046 B.C.), which followed the Xia, referred to its collection as the "Tang Criminal Code" (*Tang Xing*). However, Likui (early legalist, 455-395 B.C.), during the Spring and Autumn Period (*Chunqiu Shidai*, 722–481 B.C.) and the Warring States Period (*Zhanguo Shidai*, 403–221 B.C.), authors the first written systematic feudal code, *Law and Scripture* or *The Book of Law*. For purpose of developing a feudal economy and protecting the landlord class, Li Kui abolishes the hereditary status of the old nobility and instead enforces measures rewarding and punishing each according to what he personally deserves, and stresses nothing is more important to the reign of a king "than the prevention of robbers."[5] The conception of rule with law reached its zenith during the Tang Dynasty (*Tang Chao*, 618–907 A.D.) in the writings, *Commentary on Tang's Law* (*Tang lv Shuyi*) and *Tang's Six Canons* (*Liudian*). The *Commentary on Tang's Law* is hailed as "the earliest extant complete law code in China,"

[3] Discourse on the States (Guoyu). Yi-Pao Mei (trans.), The Ethical and Political Works of Motse (Hyperion Press, 1973). Sun Tzu, The Art of War (trans. Samuel B. Griffith), (Oxford UP, 1963). Ch'ien Mu (Qian, Mu), Traditional Government in Imperial China (Chu-tu Hsueh & George O. Totten trans., 1982).

[4] J. A. G. Roberts, A Concise History of China, (Macmillan Press Ltd, UK, 1999).

[5] Xian Dai Min Fa Xue (Modern Civil Law Study) 42 (1995). Zhaowu He et al., An Intellectual History of China 548 (Zhaowu He trans.) (1991).

whereas, *Tang's Six Canons* provided "the earliest extant perfect administrative law code."[6] These early writings evidence a Chinese consciousness about law and its place in Chinese society. These written laws caused distinctive Chinese perspectives about law to develop and culminated in a body of philosophical literature known as traditional Chinese jurisprudence.

In terms of traditional jurisprudence, traditional Confucian rules of order address Confucian rules of law, and the *ethos* and morals (*boni mores*) of a predominant traditional Confucianism and legalism. Traditional jurisprudence deals with various philosophies of proper social behavior and law from about 500 B.C. until significant Western influences in the 1800's A.D. and those of the twentieth century.[7] It is from the latter representative period that scholars extract traditional jurisprudence from a larger general philosophical literature, a literature representing the various schools of ancient philosophy. The writings of Confucianists and legalists, as regards to their writings on law, are legal philosophies. Notwithstanding other schools of traditional philosophy, such as Taoists, Ying Yang school, Logicians, Chinese Buddhists, the many of the Sung Dynasty (*Sung Chao*, 960-1279), the many of the Ming Dynasty (*Ming Chao*, 1368-1644 A.D.), and even Neo-Confucianists, the dominant legal philosophies appear to be Confucianism and legalism (or school of *Fajia*, the legalists or realists). Although Neo-Confucianism influences general philosophers who directly discuss law, Neo-Confucians have actually little to say about law.

In terms of traditional jurisprudence, Chinese legal philosophy or early jurisprudence begins with Confucius (551-479 B.C.). The *Analects* of Confucius are the principle source of traditional Confucianism. The gist of Confucianism, the orthodoxy of the traditional Chinese state, is the notion that human society expresses itself through a finite number of hierarchical relationships. These relationships imposed certain duties on, and granted certain rights to, respective individuals in such relationships. These pre-determined relationships evolved into reciprocal, if not mutual, relationships. Categorizing individuals into such relationships brings about respective assignments to related duties, because the relationships define duties. Confucianism, in essence, teaches that properly defined relationships result in desired behavior on the part of both the individual and society.[8] Another early dominant force of early legal philosophy or jurisprudence is legalism, which is mostly associated with Ha Fei Zi (Han Fei Tzu, 298-238 B.C.) and is generally distinguishable from traditional Confucianism because of its greater reliance on centralized power. Han Fei Zi is a renowned propagator of legalism, which embodies a radical reliance on centralized power and characterizes Machiavellian principles, in controlling and maximizing power.[9] Han Fei Zi is also the main representative of legalism or the school of *Fajia*. Legalism is mostly distinguishable from traditional Confucianism because of its reliance on *fa* rather than *li*, for controlling a subject people and centralizing power in a ruler. Legalism relies on harsh laws, at least initially, to promote correct behavior. Han Fei Zi synthesized the doctrines of the Shang Yang by emphasizing publicly promulgated laws (*fa*), and by providing the actual theoretical basis for legalism. Legalism became popular during the Spring and Autumn Period (*Chunqiu Shidai*,

---

[6] Zhongguo Zhengzhi Sixiang Shi, Sui Tang Song Yuen Ming Qing Juan (History of Chinese Politics) (Sui, Tang, Song, Ming, Qing Periods) 59 (Liv Zehua ed. 1996)).

[7] David A. Funk, Traditional Chinese Jurisprudence: Justifying Li and Fa, 17 S.U.L. Rev. 1 (1990).

[8] Xin Guanjie, Foreword to Analects of Confucius 4 (Cai Xiqin, trans., 1994). Lloyd Macauley Richardson, China Taken Personally, Policy Review Online, Issue 107, June 2000, (Book review on Peter Hessler, River Town: Two Years on the Yangtze, Harpercollins), http://www.policyreview.org/jun01/richardson.html.

[9] Nicolo Machiavelli, The Prince, c. 1505, published 1515.

722–481 B.C.) and the Warring States Period (*Zhanguo Shidai*, 403–221 B.C.), during which times the view was espoused that a monarch should rule according to law, as opposed to virtue.[10]

In modern China, traditional culture continues to bear relevancy, because traditional culture continues to exert its influence. The transformation of traditional culture (or philosophy) to the practical realities of modern China occurs when, "Traditional Chinese political thought fuses idealistic altruist pursuit with functional practicability, which is based on a combination of the values and ethics of Confucian, Daoist [Taoist], and Legalist traditions." Modern China's leadership or CCP leaders, though Marxist ideology still plays an important role in shaping their worldview and guiding their revolutionary practice, are still subject to the influence of traditional culture. In modern China, traditional culture remains relevant, because, "The ultimate goal of Chinese politics is to search for not only power and influence but also legitimacy of political rule that requires political leaders to behave correctly according to a moralistic ideology and rule based on benevolence." The relevancy of traditional culture is also not the exclusive province of Chinese politicians, because its relevancy equally extends to the average Chinese citizen. It is a continuing relevancy attributable to Confucius' socio-psychological thought, which touches upon many fields of social psychology. While Confucius stressed social restrictions on human beings, by demanding that individuals comply with social needs, observe social norms and see society as fundamental, he also stressed society's dependence on the individual and the individual's dynamic role in society, by advocating that individuals adopt an active attitude towards life and shoulder their social responsibilities. A fundamental aspect of Confucius' socio-psychological thinking stresses the "human" rather than divine, regulates the people with rites, spreads the "Way" and promotes harmony and the golden mean (Confucian Doctrine of the Mean and the Common, *Zhongyong*).[11] Notwithstanding a modern relevancy to Chinese politicians, the thoughts of Confucius and the traditional Confucian school, or traditionalist school, exerted great influence on the formation of the social psychology of the Chinese nation and on the social behavior of the Chinese people. The latter lends to optimizing the socio-psychological climate and producing a modern reference value for the correct handling of relations between human beings and society, and between individual human beings as China strives to build a well-off society.[12]

In terms of modern Chinese culture, and as a remnant of traditional culture, the value of a person or individual is an embodiment of society. The person is the sum of societal rules; he is the father, she is the mother, he is the son, she is the daughter, they are the employers, and other roles. In the abstract, a person or individual does not have his/her own personality, in that a personality is not detachable from society and its rules, rather directly related and linked to the same societal rules. Societal residence through the vehicle of social organizations is crucial to traditional culture. The phenomenon of tradition culture is no less an issue of morality and is best demonstrated by the words of Huan Tza, whom is said to be representative of the right wing of the School of Literarti during the pre-Qing confederation

[10] Jiang Jinsong, The National People's Congress of China 18–19 (2002).

[11] Richard Rutt, The Book of Changes (Zhouyi) 83-144 (Curzon Pr., 2002).

[12] George Xuezhi Guo, Guanxi in Chinese Politics 1 (2000) (unpublished dissertation, Univ. of Virginia), http://millercenter.virginia.edu/pubs/dissertation_chapters/2001/guo%20Chapter.pdf. Yang Zhiying, Confucius's Socio-psychological Thought and its Relevance to the Modern Era, Shandong shehui kexue (Shandong Social Science), no. 4 (2004).

of the Zhou from 298 B.C. to 238 B.C. According to Huan Tza, "A single individual needs the support of the accomplishments of hundreds of workmen. Yet an able man cannot be skilled in more than one line, and one man cannot hold two offices simultaneously. If people all live alone and do not serve one another, there will be poverty."[13] The phenomenon of the group is pervasive, because people need a social organization, and forming a social organization requires rules of conduct. In terms of modern China, and its social-political environment, including the development of law, though not necessarily true for positive law, a persistent and systemic traditional culture continues to influence the formation of social organizations and institutions. These organizations and institutions range from family relations such as father and son, to institutions such as social, economic and legal institutions.

There are, admittedly, the classical references of distinctions between Chinese culture and Western culture, such as the comparable Western virtue (*arête*), and the Confucian virtue (*de*) of the individual (*geti*). In the literature of Aristotle, Homer, Plato, Socrates and other scholars and philosophers, one finds the Western authoritative sources for virtue. For Chinese sources addressing issues of the Confucian virtue (*de*) of the individual (*geti*), there are the classic writings of the Confucius, Mencius, Xunzi and others.[14] However, in terms of the real world and what actually takes place in life, in describing individuals and relationships in China, the words (or characters) *ge ren* (individual) and *ge ren* (personality) are rarely used. The exception being when *ge ren*, though sometimes used in common language usage, is not employed in reference to an individual's personality rather the personality of the group. In traditional culture, which is still persistent and systemic in modern China, a human being is defined by such phrases as "being good" or "being a human being," all of which is reducible to defining how to handle corresponding relationships with others. In antiquity, there are various relationships such as the Emperor and *chenzi* (officials subject to the sage-king), father and son, husband and wife, teacher and student, brothers, friends, *shu ren* (acquaintances) and even between strangers. As a cultural phenomenom, some of these categorical relationships from antiquity still have validity in modern China, and count as an example the phenomenom of *guanxi* and its influence on social and economic relationships and institutions, including the social and economic constitution.

In stark contrast, and as an arguable antithesis to Chinese notions of individualism and collectivism, Eugen Ehrlich, in *Fundamental Principles of the Sociology of Law* (*Grundlegung der Soziologie des Rechts*, 1913), though primarily concerned with a significance attaching to legal capacity (*Reschtsfahigkeit*) and the development of law, uniquely addressed the Western significance of individualism and collectivism. Ehrlich writes, "The culmination of individualism is the principle that every man is an end unto himself and is not subject to any power that would use him for its own ends: neither to a domination that would subject him to the will of another nor to a domination that would subject him to the will of an association in which he does not serve himself but only the

[13] Fung Yu-lan, Selected Philosophical Writing of Fung Yu-Lan, 352-353 (Foreign Language Press, Beijing 1991).

[14] Wang Guowei, On the Institutions of the Yin and Zhou Dynasties, Gongren ribao (Sept. 1917). Aristotle's Nicomachean Ethics, (WD Ross, translation), (Clarendon Press, 1908). Wan Junren, Contrasting Confucian Virtue Ethics and MacIntyre's Aristotelian Virtue Theory, 37, Social Sciences in China (Zhongguo shehui kexue), (Summer 2003). Alasdair MacIntyre, Once More on Confucian and Aristotelian Conceptions of the Virtures: A Response to Professor Junren Wan, 58, Social Sciences in China (Zhongguo shehui kexue), (summer 2003).

whole."[15] Eugen Ehrlich's ideal of justice of individualism initially serves as antithesis to collectivism, and essentially, "dissolves all relations of dependence established by custom, i.e. slavery, domination, and subjection, and abolishes, or at least weakens, the family law powers." Consequently, "the power of the husband falls into disuse under its influence; marriage itself is loosened to a considerable extent by more easily obtainable divorces; the paternal power, guardianship, and curatorship gradually cease to be self-serving rights of a master, and become an office, the duties of which are being performed for the benefit of the person subjected to it." In comparison to Chinese antiquity, traditional culture and particularism (or particularity), the individualism described by Ehrlich stands diametrically opposed to the social and economic relationships, if not social and economic constitution, of China, in both antiquity and modernity. Nonetheless, in terms of the influence of social and economic conditions, including the development of law, there are important similarities. Ehrlich opined, "I doubt whether there is a country in Europe in which the relation between husband and wife, parents and children, between the family and the outside world, as it actually takes form in life, corresponds to the norms of the positive law; or in which the members of the family, in which there is a semblance of proper family life, would as much as think of attempting to enforce the rights against one another that the letter of the law grants to them." For Ehrlich, it was evident that positive law is far from providing a picture of what actually takes place in life.

3.2 Traditional Legal Order

Understanding traditional Chinese jurisprudence or traditional Confucianism and legalism is a difficult task for Western experts and authority. The greatest difficulty lies in engendering an understanding of Chinese concepts grounded in traditional culture. It is a difficulty only enhanced by the need to employ Western theories and models in measuring Chinese jurisprudence, from antiquity to modernity, and the tools of the Western presumed social goods of law, rule of law, and perhaps even rule by law, constitutionalism, independent judicial review, liberty and other concepts. For these reasons, in terms of Western models and tools, traditional jurisprudence is described as an on-going debate between traditional Confucianism and legalism, reflecting a discourse directed to a clash between rule by man (*fa ren*) and rule by law (*fa li*). Moreover, in terms of traditional jurisprudence, traditional Confucianism is deemed to have infused law with moral qualities by incorporating the principle of (*li*), while legalism, as an antithesis, is a harbor for positive law (*fa*). All of which profoundly effects the earlier establishment of a traditional legal order.

As for the development of a legal system (or institution) or traditional legal order, the historic development of law, which is necessarily in relation to traditional Confucian morality, is divisible into three periods.[16] First, in antiquity, and during the pre-Han period, there is the period when law (*fa*) and morality (*li*) are not conjoined and are intended for different purposes, which reflects that they developed within the realm of different

[15] Eugen Ehrlich, Fundamental Principles of the Sociology of Law (1913) 234-35, 491 (China Social Sciences Pub. House, Chengcheng Books, The President and Fellows of Harv. College, 1936).

[16] Chung-ying Cheng, Commentary on Herbert H. P. Ma's "Law and Morality: Some Reflections on the Chinese Experience Past and Present," Vol. 21, No. 4, Philosophy East and West, 461-466 (Oct. 1971).

philosophical traditions. During this period, the principle of *li* embodies morality as a separate philosophical precept and represents the rules of conduct governing relationships between men. Further, *li* stood in harmony with the universal principles of "love and righteousness" that are inherent in nature. This is the Confucian morality or *li* earlier developed by the sages into normative norms. Second, during the Han, there is a further development of law in the spirit of morality. During the on-going process of the "Confucianization of law" or "legalization of Confucianism," traditional Confucian morals mold an early legal system, which then acquires an ethical context. Thirdly, after the Chinese Revolution (1911), and during the reign of the Republic of China (ROC, *Zhonghua Minguo*, 1911-1949), law is Westernized and morality remains traditional. For Confucius, good government incorporates *li* in society, while *li* orders society and produces good government. From the traditional Confucian perspective, *li* addresses the education, cultivation and fulfillment of an individual, rather than exclusivity for government and social control. In terms of the government and social control aspects of *li*, Han Fei Zi would further develop this view of government by *li*. However, for Han Fei Zi and other legalists before the third century B.C., the effect of the traditional Confucian ideal of *li* is not recognized, rather *fa* is exclusively used for the Machiavellian purpose of political and social rectification, which meant rectifying laws clearly and establishing severe penalties. The first two periods, during the pre-Han period and then during the Han, represents the classic struggle for dominance between traditional Confucianism and legalism, or the struggle between rule by man (*fa ren*) and rule by law (*fa li*).

Dynastic history is replete with examples of the struggle or contrast between rule by man (*fa ren*) and rule by law (*fa li*). The first dynasty in traditional Chinese historiography, which is the Qin Dynasty (*Qin Chao*, 221 B.C.-207 B.C.), epitomizes this contrast. The Qin Dynasty under the rule of Qin Shi Huang (or Qinshi Huangdi) exemplifies the sometimes harshness of dynastic rule. The Qin Dynasty, especially under the rule of Qin Shi Huang, is associated with the construction of the Great Wall (completion date, 214 BC), scholars ordered burned alive (212 BC), the first Chinese peasant rebellion (209 BC) and other historical events. It is also a period witnessing the death of Han Fei Zi (233 B.C.) during his imprisonment, after attempting to urge Qin Shi Huang to treat the Han as an ally rather than as an enemy. Qin Shi Huang ruled the short-lived Qin Dynasty until 209 BC. In 210 BC, Hu Hai ascended to the throne as the second emperor (or Qin Er Shi Huang). In 207 BC, the Second Emperor (Hu Hai) commits, though by force, suicide and Zi Ying (Hu Hai's nephew) ascends to the throne. In 206 BC, Zi Ying, the Third Emperor (or Qin San Shi Huang), surrendered to Liu Bang (Gaozu or Gaodi, 256-195 BC) and his army, and later suffers the fate of execution, thus, came an end to the Qin Dynasty. In addition, the year of 206 BC marks the commencement of the Chu-Han rivalry (Xiang Yu of Chu and Liu Bang of Han rivalry or Chu-Han War), Liu Bang's defeat of Xiang Yu's forces and the 202 BC founding of the Han Dynasty (*Han Chao*, 206 B.C.-A.D. 220). Liu Bang ruled the Han Dynasty from about 206/202 BC to 195 BC.

During this period, the Confucian scholar, statesman and writer, Jia Yi (Jia Yi, Jia I or Chia I, 201-169 BC), in *Faults of Qin* (or *Guo Qin Lun*), which became a classic for its Confucian judgment of the reasons for the collapse of Qin Dynasty, "criticized the First Emperor [Qin Shi Huang] for being greedy and short-sighted and never trusting his officials nor getting to know the people." The people of Qin wanted peace under the newly unified empire, but Qin Shi Huang "cast aside the royal way by relying on private procedures, outlawing writings, making laws and penalties harsh, putting deceit first and humanity and justice last, and leading the whole world in violence and cruelty. These methods may have worked temporarily in seizing an empire, but they did not work in preserving it."[17] During this period, although Taoism was the prominent school, Jia Yi and others, such as Lu Gu and Sima Qian, pursued the ideals of the hundred schools. Jia was essentially a traditional Confucian, but still upheld the Taoist teachings. Jia Yi maintained that Tao was the basis of all things and rulers should always bear in mind the Taoist principle of non-activity, which meant that government should not overly burden the people. Following the fall of the Qin Dynasty, and then birth of the Han Dynasty, the government of the Han Dynasty would successfully rule with this Taoist policy. According to the *Records of the Grand Historian*, Prime Minister Chen Ping, Liu Bang's advisor, was asked by Emperor Wen of Han (202 BC-157 BC), "If there are officers in charge of these matters, what is your function?" Chen Ping answers, "The prime minister's duty is to help his sovereign to regulate the principles of *yin* and *yang*, to carry out projects according to the four seasons, to nurture all things, to control foreign tribes and the nobles, to rule the people with kindness and see that the ministers and officers perform their duties will."

From this relevant period, from Qin Dynasty to Han Dynasty, there is the idiom from antiquity, "agreeing on a three-point law" (*Yue fa san zhang*).[18] This idiom directly relates to Zi Ying's 206 BC surrender to Liu Bang. After Zi's surrender and eventual death, Liu Bang entered the Qin palaces. According to *Records of the Grand Historian*, "Liu Bang, entering the Qin palaces, found there hangings, curtains, hounds, horses, treasures and women by the thousands. Tempted to stay there, he ignored the advice of Fan Kuai, who urged him to camp outside. Zhang Liang said, 'You are here because Qin did not rule well. And now that you have rid the world of a tyrant, you should trade on frugality. If the moment you enter Qin you indulge in its pleasures, you will be out-doing the despot. 'Home truths grate on the ears yet are good guides to action; strong medicine tastes bitter yet helps to cure disease.' I hope you will take Fan Kuai's advice.' Then Liu Bang withdrew his troops and stationed them at Bashang." Liu Bang's greatest concern was losing the loyalty of his people. Subsequently, Liu Bang after summoning local leaders and elders announces, "You all suffered for a long time under the tyranny of Qin. Now I am to rule Guanzhong. I now decree a three-point law: Those who kill shall be executed; those who cause injury shall be punished; and those who steal and rob shall be convicted. All other laws of Qin are abolished." After local officials spread the word about this new law, Liu Bang won the loyalty of the Qin people. The phrase or idiom, "Agreeing on a Three-Point Law," became associated with concise and explicit law or rule. Liu Bang essentially abandoned the harsh Qin laws, reduced taxes and instituted three regulations or the three-point law to protect the common people, all of which made Liu Bang very popular with the people of Qin.

Notwithstanding the earlier mentioned categorizations, such as rule by man (*fa ren*), rule by law (*fa li*), positive law (*fa*) and other concepts such as natural law, difficulty still sets in when seeking to actually conceptualize the many seemingly innocuous legal concepts and terms from antiquity or traditional culture. Western normative presumed social goods, such as law and rule of law, might lend more to convenience rather than genuine understanding. This

---

[17] Sanderson Beck, China, Korea & Japan to 1875, (World Peace Communications, 2005). Zhaowu, He, Id. Selections from Records of the Historian (Shi ji xuan) 89-118, 140-42 (Sima Qian-Yang/Xianyi & Gladys Yang, trans.), (Beijing: Foreign Language Press, 2001/Beijing: Waiwen Chubanshe, 2001).

[18] Selections from Records of the Historian (Shi ji xuan), Id. The Stories Behind 100 Chinese Idioms, (Beijing: Sinolingua, 1999).

is especially true concerning the concepts of law and rule of law. If the latter concepts of law and rule of law are truly Western normative concepts, then the Chinese from both antiquity and now modernity may not cherish these presumed social goods. In addition, it is only from terms and concepts birthed in antiquity that one could possibly gleam an understanding of the influence of traditional culture on Chinese jurisprudence. In modern Chinese language, including appropriate political and legal lexicons, the concept of rule of law is, generally, describable by the word (or characters) *fazhi* or *fa-zhi*. However, the root meaning of a concept of law from antiquity is distinguishable because it lacks a similar clarity. For instance, Xu Shen (Han scholar, AD 58-147), in the *Analytical Dictionary of Chinese Language* (*Shuo Wen Jie Zi*, AD 100), when describing a judicial judgment, linked normative value judgments to judicial procedure. The ancient form of the word (or character) *fa* (or law) meant judicial judgment. In antiquity, the words (or characters) for judicial judgment comprised two parts: First, it comprised the word (or character) *shui* (or water), representing that it is even and equal to all people. Second, it comprised an ancient character for a "sacred animal" that possessed a horn for chopping away anything that is uneven. In terms of modern Chinese language, the latter "ancient character" is reducible to or simplified by the word (or characters) *qu* (or to get rid of). The combined elements of the words (or characters) for "water" and this "sacred animal" manifest metaphors in reference to law enforcement methodologies, a symbol for a value component of just and fair judging of merits and demerits, and even what is right or wrong.[19]

In the context of Chinese philosophy, the concept of "rule," as in rules of order or rule of law, is even more troubling or difficult to understand, because the word (or character) *ze* rather than *zhi* represents the concept of "rule." The word (or character) *ze* enjoys meanings exceeding the concept of "rule," because in certain contexts it also broadly translates into the phrase "law of nature." Adding confusion to the latter is a conflict with the Western normative concept of "law of nature," stemming from the earlier juristic science of the Roman *pontifices* in prehistoric times, the *Code of Justinian* (*Corpus Juris Civilis*, compiled AD 529 to AD 565), written commentaries on praetor's edicts of Roman jurisconsults, to the Enlightenment philosophies (Age of Reason, 1660-1798). Chinese scholars generally do not distinguish between the moral and natural spheres, at least not in the same context as an Enlightenment version of the "law of nature." In Western culture and jurisprudence, admittedly, jurists and legal historians struggle with the same difficulties of assigning meanings and definitions to the legal concept of "law of nature" or "natural law." Jurists and legal historians have historically and frequently used this concept differently in the same period, while conveying divergent ideas in various stages of legal history.[20]

In response to conveyances of divergent ideas concerning the concept of "law of nature" or "natural law," there have even been attempts to discard this concept as an adequate descriptor in relation to legal phenomena, all of which present problems for reviving natural law thinking. There have also been attempts to assign the concept of "law of nature" or "natural law" to customary law of divine origin, such as during the Graeco-Roman or Hellenic period, by promoting discernability between laws that are fundamental in accordance

[19] Yang Yi, Methodology for Contemporary Chinese Scholarly Research: An Overview, 60-68 Social Sciences in China (Zhongguo shehui kexue) (spring 2006).

[20] Fritz Schulz, History of Roman Legal Science, (Oxford UP, 1967). Barry Nicholas, An Introduction to Roman law, (Oxford UP, 1992). B F. Wright, Jr., American Interpretations of Natural Law, American Political Science Review, XX, 542, 543 (Aug. 1926).

with nature or ancient custom, and the conventional rules arising from ordinary human enactments. Moreover, since the Graeco-Roman or Hellenic era, the concept of natural law would continue to evolve. In particular, and as an early example of the evolution of natural law from early Greek works, there is a distinction between laws made by man, and laws that are in accordance with nature and of divine origin. An example of the latter are the Sophists directing attention toward the state and its relations to individuals, and attendant man-made *Nomoi* (law), which stood in contrast to universal laws emanating from the gods. Another example of the evolution of natural law is an earlier distinction between natural law (the universal and divine) and positive law (the local and human), which, according to Plato, in *Protagoras* (380 BC), was a distinction that the Greek Sophist Hippias of Elis promoted.[21]

Further compounding the confusion is the need to conjoin, interpret and translate the concept of rule in relation to the philosophical concept of principle (*li*), because, generally, rule is closely related to the term of principle. The latter is demonstrated by poems or odes contained in *The She King* (*Shi Jing* or *Book of Song*), which is the first record of poems collected from the *Xi Zhou* (Western Zhou) to the middle of the *Chun Qiu* (Spring and Autumn Period). For example, *Odes* 260 #1 of the *Shijing*, which is *Zheng Min* (*The Mass of Peoples*), reads, "Heaven engenders the mass of peoples; For any given thing there is a rule; The people have this normal nature; They tend to this admirable virtue." In the latter, "thing" refers to "affair" and "rule" to "law," while "thing" also refers in general to all "things" and "affairs." In this respect, "rule" became the standard, because of the placement of "rule" in parallel with both normal nature and admirable virtue. As previously mentioned, conjoining the concept of "principle" with the concept of "rule" compounds the difficulty of understanding these concepts. The philosophical concept of *li* emerged during the Warring States period, meaning essentially a model, form or pattern. During the Song Dynasty, it became more of a metaphysical concept, and subsequently meaning "principle." Chinese philosophers seem not in agreement, as to whether "principle" is independent of the material world or related to other "things." In addition, some Chinese philosophers simply do not recognize *li* as a philosophical concept. Nonetheless, what is compelling about the concept of principle is that it encompasses both natural and moral orders, which is both the "is" and "ought," because generally there is no distinction between the two. Moreover, there are other interpretations of *li*. In terms of Confucian rites and music originating in the limitation of nature, the concept of rite has also been described by the more comprehensive Chinese word (or character) of *li*, because for the ancient king (or sage king), it meant all regulations arising from the relationship between men.[22]

3.3. Chinese Renaissance Humanism

There was a Chinese Renaissance (*Zhongguo De Wenyi Fuxing*) or Chinese period of Enlightenment resembling the Western Renaissance (or *Rinascimento*) of the sixteenth

[21] John L. Myres, The Political Ideas of the Greeks, 270 (N.Y., 1927). Xenophon, Memorabilia, 4. 4. 19. Walter Eckstein, Das antike Naturrecht im sozial philosophischer Beleuchtung, chap. 11 (Wien und Leipzig, 1926). Plato, Protagoras (380 BC) (Liberal Arts Press 1956).

[22] James Legge, The Chinese Classics, Vol. IV, The She King, (Taipei: SMC Pub, 1994). Zhang Dainian, Key Concepts in Chinese Philosophy, (Edmund Ryden, trans.) (Beijing: Foreign Language Press, 2002). Fung Yu-lan, Selected Philosophical Writings of Fung Yu-lan, (Beijing: Foreign Language Press, 1998).

century that marked a turning point for Western civilization. The latter Western-style Enlightenment is gravely distinguishable from the Enlightenment sought by early Confucians and Neo-Confucians in the pursuit of *Chanism* (*Zen*), "thorough understanding" or "sudden enlightenment" (the philosophy of silence). For China, from antiquity to modernity, what would constitute Enlightenment must necessarily reflect the exigencies of China's particularism, ontological base in tradition and history as a nation. Many describe the occurrence of a first and second Chinese Renaissance. During the transition from Ming Dynasty to Qing Dynasty, there is the occurrence of what many attribute as the first Chinese Renaissance. In terms of political and social theories, the Enlightenment thoughts of Huang Zongxi (1610-1695), and others, such as Fang Yizhi, Tang Zhen and Li Zicheng, differed from all previous thoughts in the field.[23] However, Huang Zongxi's scholarly contributions to the problems of Chinese governance stand apart from others, both during the period of transition from Ming Dynasty to Qing Dynasty and even after the 1911 fall of the Qing Dynasty or Chinese Revolution (1911).

During the period from late Ming Dynasty to early Qing Dynasty, Huang Zongxi was a political theorist and philosopher. A great source of influence for Huang is his father, an official of the Ming Court, who, after imprisonment for being a follower or supporter of the Donglin Movement, dies while in prison. The Donglin Movement grew out of the 1604 restoration of the Donglin Academy (*Donglin Shuyuan*) or Guishan Academy (*Guishan Shuyuan*), growing concern for the state of Chinese governance or bureaucracy and the search for Confucian moral traditions in answer to the then contemporaneous problems of governance. As observed by Lynn Struve, in *Huang Zongxi* (2002), the foundation of Huang's outlook on life was his father, Huang Zunsu, because, during the early 1620s, Huang Zongxi witnesses the role his father plays in the Donglin partisan opposition to the arrogation of imperial power by the eunuchs.[24] Both reform politics of this period and the death of his father while in prison for opposing the eunuch faction influence Huang Zongxi's intellectual insights. Consequently, Huang Zongxi became an active participant in the Fushe Reform Movement that had succeeded a failed Donglin Movement. Following the 1644 Manchu-Qing invasion, Huang Zongxi joined the Ming loyalists in Zhejiang Province, and its offshore island strongholds, and continued to participate in the resistance against the Qing until sometime in the 1650s. His views on public law, constitutional law and the art of governing distinguished him from past and present Chinese intellectuals.

Huang Zongxi's viewpoint that the sovereign was originally one from the people would set in motion for a period the ideal of equality. It is here that Huang reminds us of Hobbes, Locke, Rousseau and other Enlightenments thinkers, because if there was one point on which they all agreed, it was "that sovereignty derived its authority from the assent of the people." Huang Zongxi in *Mingyi Daifang Lu* (*Waiting for the Dawn: A Plan for the Prince*), though not published until the twentieth century, wrote a critique of Chinese government and its authoritative nature.[25] Huang's critique focused on those who ruled or governed and those

---

[23] Zhaowu, He, Id. Shi Hu, Zhongguo De Wenyi Fuxing (The Chinese Renaisssance) (1934), (Paragon Book Reprint Corp., 1963) 295–314. Paul Johnson, The Renaissance: A Short History 3–4 (2000). Bu Xu, Postmodern-Postcolonial Criticism and Pro-Democracy Enlightenment, Vol. 25, No. 1, Modern China 117-147 (Jan. 2001).

[24] Lynn Struve, Huang Zongxi, In Encyclopedia of Chinese Philosophy (Antonio S. Cua, ed.) (Routledge, 2002).

[25] J.J. Rousseau, The Social Contract, 30 (Maurice Cranston, trans.) (Penguim, 1968). Huang Zongxi, Mingyi daifang lu. Waiting for the Dawn: A Plan for the Prince, (Trans. and intro by William de Bary) (Columbia UP, 1993). Huang Zongxi, Mingyi Daifang Lu, Sibu beiyao edition, ch. 1-3. De Bary, Wm. Theodore, Waiting for

governed, by proposing that law (*fa*) ought to serve the greater interest of all rather than the few. Huang was essentially advocating government by law and not men, or perhaps rule by law and not rule by man. For those laws that essentially enslaved the governed, Huang denounced as unlawful. In addition, for Huang Zongxi, relegating the crafts and commerce to lower status or ranking, which was often the lower of the four ranks of people, was not conducive to economic or social development. In the history of dynastic China, many scholars and reformers urged economic theories that prompted this division of labor; such as Guan Zhong (730-645 B.C.) and his "Theory (or Doctrine) of the Settlement of the Inhabitants by the Division of the Professions," Jia Yi (200-168 B.C.) and his reforms to protect agricultural production, Chao Cuo (200-154 B.C.) and his stressing of agricultural production as the indispensable means to maintain the unification of the Empire and others.[26] Huang Zongxi's economic ideals are distinguishable because they are based on the inviolability of individual rights, and stress a rule of law based on a theory strongly resembling a Western natural rights theory. It was a theory that challenged feudal despotism and promoted a republican form of government. During the moment of transition from Ming to Qing, his ideas represented the emergence of a new intellectual awakening of humanity and humanism, and in the sphere of political thought his ideas, and those of others, manifested the formation of democratic ideas with a distinctive modern hue, if not a more universal modern hue. Because of the new Enlightenment ideologues, prevailing theories of the period attempted to take a radical turn from tradition, while also attempting to influence political and philosophical thought. However, what occurs is the relegation of these novel economic, political and philosophical ideals to no more than slogans. The ideologues did not effect substantive change in governance under dynastic or imperial rule.

A post-Chinese Revolution (1911) period also witnessed a second Chinese Renaissance, which appears to have been more substantive than the first. Many refer to a Renaissance, if any, as actually occurring during this period, rather than the previously mentioned period during the transition from Ming Dynasty to Qing Dynasty. Many describe this relevant period in different terms and different histories. Depending on the perspective of the person analyzing this period or political preference such as rightist or leftist, this period represents a Chinese Renaissance, new Cultural Movement or Chinese Romanticism Movement. However, the Chinese Romanticism Movement is distinguishable from the other two descriptors, because the namesake of Chinese Romanticism is more politically motivated.

During the late Qing, changes would commence in China that would seemingly take into consideration the plight of individuals, in the sense of Western individualism or the individualized civil individual. For instance, during this period, two historical figures, Kang Youwei and Liang Qichao seemed to take the lead in what appeared to be a rising women's rights movement. Both Kang Youwei and Liang Qichao earlier emerged as important figures in the earlier days of post-Sino British Opium Wars China. In the aftermath of the Sino-British Opium Wars (1839-1842 and 1856-1860), forces urging reforms for modernization resulted in a call for a shift from dynastic government to constitutional government, and

the Dawn: a Plan for the Prince: a Study and Translation of Huang Tsung-hsi's Ming-I tai-fang lu (Columbia UP, 1993). Ching, Julia, trans. and ed., The Records of Ming Scholars by Huang Tsung-hsi; a selected translation (Univ. of Hawaii Press, 1987). Lynn A. Struve, Huang Zongxi in Context: A Reappraisal of His Major Writings, 474-502, Journal of Asian Studies, Vol. 47, No. 3. (Aug. 1988).

[26] Ulric Killion, A Modern Chinese Journey to the West: Economic Globalization and Dualism, (Nova Science Pub, 2006).

eventually contributed, though indirectly, to the 1911 fall of the Qing Dynasty. Prior to the Chinese Revolution (1911) and during the post-Sino British Opium Wars period, in order to narrow the gap between the modern West and Chinese civilization, Chinese intellectuals launched the Westernization Movement. Its purpose was to narrow or even eliminate this gap by following the guiding principle of "Chinese learning as the fundamental structure and Western learning for practical use." Although these intellectuals, as least as measured by modern Chinese scholars, would prove to be unsuccessful, they intended to build a last line of defense for Chinese culture against the West, with learning from the West serving as only a temporary expedient. By stretching their hands out to the West, many perceive them as unconsciously residing within the ranks of the builders of modern civilization in China. During this period, many also attribute the subsequent failure to some members of the official class and the gentry joining the capitalist ranks.[27] Following this period, scholars such as Kang Youwei, Liang Qichao, Tan Sitong and Yan Fu, would eventually become participants in what some describe as the second Chinese Renaissance.

There were three periods of transition, and most important, during the 1890s, an entrepreneurial class urging a constitutional monarchy, namely, Kang Youwei, Liang Qichao and Yan Fu leading the second period of transition. As a classic example of the quest for Western-style individualism, Kang Youwei, in an argument resembling a Chinese Renaissance during the transition from Ming Dynasty to Qing Dynasty, strongly advances an argument advocating sexual equality. An English translation of his argument reads, "People of the world, do you wish to eliminate the evils of private ownership? To eliminate the conflicts between countries and to rid nations of border disputes? People of the world, do you wish to give peace a chance and live in a united world of harmony? The answer lies in the independence of individuals and the equality of both sexes! And these are our God-given rights."[28]

The Qing Dynasty did fall during the Chinese Revolution (1911) and there was a movement toward greater liberalization, as the then new Chinese Renaissance (*Zhongguo De Wenyi Fuxing*) also reflected the new Cultural Movement. As an outgrowth of the May Fourth Movement, more accurately, beginning in 1915, a strong intellectual movement was well under way, known as the New Culture Movement. Members of this distinct literary gathering were Lu Xun, Hu Shi, Li Jinxi, Lin Yutang, Zhao Yuanren, Qian Xuantong, Mao Dun, Lao She and others. In January 1917, Hu Shi, an American-educated scholar, proposed a major new direction for Chinese literature and language. Hu Shi's proposed literary reforms were set forth in an article entitled *Modest Proposals for the Reform of Literature*, in the January 1917 monthly edition of *New Youth*. Hu Shi, generally, proposed the following reforms: First, literature should "depict present-day social state of affairs" and "contain lofty thoughts and sincere feelings." Second, Hu Shi proposed that the written Chinese language be brought closer to ordinary daily speech by replacing classical Chinese (*wen yan*) with the

---

[27] Wang Linmao, Further Inquiries into the Westernization Movement in the Latter Half of the 19th Century: Unconscious Moves towards Enlightenment Impelled by the Laws of Modern Civilization, Jianghai xuehan, no. 4 (2004).

[28] Jiang Jinsong, The National People's Congress of China, (Beijing: Foreign Language Press, 2002). Wong Yin Lee, Women's Education in Traditional and Modern China, Women's History Review, Volume 4, Number 3, 1. Kang You-wei, Datong Shu (The Book of Great Harmony) 379-382, as quoted in Li You-ning & Zhang yu-fa (eds.) (1975) Jindai Zhongguo Nuauan Yundong Shiliao, 1, 354 (Taipei: Zhuan Ji Wenxue). Ma Zhenchao, Recognition and Interpretation of the Concept of Human Rights in China in the 19th and Early 20th Centuries, Beijing Keji Daxue xuebao, No. 1 (2005).

vernacular language (*bai hua*) as the language for Chinese literature. His proposed reforms distanced him from other reformers, such as Liang Qichao and others. What distinguished Hu Shi's proposals from others is that he had proposed a new literary style, while other reformers, such as Liang Qichao, considered reforms as no more than the greater refinement of the classics. In Mainland China, Hu Shi's role in the new Culture Movement is distinguishable as advocating reforms of the means of literary expression rather than the content. The history of literature, actually, regards Lu Xun (1881–1936) as the greatest Chinese writer of the twentieth century, because Lu Xun's *Kuangren riji* (*The Diary of a Madman*) is the first text of Chinese modernity, and first short story written in the vernacular language (*bai hua*). Nonetheless, in April 1918, in the article *On the Constructive Literary Revolution*, which appears in the April 1918 issue of *New Youth*, Hu Shi writes, "The only aim of my theory on the construction of a new literature can be summed up in a few words: 'a vernacular literature and a literary vernacular.' We advocate the literary revolution only because we want to create a vernacular literature for China." However, in the history of Chinese literature, Hu Shi's role in the new Cultural Movement is minimized, which is attributable to politics, including the travesty of China's 1955 campaigns of "criticism of bourgeois scholarship," especially the campaign of criticism of Hu Shi.[29]

Some Chinese academics, antithetically, describe this second Chinese Renaissance Movement as a Chinese Romanticism Movement. According to this viewpoint, the innovative literature of this earlier period, which follows the May Fourth Movement, is the product of a Chinese Romanticism Movement rather than Chinese Renaissance serving as an integral part of the new Cultural Movement. Some academics characterize the lives and works of these writers as representative of the development of a new type of May Fourth-personality rather than a Chinese Renaissance in pursuit of a greater degree of humanism. Many characterize some Chinese writers, such as Lin Shu and Su Manshu, as belonging to a late Qing and early Republican precursors of the Romantics of the 1920s. Further, many describe writers such as Yu Dafu and Zu Zhimo as representative of this generation or the 1920s, and writers such as Guo Moruo, Jiang Guangci and Xiao Jun as demonstrating the transition to what is termed revolutionary Romanticism. In denial of this period representing a Chinese Renaissance, some characterize this period as Romanticism or a Romanticism Movement, reflecting sentimentalism and dynamism. In this respect, there is a relegation of the May Fourth Movement-generation to an emotional subjective strand of late Qing literature, which was a subsequent pursuant and influence of "butterfly fiction" of treaty port newspapers. All of which, supposedly, enhanced the receptivity of the May Fourth Movement-generation to the sentimentalism of nineteenth century Western fiction, or more particularly, Western or European literature.

From the viewpoints of the latter Chinese sources, the dynamics of Western culture during this post-1911 Chinese Revolution period enjoyed at best a minimum influence. The importance of this earlier generation of writers suffers minimization by a characterization of the activities of this earlier generation of writers as no more than an innovation that did not have a counterpart in the late Qing. In this respect, the second Chinese Renaissance and the activities of intellectuals aspiring to revitalize a culture seemingly drained of regenerative

[29] Wang Xuedian, Historiography in China in the Last Fifty Years, 51, Social Sciences in China (Zhongguo shehui kexue) (autumn 2004).

potentials became virtually meaningless.[30] There was an effectual dismissal of the concerns for greater humanism and democratic liberty as unimportant, as equally true for social equality for individuals, in the Western sense of individualism. The new Chinese Renaissance and new Culture Movement ended by the 1940s, and arguably so did many hopes for Western-style individualism.

In the twentieth century, there are two key periods deserving attention. One is the second Chinese Renaissance. The second is the Great Cultural Revolution (*Wenhua Da Geming*, 1966-1976). Following the May 4, 1919 Movement, the works of writers of this gathering turned towards critical realism with a strong social commentary, and art-for-art's-sake turned towards art-for-society's sake with critical realism at the helm until the 1940s. It is a period associated with a greater freedom of expression and drive toward a greater humanism in Chinese society. Scholars and social reformers of this period imported Western concepts of liberty and freedom. However, they would face the barriers of the Chinese language, especially written language or Chinese characters. For instance, when importing the Western concept of "liberty," rather than perhaps devise a new word (or characters) in the native Chinese language, the concept of liberty was simply assigned or associated with the word (or characters), *ziyou*. While *ziyou* did mean liberty, it did not connote the Western concept of liberty. For the ordinary citizen and Chinese language, *ziyou* actually conveyed a more limited, and non-political economy meaning, such as the most mundane idea of being free to do something. The barriers were the language and culture. In antiquity, the concept of *ziyou* possessed a distinguishable Sinic meaning, and not Western meaning. For the same reasons, it bore greater relevancy to traditional culture and similar ideals evolved from antiquity.

For instance, in modern China, the population of the younger generation or young iconoclasts, supposedly, challenging tradition and popular ideas is rapidly growing in numbers. In terms of the liberty they seek, one source describes them as a group resembling early American beatniks and hippies, and even Japan's earlier *shinjinrui*. In China, these young iconoclasts or new radicals are, colloquially speaking, now namely, the *linglei*, a term that did carry the negative connotation of hooligan. In 2003, the *New China New Word Dictionary* (*Xinhua Xin Ciyu Cidian*, 2003) amends the definition of *lingeli* and its association with the derogatory concept of hooligan. The *New China New Word Dictionary* now defines the word (or characters) *linglei* as an alternative lifestyle, which is a far gentler meaning than hooligan. However, China's new generation of youth, or these new *linglei*, is not concerned with matters of economic or political reform. Rather, and demonstrating their supposed novel notions of liberty, the rebellion of the *linglei* is, simply, against conformity as an exercise in self-expression, or as described by one source, a "display of self-conscious cool." For this generation born in the 1980s, their primary concern is self-expression, which gravely differs from the generation born in the 1970s and their primary concern of how to make money and enjoy life or, simply, *weile shenghuo* (make life).[31]

There is also the example stemming from the concept manifest in the words (or characters) *ren xiaoyao* (free of all constraints). The words (or characters) *ren xiaoyao*, though a concept excerpted from the writings of Zhuangzi (Taoist philosopher), can be found in the title of a popular 2003 Chinese movie; namely, *Ren Xiaoyao* (*Unknown Pleasures*), and

---

[30] Leo Ou-fan Lee, The Romantic Generation of Modern Chinese Writers (Harv. UP, 1973).

[31] New China New Word Dictionary (Shangwu Yinshuguan, 2003), [Xin Hua Xin Ci Yu Ci Dian (Shangwu Yinshuguan, 2003 Nian Ban)]. Lung-Kee Sun, The Chinese National Character: From Nationhood to Individuality (ME Sharpe, 2000). The New Radicals, Feb. 2, 2004, Times Magazine.

a 2001 song that was popular with China's younger generation, the *linglei*. For Zhuangzi, *ren xiaoyao* connoted enjoying life's pleasures and seeking absolute freedom. For instance, the butterfly in *Dreams of Being a Butterfly*, (*Discussion on Making All Things Equal* or *Zhuangzi dreamed he was a butterfly* or *Zhuang Zhou meng die*) made Zhuangzi wonder if he was a butterfly or a butterfly dreaming he was Zhuangzi. He awakes from a sleep in a garden. He dreamed of becoming a butterfly and floating among the flowers. For him, life should be a joyful process that reality should not weigh down. From antiquity, this is Zhuangzhi's interpretation of freedom. In modern China, it is noteworthy that the younger generation when seeking to express their search for freedom or liberty borrows this famous story about the butterfly.[32] While the modern concept of *ziyou* (liberty) embodies political economy connotations, it is the concept of freedom and liberty of Zhuangzi, which is free of political economy meanings and generally sought after by the younger generation.

3.4. Conclusion

Traditional Chinese rules of order fell into disfavor by those seeking to Westernize and modernize China at the turn of the nineteenth century, during the May Fourth Movement and, later, during the infamous Great Cultural Revolution. In modern China, more particularly, a post-Cultural Revolution China, although tradition fell into disfavor during the latter periods, Confucianism, now, contrarily offers hope for a more Western-oriented rule of order, model of constitutional government and rule of law, especially when compared to a governing model of one-party CCP rule. The rebirth of traditional Confucian values in modern China bolsters hope, a rebirth that the CCP sanctions and promotes, albeit for non-Confucianism ends. Assuming Confucianism can, or does, foster universal values and norms, the discovery of corresponding universal values resembling Western *ethos* may result in Confucianism's rebirth. This rebirth may eventually represent a new Chinese Renaissance humanism, perhaps the third Chinese Renaissance movement in Chinese history.

---

[32] The Complete Works of Chuang Tzu (Columbia UP, 1968). Chen Shaoming, Men, Events and Things in the Classical World: A Reflection on the Writing of Chinese Philosophy, 44-55 Social Sciences in China (Zhongguo shehui kexue) (spring 2006). Jia Zhang-Ke, writer-director of Unknown Pleasures, comments, 2003, http://www.artificial-eye.com/video/ART264/dir-2.html.

Chapter 4

SINICIZING THE BOLSHEVIK REVOLUTION

4.1. PRELUDE TO CHINESE MARXISM

In terms of traditional Chinese culture or "old" culturalism (primarily traditional Confucianism), from 1911 to 1949, and continuing to the present, traditional culture has been struggling against the forces of Western philosophy, including Marxist philosophy. Although both orthodox Marxism and Western universalism conflict with traditional culture, and even though orthodox Marxism earlier prevails over Western universalism, because of the same conflicts, struggles or paradoxical relationships, the orthodoxy of Marxism still has to be adapted, Sinicized or localized to the realities of a post-1911 China. From the 1920s, to the new millennium, this process of adapting or Sinicizing the orthodoxy of Marxism to the realities of traditional culture and society refers to the continuing attempt to finalize the localization of Marxism (*Makesi zhuyi he Zhongguo shiji xiang jiehe*). Notwithstanding the earlier brilliance and wealth of the Han and Tang Dynasties, during the earlier period of the 1920s, a compelling relevancy was a struggling rural peasant class because the Chinese economy of the 1920s is a predominantly agriculture economy, consisting of agriculture, handicraft industry and trade, and more than 90 percent of its population are farmers.[1] After Western influence, modern industries and financial institutions begin to emerge. Although there was an emergence of factories producing consumer goods such as textile, wool, toys and other products, in coastal areas such as Shanghai and Tianjin, most of the national output remained agricultural products produced by family farms, and the majority of the Chinese population were peasants. For the Chinese, their plight and the political economy of the rural areas was hardly different from the urban areas.

Shanghai provides an excellent example, in terms of both an early growth of industry and international trade, and the plight of the average Chinese citizen. About seven hundred years earlier, Shanghai emerged as shipping town on the banks of the Yangtze River (*Yangzi jiang*, *Chang jiang* or Long River) delta and its tributary, the Haungpu. The primary product of

[1] Zou Shipeng, Localization of Marxism in China and the Construction of China's Modernity, Social Sciences in China (Zhongguo shehui kexue) 12-21 (summer 2005). Mao Zedong, On Practice On the Relation between Knowledge and Practice, between Knowing and Doing July 1937, In Vol. I, Selected Works of Mao Tse-tung, Vols. I-V, (Beijing: Foreign Languages Press, 1999). Zhou Siyuan, The Chinese Communists' Inquiry into the Social Role of Intellectuals before the May 30th Movement in 1925, Social Sciences in China (Zhongguo shehui kexue) 73-83 (winter 2005). Zhang Guotao, The Political Position of Intellectual class and Their Responsibilities, in Guide, No. 6 (Dec. 6, 1922). Shanghai Historical Background, Economist.com (2006).

Shanghai's local economy was cotton, which is a produce of farmers sold to the local weaving industry. During the late seventeenth century, Shanghai comprised about 50,000 residents. However, it was foreign trade rather than local trade catapulting Shanghai's economic rise. Because of the first Sino-British Opium War (1839–1842) and the first of the Unequal Treaties (*Bu pingdeng tiaoyue*) that would eventually follow, in particular, the Treaty of Nanjing (*Nanjing tiaoyue*, 1824), five ports for British trade would be opened, one of which included the port of Shanghai, a fishing village. The Treaty of Nanjing delivered two of the richest areas in China, being Suzhou and Hangzhou, both situated in the Yangtze River delta. The close of the second Opium War (1856-1860) would produce the Treaty of Tianjin (*Tianjin tiaoyue*, 1860), which would open eleven more ports in other parts of China. Commencing in the mid-1700s, the Haungpu and Yangtze River, as a courtesy of the British East India Company, services opium trade, which ushers in foreign control of Shanghai and its growth as a trading hub. Indian-grown opium was smuggled into China at the rate of more than five million pounds of opium each year, enough for about twelve million addicts or about 10 percent of China's population. During the late Qing (1644-1911), the world witnessed in the nearly exclusive Chinese city of Shanghai, a growth of settlements controlled by foreign consults, and commencing as early as 1845, the practice of excluding Chinese residents from these settlements. By the 1850s, foreign owned businesses were, in effect, controlling Shanghai.

As for the Chinese residents, or Shanghainese, they faced low wages, heavy foreign taxation and exclusion from participation in political life. Estimates project that about three million Shanghinese lived in poverty, with squalid living conditions. In 1934, the average life expectancy was only 27 year for a Shanghinese, with workers sometimes suffering death by lead or mercury poisoning in the foreign owned factories. Shanghai of the 1920s is a spectacle inspiring something akin to terror. Some describe the 1920s, as one of working-class activism, while others, such as Zhang Guotao, perceive the Chinese people as generally lacking in political activities. However, in the 1920s, working-class activism did constitute an integral part of the rise of modern nationalism in urban areas.[2] During the Unequal Treaties period, or post-1894/95 Sino-Japanese War period, foreign interests continued to set up factories on Chinese soil, in Shanghai and other coastal cities, as permitted by the Treaty of Shimonoseki. Shanghai exemplifies the intertwined development of labor-class consciousness and nationalistic outbursts against the forces of foreign imperialism and colonialism. Shanghai had emerged as the key commercial and industrial hub, and experienced a foreign economic dominance that was obvious to Chinese eyes. However, the fact that the political economy environment of the 1920s and 1930s seemed ripe for new radical ideas does not necessarily mean that the political economy of early twentieth century China was ripe for the orthodoxy of Marxism. Notwithstanding foreign dominance of industry and international trade or, simply, foreign economic dominance, an agriculture economy, and not industrial economy, with 90 percent of its population comprising farmers is hardly amenable to the orthodoxy of Marxism.

Revolution and the classic struggle between the proletariat and bourgeois epitomize the orthodoxy of Marxism. Karl Marx's belief in the role of the proletariat as the revolutionary class is from both *The German Ideology* (*Die deutsche Ideologie*, 1845-1846) and *The*

[2] Ming K. Chan, Like Cattle and Horses: Nationalism and Labor in Shanghai, 1895-1927 (review), J. of Interdisciplinary History, Vol. 34, No. 4, 675-678 (spring 2004).

Communist Manifesto (*Das Manifest der Kommunistischen Partei*, 1848). In *The German Ideology* and in reference to the French burgers, Marx writes, "The bourgeoisie itself with its conditions, develops only gradually, splits according to the division of labour into various fractions and finally absorbs all propertied classes it finds in existence (while it develops the majority of the earlier propertyless and a part of the hitherto propertied classes into a new class, the proletariat) in the measure to which all property found in existence is transformed into industrial or commercial capital." For Marx, it is the problem of the phenomenon that subjects separate individuals to the division of labor, which is only removable by the abolition of both private property and labor. Further, *The Communist Manifesto* reads, "The history of all hitherto existing society is the history of class struggles. Freeman and slave, patrician and plebian, lord and serf, guildmaster and journeyman, in a word, oppressor and oppressed, stood in constant opposition to one another, carried on an uninterrupted, now hidden, now open fight, a fight that each time ended, either in a revolutionary reconstitution of society at large, or in the common ruin of the contending classes."[3] This historic class struggle, supposedly, results in an eventual and perhaps even a sort of Hegelian end of history synthesis rise of the working class. In *The Communist Manifesto*, Marx also emphasizes violence and conflict with the working class, and grappling power from the owners of the means of production or bourgeoisie as the road to an ideal utopia, by overthrowing bourgeois supremacy. It is a historical struggle prophesized to eventually produce the end of the nation-state, as he knew it, and all forms of government, inevitably, producing a worker's paradise or Marxian utopia.

However, in terms of late Qing China, for those advocating the orthodoxy of Marxism, and its attendant materialistic conception of history, there were no clear lines of demarcation between the historical proletariat (the class of industrial wage earners or the poorest class of working people), and bourgeois (the property-owning class, capitalist, or middle class). Given the Chinese experience and particularism, the problem of reconciling orthodox Marxism with traditional culture continues to the present day, as an ever-present reoccurring conflict, struggle or paradox. During the infamous Great Cultural Revolution (*Wenhua Da Gemming*, 1966-1976), Mao Zedong (1893-1976), though politically motivated to dislodge those in power, who supposedly favored the Soviet model of Marxism, such as Chairman Liu Shaoqi, when attacking so-called revisionists advocated that the revolution was in danger unless they could stop the emergence of a privileged class. The latter privileged class, impliedly, is the bourgeois (the property-owning class, capitalist or middle class).

A problem for both "old" Marxism (orthodox or classical Marxism) and "new" Marxism (modern, neo-classical or localized Marxism) is that modern China, or a post-World Trade Organization (WTO) China, like China of the 1920s and 1930s, is still without a genuine middle class, because modern China, as a courtesy of "poor socialism," is still experiencing a crisis of an income gap that only continues to widen. In 2003, the Chinese average per capita disposable income in urban areas was 8,472 yuan ($1,033) a year, while for farmers it was only 2,622 yuan ($319) a year. China's agriculture economy now employs about 50 percent

[3] Karl Marx, The German Ideology, Critique of Modern German Philosophy According to Its Representatives Feuerbach, B. Bauer and Stirner, and of German Socialism According to Its Various Prophets, Part I: Feuerbach, Opposition of the Materialist and Idealist Outlook, D. Proletarians and Communism, Individuals, Class, and Community, In Karl Marx & Frederick Engels, Collected Works, Vol. 5, http://www.marxists.org/archive/marx/works/cw/. The German Ideology — Die deutsche Ideologie. Kritik der neuesten deutschen Philosophie in ihren Repräsentanten Feuerbach, B. Bauer und Stirner, und des deutschen Sozialismus in seinen verschiedenen Propheten — is the joint work of Marx and Engels which they wrote in Brussels in 1845 and 1846. Id. Karl Marx & Friedrich Engels, The Communist Manifesto (1848).

of the labor force, which constitutes about 630 million persons or half of China's population, mostly comprised of the poverty-stricken, ethic minority, rural areas and remote areas, in the central and western regions.[4] Modern China is still a farmer culture, and the only difference is that some went to the city earlier, and some went later. In modern China, there does not exist a discernible middle class (or bourgeois), and the lines between the historical proletariat and bourgeois of the orthodoxy of Marxism remains difficult to discern.

The political economy of this period, from the late Qing Dynasty to the 1920s, produced a struggling peasant class, or perhaps more accurately, continued the problem of a historically struggling peasant class. It was also a period of heavy taxation associated with reforms of the Qing Dynasty and peasant revolts or uprisings, such as the Wuhan Uprising (or Wuchang Uprising or *Wuchang Qiyi*, October 10, 1911). The Wuhan Uprising was followed by the Chinese Revolution (Xinhai Revolution, *Xinhai Geming*, 1911) and the fall of the Qing Dynasty. The Chinese Revolution actually spanned a period from October 10, 1911 to the February 12, 1912 founding of the Republic of China (R.O.C., *Zhonghua Minguo*). It is subsequent to this period that Mao Zedong earlier links the communist movement to a rural peasant class rather than the orthodoxy of Marxist dogma, when attempting to adapt, Sinicize or localize the orthodoxy of Marxism to traditional culture or "old" culturalism. Mao Zedong in *On Practice* (*Shijian lun*, 1937) wrote, "There used to be a number of comrades in our Party who were dogmatists and who for a long period rejected the experience of the Chinese revolution, denying the truth that 'Marxism is not a dogma but a guide to action' and overawing people with words and phrases from Marxist works, torn out of context." Despite the fashionable ideology of the period, the 1920s and 1930s, which promotes revolution rather than reforms, the experience of the Chinese revolution, by necessity, interlinks with the dynamics of traditional culture, because nationalism's denial of culturalism has always been problematic. Although the orthodoxy of Marxism would eventually not prevail, Marxism, though with distinctive Chinese characteristics, still took root in China. The dynamics of a persistent and systemic traditional culture necessitates the adaptation, Sinicization or localization (*difang hua*) of orthdox Marxism.

Although many forces contributed to Marxism taking root in China, one of the most important forces or causes was the relegation of traditional culture to minimum importance, if not simply its denial. Traditional culture suffered from being associated with the former Qing Dynasty, which was the last dynasty, and also suffered disfavor by those seeking to modernize or Westernize China. Following the post-Sino British Opium Wars period (1839–1842 and 1856–1860), Boxer Rebellion (Boxer Uprising or *Yihetuan Qiyi*; literally, The Righteous and Harmonious Fists, 1900), Chinese Revolution (1911), Paris Peace Conference (1919), Treaty of Versailles (1919), May Fourth Movement (*Wu shi yundong* or New Culture Movement, 1919) and other conflicts, traditional Confucianism as representative of "old" culturalism suffered disfavor by those seeking to defend and regenerate China. This period also manifest a search for nationalism, which subsequently suffered from the exclusion of traditional culture. Following the Sino-British Opium Wars, structural changes engulfing Chinese society drastically accelerated during the late Qing. Sun Yatsen (Sun Zhongsan,

[4] Income gap between the poor and other groups widens, May 19, 2005, People's Daily. Angang Hu & Yizhi Xiong, The Strategy of Knowledge-based Development: China's Long-run Future, Social Sciences in China (Zhongguo shehui kexue) 24-25 (winter 2003). Gregory Chow, The Chinese Economy, 1901-2000, Perspectives, Vol. 2, No. 6 (June 30, 2001). Gao Jianqu, Zui qin de Xiongdi (My Close Brother), Shaanxi Ribao 2004 4 yue 11 ri (Shaanxi Daily, Apr. 11, 2004).

1866-1925), though during late Qing intending to build a democratic China based on a Western model by reformist policy rather than revolution or revolt, as leader of the Revolutionary Alliance (*Tongmenghui*) pledged, "We will all fight those who dare to restore the emperorship."[5] For these reasons, and others, the Chinese revolution (1911) opposed China's modernization by the Qing Dynasty, or remnants of those forces associated with traditional culture.

Many forces contribute to the relegation of "old" culturalism to minimum importance. The same forces would later influence the growth of Marxism. In the aftermath of historical events such as the Chinese Revolution (1911), Paris Peace Conference (1919), Treaty of Versailles (1919) and the May Fourth Movement (1919), China begins to gradually move toward Marxism. Notwithstanding the aforementioned forces, there was also the humiliation of the Unequal Treaties, which are generally, the Treaty of Nanking 1842; Treaty Aigun (1858); Treaty of Tientsin (1858); Treaty of Shimonoseki (1895); Convention of Peking (1860); Second Convention of Peking (1898); Treaty of 1901 (Boxer Protocol); Twenty-One Demands (1915); Sino-Portuguese Treaty of Peking (with Portugal) and other pacts. The humiliation of the Unequal Treaties would also serve as a force, though not as prominent a force as the later Bolshevik Revolution, moving Chinese intellectuals away from a path of modernization focused on imitating Western capitalist models.

4.2. The Bolshevik Revolution

The previously mentioned events of 1919, though important, would pale in comparison to the later magnitude and influence of the Bolshevik Revolution. A Bolshevik Revolution commenced in 1917 had not yet worked itself out by 1919. As of 1919, and corresponding to historical events such as the Paris Peace Conference (1919) and Treaty of Versailles (1919), civil war in Russia between the Bolsheviks, and an assorted array of anarchists, liberals, various nationalists groups and the remnants of the old regime or guard, was still pending. As the world watched, it was difficult to know what was actually occurring in the Russian heartland. As of 1919, it was not yet a certainty that the Bolsheviks and its Red Army would be victorious over the White Army, the anti-socialists. In 1919, Russia was a relatively unknown country. In later years, especially commencing in the 1920s and 1930s, China and the world would witnessed the strong and residual influence of Lenin (Vladimir Ilyich Lenin, 1870-1924) and the Bolsheviks-led first communist revolution of the twentieth century, which is the second phase of the Russian Revolution of 1917 - the Bolshevik Revolution (October Revolution, November Revolution or Red October). At the close of the Bolshevik Revolution, the Lenin-led Bolsheviks and their Red Army eventually defeated the White Army (the anti-socialists) and, in 1922, the former Soviet Union is born.

The Bolshevik Revolution would greatly influence both China and the world, especially as a model against the perceived threats of imperialism and colonialism. *Time* magazine describes Lenin as a person driven by ideological zeal that reshapes Russia and elevates

[5] Chi Yunfei, Late Qing Social Divisions and Social Stratification, Shixue jikan, no. 4 (2003). S.A.M. Adshead, China in World History (2000).

communism into a potent global force.[6] In 1918, Lenin split with the Left Social Revolution and renames the Bolsheviks, as the Russian Communist Party. Many hail Lenin as the initiator of the central drama or the greatest tragedy of our era, which was the rise of totalitarian states. In the twentieth century, Lenin, during his years as the leader of the Bolshevik party and as the first premier of the former Soviet Union, though a relatively short period from 1917 to 1924, creates a model for his successors, Stalin (Joseph Vissarionovich Stalin, Josef Stalin, or Ioseb Jughashvili, 1878-1953) and Khrushchev (Nikita Khrushchev or Nikita Sergeyevich Khrushchyov, 1894-1971). However, the influence of Lenin, Leninism and the Bolshevik Revolution would reach far beyond the boundaries of the newly formed Soviet Union. The influence of Lenin, Leninism and the Bolshevik Revolution would not be limited to his successors because Lenin had created a model of Marxism that would be followed by other world leaders and rulers, such as Mao Zedong, Adolph Hitler (1889-1945) (*Führer* (Leader) of Nazi Germany (Third Reich) 1934-1945), Pol Pot (1925-1998) (or Saloth Sar, Ruler of Khmer Rouge and Prime Minister of Cambodia (Democratic Kampuchea) 1976-1979), Castro (or Fidel Alejandro Castro Ruz, President of Cuba) and others.

Francis Fukuyama writes, "But much of the Right believed that a 'failed society' like the Soviet Union had nonetheless found the key to power through the intervention of Leninist totalitarianism, by which a small band of 'bureaucratic-dictators' could bring to bear the power of modern organization and technology and rule over large populations more or less indefinitely. Totalitarianism had succeeded not just in intimidating subject populations, but in forcing them to internalize the values of their communist masters."[7] Further, Fukuyama writes, when comparing rightist to leftist, "Radical totalitarianisms of the Left seek to 'claim jurisdiction over the whole of the society,' and violate 'internalized values and habits.'" The thoughts of Lenin and Leninism require an adaptation of Marxist philosophy to the new era, the twentieth century, which was an earlier era many deem as subject to the forces of imperialism and colonialism. In 1924, Li Dazhao (Li Ta-chao, 1888-1927) describes China as "now subjected to the oppression of foreign imperialist countries." Li Dazhao presented the questions of "who can put up resistance against them? The bourgeoisie, the petty bourgeoisie, or the intellectual class?" Li answers these questions, "No. None of them. Only the proletariat. And only the proletariat is the vanguard of the nationalist revolution."

It was a great shock or awe, depending on one's perspective, rightist or leftist, when the Lenin-led Bolsheviks were victorious over the White Army of the anti-socialists. In the post-Bolshevik Revolution period, the victorious Bolsheviks called on the left-wing forces of the world to purse the path to revolution. The threat to the Western world and anti-socialist world was clear. What followed were successful, though many were brief, revolutions, such as in Austria-Hungary (fall of monarchy), Germany (fall of monarchy), Bavaria (briefly communist government), and Hungary (briefly communist government), and other examples of revolutions from workers and soldiers taking power, to demonstrations and strikes. In terms of China, in 1949, what would eventually follow would be the consternation in the advanced capitalist world when China "went communist" and the joy of the majority of the populations

[6] David Remnick, V.I. Lenin, Apr. 13, 1998, Time magazine. The Communist Split, Apr. 24, 1962, Time Magazine. Li Dazhao, Mourning over the Death of Lenin and Commemorating the February Seventh Massacre, (Feb. 1924), In Collected Works of Li Dazhou.

[7] Francis Fukuyama, The End of History and the Last Man, 8-9 (Free Press, 1992).

in the Third World.[8] The Soviet Union (USSR, Union of Soviet Socialist Republics or Russian Soviet Federated Socialist Republic, RSFSR) was a communist state that existed from 1922 to the end of cold war (1945-1991). In later years, the greatest influence of the Lenin, Leninism and the Bolshevik Revolution would be a relationship between China and the former Soviet Union that would span decades, and continues in the new millennium, though it is now a relationship between China and the post-1991 Russian Federation (Russia).

In later years, the Unequal Treaties, admittedly, posed a problem, dilemma, or perhaps even paradox, for China in its relations with the former Soviet Union. During the cold war and a period of tenuous Sino-Soviet relations, modern China or post-1949 China would find that its biggest obstacle to full national independence would be its ally, the former Soviet Union. Ironically, the Soviet Union also enjoyed benefits or privileges from the infamous Unequal Treaties. Official Sino-Russian relations and China's first treaty with a foreign power or foreign barbarian date to the Ming-Qing Dynasties, which follow China's (the Manchu) penetration into Turkistan at a time when the Russians were expanding their empire in Asia. In 1650, the Russians establish a fort near the Amur River (River of the Black Dragon), an area the Manchu deem a part of their territory, and, in 1685, the Manchu destroy the Russian settlement. What follows is the Treaty of Nerchinsk (1689), which is important as the first Chinese treaty with a European power.[9] In 1727, Emperor Yung-cheng consents to a Russian request for a revision of the old treaty, which results in the Russians receiving permission to set up a legation, a commercial agency in Peking (Beijing) and a church. Although later, during the Ch'ien-lung period (1736-1796), fighting continues and ends with the 1739 agreement and Russian colonialists (Mongols, then called Kalmuks) ceding half their territory (the Ili region) to Manchu China, the 1754 peace and, finally, decisive Chinese victory in 1755, for China the Treaty of Nerchinsk is of historic consequence because it marks the beginning of foreign capitulations.

The paradox of Sino-Russian treaties continues to haunt Sino-Russian solidarity in a post-1911 China and post-1949 China. The passing from old China to post-1949 China of the August 1945 Sino-Soviet Treaty of Friendship, Alliance and Mutual Assistance (*Zhongsu Youhao Tongmeng Huzhu Tiaoyue*, Sino-Soviet Treaty of Friendship and Alliance), is one of the most unjust treaties that continues to challenge solidarity. This post-World War II treaty between China and the Soviet Union forced China to renounce its sovereignty over Outer Mongolia, by acceding to the independence of Outer Mongolia; concede the Soviet Union's Port Lüshun (or Port Arthur, the Northeast naval base); and jointly run with the Soviet Union, the Chinese Changchun Railway (between Manchuria and Dalian).[10] Port Arthur refers to the former Soviet Union's naval base or Lüshunkou (Lushun or literally, Lüshun Port), now a part of Dalian (Liaodong peninsula). On February 14, 1950, following promptings from China, the parties or countries sign a new Sino-Soviet Treaty of Friendship and Alliance. However, the new Sino-Soviet Treaty of Friendship and Alliance was also problematic because it produced subsidiary agreements or Sino-Soviet joint ventures, which Chinese

---

[8] Utsa Patnaik, Experimenting with Market Socialism, 16 Frontline, No. 21 (Oct. 9-22, 1999). Margaret O. MacMillan, Lessons of History: the Paris Peace Conference of 1919, Foreign Affairs and International Trade Canada, http://www.dfait-maeci.gc.ca/department/skelton/paris_peace_conference_1919-en.asp.

[9] Wolfram Eberhard, A History of China (Germany, 1948) (Kessinger Pub, 2004).

[10] Yang Kuisong, The Sino-Soviet Alliance and Nationalism: A contradiction, Social Sciences in China (Zhongguo shehui kexue) 86-99 (summer 2005). Modern Chinese History Teaching and Research Group, Selected Materials of Modern Chinese Diplomatic History (1840-1949) 261-272, In Vol. II, (Shanghai: People's Pub. House, 1977).

leaders such as Mao Zedong and Zhou Enlai would later assess as not serving the greater interests of China.[11]

This dispute between China and its ally, the former Soviet Union, would be one of many faced by a new China or post-1949 China. Although the new Sino-Soviet Treaty of Friendship and Alliance would end in 1979, there was an earlier split in the early 1960s between the two countries. These troubles and challenges to Sino-Soviet solidarity mostly revealed themselves after the 1949 founding of modern China. In the 1920s and 1930s, the early Chinese communists would often succumb to Lenin's insistence, and then to Stalin's insistence, in order to avoid impairing the solidarity between China and the former Soviet Union, such as what occurred in the 1950 signing of the new Sino-Soviet Treaty of Friendship and Alliance, and it attendant subsidiary agreements. In the 1950s and 1960s, Chinese leaders for the sake of solidarity would succumb to Stalin, and then Khrushchev. In the interim, the influence of the Bolshevik Revolution and Marxism continued to grow in the China of the 1920s and 1930s, and in subsequent years.

During the 1919 era of the Paris Peace Conference, Treaty of Versailles and the May Fourth Movement, a pending outcome of the Bolshevik Revolution grew from a domestic or national concern of civil war in the relatively unknown Russia territory, to an issue of world prominence. The fear or hopes, depending on one's political preference such as left-wing or right-wing politics, of the Bolshevik Revolution would affect the Paris Peace Conference and the Treaty of Versailles, while also serving as one of the catalysts, if not the primary catalyst, for the May Fourth Movement. However, and notwithstanding the events of 1919 and the Bolshevik Revolution, it is the May 30th Movement (1925) that is, generally, recognized as serving as the moment of crystallization, in terms of the pursuit of revolutionary policy by early Chinese communists.

4.3. Reformist Policy-Revolution Debate

Mao Zedong, in *Analysis of the Classes in Chinese Society* (*Zhongguo shehui ge jieji de fenxi,* 1926), addresses the questions of "who are our enemies" and "who are our friends," as questions of the first importance for the revolution.[12] In terms of the orthodoxy of Marxism, this necessitates addressing the issue of the condition of the classes in Chinese society. Mao wrote of the May 30th Movement, "But in times of war, that is, when the tide of the revolution runs high and the dawn of victory is in sight, not only will the left-wing of the petty bourgeoisie join the revolution, but the middle section too may join, and even right-wingers, swept forward by the great revolutionary tide of the proletariat and of the left-wing of the petty bourgeoisie, will have to go along with the revolution. We can see from the experience of the May 30th Movement of 1925 and the peasant movement in various places that this conclusion is correct." The May 30th Movement was generally an anti-imperialist movement and its driving forces are the May 30, 1925 massacre of the Chinese by the British police in Shanghai, and other earlier causes.

[11] The Report to Stalin on 1 February 1950 by Vishinsky on the Progress of Negotiation with Zhou Enlai, Dangshi Yanjiu Ziliao, No. 5 (1998).

[12] Mao Tse-Tung, Analysis of the Classes in Chinese Society 13-21, In Selected Works of Mao Tse-tung, Vol. 1 (Peking: Foreign Languages Press, 1967).

In early May 1925, Japanese imperialists and Northern warlords attempt to suppress major strikes in Japanese owned textile mills in Tsingtao (Qingdao) and Shanghai. On May 15, 1925, many attribute the cause of the death, by shooting, of worker Ku Cheng-hung, while wounding others, to Japanese textile mill-owners. On May 28, 1925, the target of blame for the death of eight workers is the reactionary government in Qingdao. Mao wrote, "On May 30 more than two thousand students in Shanghai agitated in the foreign concessions in support of the workers and for the recovery of the foreign concessions. They rallied more than ten thousand people before the British police headquarters, shouting such slogans as 'Down with imperialism!' and 'People of China, unite!' The British imperialist police opened fire, killing and wounding many students. This became known as the May 30th Massacre. It immediately aroused country-wide indignation, and demonstrations and strikes of workers, students and shopkeepers were held everywhere, forming a tremendous anti-imperialist movement." In the aftermath of the May 30th Movement, it would be the task of Mao and other Chinese intellectuals to give birth to Chinese Marxism or Mao's socialism, by adapting, Sinicizing or localizing the orthodoxy of Marxism. As earlier mentioned, this was the period, the 1920s, of the intertwined development of labor-class consciousness, nationalistic outbursts against foreign imperialism and the rise of modern nationalism. While the May Fourth Movement and other historical events of 1919 served as catalysts to the road to Marxism, it was after the May 30th Movement that the Chinese people really began talking about class struggle. Luo Zhitian describes the May 30th Movement as a watershed event in the history of Chinese communism, because "It was the epoch-making change embodied in the May 30th Movement that pushed the May Fourth Movement into the past."[13]

As Karl Marx and Frederick Engels wrote, "All fixed, fast-frozen relations, with their train of ancient and vulnerable prejudices and opinions are swept away, all new-formed ones become antiquated before they can ossify. All that is solid melts into air, all that is holy is profaned."[14] The force of Marxism would only grow in influence following the Bolshevik Revolution, which served to arouse the imagination of Eastern Marxists. For Chinese intellectuals pursuing Marxist ideology, the Bolshevik Revolution answered the question of whether a backward country could seize state power and commence the pursuit of modernization. Mao Zedong wrote, "The salvoes of the October Revolution [or Bolshevik Revolution] brought us Marxism-Leninism. The October Revolution helped progressives in China, as throughout the world, to adopt the proletarian world outlook as the instrument for studying a nation's destiny and considering anew their own problems."[15]

Following the end of World War I, Western countries or powers dominating the Paris Peace Conference (1919) and to the shock and dismay of the Chinese delivered former German privileges in China to Japan. During the post-World War I era, following the November 11, 1918 signing of the Armistice, participating countries agree to convene the Peace Conference in Paris. In 1919, the Paris Peace Conference convenes, though there were several meetings. The primary source of China's discontent with the Paris Peace Conference

---

[13] Zhou Siyuan, Id. Luo Zhitian, Relations of Hu Shi with the CPC during the Several Years before the Northern Expedition, Jindaishi yanjiu, no. 4 (2003).

[14] Zuo Shipeng, Localization of Marxism in China and the Construction of China's Modernity, Social Sciences, (Zhongguo shehui kexue) 12-21 (summer 2005). Karl Marx and Frederick Engels, Selected Works, Vol. I, 35 (Foreign Languages Pub. House, 1951).

[15] Mao Zedong, Selected Works, Vol. IV, 413 (Foreign Language Press, 1961).

was the resulting final draft of the Treaty of Versailles (June 28, 1919).[16] In particular, Part IV, German Rights and Interests outside Germany, Section VIII, Articles 156-158, of the Treaty of Versailles (1919), transferred German concessions in Shandong, China to Japan, rather than returning sovereign authority to China. Section VIII, Article 156, reads: "Germany renounces, in favour of Japan, all her rights, title and privileges particularly those concerning the territory of Kiaochow [Jiaozhou], railways, mines and submarine cables which she acquired in virtue of the Treaty concluded by her with China on March 6, 1898, and of all other arrangements relative to the Province of Shantung [Shandong]. All German rights in the Tsingtao-Tsinanfu [Qingdao-Jinan] Railway, including its branch lines together with its subsidiary property of all kinds, stations, shops, fixed and rolling stock, mines, plant and material for the exploitation of the mines, are and remain acquired by Japan, together with all rights and privileges attaching thereto. The German State submarine cables from Tsingtao [Qingdao] to Shanghai and from Tsingtao [Qingdao] to Chefoo [Zhifu], with all the rights, privileges and properties attaching thereto, are similarly acquired by Japan, free and clear of all charges and encumbrances."

There are also the noteworthy conveyances in Articles 157 and 158. Section VIII, Article 157, reads: "The movable and immovable property owned by the German State in the territory of Kiaochow [Jiaozhou], as well as all the rights which Germany might claim in consequence of the works or improvements made or of the expenses incurred by her, directly or indirectly, in connection with this territory, are and remain acquired by Japan, free and clear of all charges and encumbrances." Finally, Section VIII, Article 158, reads: "Germany shall hand over to Japan within three months from the coming into force of the present Treaty the archives, registers, plans, title-deeds and documents of every kind, wherever they may be, relating to the administration, whether civil, military, financial, judicial or other, of the territory of Kiaochow [Jiaozhou]. Within the same period Germany shall give particulars to Japan of all treaties, arrangements or agreements relating to the rights, title or privileges referred to in the two preceding Articles."

The resulting consequence is a new spark for the fervor for revolutionary jargon. Notwithstanding China's eventually withdrawal from the Treaty of Versailles (1919), on the historic date of May 4, 1919, students in Beijing "rose in a patriotic demonstration to... people all over the country, especially the young intellectuals, as they responded vehemently. Thus began the May Fourth Movement."[17] Many describe the latter movement as an anti-imperialist and anti-feudal demonstration. Subsequent to the May Fourth Movement, various schools of communism or socialism grew increasingly popular in Chinese ideology, and in their intended evolutionary course. However, the earlier event sparking a critical move towards revolutionary discourse in the political arena was undoubtedly the Chinese Revolution (1911), and the other previously mentioned historical events of 1919. There would later, of course, be the crystallizing event of the May 30th Movement (1925).

Before and after the Chinese Revolution, including the late Qing Dynasty, one of the great debates of the period turns on the issue of reform policy versus revolution, as a means of modernizing or Westernizing China in the twentieth century. For the youthful Chinese students, revolution, and not reformist policies, offers the only means for facilitating social

---

16 The Treaties of Peace 1919-1923, New York: Carnegie Endowment for International Peace, 1924.

17 Zhaowu He, et al., An Intellectual History of China, 548 (Zhaowu He trans.) (1991). Vera Schwarcz, The Chinese Enlightenment: Intellectuals and the Legacy of the May Fourth Movement of 1919, 12–27 (1990).

progress and the road to modernization. Some sources contend that for many Chinese students of this period a preference for revolution, including violent revolution, may have roots in antiquity, traditional culture and history. As characterized by the Chinese scholar, Zhang Hailin, during the period of the Chinese Revolution (1911), "there was another deeper-seated ideological reason, i.e., peasant revolts and violent revolutions in Chinese history still had a great effect on radical revolutionaries." In modern China, there are many that would attribute violent revolutions in Chinese history, including peasant revolts, as having influenced the preference for revolution rather than reformist policy.[18] There are many, including Mao Zedong, subscribing to a correlation between a Chinese history of peasant revolts and a propensity for revolution rather than reformist policies. There have been many peasant uprisings in history, which many describe as a history of revolutions.

One source contends revolution is a word (or characters) that even Confucius uses for describing the Shang Tang (or Cheng-Tang) Revolution. The Shang's (pre-Qin confederation, 1766-1122 B.C.) founder, Shang-Tang (Tian Yi or Heavenly Yi), claimed that Lord Highness (Heaven) instructed him to campaign against the Xia's Lord Jie, because of Jie's corruption, lasciviousness and cruelty. The last Xia ruler, Lord Jie, had refused to take admonition by claiming that the "mandate" was with him the minute he was born. Shang-tang, as the founder of the pre-Qin confederation of the Shang, "was who to great valour added the virtues of humanity and justice." From Confucius first describing the Shang Tang replacement of the pre-Qin confederation of the mythical Xia as a revolution, to Sun Yat-sen's "call for" a revolution, when seeking to overthrown Manchu rule of the late nineteenth century or late Qing, and considering the many peasant revolts in between, revolt and revolution did constitute a part of dynastic history. At the turn of the twentieth century and during the late Qing, W.A.P. Martin, in *The Awakening of China* (1907), wrote, "Revolutions many and startling are to be recorded: some, like that in the epoch of the Great Wall, which stamped the impress of unity upon the entire people; others, like the Manchu conquest of 1644, by which, in whole or in part, they were brought under the sway of a foreign dynasty."

Mao Zedong, in *The Chinese Revolution and the Chinese Communist Party* (*Zhongguo geming yu Zhongguo gongchandang,* 1939), wrote that the "principal contradiction in feudal society was between the peasantry and the landlord class. The peasants and the handicraft workers were the basic classes which created the wealth and culture of this society."[19] Mao offered the following examples of peasant revolts or violent revolution against landlord rule or feudal rule. According to traditional Chinese historiography, China was first united by Qin Shi-huang (Yellow Emperor of the Qin clan), who was the first Emperor of the Qin Dynasty (*Qin Chao* 221 B.C. - 206/207 B.C.). During the Qin Dynasty, in 221 B.C., there is the first great peasant uprising of Chen Sheng, Wu Kuang, Hsiang Yu and Liu Pang. In 209 B.C., Chen Sheng and Wu Kuang organized a revolt in Chihsien County (now Suhsien County in Anhui Province) against the tyranny of the Qin Dynasty. Hsiang Yu and Liu Pang were the most prominent of those who rose in response to this armed uprising all over the country,

---

[18] Zhang Hailin, On the "Revolution Worship" during the Revolution of 1911, Nanjing Univ., Nanjing Daxue xuebao, No. 3 (2002). An Xiang, An Xiang's China's Wars: The Zhou Dynasty Part II, June 14, 2006. Volume: 4, Issue 43, History at Orbat.com, May 31, 2006. W.A.P. Martin, The Awakening of China, (Doubleday, Page & Co, rpt. 1907).

[19] Mao Zedong, The Chinese Revolution and the Chinese Communist Party, December 1939, in Vol. II, Selected Works of Mao Tse-tung, Vols. I-V (Beijing: Foreign Languages Press, 1999).

with Hsiang Yu's army annihilating the main forces of the Qin, and Liu Pang's troops taking the Qin capital. The latter struggle also births the founding the Han Dynasty.

During the Han Dynasty (206 B.C.-A.D. 220), there are the uprisings of Hsinshih, Pinglin, the Red Eyebrows, the Bronze Horses and the Yellow Turbans, which are peasant uprisings in the latter years of the Western Han Dynasty. In A.D. 8, Wang Mang overthrew the reigning dynasty and ascends to the throne, but the starving masses in Hsinshih (now Chingshan County in Hubei] and Pinglin (now Suihsien County in Hubei) rose in revolt. The Bronze Horses and the Red Eyebrows are the peasant forces that revolt during his reign in what is now central Hubei and central Shantung Provinces. In A.D. 184, the Yellow Turbans, also stage a peasant revolt. In the Sui Dynasty (581-618), during commencement of the seventh century, there are the uprising of Li Mi and Tou Chien-theh, who are leaders of peasant uprisings against the Sui Dynasty in Henan and Hubei. In the Tang Dynasty (618-907), there are the uprisings of Wang Hsienchih and Huang Chao. First, in A.D. 874, Wang Hsien-chih organizes an uprising in Shandong and then, in the following year, Huang Chao organizes an uprising to support him. In the Sung Dynasty (960-1271), during the twelfth century, there are the peasant uprisings of Sung Chiang and Fang La along the borders between Shandong, Hubei, Honan, Henan and Jiangsu, while Fang La was active in Zhejiang and Anhui. In the Yuan Dynasty (1271-1368), there is the 1351 uprising of Chu Yuan-chang, in revolt against the rule of the Yuan (Mongol) Dynasty. In 1368, Chu Yuan-chang eventually succeeds in overthrowing the rule of the Mongol Dynasty. Finally, from the Ming Dynasty (1368-1644), to the uprising known as the War of the Taiping Heavenly Kingdom (1851-1864) during the last dynasty in Chinese history, being the Qing Dynasty, there is the uprising led by Li Xiucheng (1823-1864).

For Mao Zedong, a history of peasant revolts did not necessarily mean that violent revolution ought, or ought not, to be condemned. Rather, Mao perceived the problem of peasant uprisings and wars as the problem of lack of what he deemed "correct" leadership, such as what the proletariat and the Communist Party provide today. Mao opined, "Every peasant revolution failed, and the peasantry was invariably used by the landlords and the nobility, either during or after the revolution, as a lever for bringing about dynastic change." Despite social progress being made after each great peasant revolt, Mao contends, "the feudal economic relations and political system remained basically unchanged." Mao observed that only within the past hundred years had a change of a different order occurred. In comparison to antiquity, the early Chinese communists perceive the peasant revolt as now wearing the dress of modern democracy and freedom, though now Chinese communists-defined concepts, which had resurfaced in twentieth century China.

Nonetheless, a post-Chinese Revolution (1911) period would witness an early, perhaps even premature, test of constitutional government by a Sun Yatsen-led China, or Republic of China (R.O.C.). Reflecting on the failings of the Chinese Revolution, Sun wrote a *General Outline for China's Constitution*. He divided the so-called democratic revolution into the phases of the military, tutelary and constitutional government. For Sun Yatsen, "in the future revolution, we should try not only to destroy, but also to construct." Sun Yatsen would return to the ideals of constitutionalism and an earlier preference for reformist policy, or gradual reformism. Revolution, especially violent revolution, at least for some such as Sun Yatsen, was impractical, as revolution sought immediate changes that would eventually fail, or perhaps even reverse previous successes. It bears remembering that during the late Qing, Sun Yat-sen accused Manchu rulers of the Qing Dynasty of despotic rule over the Chinese people, which "violated their inalienable rights of life, liberty and property," and further, "suppressed their liberty of speech and association, and deprived them of their rights without due process of law."

4.4. Localization of Marxism

The Chinese Revolution (1911), effectually, ended the late-Qing debate between reformist policy and dynastic or imperial rule. After the Chinese Revolution, the failure of democratic constitutionalism in the first years of the republic equally contributed to the transition to revolutionary discourse, and ending the debate between reformist policy and revolution. The early communists advocated a class revolution, the Youth Party advocated an "all-people's" revolution and even the *Kuomintang* (Guomindang), though it would turn anti-communist by 1927, advocated a nationalist revolution. One Chinese scholar, Wang Qicheng, opined that from a semantic perspective, the Guomindang/communist slogan "Down with imperialism" differed little from the Youth Party's call to "resist foreign aggression." However, the former implied a Leninist world revolutionary front that would that call for China's national liberation and the overthrow of both China's feudal past and Western capitalist imperialism. As Karl Marx once warned, if confined to a region, communism cannot survive. In order for communism to survive and grow in a relatively backward country, it must take the initiative of expanding its communications with an outside world and actively pursue becoming a world-influencing power in the international community.[20]

In the 1920s, the *Kuomintang* and Communist Party joined forces to suppress the Youth Party, and in 1927, there was a total break between the *Kuomintang* and Communist Party. Earlier tensions were rising between the *Kuomintang* and the Communist Party during their joint military campaign against warlords, namely, the Northern Expedition (*Bei Fa*, 1926-1927). Tensions arising during the Northern Expedition were heightened when followed by the early anti-communist purges of April 12, 1927, by Jiang Jieshi (or Chiang Kai-shek's Nationalists or *Kuomintang*) (1887-1975), and then on July 15, 1927, by Wang Jingwei, which resulted in a final split between the Communist Party and Jiang Jieshi's Nationalists or *Kuomintang*. The Han Chinese later describe Wang Jingei (1993-1944) as a traitor, because he subsequently split with the *Kuomintang* and forms a Japanese supported collaborationist government in Nanjing, in Jiangzu Province. Nonetheless, and despite the *Kuomintang* turning anti-communist and the Youth Party opposing both the *Kuomintang* and Communist Party, during the 1920s, Marxism, though with Chinese characteristics, became the predominant trend or ideology.

An immediate consequence would be the July 1921 birth of the CCP, in Shanghai, when the First National Congress convenes. Following the founding of the CCP, the party announced that the revolution is a socialist one and defined the tasks of the CCP as "overthrowing the power of the capitalist class, eliminating the capitalist system of ownership, and establishing the dictatorship of the proletariat." In July 1922, and following

[20] Wang Qisheng, "Revolution" and "Counter-Revolution": Interaction among the Three Major Political Parties in China in the 1920s, 79-92, Social Sciences in China (Zhongguo shehui kexue) (winter 2004). The first program of the Communist Party of China, In Selected Documents of the Central Committee of the Communist Party of China, Vol. I (Party School of the CC of the CPC Press, 1982), 5. Zhao Xingliang, Is Globalization in Favor of Socialism?, no. 7 (2002).

the 1922 meeting of Communist International, during the Second National Congress, the CCP fully embraces Lenin's theory or Leninism regarding nationalities and colonies as the party's guiding principle of the Chinese democratic revolution.[21] The two conferences reflected a common spirit or goal of pursuing a nationalist revolution. This commonality and purpose of goals also lends explanation to why and how during the early 1920s the *Kuomintang* and Communist Party joined forces, though briefly. The earlier joint conferences convened in 1922 and resulting in the common spirit of pursuing the nationalist revolution, led to the decision of the CPC to support and participate jointly, though briefly, in *Kuomintang* undertakings, such as the earlier mentioned Northern Expedition. However, the unexpected and future consequences for a modern China, post-1949 China, and even a post-WTO China would be the CCP's views on constitutional theory and practice; China becoming a communist state; and China selecting democratic centralism rather than separation of powers as an underlying principle of governance and other consequences. It was a period when young communist leaders considered parliamentary forms of government to be both infeasible and a tool of the capitalists.[22]

In the 1930s, there was also an attendant growth of the popularity of Marxism as the ideological mainstream among the Chinese literati and students. During the 1930s, Marxism only grew in influence and prominence. As previously mentioned, in the 1920s, the world witnessed Mao Zedong's linking of the communist movement to a rural peasant class, but not the orthodoxy of Marxist dogma. In addition, during the earlier Yan'an (Yenan) period of the 1930s, Mao Zeong formally announced his variation of what can variously be described as Marxism with Chinese characteristics, Sinicized Marxism, localized Marxism, Mao's socialism, or even the Maoist International Movement (MIM). The latter, the MIM, described itself as upholding "the revolutionary communist ideology of Marxism-Leninism-Maoism," as "an internationalist organization that works from the vantage point of the Third World proletariat."

During the Yan'an period, Marxism is heavily subject to the process of adaptation, Sinicization or localization. The city of Yan'an, in Shaanxi Province, China, is on the Yen River. Yan'an was the end of the route for the famous long march, the incredible Long March of 6,000 miles (9,660 km.) by ill-equipped revolutionary soldiers of the Red Army (1934–35). Yan'an also served as the *de facto* capital (1936-47, 1948-9) of the Chinese communists, who established arsenals, colleges and a military academy there, such as the Anti-Japanese Military and Political College. During World War II, loess caves serve as homes and air raid shelters.[23] During the Yan'an period or the 1930s, Mao imbues Marxism with Chinese characteristics, or perhaps commences the process of Sinicizing or localizing Marxist philosophy, in the publications *On Practice* (*Shijian lun*, 1937) and *On Contradiction* (*Maodun lun*, 1937). The latter publication *On Contradiction* is subsequent to *On Practice*,

[21] Zhou Siyuan, Id. Xiang Qing, A Historical Survey of the Relationship between the Communist International and the Chinese Revolution, 25-30 (Guangdong: People's Pub. House, 1983).

[22] Jiang Jinsong, The National People's Congress of China 18–19 (2002). Zhou Enlai Tong Yizhan Xian Wen Xuan (Selected Works of Zhou Enlai United Front) 141 (1984). Mao Zedong Xuanji (Selected Works of Mao Zedong) 628–29 (1966).

[23] Maoist International Movement (MIM) About MIM, http://www.etext.org/Politics/MIM/. J. Myrdal, Report from a Chinese Village (M. Michael, trans.); J. K. Emmerson, A View From Yenan (1985). Mao Zedong, On Practice On the Relation between Knowledge and Practice, between Knowing and Doing July 1937, In Vol. I, Selected Works of Mao Tse-tung, (Beijing: Foreign Languages Press, 1999). Mao Zedong, On Contradiction, Aug. 1937, Id.

and is actually the product of a series of lectures at the Anti-Japanese Military and Political College. Mao also later revises *On Contraction* for inclusion in the *Selected Works of Mao Tse-tung* (*Mao Zedong Xuanji*, 1966). Mao's attempt to Sinicize or localize Marxism did create rifts, though manageable, between the early Chinese communists and the former Soviet Union. It was a rift, though manageable, that survived many decades, including the period of the 1949 founding of modern China. In the late 1950s, the rift intensified, and in the early 1960s, found itself an unmanageable rift challenging a former solidarity.

However, notwithstanding Mao's socialism, especially during the 1920s and 1930s, as a challenge to orthodox Marxism, Chinese Marxism, communism or socialism continues to evolve in modern China or post-1949 China, and continues to evolve in a post-WTO China or post-2001 China. As previously mentioned, the 1950s witnessed a turn for the worst in Sino-Soviet relations, which eventually, in the 1960s, led to a split between China and the former Soviet Union. In terms of Sino-Soviet relations, during the mid-1950s, a post-World War II era was experiencing the balance of power, in the process of seeking a fix under the cold war structure and politics. It was also an era of difficult relations between China and the former Soviet Union, as many factors contributed to a split between the two countries. Commencing in the 1950s, growing tensions make the goal of maintaining solidarity on the communist front increasingly difficult.

A list of these factors, though not exhaustive, contributing to the split between China and the former Soviet Union are: the 1945 Sino-Soviet Treaty of Friendship, Alliance and Mutual Assistance, and its attendant subsidiary agreements; cold war diplomacy; domestic instability such as severe recession commencing in the 1950s and continuing in the 1960s; the "Western threat," in particular, the United States as China's main threat; Jiang Jieshi's Nationalists or *Kuomintang*, and the problems of the Republic of China, Taiwan, cross strait relations, and possible U.S. military intervention; the June 25, 1950 outbreak of war on the Korean Peninsula and Kim Il Sung; Stalin and the former Soviet Union's reluctance to provide air cover or support for the Chinese People's Volunteers (CPV) in the Korean War; Khrushchev and unfulfilled Sino-Soviet military cooperation during the 1950s, such as the issues of the long-range radio station and a combined naval fleet; the Indo-China war and the Vietnamese-American negotiations from the Geneva Conference of 1954 to 1973 (Richard Nixon presidency, Paris Peace Accords, and end of war); the Sino-Indian border conflict of 1962, the disputed McMahon line, and Khrushchev's reversed policy of peaceful coexistence towards India and promise to provide military aid to India; and the Rebellion in Tibet in 1959.[24]

In the 1960s and 1970s, China began to emerge as a world player, as it plays the strategic game alongside the former Soviet Union and the United States, in the Asia region. In the years that followed, China became increasingly intolerant of succumbing to the insistence of

---

[24] Zhang Baijia, Cross the Yalu River – How China Handled a Crisis and Decided to Enter the Korean War, Social Sciences in China, 109-117 (Zhongguo shehui kexue) (summer 2003). Shen Zhihua, Khrushchev, Mao Zedong and the Unfulfilled Sino-Soviet Military Cooperation, 118-12 (summer 2003). S. Khrushchev, Missiles and Crisis – Khrushchev in his Son's Eyes, transl. Guo Jiashen, et. al., (Beijing: Central Compilation and Translation Press, 2002). Qu Xing, Chinese and Vietnamese Views on the Indo-China War: Strategic Unity and Tactical Differences, 127-135, Social Sciences in China, (Zhongguo shehui kexue) (summer 2003). T.N. Kaul, A Diplomat's Diary, 1947-1999: China, India and USA, The Tantalizing Triangle, 77-78 (New Delhi: Macmillan India Limited, 2000). Paris Peace Accords, Agreement on Ending the War and Restoring Peace in Vietnam, signed in Paris and entered into force January 17, 1973, http://www.aiipowmia.com/sea/ppa1973.html.

the Soviet Union and its leaders, as it had done so in past eras. The close of cold war and fall of the former Soviet Union would see the birth of the Russian Federation (Russia) and a new era in Sino-Russian relations. On July 16, 2001, in Moscow, then China President Jiang Zemin and Russian President Vladimir Putin sign a milestone agreement, namely, the Treaty of Good-Neighborliness and Friendly Cooperation between the People's Republic of China and the Russian Federation (*Zhong e ruo si mulin youhao hezuo tiaoyue*).[25] In countering a history of Sino-Russian relations that experiences both alignment and confrontation during the twentieth century, the treaty stipulates that new Sino-Russian relations reflect common grounds on the principles of peaceful co-existence or mutual respect to sovereignty and territorial integrity, mutual non-aggression and non-interference into each other's internal affairs. The treaty also stipulates the principles and directions for future bilateral cooperation in the fields of politics, economics, trade, science and technology, culture and international issues. According to Kong Quan, China Foreign Ministry spokesman, "With non-alignment, non-confrontation and not attacking a third country as its central theme, the treaty not only acts as a guideline for good-neighborly relations and cooperation between the two countries, but sets a model for the establishment of new international relations quite different from that of the cold war. In keeping with the spirit of the treaty and for the sake of world peace and development, the two sides are to take effective measures to promote political mutual trust and strategic cooperation." The clearest evidence of the new era of Sino-Russian relations and cooperation are the Boao Forum for Asia (BFA) and the Shanghai Cooperation Organization (SCO), both of which are China-established bodies. There is also the voting record of China and Russia as permanent members of the United Nations Security Council.[26]

In the new millennium, it is China, and not the former Soviet Union or now Russia, which is evolving into the leading Marxist, communist or socialist country. From the 1920s to the new millennium, China evolved into a world player and is no longer a puppet of the former Soviet Union, or mere pawn in the international communist movement. Rather, China is now a leading world player in the international community. China has, in effect, adapted, Sinicized or localized the Bolshevik Revolution. As for Marxism, China after borrowing the Western philosophy of Marxist philosophy, gave it a Chinese name, Mao's socialism, and then commences the process of adapting, Sinicizing or localizing Marxism, and is continuing to do so, in an attempt to finalize its adaptation, Sinicization or localization. China also borrowed Soviet models of industrialization and planning, and then jointly pursued a socialist-political polity and capitalist-economic policy. It is no less different than when China borrowed Buddhism during the Han Dynasty, because the Taoists, after accepting the heavens and hells from Buddhism, gave them Chinese names and invented Chinese Gods that would preside over them.[27]

---

[25] Li Yan, Milestone of Sino-Russia Relations: Commentary, July 16, 2002, People's Daily. Treaty of Good-Neighborliness and Friendly Cooperation between the People's Republic of China and the Russian Federation, Zhong e ruo si mulin youhao hezuo tiaoyue, July 16, 2001, Xinhua, http://news.xinhuanet.com/ziliao/2002-08/21/content_532202.htm. Sino-Russian Treaty for Friendship Takes Effect, Mar. 1, 2002, People's Daily. Commentary: Treaty Opens New Chapter for Sino-Russian Relations, July 16, 2001, People's Daily.

[26] Backgrounder: Chronology of Boao Forum for Asia, June 25, 2004, People's Daily. China and the Shanghai Cooperation Organization, China.org.cn (May 13, 2003), http://www.chinataiwan.org/web/webportal/W5042136/A5046305.html.

[27] Shi Hu, Zhongguo De Wenyi Fuxing (The Chinese Renaisssance) (Beijing: Foreign Language Teaching and Research Press, 2002).

4.5. CONCLUSION

In the 1920s and 1930s, the influence of Marxism was everywhere. Speaking of this transitional period, Zhang Dongxun (1886-1973), one of the liberals during the period from 1931 to 1935 and standing in opposition to those favoring what Edmund S.K. Fung characterized as a neo-dictatorship, wrote, "It seems to me some people are anti-Marxists, but their own thoughts fall into the conventional rut of Marxism. The danger of Marx lies not in what he advocated, but in the conceptual categories he set up. Unconsciously, people's heads are encased by these categories beyond their own expectations, just as the Monkey King could never get out of Buddha's palm as the common saying puts it."[28] Zhang Dongxun was referring to the classic fictional novel *The Journey to the West* (*Xi You Ji*).

One of the main characters in *The Journey to the West* is a monkey, namely the Monkey King, Sun Wukung, or as he sometimes fancied himself, "The Great Sage, Equal to Heaven." The Monkey King in a dispute with a Buddhist Patriarch or Tathagatha over access to the Heavenly throne in the Celestial Palace entered into a wager. The Buddhist Patriarch said, "If you have the ability to somersault clear of this right palm of me [mine]. I shall consider you the winner.'" In this famous tale, after the Monkey King lost the wager, though he could somersault a hundred and eight thousand miles, the Buddhist Patriarch tossed him out of the West Heavenly gate, and then pinned him by five connected mountains (the Five-Phases Mountain: metal, wood, water, fire and earth). No matter how high the Monkey King could somersault, he could never jump clear of the Buddhist Patriarch's palm. Borrowing from the tale of the Monkey King, it seems fitting to suggest that the future of China may, though problematic, lie firmly embedded in the palm of Marxism, Leninism or Mao's socialism, and what was termed in 1922 as the party's guiding principle of the Chinese democratic revolution. Because of the victory of Marxism and advocates for historical materialism, from modern China or post-1949 China, to a post- WTO China or new millennium-China, China's governing polity still hails Marxism as the official ideology, which still carries the burden of legitimizing itself as the official ideology of modern China.

During the 1920s and 1930s, the consequences of the then successful Bolshevik Revolution of 1919 as the model for future communist states are obvious. It was clear to the leading Chinese intellectuals of the period that the Bolshevik Revolution could be adapted, Sinicized or localized. The success of the Bolshevik Revolution of 1919, in important part, served as a primary catalyst for commencing the process of attempting to adapt, Sinicize or localize orthodox or classical Marxism. Although this process of localizing Marxism commences in the nineteenth century, it is a process continuing in modern China with modern party ideologies, such as Jiang Zemin's Theory of the Three Represents and the goals of building a *xiaokang* and harmonious "socialist" society, and harmonious socialist world, serving as tools for localizing Marxism and as achievements of the localization of Marxism.[29]

---

[28] Edmund S. K. Fung, In Search of Chinese Democracy. Civil Opposition in Nationalist China 1929-1949, (Cambridge UP, 2000). Zhang Taiyuan, Liberalism and Marxism: the Attitude of Independent Review toward Communist Party of China, 84-94, Social Sciences in China, (Zhongguo shehui kexue) (summer 2003). Chen Duanzhi, Historical Evaluation of the May Fourth Movement (Shenghuo Shudian, 1936). Hu Qiuyuan, An Outlined History of Chinese ideology in the Past 130 Years, (Taipei: Xueshu Publishing House, 1983). Zhang Dongxun, On the Question of Classes, Vol. 1, No. 4, 1-19 (Zaisheng, August 1932). Anthony C. Yu, (tr.), The Journey to the West, Vols I-IV; Vol I, ch. 7. (Univ. of Chicago Press, 1977).

[29] "Three represents": guiding ideology requires long-term adherence to, News of the Communist Party of China, Sept. 23, 2004, http://english.cpc.people.com.cn/66106/4480431.html.

Problematic, and serving as one of the major consequences in modern China, an earlier Sinicization of the Bolshevik Revolution and ongoing process of adapting, Sinicizing or localizing Marxism continues to influence modern legal and economic reforms, while also failing in the capacity and capability of resolving pending paradoxical interrelationships between competing sources of order.

Chapter 5

DEFINING PRAGMATIC NEO-LIBERALISM

5.1. DEFINING LIBERALISM

Classical liberalism, generally, characterizes Western notions of individual liberty, limited government and rule of law. Classical liberalism also embodies Western values, such as profit, free-market, private property and economic initiative. Liberalism is a political theory of rights that attempts to forge a social theory focusing on establishing the equality of all men before law. A problem of liberalism is that its excesses and abuses, historically, contribute to various revolutions, anti-clericalism, the rejection of legitimate authority and other tragedies. In its origins, it is an attempt to end the social intolerance strife that plagues Europe after the Reformation. Success of liberalism is contingent on establishing a culture founded on the idea of a civil liberty secured by a doctrine of pluralism. The gist of liberalism in formulating this idea of civil liberty is respect for civil liberty and individual human rights. However, Western classical liberalism, admittedly, achieves little success in terms of its historic manifestations. In France, at the close of the French Revolution (1789-1799) and in other parts of Europe, both revolutionary purposes and the promotion of moral license on the part of secular humanists subvert liberal ideals. Problematic and presenting a challenge to liberalism is that in time, counter deviancies develop in opposition to the original liberal agenda, because they lack practical continuity with the elemental principles of classical liberalism. A French Revolution that initially hails itself as the liberal revolution, antithetically, becomes a pillar of religious intolerance.[1] One source observed that the great movement for reform had only succeeded by the smallest of margins. Following victory and removal of the menace to society and the rebels, the Protestant camp dissolved into seemingly infinite numbers of smaller hostile groups. These smaller groups then set about the business, though on a much smaller scale, of repeating all of the errors that their enemies had been guilty of during the heyday of their power. Rather than make the history of humankind simpler and more harmonious, they (Protestantism) seemed to have made it more complicated and less orderly. Perhaps the problem was not so much the fault of the Reformation, rather more so the inherent weaknesses in the mental habits of most people.[2]

---

[1] Michel Therrien, John Paul II's Use of the Term Neo-Liberalism in Ecclesia in America, (Apr. 8, 2000), Action Institute for the Study of Religion and Liberty.

[2] Hendrik Willem Van Loon, Tolerance (1925).

In terms of the history of Western civilization and culture, it is a problem that dates back to primitive and ancient societies as the clash between rules of order and the various rules of religions, *ethos* and morals (*boni mores*). In addressing this earlier clash or struggle of higher ideals, the Greek Sophists delineated between nature (*Physis*) and law (*Nomos*). In so delineating this clash, the Sophists would cast laws as being artificial and man-made, and violating natural freedoms. In Greek mythology, *Nomos* is the *Daemon* (spirit) of laws, statutes and ordinances. In particular, *Nomos* was the husband of Eusebia (Piety) and the father of Dike (Justice), and is sometimes associated with Zeus. In Greek mythology, there is a struggle between rationalism and chaos, and law and nature. It is a struggle between *Nomos* (law, order and rationalism) and *Physis* (nature). The gods of mythology came to bring order to their world, with the god Apollo serving as the exalted representative of *Nomos* among the gods themselves. The god Apollo did so by fighting against *Physis* (the dragons and sea monsters). *The Homeric Hymns,* or *Orphic Hymn* #64 to *Nomos*, in part, reads, "Hymn to *Nomos* (law). The holy king of Gods and men I call, heavenly *Nomos*, the righteous seal of all: the seal which stamps whatever the earth contains, and all concealed within the liquid plains: stable, and starry, of harmonious frame, preserving laws eternally the same. Thy all-composing power in heaven appears, connects its frame, and props the starry spheres; and unjust envy shakes with dreadful sound, tossed by thy arm in giddy whirls around. 'Tis thine the life of mortals to defend, and crown existence with a blessed end; for thy command alone, of all that lives, order and rule to every dwelling goes."

Greek thought generally comprises two viewpoints, which is positive law and coercion, and Sophist's law as an expression of reason and self-interest. In opposition to the Sophists are Platonic and Aristotelian thoughts. Plato denied that law was mere coercion or coercive power, relying more on reasoning in explanation of law. In contrast, Aristotle viewed law in terms of reason and order. In terms of ancient Athenian law, there was also the distinction between a *Nomos*, which is comparable to modern constitutional laws, and a *Psephisma* that is akin to a decree. Following the introduction of a *Psephisma*, as a fundamental principle, in the form of a decree (*Psephisma*), whatever its content, a *Psephisma* could not conflict with a *Nomoi* in either form or substance. The body politic then proposes the now illegal decree (*Psephisma*) as criminal, thereby criminal liability attached and gave rise to a public right of action. There were also those decrees (*Psephisma*) that conflict with a *Nomoi*, which are, simply, voidable. What is more compelling about the concept of *Nomos* are its modern translations, such as the 1933 translation of *Nomos* from the French spelling found in Emile Durkheim's *Suicide* (1897), which translates as an "absence of accepted social values."

From early Greek thought to the Enlightenment era (Age of Reason, 1660-1798), it is the self-interest of the individual that would be produced by this clash, and while seemingly denying the congruence between natural reason and positive law allowed the self or newly constituted particularized (individualized civil) individuals to rationalize the place of law in society. For Western philosophical forms, from the works of Homer, Aristotle, to Plato and others, the bearer of virtue (*arête*) was an individual with a clearly defined social role, which is the particularized (individualized civil) individual.[3] The Enlightenment era also symbolizes the birth of the modern science of law, because the seventeenth century witnesses the sixteenth century-divorce of jurisprudence from theology. Roscoe Pound writes, "As the

[3] Wan Junren, Contrasting Confucian Virtue Ethics and MacIntyre's Aristotelian Virtue Theory, 37, Social Sciences in China (Zhongguo shehui kexue) (summer 2003).

seventeenth and eighteenth centuries saw it, the problems of the science of law were to ascertain by reason the content of the postulated social compact; to discover the rules demonstrated by reason as those to which an ideal man would conform in an ideal state of things and work out a technique of formulating and applying these rules; and to discover the qualities, demonstrated by reason as those of an ideal man by virtue of which he ought to have certain things and be free to do certain things, and formulate them as natural and so legal rights."[4] On reshaping these new rules of order, Pound further writes, "These were theoretical ways of putting a practical problem of directing legal growth in the reshaping of the authoritative legal materials which followed the transition from the relationally organized society of the Middle Ages to the society organized on a basis of free individual competitive acquisition and self-assertion which governed in the maturity of modern law."

During this period, the moral science of economics or political economy also emerges. The inherent notions of natural law manifest in the *physis - nomos* dichotomy, as a predominant philosophical form of Western culture and society, also, eventually, lays the foundation for economics and other social sciences. Joseph A. Schumpeter (1883-1950), and others, attributable this evolution to economics to earlier thoughts of Saint Thomas Aquinas (1225-1274) and his advocacy of religion based on reason and experience or natural religion (natural theology or *theologia naturalis*) rather than revealed religion, and even the Scholastics.[5] It is a history spanning from Aristotle's (384-322 BC) approach to economics or *oeconomica* in his *Nichomachean Ethics* (*Ethica Nicomachea*) and *Politics* (*Politica*); Scholasticism (*scholasticus*) and its relation of economics to broader theological and moral concerns; the natural law perspectives of Hugo Grotius (1538-1645) and Samuel von Pufendorf (1632-1694); to Francis Hutcheson (1694-1746), the teacher of Adam Smith, whom perceived economics as operating within the law of nature or jurisprudence, which operated within the bounds of moral philosophy. Adam Smith, as influenced by Francis Hutcheson, also considered economics or political economy as being the subject of moral philosophy. Adam Smith in his classic publications of *The Theory of Moral Sentiments* (1759) and *The Wealth of Nations* (*An Inquiry into the Nature and Causes of the Wealth of Nations*, 1776) fully embraces the idea that "economic growth was itself intimately connected with morality; this is seen in both the moral effects and in the moral prerequisites of growth."[6]

The theory of the social contract or contractarianism would later echo this new enlightened individual, or newly constituted individualized civil individual. It would also represent the advance of reason, grounded in René Descartes' (1596-1650) rationalism (Cartesian rationalism or Constructivist rationalism). Radical doubt was a critical feature of Descartes' method, or the Cartesian method, as expressed by his often-quoted phrasing, "we must doubt everything (*de omnibus dubitandum*)." Descartes, in his *Discourse on Method* (*Discourse on the Method of Rightly Conducting the Reason and Seeking the Truth in the Science* or *Oeuvres de Descartes*, 1637), wrote, "It is well to know something of the manners of various peoples, in order more sanely to judge our own, and that we do not think that everything against our modes is ridiculous, and against reason, as those who have seen

---

4 Roscoe Pound, Introduction, 234-35, 491, In Eugen Ehrlich, Fundamental Principles of the Sociology of Law (1913) (China Social Sciences Publishing House, Chengcheng Books: The President and Fellows of Harvard College, 1936).

5 Joseph A. Schumpeter, History of Economic Analysis, (E. Schumpeter, ed.) (Oxford UP, rev. ed, 1996).

6 Aristotle's Nicomachean Ethics, (WD Ross, trans.) (Clarendon Press, 1908). James E. Alvey, A Short History of Economics as a Moral Science, Vol. 2, No. 1, Journal of Markets and Morality (spring 1999).

nothing are accustomed to think."[7] This comparison of different places, customs and other worlds would later be echoed in the works of Montesquieu (or Charles-Louis de Sécondat, Baron de la Brède et de Montesquieu, 1689–1755), such as *Persian letters* (*Lettres Persanes*, 1721) and *The Spirit of Laws* (*De l'esprit des lois*, 1748). For Descartes, it was essential to read "the book of the world" and the evidence of his senses. In *Discourse on Method*, Descartes writes, "Good sense is, of all things among men, the most equally distributed; for every one thinks himself so abundantly provided with it, that those even who are the most difficult to satisfy in everything else, do not usually desire a larger measure of this quality than they already possess. And in this it is not likely that all are mistaken the conviction is rather to be held as testifying that the power of judging aright and of distinguishing truth from error, which is properly what is called good sense or reason, is by nature equal in all men; and that the diversity of our opinions, consequently, does not arise from some being endowed with a larger share of reason than others, but solely from this, that we conduct our thoughts along different ways, and do not fix our attention on the same objects." As concerns the book of the world, Descartes further writes, "For these reasons, as soon as my age permitted me to pass from under the control of my instructors, I entirey abandoned the study of letters, and resolved no longer to seek any other science than the knowledge of myself, or of the great book of the world."

While the philosophy of Descartes would later espouse the famous phrase, "I think, therefore I am" (*cogito ergo sum*), he remained the great doubter and committed to the method of doubt. In later years, though opposed by Leibnitz (Gottfried Wilhelm Freiherr von Leibnitz, 1646-1716) and his rationalism and optimism in Germany, and then opposed by Henry More (1614-1687), a friend of Isaac Newton (1642-1727), and the other Cambridge Platonists in England, Descartes' rationalism conquered France. In terms of the advance of reason, as grounded in Descartes' rationalism, there are the classic interpretations of social contract theory written by Thomas Hobbes (1588-1679) in *Leviathan* (1651), John Locke (1632-1704) in *Two Treatises of Government* (1689) and Jean-Jacques Rousseau (1712-1778) in *The Social Contract* (*Du Contrat Social*, 1762). It is the social contract and not anarchic society serving the greater interest of civil individuals. The concept of the enlightened self-interest, especially as advocated by Thomas Hobbes, also characterizes nineteenth century utilitarianism.[8] Immanuel Kant (1724-1804) and other proponents of utilitarianism, such as John Stuart Mill (1806-1873), perceived liberalism as promoting a vision of the human good, which would be the autonomous or rational self-directing individual in civil society.

However, and notwithstanding the efforts of iconoclasts of this era such as Locke, Bayle (Pierre Bayle, 1647-1706) and his *Various Thoughts on the Occasion of a Comet* (*Pensées diverses sur la comète*, 1682), Voltaire (Francois Marie Arouet, 1694-1778) and his *Candide*

---

[7] Descartes, Discourse on Method, Part I, Oeuvres de Descarte, publiées par Charles Adam et Paul Tannery, 12 vols., (Paris, 1897-1910). René Descartes, Discourse on Method Vol. XXXIV, Part 1 (P.F. Collier & Son, 1909–14). J. Bronowski & Bruce Mazlish, The Western Intellectual Tradition from Leonardo to Hegel 216-229 (Harper & Row, 1975). Montesquieu, Persian Letters (C. J. Betts trans.) (Penguin, 1973). Montesquieu, The Spirit of Laws, In Great Books of the Western World (Robert Maynard Hutchins ed., 1952). Robert Latta, Leibniz: The Monadology and other Philosophical Writings (Oxford UP, 1925).

[8] Concept of Law, Vol. 3, In The Dictionary of the History of Ideas: Studies of Selected Pivotal Ideas, (Philip P. Wiener, ed.) (Charles Scribner's Sons, 1973-74). F. A. Hayek, Law, Legislation, and Liberty, Vol. I, 5-6 (Univ. of Chicago Press, 1973-79). Thomas Hobbes, Leviathan (1651). John Locke, Two Treatises of Government (1689). Jean-Jacques Rousseau, Social Contract (1762) (Penguin, 1968). George Crowder, Galston's Liberal Pluralism, Paper for APSA Conf., Univ. of Adelaid, 2004.

(*Optimism*, 1759) and other Enlightenment thinkers,[9] in the quest for a perfect order Jeremy Bentham (founder of utilitarianism, 1748-1832) directly addresses the rigidity of primitive law and its association and identification with religion, and this sets him apart from others. Bentham addresses the problem of views on life and conduct that had chained down humankind since these views were first consolidated into a systematic form. He did so, by placing a distinct object before England to aim at in the pursuit of improvement or, simply, a clear rule of reform. Bentham, by placing such an object before England, made the good of the country take precedence over other objects, thereby giving escape to a current that had long been trying to find a way out. It is the same happiness of humankind, though conceptually different, seen in earlier Ancient legal literature, from the Greeks and their tribunals as seen in the Orators preserved by Aristotle in *Treatise on Rhetoric* (*Ars Rhetorica*), Roman *pontifices* in prehistoric times, *Law of the Twelve Tables* (*Lex Duodecim Tabularum*, published 451-450 B.C.), *Code of Justinian* (*Corpus Juris Civilis*, compiled AD 529 to AD 565), to written commentaries on praetor's edicts of Roman jurisconsults. For the Romans and Roman jurisconsults, it is seen "as the object of remedial legislation" that is offered to "the overshadowing claims of the Law of Nature,"[10] which is a consequence of associating the Roman Law of Nations (*Jus Gentium*) with the Law of Nature.

Liberalism is truly the product of history, and an evolutionary development of Western culture and its philosophical forms. While these Western rules of order or philosophical forms, as true of all organic systems, experience growth and development, though periodically expanding and contracting, such as the close of the French Revolution and subversion of liberal ideals, they, still, continue a historical growth and evolutionary development. Classical liberalism would stay the course of history and experience an evolutionary development that could hardly have been reasonably anticipated by its original authors, from the Greeks, Romans, to Enlightenment thinkers. It is a history far exceeding boundaries of the theological-political problem of the question of the political role of revealed religion, being Christianity.[11] It is a consequence of classical liberalism having roots in the Enlightenment era and an ancient period preceding the Enlightenment era. Classic liberalism, admittedly, commenced as a social philosophy or moral philosophy. There were originally no discernible differences between political liberalism and economic liberalism, because until about the 1850s economics was not a separate discipline. In the context of ideas supporting a free market, market economy and international economics or simply economics, liberalism would evolve to economic liberalism, which is often definable as *laizzez-faire* capitalism.

Ludwig von Mises (1881-1973) wrote, "The history of civilization is the record of a ceaseless struggle for liberty. The grand idea of liberty is peculiar to the West and separates the East from the West, because he [Ludwig von Mises] concluded that the people of the East

---

[9] Pierre Bayle, Various Thoughts on the Occasion of a Comet (Robert C. Bartlett, trans.) (Albany. St. UP, 2000). Voltaire, Candide (1759) (John Butt, trans.) (Penguin, 1990).

[10] Jeremy Bentham, A Fragment of Government, 3 (J.H. Burns & H.L.A. Hart, eds.) (Cambridge UP, 1988). Kenneth W. Dam, The Law-Growth Nexus 5 (Brookings Inst. Press, 2006). Aristotle, Treatise on Rhetoric (Theodore Buckley, trans.) (Prometheus Books, 1995). Fritz Schulz, History of Roman Legal Science, (Oxford UP, 1967). Barry Nicholas, An Introduction to Roman law, (Oxford UP, 1992). Sobei Mogi, Otto von Geike, his political teachings and jurisprudence, (P.S. King & Son, 1932). Henry Summer Maine, Ancient Law Its Connection with the Early History of Society, and its Relations to Modern Idea, 70-87 (1861) (China Social Sciences Publishing House, Chengcheng Books, 1999).

[11] Pierre Manet, An Intellectual History of Liberalism (Princeton UP, 1996).

never conceived the idea of liberty."[12] The history of Western civilization and culture may well substantiate the earlier contention of Ludwig von Mises. In terms of the history of Western civilization and culture, the Greek articulated liberty and Rome produced a model of law.[13] For Mises, nobody could ever successfully contest the cities of ancient Greece as creating the idea of liberty, and "the writings of Greek philosophers and historians transmitted it to the Romans and later to modern Europe and America. It became the essential concern of all Western plans for the establishment of the good society. It begot the laissez-faire philosophy to which mankind owes all the unprecedented achievements of the age of capitalism." For Mises and no doubt other liberals or libertarians, "The meaning of all modern political and judicial institutions is to safeguard the individuals' freedom against encroachments on the part of the government. Representative government and the rule of law, the independence of courts and tribunals from interference on the part of administrative agencies, habeas corpus, judicial examination and redress of acts of the administration, freedom of speech and the press, separation of state and church, and many other institutions aimed at one end only: to restrain the discretion of the officeholders and to render the individuals free from their arbitrariness."

In addition, the liberal ideal of individuals being free from arbitrariness reflects groundings in notions of free enterprise and free markets, which imply the removal of barriers to trade and cessation of government-bestowed privileges, such as subsidies and monopolies. For instance, Adam Smith's argument against governmental intervention stems from a philosophy of *laissez faire* economics that assumed the existence of perfectly competitive markets.[14] The two major thesis of Adam Smith was that government should pursue a policy of *laissez faire* economics and that the resulting distribution of income should be unequal. Albeit reality may often suggest otherwise, the latter became the economic ideology of Western civilization and culture, an ideology that Western culture has attempted to promote in non-Western countries. Inherent in Adam Smith's argument and philosophy of *laissez faire* economics is a market economy with flexible prices that is full of self-correcting mechanisms, or what one source colloquially describes as self-correcting thermostats.[15]

The latter also, admittedly, presents issues of reconciling the often-seeming conflict between the social goods of liberty and equality. As observed by Alexis de Tocqueville (Alexis-Charles-Henri Clérel de Tocqueville, 1805-1859), it is the tension between the two that is as "necessary and ineradicable," as the inequality out of which it grows.[16] A problem of efforts expended to correct the resulting imbalance by giving the disadvantaged equal dignity often only results in the violation of the liberty, freedom or rights of others. Francis

---

[12] Richard M. Ebeling, (ed.), Money, Method, and the Market Process: Essays by Ludwig von Mises (Kluwer Academic Pub, 1990).

[13] James Kurth, The Fate of the West in the Age of Globalization: Triumph or Twilight?, Vol. 1, No. 10, FPRI newsletter (2000).

[14] Harry Landreth, History of Economic Theory, Scope, Method, and Content, 41-43, 285 (Houghton Mifflin, 1976). Adam Smith, The Wealth of Nations (Bantam Dell, 2003). Manfred B. Steger, Globalism: The New Market Ideology 10 (Rowman & Littlefield, 2002). Karl Marx, Grundrisse: Foundations of the Critique of Political Economy, 81-114 (Martin Nicolaus, trans.) (Penguin, 1993).

[15] Mason Gaffney, Characteristics of Macro-Economics as a Field Study: A Study, Univ. of California, (1991), unpublished, http://www.economics.ucr.edu/people/gaffney/Econ2S04FieldStudy.pdf.

[16] Francis Fukuyama, The End of History and The Last Man, 292-93 (Free Press, 1992). Alexis de Tocqueville, Democracy in America, Vol. 2 (Henry Reeve, trans.) (Lawbook Exchange, 2003). Karl Marx, Critique of the Gotha Programme (1875), 13-30, In Marx/Engels Selected Works, Volume Three (Moscow, Progress Publishers, 1970).

Fukuyama writes, "There is no fixed or natural point at which liberty and equality come into balance, nor any way of optimizing both simultaneously." At the other extreme, there is Marxism and its materialistic conception of history, which also does not resolve the dilemma between liberty and equality. Marxist ideology intending to promote the perfect social equality or Marxian utopia, only, inevitably, does so at the expense of liberty. Marxism does so, by the elimination of natural inequalities "through the reward not of talent, but of need, and through the attempts to abolish the division of labor." As observed by Karl Marx, in *Critique of the Gotha Programme* (*Kritik des Gothaer Programms*, 1875), "from each according to his ability, to each according to his needs," because a primary concern for Marx was, "the enslaving subordination of the individual to the division of labor." The theoretical limitations of Marxism for resolving the tension between liberty and inequality is the essentialization of class struggle and revolution. As previously mentioned, classical liberalism characterizes Western notions of individual liberty, limited government and rule of law, and embodies Western values such as profit, free-market, private property and economic initiative.

Moreover, Karl Marx did not necessarily disagree with Adam Smith's thesis that the resulting distribution of income should be unequal. Marx, in *Grundrisse: Foundations of the Critique of Political Economy* (*Grundrisse der Kritik der Politischen Ökonomie*, 1939-41), even concedes the correctness of Adam Smith in throwing out every limited specification of wealth-creating activity, and on the resulting general abstraction of the abstract universality of wealth-creating activity. Marx further opines that Adam Smith from time to time fell back into the physiocratic system. As for the physiocrats, such as François Quesnay (1694-1774), Marquis de Mirabeau (or Victor de Riqueti, whom coined the term mercantile, 1715-1789), Mercier de la Rivière (Paul Pierre le Mercier de la Rivière, 1720-1794) and others, they were a sect of French Enlightenment thinkers of the 1760s, distinguishable for the economic idea that only agriculture yields a surplus or net product. Nonetheless, the physiocrats did speak against the worst features of mercantile economics and pursued *laissez-faire* economics, by calling for the removal of restrictions on internal trade and labor migration, the abolition of the *corvée* (or practice of unpaid labor for a day), the removal of state-sponsored monopolies, the dismantling of the guild system and other restrictions. They especially disliked the Colbertiste-policies that are associated with Jean-Baptiste Colbert (1619-83), the finance minister for Louis XIV from 1665 to 1683, which produced the state-sponsored monopolies and protective tariffs. During the absolutism of Louis XIV (*Louis-Dieudonné*: King of France, Sun King or *Le Roi Soleil*, 1643-1715) and before the close of the seventeenth century, Fénelon (the priest), Vauban (the military engineer) and Boisguillebert (Vauban's cousin) wrote in support of reform, while Boisguillebert was actually the first to speak of *laissez faire* and *laissez passer* (*laissez faire*, *laissez aller*, *laissez passer*, literally, let do, let go, let pass).[17] However, their want of reform lacked a systematic analysis of economics, a task they would leave for the economists or physiocrats. In addition, and resembling social contract theorists such as Hobbes, Locke, Rousseau and others, though there were differences, for physiocrats the natural order (*ordre naturel*) were the laws of nature, which were God-

[17] Jean-Baptist Say, A Treatise on Political Economy 5-6 (Claxton, Remsen & Haffelfinger, 1880). J. Bronowski & Bruce Mazlish, Id., 436—56. Charles Woolsey Cole, French mercantilism, 1683-1700 (Octagon Books, 1965). Patrick A. Messerlin, France and Trade Policy: Is the 'French Exception' Passee?, Intern'l Affairs, Vol. 72, No. 2, 293-309, New Currents in Trade Policy Thinking (Apr. 1996). Charles Woosley Cole, Colbert and a century of French mercantilism, (Archon Books, 1964).

given and inalienable, thereby humankind's only choice was to structure their polity, economy and society in conformity with the natural order or go against the natural order. Marx, in *Grundrissee*: *Foundations of the Critique of Political Economy*, concedes, in part, the correctness of this idea (the philosophy of *laissez faire* economics), which was grounded in liberalism. Marx wrote, "This is correct in one respect. Not in another. Indifference towards any specific kind of labour presupposes a very developed totality of real kinds of labour, of which no single one is any longer predominant. As a rule, the most general abstractions arise only in the midst of the richest possible concrete development, where one thing appears as common to many, to all. Then it ceases to be thinkable in a particular form alone."

Earlier notions of Adam Smith, capitalism and classical liberalism continued to evolve by the works of others, such as the anti-mercantilist David Hume (1771-1776), Thomas Malthus (1766-1834), David Richardo (1772-1823) and his famous treatise *On the Principles of Political Economy and Taxation* (1817), though he and later others would commence the problematic tendency towards positivism in economics, and many others.[18] In terms of positive economics, according to Milton Friedman, the positive-normative economics dichotomy represents the divide between positive economics as having to do with "what is," and normative economics addressing "what ought to be." Moreover, positive economics is a social science that is subject to the same checks based on evidence as other sciences, while normative economics with its moral and ethical aspects goes beyond what science "can say." For this reason, economics, including positive economics, often cannot rely on experimental methods to verify its hypotheses, in many cases. Commencing in the 1970s, and highlighting such distinctions, the Western economic model of capitalism experienced profound changes because of information technology, globalization and financial deregulation. The discipline of economics earlier birthed would produce in the later part of the twentieth century the ideas of economic liberalism, economic globalization and a new capitalism, such as global capitalism. Adam Smith could not have reasonably foreseen this evolutionary path and subsequent development of political economy. Moreover, and despite a growing proclivity toward positivism in political economy or economics, excepting for the Chicago imperialists or avowed Marshallians of the second Chicago school (1960s), the observations of Alfred Marshall (1842-1925), the father of neoclassicism, still hold true.

Alfred Marshall observed that economics, not unlike law, "is a biased undertaking in that the use of any particular economic model embraces specific assumptions and value statements and consequently any outcome generated by the use of such a model will be biased." A definition of economics had to encompass the terms of political economy and economics, because the concept of political economy implies an interrelationship between economics and politics, then economics, as a social science, intimately connects with normative judgments. Since economics served a moral purpose, there was not a clear line between science and art. Marshall listed what he deems some practical issues of economics, "How should we act so as to increase the good and diminish the evil of economic freedom, both in its ultimate results and in the course of its progress?... Taking for granted that a more equal distribution of wealth is to be desired, how far would this justify changes in the institutions of property, or

[18] David Ricardo, On the Principles of Political Economy and Taxation (London: John Murray, 1821/First published: 1817). Deepak Lal, Reviving the Invisible Hand: The Case for Classical Liberalism in the Twenty-first Century, (Princeton UP, 2006).

limitations of free enterprise even when they would be likely to diminish the aggregate of wealth?" Alfred Marshall addressed the same normative themes in his classic *Principles of Economics* (1890) and other works.[19] Marshall, in *Principles of Economics*, writes, "But ethical forces are among those of which economists has to take account. Attempts have indeed been made to construct an abstract science with regard to the actions of an 'economic man,' who is under no ethical influences and who pursues pecuniary gain warily and energetically, but mechanically and selfishly. But they have not been successful, nor even thoroughly carried out. For they never really treated the economic man as perfectly selfish." For these reasons, Marshall's definition of economics, in *Principles of Economics*, "is a study of mankind in the ordinary business of life; it examines that part of individual and social action which is most closely connected with the attainment and with the use of the material requisites of well being. Thus it is on the one side a study of wealth; and on the other, and more important side, a part of the study of man."

Commencing with Alfred Marshal, the father of neoclassical economics or neo-classicism, whose major contributions are from the mid-1880s, to mid-1920s, the subject of political economy experienced important changes. From Marshall and William Stanley Jevons (1835-1882), one can trace an earlier growing influence of positivism in the discipline of political economy or economics. The earlier ideas of Jevons, during the 1870s and 1880s, are also associated with the transition from classical political economy to modern economics. Alfred Marshall, though opposing William Stanley Jevons in many areas, made a critical decision to support Jevons's earlier calls for adopting a new name for the discipline of political economy. Marshall considered economics as a separate science with pure aspects. Marshall wrote, "It is better described by the term 'Economics' than by the term 'Political Economy.'"[20] For example, Alfred Marshall entitles his classic treatise as *Principles of Economics* (1890) and not *Principles of Political Economics*. Although the latter went against the conventionalism of classical economists during this era, the term "economics" is now widely accepted. Marshall was primarily motivated to obtain the independence of economics from other majors at his university, Cambridge, such as the moral science majors and history majors. In 1903, Marshall was victorious and what followed was, "the establishment of a separate School and Tripos [Majors] in Economics and associated branches of Political Science." In terms of the history of economics, what followed over the years was the growing influence of positivism, an unintended consequence of Alfred Marshall, though not necessarily of William Stanley Jevons. For Alfred Marshall, economics had always served a moral (*boni mores*) purpose, and there was not a clear line between science and art. Marshall could not have foreseen this by-product of his personal battle to establish economics as a major separable from other majors, especially, the problematic contagion effects of the amoral, apolitical and atheoretical proclivities of positivism in liberal economic theory. The result is a growing influence of positivism in liberal economics, or man as "he is" or economics as "it is" rather than "what ought to be."

---

[19] Landreth, Id. Alfred Marshall, Principles of Economics (1890), vi, 31-34, 594-95, 660-61 (Macmillan, 1920). The Chicago School, http://cepa.newschool.edu/het/schools/chicago.htm. Alfred Marshall, Principles of Economics (1890), 32, 36 (London: Macmillan, 8th ed., 1920).

[20] James E. Alvey, A Short History of Economics as a Moral Science, Vol. 2, No. 1, Journal of Markets and Morality (spring 1999). John Maynard Keynes, The Collected Writings of John Maynard Keynes, 30 vols. (D. E. Moggridge & E. Johnson, eds.) (London: Macmillan, 1973—1989), Vol. 10, 222.

5.2. Economic Liberalism and Pragmatic Neo-Liberalism

In the late nineteenth century, international trade is primarily contingent on liberal national legislation, bilateral trade agreements and Treaties of Friendship, Commerce and Navigation. The Great War (World War I, 1914-1918) ensues and causes collapse of this earlier trading system, and protectionism and currency instability follow in the inter-war period or interbellum, the period between the end of World War I and the beginning of World War II, from 1918-1939. The Bretton Wood Conference convenes prior to the close of the Second World War (World War II, 1939-1945). In 1944, and near the close of the Second World War, the Bretton Wood Conference creates the multilateral trading system. Today's global international economic regulations are the product of the multilateral trading system created by the Bretton Wood Conference. The objectives of the Bretton Wood Conference are twofold: "First, to advance the reduction of tariffs and other barriers to international trade." Second, "to create a global economic framework to minimize the economic conflicts among nations, which, at least in part, were held to have been responsible for the outbreak of the Second World War." The result of the Bretton Wood Conference in 1944 is the creation of three basic international economic institutions regulating money and trade, which are the International Monetary Fund (IMF), the International Bank for Reconstruction and Development (IBRD) (or World Bank) and the General Agreement on Tariffs and Trade (GATT).[21] Notwithstanding the hopes and aspirations embodied in the Bretton Wood Institutions (BWIs), the problems causing the collapse of the trading system during the inter-war period, which were primarily protectionism and currency instability, persist to this day. Both developed and developing countries, including the People's Republic of China (China), contribute to the ongoing problems of protectionism and currency instability. In particular, in terms of global trade and evolving global international economic regulations, there have been charges of both protectionism and currency manipulation against a post-WTO China.

Many hail the Bretton Wood Conference as one of the most successful economic conferences, which is a conference that births international economic institutions or BWIs that continue to evolve and experience profound challenges in a post-World War II world. While many hail GATT as a major trade organization and trade treaty, GATT, technically, is a treaty that never came into force, because there was never an intent that it becomes an organization. Designers of these institutions originally intend to create by a treaty-charter, the International Trade Organization (ITO), which would be the institutional framework to which GATT would attach. Following a 1951 U.S. Congressional refusal to approve the ITO Charter, the GATT came into force in 1948 by the terms of the Protocol of Provisional Acceptance Application, and evolves into a major trade organization. On January 1, 1995, the World Trade Organization (WTO) enters into force, and encompasses the GATT, various supplementary agreements and codes, and a reform of the dispute settlement system. Consequently, both the WTO and GATT continue to regulate international trade. GATT is not the only international economic institution that experiences an evolution, because other economic institutions also evolve. Both the World Bank and IMF have also needed to adapt to changing social environments and international political economy concerns, and needed reforms of these institutions are routinely the subject of public debate. For example, in terms of the evolution of the IMF, economic liberalism would influence its evolution from

[21] Peter Malanczuk, Akehurst's Modern Introduction to International Law 231 (Routledge, 1997).

bimetallism (before 1875), the classical gold standard (1875-1914), inter-war period and its lack of coherent international monetary system (1915-1944), Bretton Wood system (1945-1972), to the contemporary flexible exchange rate regime period (since 1973).[22]

In subsequent years, liberalism and the various international economic institutions, including the BWIs, would have their trials and tribulations. In the 1970s and 1980's, the concept of neo-liberalism (or economic liberalism) begins to emerge with the debt crises in developing countries. In the 1970s, and pursuant to growing interests in international economics, the antagonists of economic liberalism and globalization commence usage of the nomenclature of neo-liberal, while those supporters subscribing to its tenants would rather prefer to themselves as simply libertarians, free marketers or conservatives. Neo-liberalism is also the name often given to the political-economic restructuring or reform programs proposed for developing countries by developed country economists, the IMF and World Bank, and some refer to the structural adjustment programs of the BWIs as simply neo-liberal reforms.[23]

The history of neo-liberalism is traceable to classical liberalism. Western classical liberalism, generally, stems from the eighteenth and nineteenth century liberal movements for individual freedom from restrictions by the state on individual human rights, civil rights and property rights. A criticism of neo-liberalism is that it arguably extends the same individual rights to transnational corporations and banks, and moves the rights of property from the status of a social right to that of a fundamental right. The complaint being that Western neo-liberalism treats transnational banks and corporate entities as equal, for instance, to a small farmer in China. The antagonists complain that while neo-liberalism grants significantly more freedom to corporate entities, a problem of neo-liberalism is that, historically, it does not extend the same freedoms to indigents and working people.

In subsequent years, the concept of neo-liberalism (or economic liberalism) would experience a further, though slight, evolution, eventually manifesting itself as what is termed by some as pragmatic neo-liberalism (or pragmatic economic liberalism). As earlier mentioned, the origin of Western neo-liberalism in the 1970's and 1980's evolves from the IMF and World Bank providing economic assistance to developing countries. What presented a problem for many developing countries is that economic assistance was, and continues to be, contingent on implementation of neo-liberal reforms. The neo-liberal reforms, generally, encompass privatization, free markets, de-regulation, austerity and comparative advantage. Globalization, or the pursuit of a new global economy, results in the need for neo-liberal policies. Due to some failures of neo-liberal reform policies of international economic institutions, including the BWIs such as the IMF and World Bank, economic liberalism inherits a new name or nomenclature of pragmatic neo-liberalism, with usage of the adjective of pragmatic intending to change the face of neo-liberalism. It is the strategy of the BWIs to present a kinder and gentler image of globalization, or the new global economy, to the world, especially developing countries and economies. The rhetoric of pragmatic neo-liberalism is

---

22 John H. Jackson, The World Trade Organization, (Royal Inst. of Int'l Affairs, 1998). Margaret Garritsen de Vries, The IMF in a Changing World (IMF, 1986). Edwin M. Truman (ed.), Reforming the IMF for the 21st Century, Special Report 19, (Inst. for Int'l Econ., 2006). Jessica Einhorn, Reforming the World Bank, Foreign Affairs, Jan/Feb 2006. Fan, DeCheng (ed.), Fundamentals and New Concepts for Economics & Management (Beijing: Foreign Language Teaching and Research Inst., 2001).

23 World Bank Documents, http://www.worldbank.org. NACLA Report on the Americas, Vol. XXX, No 4, 20, Jan/Feb. 1997. Russ Kleinbach, (presentation), Sustainable Development and Neo-Liberalism, Conference, American Univ. (Kyrgyzstan), May 30, 1999, http://faculty.philau.edu/kleinbachr/neo-liberalism.htm.

people-friendly, but remains in identity neo-liberalism. During the 1990s, the World Bank and the IMF adopted this gentler approach, or political rhetoric, because of first decade failures in an earlier development philosophy. In the early 1980s, because of criticisms, from the right and left, the BWIs reposition and reinvent themselves as champions of the world's poor. The IMF follows suit and reinvents itself after the alleged bungling of the 1997-98 East Asian, 2000 Mexico financial crises and the 1999-2002 Argentine financial crisis. In particular, antagonists of neo-liberalism frequently cite the Argentine financial crisis as an example of the failure of neo-liberalism. However, wholly blaming the BWIs, or these international economic institutions, such as the IMF, World Bank, GATT and the WTO, for these crises is problematic. The 1997-98 East Asian financial crisis presents a classic example of this wrongfully attributing of a financial crisis to these international economic institutions.

China, though surviving the 1997-98 East Asian financial crisis, presents a prime example of the problem of arguments from the various antagonists of neo-liberalism and the many dependencies theories, including the growth of distinctive Asian development models and theories. An earlier 2004 OECD study foretold that China's growth is losing its dynamism. Assuming this prediction is true, China should pursue more orthodox or even Western models of development, or development theory rather than dependency theory. A case in point is the East Asian financial crisis, which brought into question whether too much been expected from Asian industrialization or whether the Asian development model, in relying on foreign capital, lacked substance. Public debates ensued concerning reactions to the Asian financial crisis and to the correctness of the IMF's prescription, especially what Asian economies deemed rigorous conditionalities of the IMF and World Bank. There was also the problem of an influx of international short-term capital. During this period, the United States, Europe and Japan endure criticism for doing too little, too late, for a financial crisis that left the East Asian region feeling the blunt of uncertainty about the future. Some describe the East Asian financial crisis as Asian economies failing to pursue an industrialization pattern reflective of Asian reality. While Asian economies depended on international short-term capital via financial liberalization for combating capital shortages, if they would have developed soft infrastructures such as human resources, and hard infrastructures such as roads, factories and transportation, and then pursued a more orthodox industrial development path of cultivating industries, this problem would have never intensified to the degree that it did.[24] Subsequent assessments of the East Asian financial crisis differ, as some argue that export orientation is the major source of growth competitiveness, while others argue that imports have a stronger effect on productivity than exports. The latter presents the consequences of China restricting imports or import-based growth via a distinctive model of Chinese regionalism, pursuing nationalistic or ideological motivations, pursuing political rather than economic motivations, or even exalting dependency theory and its traditional or state-control approach, over Western development models or theories. For these reasons, many rightly blame national governments for the East Asian financial crisis, rather than the international economic institutions and BWIs.

[24] M. Ulric Killion, Chinese regionalism and the 2004 ASEAN-China Accord: the WTO and legalized trade distortion, 31 N.C. J. Int'l L. & Com. Reg. 1 (2005). Robert Z. Lawrence & David E. Weinstein, Trade and Growth: Import-Led or Export-Led? Evidence from Japan and Korea, In Rethinking the East Asia Miracle 379-407 (Joseph E. Stiglitz et. al. eds., 2001). Huijong, Wang, Integrated Study of China's Development and Reform Preliminary Exploration of Social System 327-338 (Beijing, Foreign Language Press 2003).

Many, admittedly, fault the IMF and World Bank for initial misdiagnoses and for prescribing inappropriate solutions that worsened the crisis and its effects. There was, and is, a commonly held view in East Asia, especially South Korea and the Association of Southeast Asian Nations (ASEAN), that they had been let down by the West, in particular, the U.S. and Japan, during the East Asian financial crisis. The view of these countries that they had been let down, and more assistance should have come from the West, is based on a belief that the West, or the G-7 nations, being France, the United States, Britain, Germany, Japan, Italy, Canada, and the European Community, now G8 with full Russian participation, made the financial crisis worst by pulling from their region funds from their banking and financing institutions.[25] In particular, developing economies deemed the requirement for assistance from these international economic institutions as overly rigid conditionalities. For instance, the Articles of Agreement of the International Monetary Fund, Article V, section 3(a), provides, "The Fund shall adopt policies on the use of its general resources, including policies on stand-by or similar arrangements, and may adopt special policies for special balance of payments problems, that will assist members to solve their balance of payments problems in a manner consistent with the provisions of this Agreement and that will establish adequate safeguards for the temporary use of the general resources of the Fund." The perceptions of many developing economies, though suspect, is that the G-7, now G-8, nations either refused to assist, as in the case with the United States and Japan concerning Thailand, or when assisting, as through the IMF, imposed seemingly excessive and stringent demands. Despite the merits of these contentions, there was a consensus among Asian economies that they should reduce their dependence on the G-7 nations and multilateral financial institutions such as the IMF and World Bank.

Nonetheless, commencing in 2000, the IMF's Enhanced Structural Adjustment Facility reinvents itself as a friendlier Poverty Reduction and Growth Facility (PRGF). The World Bank and IMF initiate efforts to build partnerships with recipient governments, nongovernmental organizations (NGOs), enhance participation of recipient governments in the design of adjustment programs, augmentation of human capital, and address problems of governance, corruption and human rights.[26]

5.3. The Antagonists of Globalization

The late twentieth century also witnesses the birth of the new antagonists to economic liberalism and economic globalization. In this new era of economic globalization, the antagonists and their dependency theories would call into question the orthodoxy of neo-

[25] M. Ulric Killion, The New Millennium: APEC and Emerging China 1-45, In New Developments in Macroeconomics Research, editor: Lawrence Z. Pelzer (Nova Science Pub, 2006). Shalendra D. Sharma, Beyond ASEAN and APEC: Towards a New Asia-Pacific Economic Regionalism, Vol. 14, No. 3 East Asian Review, 37-48 (autumn 2002). Univ. of Toronto G8 Information Center: What is the G8?, http://www.g7.utoronto.ca/what_is_g8.html. Association of Southeast Asian Nations, Overview, http://www.aseansec.org/64.htm. In 2006, ASEAN member countries are Indonesia, Malaysia, Philippines, Singapore, Thailand, Brunei Darussalam, Vietnam, Laos, Myanmar and Cambodia.

[26] Dickson Eyoh & Richard Sandbrook, Pragmatic Neo-liberalism and Just Development in Africa, Univ. of Toronto, CIS Working Paper 2001-1. Robert Dahlberg & Marc Uzan, The Future of the Bretton Wood Institutions: The European Contribution to the Debate on the New Financial Architecture, American Council on Germany Reinventing Bretton Wood Committee, Paris, Sept. 2000.

liberal theory, and its attendant development models and theories. The antagonists and dependency theories are many and continue to evolve, and count as examples the Marxist models of dependency theory and world system theories. The latter world system theories are essentially Marxist theories, which are describable as a compromise, synthesization and continuation of Marxism. In terms of the issues of endless capital accumulation, theory of surplus value, theory of imperialism and other theories, world system theorists, such as Immanuel Wallerstein and others, reached the same conclusions of Lenin (Vladimir Ilyich Lenin, 1870-1924) and Bukharin (Nikolay Ivanovich Bukharin, 1888–1938), which is a prophecy of the birth of socialism from the disintegration of the capitalist world economy. Dependency theory is also describable as a modern theory that refutes Marxism, while world system theory develops dependency theory. In terms of North (developed countries)-South (developing countries) relations and East-West relations, and presenting a potential problem for liberalism and economic liberalism, there are the growth of distinctive Asian development models and theories. In terms of dependency theory, historically, there are the developed countries members of the Organization of Economic Co-operation and Development (OECD), and the so-called dependent countries such as Latin American, Asian and African countries. The latter developing countries, including least developed countries (LDCs), have, historically, experienced low per capital gross national products (GNP) and relied heavily on the export of a single commodity for foreign exchange earnings. In the 1990s, dependency theory evolves from its Latin origins *dependencia* and the traditional or state-control approach to markets in Latin America.[27]

For neoclassical economics or neoclassicism, dependency theory and the anti-globalization movement stemming from fears of global capitalism, within and without the academic community, has been problematic. In the late 1950s, the study of Paul Prebisch and his colleagues, with the support of the United Nations (UN) Economic Commission for Latin America, originally developed the idea of dependency theory in the Prebisch-Singer hypothesis or Singer-Prebisch thesis. Dependent theory develops in response to growing concerns that economic growth in developed countries does not necessarily lead to commensurate growth in developing countries. In 1948, after being appointed director of the Economic Commission for Latin America (ECLA or CEPAL), Paul Prebisch released a study referred to as the Prebisch-Singer hypothesis or Singer-Prebisch thesis. In the 1960s, economists at the ECLA developed an extension of Paul Prebisch's hypothesis on structuralism into dependency theory, which, generally, finds that economic development of the periphery is a nearly impossible task. The Prebisch-Singer hypothesis suggests that developing countries exporting goods would be able to import less and less for a given level of exports. The study suggested that economic activity in developed countries might lead to serious economic problems in developing countries. The study challenged neoclassical theory and its assumption that economic growth was Pareto optimal and beneficial to all parties (or countries), even if the parties (or countries) do not equally share benefits. One of the core propositions of dependency theory is that developing countries are simply poor. The state of

[27] Immanuel Wallerstein, The Modern World-System, Capitalist Agriculture and the Origins of the European World-Economy in the Sixteenth Century, Vol. I (Academic Press, 1974). Immanuel Wallerstein, The Modern World-System: Mercantilism and the Consolidation of the European World-Economy, 1600-1750, Vol. II (Academic Press, 1980) Immanuel Wallerstein, The Modern World-System, The Second Great Expansion of the Capitalist World-Economy, 1730-1840's, Vol. III (Academic Press, 1989). Jiang Hua, The Marxist source of the World-System Theory, Zhonggong Zhejiang Shengwei Dangxiao xuebao, no. 2 (2005).

poverty of these developing countries is attributable to the many developing countries lagging behind the scientific transformations or the Enlightenment values of the European states or Western developed countries. Consequently, and pursuant to the Prebisch-Singer hypothesis, these developing countries are poor because of their coercive integration into a Western economic system as producers of raw materials or as repositories of cheap labor, and denial of an opportunity to market their resources.[28]

For the antagonists of the orthodoxy of economic liberalism, from the late 1940s to the 1980s, dependency theory (*dependencia* or *dependencia* school) ruled. Notwithstanding Raul Prebisch's 1950 hypothesis, dependency theory is also traceable to the early twentieth century, the 1920s and 1930s, which is during the era of the Great Depression (1892–1933). It was especially during the year of 1929, when the Great Depression severely struck North America. During this period, many Latin American countries or economies suffered from the collapse of prices in goods, which had a devastating affect on their export-oriented economies. The idea of dependency theory begins to take root as a rationale for state dominance and its attendant high import barriers, closed economy and, eventual, demotion of the market. As part of this rationalization, national security served as justification for governments to take over strategic sectors of a domestic economy, in order to meet the needs of the domestic economy rather than those of international investors. A classic example is the founding of the state oil companies in struggling Latin American economies. The post-World War II period witnessed a shift to a greater reliance on the state. The shift to greater state reliance is the by-product of an emergence of the Western welfare state, Keynesian interventionism, the prestige of Marxism and the former Soviet Union, and growing anti-Americanism. In response to these growing international political economy concerns, the antagonists responded. Consequently, there is the birth of *dependencia* theorists, who problematically begin to deny the benefits of economic liberalism and global trade. Prebisch, though earlier a disciple of neoclassical theory, following his experiences in the 1930s as director of Argentina's central bank and witnessing the near financial ruin of both Argentina's central bank and Argentina's financial structure, wrote, "The first great crisis of capitalism -- the Great Depression -- prompted in me serious doubts regarding those beliefs."[29] Most problematic and disconcerting about dependency theory, and its variant of the traditional or state-control approach, is the denial and rejection of the benefits of economic liberalism, global trade or the world multilateral trading system. No doubt, a later Argentinean financial crisis, though birthing the Paris Club (and its debt rescheduling or debt cancellation), during the Peronist Unrest of 1956 only buttressed an advocacy for *dependencia* theory.

Many perceive the influence of dependency theory (or *dependencia*) as having waned during the 1980s. However, the influence of dependency theory remains and finds new outlets in a post-WTO world. For instance, the development theory-dependency theory dichotomy bears great relevancy and similarities to the prevalently growing post-WTO problem of proliferating regional trade agreements or free trade areas, the most common form of which

---

[28] Paul Prebisch, The Economic Development of Latin American and its Principal Problems (1949). Paul Prebisch, Hacia una dinámica del desarrollo latinoamericano (1963 ECLAC Report). Karl Marx, The Future Results of the British Rule in India, Aug. 8, 1853, N.Y. Daily Tribune. Andre V. Mollick & Joao Ricardo Faria, Albuquerque, Pedro H. & Leon-Ledesma, Miguel A., Can Globalisation Stop the Decline in Commodities' Terms of Trade? The Prebisch-Singer Hypothesis Revisited (Feb. 2006), http://ssrn.com/abstract=860224.

[29] Daniel Yergin & Joseph Stanislaw, Commanding Heights (Simon & Schuster, 2002).

are the euphemistically named free trade areas (FTAs).[30] In this respect, dependency theories remain influential in the anti-globalization movement. It does so by having evolved and birthed new variants and possibly a new aberrant in the form of the problem of post-WTO growing regionalism. The growing proliferation of FTAs poses a threat to the WTO goal of free trade and fair trade because political considerations for entering FTAs may override economic considerations. The debate contrasting regionalism with multilateralism in trade has yet to be resolved. Some critiques perceive liberalization as the cause of social and economic problems, rather than as a solution. In this respect, Asian regional bodies, by adopting a neo-liberal agenda, adopted an incorrect model. Other criticisms simply center on the adoption of economic liberalization or neo-liberalism. This is mostly an issue of state sovereignty that results from models of regionalism embracing both developed and developing economies. Some development theorists, in challenging liberalization as the best option, argue that the retention of state control over strategic economic instruments and sectors provides more options for development. There are also criticisms that focus on economic liberalization, simply in terms of it being desirable or not, while others direct attention to a desirability that is contingent upon the context in which liberalization is to occur. Some critics, such as liberal economists, encourage a multilateral approach rather than a regional approach to trade liberalization. For such critics, regionalism is a second best choice to multilateralism.[31]

The development-dependency theories dichotomy addresses many of the same concerns associated with the debate concerning the regionalism-multilateralism dichotomy, especially the issue, if not rationalization, for the retention of state control over strategic economic instruments and sectors in promoting economic development. Dependency theory, and its variants of the traditional or state-control approach, still, though indirectly, continues to challenge economic liberalism, global trade, or the world multilateral trading system, especially its international economic institutions, such as the IMF, World Bank, GATT and the WTO.

5.4. CONCLUSION

Despite the efforts of the BWIs at repositioning and reinventing themselves, there is the maintenance of elemental principles of a core policy, especially in terms of an American consensus or Washington consensus that assumes adjusting firms, governments, employees, farmers, and citizens serve the greater good in general to the exigencies of competition within increasingly deregulated and global markets. The American consensus or Washington consensus refers to the policies of neo-liberal economists, which are, essentially, policies for promoting economic growth in Latin American countries and other countries, by promoting free market oriented economic reforms. The pragmatic extensions of neo-liberalism,

[30] T.N. Srinivasan, (presentation), Preferential Trade Agreements with Special Reference to Asia, Asian Economic Outlook Workshop, Manila, Nov. 2001, (on file with Yale Univ.), http://www.econ.yale.edu/~srinivas/PrefTradeAgreements.pdf.

[31] National Foreign Trade Council, Vision 2005: Free Trade and Beyond, Recommendations for the Doha Development Agenda, May 22, 2002, http://www.nftc.org/default/trade/NFTC_Doha_Round_ Position_ Paper_May_2002.pdf. Arvind Panagariya, Regionalism in Trade Policy: Essays on Preferential Trading 47-111 (1999). Paul Bowles, APEC: Progress Based on the Wrong Model?, 6 Can. Bus. Econ. 48 (1997).

therefore, supplements this core notion, in that, they present neo-liberalism with a more human face.

In this respect, China presents a classic case study. Many hail China for its burgeoning economic growth, and as a model economy for economic growth, economic development and economic globalization for many Asian, Latin American and African countries. However, despite the development verbiage, or more accuracy, the verbiage of dependency theory and its traditional or state control approach of Asian development or Asian values, in terms of China and other countries, both developed and developing countries, there are direct consequences and benefits flowing from the international economic institutions, including the BWIs, such as the World Bank, IMF and WTO. In the future, or post-Enlightenment period, liberalism would find itself cast in terms of liberal economic theory, and economic liberalism (or neo-liberalism) would become a mainstay in promoting, fostering, managing and regulating international trade in a global market. In the late twentieth century and, now, new millennium, economic liberalism will also produce new and evolving consequences and benefits of world trade.

Chapter 6

Liberalism and Marxism

6.1. Liberal and Economic Liberal Norms

There are several Western models and theories addressing the issues of transplanting and borrowing laws and legal systems. However, in terms of the issues of complementary or paradoxical interrelationships between social norms, economics norms and legal norms, the issue is broader than the problem of transplanting and borrowing laws and legal systems. Western culture has also attempted to promote in non-Western countries, the economic or political economy ideology of Western civilization and culture. In the future or post-original Enlightenment project period, or even perhaps a period of a moderate Enlightenment, liberalism would eventually be cast in terms of economic liberalism and its liberal economic theories. Commencing in the 1970s, economic liberalism or neo-liberalism would become a mainstay in managing and regulating international trade in a global market. The Western economic model of capitalism experienced profound changes beginning in the 1970s, because of information technology, globalization and financial deregulation. In terms of Western development taxonomies, the latter reflects a distinctively West centric view of reality, which is characterized by Western notions of individual liberty, limited government and rule of law. Despite the antagonists against liberalism and economic liberalism and its liberal economic theories, who contest economic globalization and the phenomenon of the rich Western market (liberal) democracies, there are a host of benefits stemming from the ideals embodied in the concepts of liberalism and economic liberalism. A sampling of the benefits are the effective and efficient management and regulation of international trade in a global market, the creation of international economic institutions and international intergovernmental organizations that promote world poverty reduction and sustainable development policies and programs, programs and institutions fostering increased employment rates and the sharing of technology with developing countries, and a host of other benefits. There are also the potential benefits stemming from the historic ideas birthed by Immanuel Kant's essay in *Perpetual Peace: A Philosophical Sketch* (*Zum ewign Frieden: Ein philosophischer Entwurf*, 1795).[1]

[1] Robin Matthews, A New Model of Strategy Applied to the Russian Situation, Kingston Business School Occasional Paper Series No. 38 (Dec. 1999). Immanuel Kant, Perpetual Peace (1795), 10–23 (Lewis White Beck, ed., Bobbs-Merril 1957). Immanuel Kant & Kehrbach Karl, Zum ewigen frieden. Ein philosophischer entwurf (Leipzig: P. Reclam jun, 1881). Immanuel Kant, Perpetual Peace: A Philosophical Sketch, 93-130, In Hans Reiss, ed. Kant's Political Writings (Cambridge UP, 1970).

In the historical search for a perfect order, utopia or perpetual peace, the thoughts of many scholars and philosophers from different disciplines and eras precede and succeed the thoughts of Immanuel Kant in *Perpetual Peace*. In terms of early thoughts antedating Kant, it is a history that has an origin dating back as far as Pierre du Bois (1255) and his pamphlets written from 1300 to 1314, and his, as King's adviser, proposal to the King of France to form a European federation to be led by France, with the pope as titular head and possibly regaining Holy lands; and Dante Alighieri (Durante degli Alighieri, 1265-1321), and his *De Monarchia* (vision of a restored Roman world empire, 1313) and notions of a self-asserting political elite. Kant's thoughts in *Perpetual Peace* can also be traced to others, such as Hugo Grotius (1538-1645) and his *De iure belli ac pacis* (*On the laws of war and peace*, 1625), and proposed periodic congresses of princes; Gottfried Leibnitz (Gottfried Wilhelm Freiherr von Leibnitz, 1646-1716) and his "collection of documents of the law of peoples" (*Corpus Juris Gentium* or *Codex juris gentium diplomaticus*, 1693), and then later to the Abbé de St. Pierre (Abbé Charles-Irénée Castel de Saint-Pierre, 1658-1743) and his eighteenth century Project for Perpetual Peace (*Paix Perpetuelle*, 1712, and expanded English version, *A Project for Settling an Everlasting Peace in Europe*, 1714), in creating a detailed plan for the foundation of perpetual peace, and others. During the late eighteenth century, Immanuel Kant's *Perpetual Peace* essay coincided with Napoleon's revolutionary wars and a European continent in search of a lasting peace or perpetual peace, if not a utopia. Indeed, a French Revolution would promote the idea that reason in politics was plausible. As one source observed, "Amid fear and uneasiness in Europe, the French Revolution promoted the idea among many, including Immanuel Kant, that reason itself could be realised in politics." However, Kant did not follow Dante's proposed political elite in answer to the quest for peace in Europe. Rather, he perceived a European peace as being achieved by increasing the rule of law in relations between states.[2]

Immanuel Kant, in *Perpetual Peace*, in the Second Definitive Article for a Perpetual Peace "The Law of Nations Shall be Founded on a Federation of Free States," writes, "For states in their relation to each other, there cannot be any reasonable way out of the lawless condition which entails only war except that they, like individual men, should give up their savage (lawless) freedom, adjust themselves to the constraints of public law, and thus establish a continuously growing state consisting of various nations (*civitas gentium*), which will ultimately include all the nations of the world." For a Kantian perpetual peace, the state of peace must be established, and it could only be established by the application of the his three definitive articles, namely: "The civil constitution of each state shall be republican" and "The rights of men, as citizens of the world, shall be limited to the conditions of universal hospitality," and the previously mentioned Second Definitive Article, "The law of nations shall be founded on a federation of free states." More generally, for Kant, the process of formalizing his ideal lasting peace, world peace or perpetual peace requires a legal constitution that embodies civil rights of individuals (*jus civitatis*), international rights of states in their relations with one another (*jus gentium*) and cosmopolitan rights, which are

[2] Hugo Grotius, The Law of War and Peace (1625), (Francis W. Kelsey, translator) Three volumes (Clarendon Press, 1925). Herfried Münkler, Kant's "perpetual peace": utopia or political guide?, 27 May 2004. Caspian Richards, A commentary on the 'Perpetual Peace' of Immanuel Kant, Vol. 2, Paideusis-Journal for Interdisciplinary and Cross-Cultural Studies, 1999. John Howard Yoder, History of Religiously Rooted NonViolence: A Series of Working Papers of the Joan B. Kroc Instit. for Intern'l Peace Studies (1994), http://www.nd.edu/~theo/research/jhy_2/writings/history/worldorder.htm.

between individuals and states that coexist in an external relationship of mutual influence; to wit, citizens of a universal state of humankind (*jus cosmopoliticium*).

Immanuel Kant's *Perpetual Peace* essay has been translated as promoting a democratic peace thesis, liberal peace and a cosmopolitan peace, as the most viable means for achieving world peace among nations and other benefits. A Kantian perpetual peace inspires the concept of cosmopolitan democracy, which promotes models of a world of peace, democracy, equality and justice.[3] In terms of the democratic peace thesis, there is substantive empirical evidence supporting the proposition that democratic states have not initiated and are not likely to initiate interstate wars against each other. Empirical work analyzing international wars since 1817 by scholars, such as Michael Doyle, Bruce Russett, Rudolph J. Rummel and others, substantiate the democratic peace thesis. The conclusion from the study of wars over the past two centuries is that while liberal nations often go to war against non-liberal nations, liberal nations evidence a proclivity to stay at peace with other liberal nations. From 1816 to 1991, there were not any liberal nations or democracies at war with one another, from a group comprising 353 pairings of nations engaged in major international wars. One source observed, the "democratic peace theory is an example of a social science theory having a clear and speedy impact on government policy." Ludwig von Mises (Ludwig Heinrich Elder von Mises, 1881-1973), in *Liberalism in the Classical Tradition* (1927), writes, "For the liberal, the world does not end at the borders of the state. In his eyes, whatever significance national boundaries have is only incidental and subordinate. His political thinking encompasses the whole of mankind. The starting-point of his entire political philosophy is the conviction that the division of labor is international and not merely national. He realizes from the very first that it is not sufficient to establish peace within each country, that it is much more important that all nations live at peace with one another. The liberal therefore demands that the political organization of society be extended until it reaches its culmination in a world state that unites all nations on an equal basis."[4]

In the context of East Asia, admittedly, the democratic peace thesis remains difficult to substantiate or unsubstantiate by empirical evidence. One study conducted by Edward Mansfield and Jack Snyder, the Mansfield-Snyder study, while admitting there is some truth in the democratic peace thesis, perceived transitioning democracies in some former countries or parts of Soviet bloc as historically being war-like. The Mansfield-Snyder study found that the democratic peace thesis is inapplicable to internal conflicts of nations, and many security problems in East Asia address internal conflicts. In terms of East Asia, the Mansfield-Snyder study finds that it is difficult to conclude whether the process of democratization has yet to produce discernible peace dividends. The study finds that the dangerous transition to democracy to be problematic, because of the problem of internal conflicts in East Asia,

---

[3] Benjamin Solomon, Kant's Perpetual Peace: A New Look at this Centuries-Old Quest, OJPCR, Issue 5.1 (summer 2003). James Lee Ray, Does Democracy Cause Peace?, Annu. Rev. Polit. Sci., 1:27-46 (1998). Roland Rich, Democratic Peace Theory: What Relevant to East Asia? Centre for Democratic Instits., 2003. Michael Doyle, Kant, Liberal Legacies, and Foreign Affairs 3-57, In Sean Lynn-Jones Michael Brown, & Steven Miller, eds., Debating the Democratic Peace (Cambridge: MIT Press, 1996). Bruce Russett, The Fact of Democratic Peace, In Sean Lynn-Jones Michael Brown, & Steven Mille, eds., Debating the Democratic Peace (MIT Press, 1996), 58-81. R.J. Rummel, The politics of cold blood, Society, Vol. 27 (Nov/Dec., 1989), 32-40.

[4] Ludwig von Mises, Liberalism in the Classical Tradition, (German ed., 1927), (Ralph Raico, trans., Foundation for Economic Education, 1985). Jörg Guido Hülsmann, Who was Ludwig von Mises?, 2003, http://www.anb.org/articles/14/14-01132.html.

pushing countries such as Russia and China toward democracy may actually bring war in the short term.

In the new millennium, the difficulties of the democratic peace thesis are undoubtedly attributable, in part, to the yet to be fulfilled prophecy of Francis Fukuyama (1992). Fukuyama addresses the old question, "Whether, at the end of the twentieth century, it makes sense for us once again to speak of a coherent and directional history of mankind that will eventually lead the greater part of humanity to liberal democracy?" Fukuyama affirmatively answered the latter question based on two separate reasons -- economics and the struggle for recognition. He foresaw all nations converging to liberal democratic political economies. For Fukyuman, the end of cold war (1945-1991) and fall of the Berlin Wall (*Berliner Mauer*, 1961-1989) marked the end of history or end of the struggle between ideologies, with the world settling on liberal democracy. Notwithstanding Fukuyama's yet to fulfilled prophecy and the struggle for recognition, the relationship between economics and liberal democracy is all-important. The consequence of the end of the cold war era and rise of economic globalization pointed the direction in history towards a new world order, or perhaps even a new utopian international reality. As described by Louise Fawcett, in a new international reality, "Where–as different scholars predicted–history, geography, and ideology would become things of the past, subsumed in a new, highly interpenetrated and interconnected international order," the vision of a new international order parallels the idealistic thinking that followed the First and Second World Wars.[5] For Fawcett, "The end of a major war, even a 'cold' one, not unnaturally gives rise to hopes for the evolution of a just, peaceful, and prosperous international order." His vision is in harmony with the democratic peace thesis, or Kantian perpetual peace, which says, "Democracies do not fight each other." The democratic peace thesis evolves into cosmopolitan democracy, and then evolves into models of world peace, democracy, equality and justice. Indeed, it seems a truism that the democratic peace thesis more readily comes to fruition through the vehicles of liberalism or economic liberalism, rather than a Marxian materialistic concept of history.

Cosmopolitan law, in conjunction with international law, generally provides states with incentives for moral (*boni mores*) commitments, and facilitates the spirit of commerce and trade, especially international trade, to promote peace and not war. Cosmopolitan law fills the gap between traditional international law, which applies primarily between states, and domestic constitutional law that regulates relations between a state and its own citizens, subsequently producing corresponding cosmopolitan rights and a universal state of humankind (*jus cosmopoliticium*). Liberal economic theory and its attendant comparative advantage theory posit that cosmopolitan ties evolve from cooperative international divisions of labor and free trade. Economies are better off than they would have been under autarchy (or autarky), acquiring incentives to avoid breaking economic ties. Open markets, as a corollary of free trade, are contingent on the assumption that legal rights and agreed upon prices will determine the next set of transactions and not by coercion, thereby avoiding military conflicts among liberal states and enhancing the security of all, by means of an

[5] Francis Fukuyama, The End of History and the Last Man (Free Press, 1992). Louise Fawcett, Conclusion: Wither the Third World, In The Third World Beyond the Cold War Continuity and Change 245 (Louise Fawcett & Yezid Sayigh eds.) (Oxford UP, 1999). Benjamin Solomon, Kant's Perpetual Peace: A New Look At This Centuries-Old Quest, 5.1 Online J. of Peace and Conflict Resolution, ¶ 106 (summer 2003), http://www.trinstitute.org/ojpcr/5_1solomon.pdf. Michael W. Doyle, Liberal Internationalism: Peace, War and Democracy, Nobelprize.org, ¶ 6, http://nobelprize.org/peace/articles/doyle/html.

alliance that naturally results in economic interdependence.[6] As international economic interdependence lessens the need for governmental planning as to production and distribution, foreign states become less responsible for outcomes. The international market thereby evolves into a greater interdependence of commerce and trade, and the international contacts of state officials, who, ultimately, serve as lobbyists for mutual accommodation. Merchants of commerce and trade accordingly create interests in favor of accommodation, while offering a variety that ensures no single conflict challenges this relationship. A combination of trust, property rights and the rule of law make economic and non-economic disputes easier to resolve. These cosmopolitan sources of liberal peace, such as democracy, cosmopolitan law, international law, international markets and free trade, foster cosmopolitan ties lending to multilateralism, and not unilateralism. Liberal institutions, liberal ideals and transnational ties function as important factors to promote sustained liberal peace by encouraging the traits of liberal polities and economies together. It is in this manner that a Kantian perpetual peace comes to fruition. In conjunction with empirical evidence indicating that democratic states are not likely to initiate wars against each other, there appears to be a causal relationship between free trade and the democratic peace thesis or Kantian perpetual peace.

Francis Fukuyama essentially presented an earlier prophecy of the eventual triumph of political and economic liberalism. Although in subsequent years, Fukuyama (2000) slightly modified his "end of history" thesis, he remains committed to the idea of the United States using its power to promote democracy in the world.[7] However, it would be power used in accord with the ideals of "realistic Wilsonianism" and military intervention as a last resort and only when conjoined with other measures, because an American pre-emptive first-strike doctrine only challenges the ideals of "realistic Wilsonianism." On September 12, 2001, President Bush announced the Bush doctrine of pre-emptive first strike, which the UN General Assembly and Security Council, implicitly, authorized by UN Resolution 678 (1990), UN Resolution 687 (1991) and UN Resolution 1441 (2002). Fukuyama (2006) writes, "The so-called Bush Doctrine that set the framework for the administration's first term is now in shambles. The doctrine, which is elaborated, among other places, in the 2002 National Security Strategy of the United States, announces that, in the wake of the Sept. 11 attacks, America would have to launch periodic preventive wars to defend itself against rogue states and terrorists with weapons of mass destruction; that it would do this alone, if necessary; and that it would work to democratize the greater Middle East as a long-term solution to the terrorist problem." For American international relations, a perceived failure in Iraq challenges the ideals of "realistic Wilsonianism," and promotes, instead, the restoration and authority of foreign policy realists in the tradition of Henry Kissinger (former U.S. Secretary of State from 1973 to 1977).

---

6 M. Ulric Killion, China's Foreign Currency Regime: The Kagan Thesis and Legalification of the WTO Agreement, Vol. 14 Minn. J. Global Trade 43 (winter 2004). Pauline Kleingeld, Kants politscher Kosmopolitismus; in 5 Ann. Rev. L. Ethics (1997), http://www.str2.jura.uni-erlangen.de/JRE/vol05/a5-klein.htm. Richard N. Block, et al., Economic Perspectives on International Labor Standards, 11 MSU-DCL J. Int'l L. 417, 419–421 (2002).

7 Francis Fukyuman, Our Posthuman Future: Consequences of the Biotechnology Revolution (Farrar Straus & Giroux, 2002). Amy E. Eckert & Manooher Mofidi, Doctrine or Doctrinaire—the First Strike Doctrine and Preemptive Self-defense under International Law, 12 Tul. J. Int'l & Comp. L. 117, 119 (2004). Francisco Vázquez Ahued, America at the Crossroads: Democracy, Power, and the Neoconservative Legacy - Francis Fukuyama, Politics & Policy, Volume 34, Issue 3, 661 (Sept. 2006).

Nonetheless, the goals of promoting political and economic liberalism remain in tact. The subjects of dispute are the means for achieving greater political and economic liberalization, such as military, non-military and other means. For Western liberalism, there are problems of non-Western normative rules of order. Samuel P. Huntington, generally, describes the major cultures of the world as the West, Islam, China, "the Orthodox world," Africa, South America, India and Japan. Huntington also, borrowing from the *World Christian Encyclopedia* (1982), outlines the major religious traditions as Western Christian, Orthodox Christian, Muslim, nonreligious, Hindu, Buddhist, tribal, atheist and Chinese folk.[8] Non-Western cultures are dominant representatives in the latter categorizations, especially in Asia and East Asia. Liberalism and economic liberalism manifest Western rules of order standing in direct contrast to prevailing dominant, non-Western rules of order in other cultures and nations, such as the prevailing traditional rules of order, as manifest by Confucianism, Islamism, Buddhism and other culture-specific norms.

China is especially problematic when one considers the dynamics of Chinese politics and its history of constitutional government dating from the Sino-British post-Opium War (1839-1842) to modern China or a post-1949 China, with its many twists and turns, especially in terms of sovereignty and nationalism. For China, this historical journey of political growth parallels a history of international law and trade, from the original preferential trading arrangements of the British Empire (Opium Wars), to the WTO and its dialectic and economic visions of world order. Twice, from 1839 to 1842 and again from 1856 until 1860, the Chinese government sought to oust the British trade. China's historical journey, at least in the sense of classical international law (1648-1918) and modern international law, presents problems for Western institution building such as that undertaken by Western developed countries. A complex problem only compounded by the influence of traditional culture (primarily traditional Confucianism), ideology, nationalism and Marxism.

In terms of distinguishable historical, cultural and legal particularities, the situation is no less dramatic with other non-Western cultures and developing countries such as Afghanistan and Iraq. Edward W. Said observed that Chinese, Indian, Egyptian and Greek civilizations manifest anachronisms in modernity, offering at best marginally practical working political and legal ideologies in today's world. Said writes, "There are, of course, many religious, psychological, and political reasons for this, but all of these reasons derive from a sense that so far as the West is concerned, Islam represents not only a formidable competitor but also a late coming challenge to Christianity." Further, Edward W. Said writes, "Islam was believed to be a demonic religion of apostasy, blasphemy, and obscurity …It was as if a younger, more virile and energetic version of Christianity had arisen in the East …Only Islam seemed never to have submitted completely to the West; and when, after the dramatic oil-price rises of the early 1970s, the Muslim world seemed once more on the verge of repeating its early conquests, the whole West seemed to shudder." Problematic for Western institution building in non-Western countries and cultures is that Islamic political ideology is a worldwide

[8] UN, Resolution 678, S/RES/0678 (1990), Adopted by the Security Council at its 2963rd meeting on 29 November 1990. UN, Resolution 687, S/RES/687 (1991), Adopted by the Security Council at its 2981st meeting, on 3 April 1991. UN, Resolution 1441, S /RES/1441 (2002), Adopted by the Security Council at its 4644th meeting, on 8 November 2002. Francis Fukuyama, After Neoconservatism, Feb. 19, 2006, NY Times Magazine. Samuel P. Huntington, The Clash of Civilizations and the Remaking of World Order 19 (1996). David B. Barret, ed., World Christian Encyclopedia: A comparative study of churches and religions in the modern world (Oxford UP, 1982).

phenomenon, representing a "complex iteration of Quranic inspiration and reformist, fundamental orientation."[9] In the Arab and Muslim world, the seventh century precepts of the Prophet Muhammad (c. 570-632), God's prophet to whom the Qur'an was revealed, still bears relevancy and remains the substantive rule of order.

F.A. Hayek (Friedrich August von Hayek, 1899-1992) perceived the problem of institution building, as one of a "complex relationship between values and facts." It is a problem of blending these values and facts, and a resulting complex social structure "that exist only because the individuals composing them hold certain values." Hayek posits in terms of proposed modifications or improvements of existing orders that, "he [social scientist] will have to accept the values which are indispensable for its existence, as it would clearly be inconsistent to try to improve some particular aspect of the order and at the same time propose means that would destroy the values on which the whole order rests." Hayek is addressing the problem confronted by social scientists seeking to study complex social structures, which only exist because individuals hold certain values. Following David Hume (1711-1776), Hayek told us that we could never know why many valuable and important customs and systems evolved and desires that we give vestigial practices the benefit of our doubt, if not more. A phrase attributable to Robert Frost: "Never pull down a fence until you know why it was put up," succinctly and colloquially brings life to Hayek's viewpoints. Hayek, like David Hume and Edmond Burke (1729-1797), was not a proponent of grand plans for social reorganization of society, because social organizations will evolve organically in the course of history from diverse political, cultural and social circumstances.[10] Notwithstanding an adoption for other reasons or by accident, these are the processes that "enabled the group in which they had arisen to prevail over others." Hayek describes the resulting order as a "state of affairs in which a multiplicity of elements of various kinds are so related to each other that we may learn from our acquaintance with some spatial or temporal part of the whole to form correct expectations concerning the rest, or at least expectations which have a good chance of proving correct." However, scholars such as Burke, Hume and Hayek were often critical of rationalist theories of natural law and social contract theories, because ideals focused on unplanned historical evolutions of political and social norms better describe their theories.

For liberalism or economic liberalism, non-Western rules of order are problematic. Michael W. Doyle finds a Kantian perpetual peace to be objectionable, because of the normative explanation for liberal peace. It is the problem of Western normative norms that apply to "all statespersons as moral agents, as human beings, anywhere, whatever their state structure. Yet states other than liberal states do not maintain peace (and liberals maintain peace only with each other)."[11] In the new millennium, the problem remains how best

[9] Maimul Ahsan Khan, Human Rights in the Muslim World Fundamentalism, Constitutionalism, and International Politics, (Carolina Academic Press 2003). Edward W. Said, Covering Islam: How the Media and the Experts Determine How We See the Rest of the World, 4-5 (rev. ed. 1997).

[10] Peter G. Klein, Biography F. A. Hayek (1899-1992), Ludwig Von Mises Instit., http://www.mises.org/content/hayekbio.asp. F. A. Hayek, Law, Legislation and Liberty, Three volumes, (Univ. of Chicago Press, 1973-79), 111-112. Julian L. Simon, Hayek's Road Comes to an End, The Independent Institute, Commentary Apr. 13, 1992.

[11] Edward Mansfield & Jack Snyder, Democratization and War, Foreign Affairs, May/June 1995. Samuel P. Huntington, The Clash of Civilizations and the Remaking of World Order 19 (1996). Richard Pierre Claude & Burns H. Weston (eds.), Human Rights in the World Community, 3-4 (Univ. of Penn. Press, 1992). Michael W. Doyle, Ways of War and Peace (W.W. Norton, 1997). Zeev Maoz & Bruce Russett, Alliance, Contiguity,

Western culture can promote in non-Western countries, the economic or political economy ideology of Western civilization and culture.

6.2. THE "OTHER" WORLD AND MARXISM

The issues of transplanting laws and legal systems, including normative norms, directly relate to issues of transplanting or borrowing liberalism or economic liberalism. In the real world, it is often difficult to discern between politics and economics, economics and law, or even between politics and law. A failure to accomplish this feat, in terms of real world applications of the respective disciplines or sciences, only begs the question of whether someone should have done so, because given a failure to do so, leaves us without a hierarchy that describes effective institution building or reforms. More particularly, in the efficient and effective building or reform of systems or institutions, do efficient and effective reforms require first the building of a political system rather than a legal system or economic system, or first the building of a legal system or economic system, and which one of this trio of systems (or institutions) should be secondly built, then thirdly built. A complex gathering of issues that becomes even more complex when a quadruple set of systems or institutions is constructed, this includes a fourth entity of a society's infrastructure of social norms, the social system. It now seems a tacit assumption of liberalism or economic liberalism that this trio, if not quadruple, of systems or institutions should be conjoined in effective institution building, rebuilding or reforms, because the roots of economic liberalism, being classic liberalism, is moral and social philosophy.

In Western theory, it is now conventional wisdom that "law reform projects should be assessed not in isolation, but within a broader context of economic policies."[12] Western experts and authority, generally, summarize Chinese economic growth and development policies as reflecting a choice between two alternative patterns or policies: "big bang" approach or reforms and "gradualist" approach or gradual reforms. Antithetically, there are also contradistinguishable models to the "big bang" reforms – "gradualist" reforms dichotomy. For instance, two Chinese academics, Zhou Bing and Jin Tao, promote a transformation that isolates transformation from reforms, which results in severing the links between economic transformation and political reforms as a premise for successful economic transformation. Another source, Fang Gang and Wing Thye Woo, offers "parallel partial progression (PPP)" as an alternative reform policy, which focuses on commencing reforms in as many areas as possible without waiting on subsequent developments in each area, rather than "sequencing" and one reform measure being contingent on completion of an earlier reform measure.[13] There are many contradistinguishable models residing between the disciplines of Western conventionalism, and the orthodoxy and unorthodoxy of Marxism.

Wealth and Political Stability: Is the Lack of Conflict among Democracies a Statistical Artifact?, Vol. 17, No. 3 Int'l Interactions, 245-268 (1992).

[12] Katharina Pistor & Phillip A. Wellons, Asian Dev. Bank, Executive Summary: The Role of Law and Legal Institutions in Asian Economic Development 1960-1964 16 (1998). Wing Thye Woo, A United Front for the Common Objective to Understand China's Economic Growth: A Case of Nonantagonistic Contradiction, Wu vs. Woo, Issues & Studies 39, no. 2 (June 2003), 1-23. Zhang Jun, Capital Formation, Industrialization and Economic Growth: Characteristics of China Structural Reform, Jinji yanjiu, no. 6 (2002).

[13] Zhou Bing & JinTao, The Way the Economic System is Transformed and How it is Determined, Social Sciences in China, 97-109 (spring 2006). Fan Gang & Wing Thye Woo, "Sequencing" or "Parallel Partial Progression;"

However, the latter conventionalism and its language of "a broader context of economic policies" neither buttresses Marxian analysis and its economic determinism, nor substantiate a causal influence of legal, political, religious, artistic and other philosophical forms in Marxist, communist or socialist societies. A persistent problem of Marxian analysis is social, legal and political systems or institutions being defined and confined in their development by the fundamental and exclusive causal influence of economic determinism. Since the late nineteenth century, and as observed by academic Maurice Finkelstein, "All sociological theories of jurisprudence recognize at the outset that law is only one of the means of social control and not necessarily the best." Finkelstein counts as examples, those situations "when it is the part of wisdom to intrust social control to the various moral and psychological forces of the community," such as the *fas* (the lawful or will of the gods) and *boni mores* (morals) of primitive societies.[14] These moral and psychological forces are concepts borrowed from Roman law, from the juristic science of the Roman *pontifices* in prehistoric times, the *Law of the Twelve Tables* (*Lex Duodecim Tabularum*, published 451-450 B.C.), to the *Code of Justinian* (*Corpus Juris Civilis*, compiled AD 529 to AD 565). They are generally described as -- *fas*, *jus* and *boni mores*, and most laws of the kings were rules of the *fas*, -- that is, of religious duty. Indeed, the latter forces of a community, or a culture and society, stand diametrically opposed to Marxian analysis and its economic determinism.

Eugen Ehrlich (Austrian legal scholar, 1862-1922), in *The Sociology of Law* (1922), perceives social order as being based on fundamental social institutions, such as marriage, family, possession, contract and succession. It is a social order perceptible to the senses of those persons standing in social relations to the acts of others, in their respective dealings according to established norms. However, in terms of Marxist, communist or socialist rules of order, Eugen Ehrlich, in *Fundamental Principles of the Sociology of Law* (*Grundlegung der Soziologie des Rechts*, 1913), by analogy, presents Marxism as a contradistinction to traditional Chinese culture and Western universalism. As pertains to law and legal order, Marxists follow a contradistinction to traditional Chinese culture and Western universalism, in the pursuit of a Marxist, communist or socialist philosophy of history. While a Marxist conception of law, or perhaps more accurately positive law, admittedly, presents itself as a coercive order of law and as being derived from social life as a whole, it is still problematically confined by Marxian analysis and its economic determinism. Marxists observe, historically, a great contrast in social order between the rich and poor, manifesting an inequitable burden of work for the poor, an unfair exchange providing for the bare necessities of life and a legal order compelling the poor to render valuable services in an unfair exchange for services of much less value. All of which for Marxists are consequences of a materialistic conception of history. Commencing with the older economic organization of humankind, the ordering of the clan and family, the household as a self-sustaining economic unit and industry "carried on" by organized crafts, according to Engels (Friedrich Engels, 1820-1895) and others, there exist an "equal division of the fruits of labor among all who participated therein was secured." Marx (Karl Heinrich Marx, 1818-1883) and Marxists

Incoherence Cost and the Optimal Path of Institutional Transformation, Social Sciences in China, 87-96 (spring 2006).

[14] Maurice Finkelstein, The Functional View of Legal Liability, Int'l Journal of Ethics, Vol. 34, No. 3, 243-253 (Apr., 1924). Mary Emily Case, Did the Romans Degenerate?, Int'l Journal of Ethics, Vol. 3, No. 2, 165-182 (Jan., 1893). Fritz Schulz, History of Roman Legal Science, (Oxford UP, 1967). Barry Nicholas, An Introduction to Roman law, (Oxford UP, 1992).

perceive the latter state of affairs, when subject to influence of capitalism, as "continually shifting to the disadvantage of an ever increasing majority of those who have not and to the advantage of an ever decreasing number of those who have." The great majority perceived an advantage to sustaining the older economic order. In comparison, a later capitalistic order was antithetically maintained exclusively by the state, or the sovereign power of the state, as a powerful and elaborate organization of those "who have for the protection of the legal order, which is based on property, contract, and the law of inheritance." Consequently, the Marxists urge those "who have not to oppose to the organization of those who have the organization of the masses in order to bring about a legal order which is more favorable to the latter." A critical component of Marxist legal order is the contention of a small, yet ever decreasing, minority of "those who have against the great mass of those who have not."[15]

Marx, in the preface to *A Contribution to the Critique of Political Economy* (*Grundrisse der Kritik der politischen Ökonomie/Rohentwurf*, 1859), which also sets forth his materialistic conception of history, examined the system of a bourgeois economy in ranking order as capital, landed property, wage-labor, the State, foreign trade and world market.[16] While Marx indicated that he had studied jurisprudence, he approached the study of jurisprudence as being subordinate to both philosophy and history. Marx wrote, "The first work which I undertook to dispel the doubts assailing me was a critical re-examination of the Hegelian philosophy of law; the introduction to this work being published in the *Deutsch-Franzosische Jahrbucher* issued in Paris in 1844. My inquiry led me to the conclusion that neither legal relations nor political forms could be comprehended whether by themselves or on the basis of a so-called general development of the human mind, but that on the contrary they originate in the material conditions of life, the totality of which Hegel, following the example of English and French thinkers of the eighteenth century, embraces within the term 'civil society;' that the anatomy of this civil society, however, has to be sought in political economy." Marx, in terms of the productive forces determining the relations of production, writes, "In the social production of their existence, men inevitably enter into definite relations, which are independent of their will, namely relations of production appropriate to a given stage in the development of their material forces of production. The totality of these relations of production constitutes the economic structure of society, the real foundation, on which arises a legal and political superstructure and to which correspond definite forms of social consciousness. The mode of production of material life conditions the general process of social, political and intellectual life. It is not the consciousness of men that determines their existence, but their social existence that determines their consciousness. At a certain stage of development, the material productive forces of society come into conflict with the existing relations of production or - this merely expresses the same thing in legal terms - with the property relations within the framework of which they have operated hitherto. From forms of development of the productive forces these relations turn into their fetters. Then begins an era of social revolution."

Karl Marx, in *A Contribution to the Critique of Political Economy*, further observes, "The changes in the economic foundation lead sooner or later to the transformation of the whole

---

[15] Eugen Ehrlich, Fundamental Principles of the Sociology of Law (1913), (China Social Sciences Publishing House, Chengcheng Books, Ltd.: The President and Fellows of Harv. College, 1936). Eugen Ehrlich, The Sociology of Law 36 Harv. L. Rev. 128 (Nathan Isaacs, trans., 1922).

[16] Karl Marx, (Preface), A Contribution to the Critique of Political Economy (1859). Karl Marx, The Portable Karl Marx 158-61 (Eugene Kamenka, trans.) (Penguin, 1983).

immense superstructure." In terms of these transformations, it was critical to discern between material transformations of the economic conditions of production that are determinable with the precision of natural science, and those ideological forms by which people become conscious of this conflict and willing to fight it out for, such as the legal, political, religious, artistic and other philosophical forms. Consequently, productive forces determine the relations of production, and, in turn, the production relations create the economic basis of society, which determines all social institutions and ideas that make these production relations possible. This superior economic basis of society shapes "the general process of social, political and intellectual life." Marx and his theory of history or materialistic conception of history, and its attendant concepts of base and superstructure, essentially analyzed the economic structure (*Struktur*) of society as constituting the genuine basis on which legal and political superstructures (*Überbau*) should be erect. For Marx, it was from these superstructures that social consciousness corresponds. A Marxist perspective views the basic structure of society as being economic or material, thereby determining the rest of social life, being the spiritual or ideological and other philosophical forms.

Niklas Luhmann (1927-1998), whom viewed and treated social systems from an ontological perspective or, more particularly, hailing that systems exist, in *A Sociological Theory of Law* (*Rechtssoziologie*, 1985), describes the social teachings of Karl Marx as reacting to an elemental tenet of modern social development, which constitutes a transition of the primacy of social meaning from politics to economics. Marx viewed the primacy of economics, as he related economics to materialism or the materiality of human needs, as "an ahistorical-anthropological truth and formulates a theory of natural-legal, dialectical and societal development within this framework." For Marx, the impetus for development always originates in changing productive forces and relations of productions that satisfy material needs. A basic tenet that these contradictions are unstable continues to drive Marxism and serve as the originators of change. Marx was concerned with the social contradictions that accumulate when developing production and satisfying needs, and perceived the role of law as addressing these contradictions. The law does so by an allocation of unequal opportunities to individuals and by, most importantly, granting and protecting property. Marxism remains problematic, because according to the teachings of Marx, "if the whole body of law is designed according to the interest of owners and administered by them, this legal change can only take the form of a *revolution*." Luhman, in translating Marxist theory, writes, "During the course of society development, then, the socialization of needs (distribution) from decisions regarding production, and substitutes rationality for objectivised and interest-oriented (class-oriented) law." However, Luhmann's personal views differed from Marxist theory, because Niklas Luhmann, antithetically, viewed all collective human life as being directly or indirectly affected by law. For Luhmann, law resembles knowledge, as one of the essential facts of the social condition, because a lasting social order must be based on law and "a minimum amount of legal orientation is indispensable everywhere."[17]

[17] Karl Marx, Das Kapital, (Gateway eds., 1999). Niklas Luhmann, A Sociological Theory of Law (Elizabeth King & Martin Albrow, trans., 1985).

6.3. Conclusion

For these reasons and others, a successful re-building or reform of Marxist, communists or socialists systems or institutions is contingent on an institutional analysis within a Marxian framework or Marxist political economy, which is the very heart of Marx's project for a future Marxian utopia, or even perpetual peace.[18] A primary concern of a Marxian framework or Marxist political economy is the subject of the relations of production. A Marxian framework, generally, operates through the vehicle of institutional economics serving as a theoretical system in the analysis of society's institutions, including social, political, legal and economic institutions. In terms of Marxist political economy, there is an elemental institutional analysis forthcoming from the basis premises that productive forces determine production relations, economic foundation decides superstructures or society's institutions and ideas and a core segment that covers the social division of labor. In terms of liberal or liberal economic norms and institution building or reforms, Marxist political economy is problematic as a force driving institutional research and analysis, while also being hailed as the primordial explanatory system for institutional phenomena.

Experimentation in reforms or a "gradualist" approach by China, though many Western experts disagree, may reflect conventional wisdom of not pursuing reforms in isolation, because a "gradualist" approach may evidence some influence of Western theories or rules of order. However, there remains the problematic influence of the interrelated paradoxical Western theories or rules of order producing paradoxical consequences. As observed by Qian Mu (Mu, Ch'ien, 1895-1990), "In discussing the history of Chinese economic thought, one must give careful attention to the political conditions prevalent at the time of the origin of new economic institutions."[19] On-going reforms present problems of reforming or building social-economic, political and legal systems or institutions, which challenge Marxian analysis and its economic determinism. The same concerns addressing the issue of transplanting law and legal systems equally apply to the issues of transplanting liberalism or economic liberalism. For China, the problem of transplanting and borrowing Western liberalism or economic liberalization, and Western laws and legal systems, presents the issues of transplanting and borrowing Western normative norms, or "other" cultural values, *ethos* and morals. A problem is growing anti-American sentiment, such as associated with the invasion of Iraq and growing in other parts of the world, such as China, Russia, North Korea and other non-Western countries, which only enhances the difficult of accomplishing this feat.

---

[18] William James Booth, Explaining Capitalism: The Method of Marx's Political Economy, Political Studies 37 (4), 612-625 (1998). Li Shenglong, The Overall Structure of the Institutional Analysis Theory of Marxism, Jingjixue dongtai, no. 5 (2003). Yu Wujin, Drawing Inspiration from Marx's Diagnosis of Modernity, Sun Hui, Marx's Ontology and Its Significance in Our Times, 3-11 Social Sciences in China (Zhongguo shehui kexue) (spring 2003).

[19] Ch'ien Mu (Qian Mu), Traditional Government in Imperial China, (Chu-tu Hsueh & George O. Totten trans., 1982). America's Image Problem Complicates War on Terror, Mar. 12, 1999, Detroit News.

Chapter 7

TRANSPLANTING LAW AND ECONOMICS

7.1. DEFINING LIBERTY FOR CHINESE LIBERAL COTERIE

When importing the Western concept of liberty into a Chinese political economy lexicon of liberty, rather than devise a new word or character(s) for liberty in the native Chinese language (Mandarin or *Putonghua*), culture, ideology, thought system and appropriate lexicon, they (the Chinese) simply assigned the Western concept of liberty to the word (or characters) *ziyou* or *zi-you*. In terms of traditional Chinese culture (primarily traditional Confucianism) and language, while the word (or characters) *ziyou* did convey an earlier Chinese conceptualization of liberty from antiquity, *ziyou* did not connote the Western concept of liberty and its attendant political economy consequences. In antiquity, the word or (characters) *ziyou* for the ordinary Chinese citizen conveyed a limited and, especially, non-political economy meaning manifesting the most mundane ideas of simply being free to do something in their daily lives, such as free to go for a walk. There are many examples of the usage of *ziyou* from antiquity, in the classics, literature and history. For instance, where Zheng Xuan's (127–200) commentary to the passage, in the *Liji* (*Book of rites*), reads, "while one may ask for an audience, one may not ask for retreat," one finds the following usage, *Qu zhi bugan ziyou* (To leave or stay is not up to one's own liking).[1] There is the classic *Sanguozhi* (*Records of the Three States*) that reads, *Jiedu bude ziyou* (Revenues may not be settled arbitrarily). From the Han Dynasty (BC 206-AD 220), there is also the example from a verse of a prominent classic poem from the *yuefu* (or *Yuefu Shiji*) entitled, *Kongque dongnan fei* (*A Pair of Peacocks Southeast Fly* or *Southeast the peacock flies*), which reads, *Wu yi jiu huaifen, ru qi de ziyou* (For a long time I've found her infuriating/How dare you try to have your own way.[2] In antiquity, usage of the word (or characters) *ziyou* was substantially

---

[1] Xiong, Yuezhi, 'Liberty', 'Democracy', 'President': The Translation and Usage of Some Political Terms in Late Qing China, Liji (Book of rites, rpt. 1980). Shisanjing zhushu (The Thirteen Classics with annotations and notes) (edited by Ruan Yuan BC) (Beijing: Zhonghua shuju, 1512). Chen, Shou (233–297), Sanguozhi (Records of the Three States), (Beijing: Zhonghua shuju, 1962). The Columbia Book of Chinese Poetry, (Columbia UP), 82–92; 93.

[2] From Han Dynasty (BC 206-AD 220), Kongque Dongnan Fei (A Pair of Peacocks Southeast Fly) is a classic poem from the Yuefu (or Yuefu Shiji), also representative of the triad of pre-Tang poetic heroines (Luofu, Cai Wenji and Lan-zhi). As recounted in poem, "Lanzhi's mother-in-law sends her home; she commits suicide when her parents try to force her to remarry, at which point her husband Jiao Zhongqing commits suicide." Guo, Maoqian, ed., Yuefu Shiji (Anthology of Yuefu [Music Bureau] Poetry), 12 vols. (Beijing, 1955).

different from its usage commencing in the late nineteenth century or late Qing (Qing Dynasty, 1644-1911). The problem of the word (or characters) *ziyou*, especially in the post-Qing period, is that the Western conceptualization of liberty is not native to China in its etymology and content.

Nonetheless, assuming the concept of liberty now enjoys a political connotation in modern China, such as radicalism in the political environment, the concept of legal borrowing may explain the transmutation rather than the transplant or integration into its political or legal system of Western liberty to a modern Chinese lexicon of liberty. In the Chinese language, the word (or characters) *zi you* primarily translate into the English words of "liberty" and "freedom," and then "liberal," which may also intimate an artificial rather than natural transmutation. The word (or character) *zi* translates into "oneself" or "one's own." The word (or character) *you* translates into "cause," "reason," "because of" or "due to." The word (or character) *you* standing alone is a function word constituting an adverb, which is without concrete meaning. However, the word (or character) *zi* when combined with the word (or character) *you* produces *zi you* and results in formation of a notional word (or characters) that has concrete meaning as a noun. In terms of a modern Chinese concept of liberty conceptualizing a Western concept of liberty and its attendant political economy consequences, the word (or characters) *zi-you* (or *ziyou*) produced nouns with concrete meanings (or etymologies): liberal (*ziyou* or *ziyou pai*), neo-liberal (*xin ziyou* or *xin ziyou pai*), liberalism (*ziyou zhuyi*) and neo-liberalism (*xin ziyou zhuyi*).

This does not mean that the word (or characters) *ziyou* became the exclusive province of political, legal, political economy lexicons, or other appropriate lexicons. For instance, modern China and its new generation of youth, those born in the 1980s, intended to give a different interpretation to notions of freedom and liberty. They are the so-called new *linglei*, or new iconoclasts, which have supposedly pitted themselves against conformity and conventionalism as an exercise in self-expression. While the new iconoclasts pride themselves as fighting against conformity and conventionalism, they instead substantiate the force of cultural enculturation, which is defined as, "the total activity of learning one's culture."[3] This new interpretation of notions of freedom and liberty reflect non-political economy meanings, which are hardly distinguishable from meanings in antiquity. The plight of the new iconoclasts serves to symbolize the continuing struggle between the relatively short-term processes of borrowing, assimilation, diffusion and acculturation, and the long-term and historical process and force of cultural enculturation. However, and notwithstanding examples such as the new *linglei*, one can still reasonably deduce that the conceptualization of Chinese neo-liberalism is too some extent linguistically rooted in Western liberalism. Although not necessarily importing an effective transplant of liberalism, the latter lends credence, too some extent, to cultural borrowing, in particular, legal borrowing and the dynamics of legal borrowing.[4] The question of whether cultural borrowing occurs, admittedly, during legal borrowing from an original Western donor country, as a sort of reverse cultural assimilation, diffusion or acculturation, is perhaps a matter of degree and extent. The problem of transplanting and borrowing laws and legal systems, including economic systems, also presents issues of measuring the effectiveness and efficiency of transplanting and borrowing

---

[3] Larry A. Samovar, Richard E. Porter & Lisa A. Stefani, Communication Between Cultures, 38-39 (Wadsworth Pub, 2000).

[4] Katharina Pistor & Philip A. Wellons, eds., The Role of Law and Legal Institutions in Asian Economic Development 1960-1995, (Oxford UP, 1998).

or diffusion, which is dependent on the models, methodologies and tools for doing so. In addition, there are several Western models, methodologies and tools, for measuring transplantation and borrowing.

7.2. Transplantation Model – Ugo Mattei Model

Ugo Mattei provides a very straightforward and pragmatic model for understanding the process of transplanting and borrowing laws and legal systems, including economic systems.[5] Mattei provides three generally described historical patterns, or models, for transplanting law in intended recipient countries. Ugo Mattei's first model is one of "direct imperialistic/colonial rule, or imposition of legal patterns by military force." Classic examples are military conquests in the Kingdom of Belgium (Belgium) and Japan, and there are other examples. Napoleon Bonaparte, after his conquest of Belgium in 1795, transplants the Napoleonic Code (French civil codes or *Code civil des français*), and modern Belgium's civil and penal codes still reflect similarities from the original *Code civil des français*. Francis Fukuyama writes, "In light of the broad movement of civilization, even bloody wars like those of Napoleon could be interpreted by philosophers as socially progressive in their results, because they fostered the spread of republican government."[6] In terms of Japan, there are American General Douglas MacArthur's (1880-1964) reforms, or post-War World II U.S. reconstruction in Japan (1945 to 1951). In "Occupied Japan," General MacArthur, as Supreme Commander of the Allied Powers (SCA), oversaw an American-led reconstruction, re-organization and re-supply of the Japanese people. What aids the reconstruction of Japan is that during the Meji Restoration (*Meiji-ishin*, 1866-1869 and 1940s), Japan earlier industrialized and made institutional and infrastructure changes. General McArthur's occupation forces did not experience problems in implementing the Ladejinsky/McArthur land reforms in Japan and then later in Taiwan (Republic of China, R.O.C.). However, in 1949, Wolf Ladejinsky, the Agricultural attaché in Tokyo, when charged with the task of doing the same in Mainland China faced an impossible task, because the Chinese communists (Red Army) had expanded its power during the civil war against Jiang Jieshi's (Chiang Kai-shek, 1887-1975) Chinese Nationalist Party (*Kuomintang*). The Red Army had swept down from the north, and forced the Nationalist army and government to take refuge in Taipei, Taiwan (Formosa). The Chinese communists subsequently organized their own land reform, which, as observed by Ladejinsky, involved using a great deal of force and violence.

Another example is institution building, including socio-economic, legal and political institutions, by military force and coercion, such as the cases of Afghanistan and Iraq, especially in their bid for democratically elected legislatures. In both cases, military impetus prompts institution building. In terms of success or failure, there are hopes of hailing Afghanistan's earlier democratic elections as a model of success that Iraq will subsequently follow. Admittedly, in September 2004, the White House (President George W. Bush) announced an achieved success, though perhaps prematurely. A September 2004 press

---

[5] Ugo Mattei, A Theory of Imperial Law: A Study on U.S. Hegemony and the Latin Resistance, Global Jurist Frontiers: Vol. 3: No. 2, Article 1 (2003), http://www.bepress.com/gj/frontiers/vol3/iss2/art1. Ugo Mattei, A Theory of Imperial Law: A Study on U.S. Hegemony and the Latin Resistance, 10 Ind. J. Global Leg. Stud. 383, 388-89, (winter, 2003).

[6] Francis Fukuyama, The End of History and the Last Man, 4 (Free Press, 1992).

release, in part, reads, "Today, because we acted to liberate Afghanistan, a threat has been removed, and the American people are safer… Iraq is now becoming an example of reform to the region. Iraqi security forces are fighting beside coalition troops to defeat terrorists and foreign fighters. Today, because America and our coalition helped to end the violent regime of Saddam Hussein, and because we are helping to raise a peaceful democracy in its place, the American people are safer."[7] However, as observed by Peter L. Berger, "Bin Laden's network -- which also values technical proficiency, albeit of a rather specialized kind -- is as cosmopolitan as the cosmocrats." Al Qaeda global bases are in the Pakistan-Afghanistan border region, Iraq and Europe and, presently, preparing to expand to the Middle East, Africa and South Asia.

Since the Iraq War (Second Gulf War) was commenced, there have been pundits subscribing to a theory that an America-led war, in conjunction with coalition forces, against Iraq is illegal in terms of international law. The latter presents the issue of whether war against Iraq, especially for purpose of institution building, is illegal under the principle of *justum bellos* or *jus ad bellum* (just war). Hans Kelsen (1881-1973), in *The Pure Theory of Law* (*Reine Rechtslehre*, 1934), describes two theories of just war. The first holds that according to general international law, war is neither a delict nor a sanction; every state may go to war for whatever reason, without violating international law. The second holds that war, even according to general international law, is permissible only as a reaction against a violation of international law. War, like reprisal, is itself a delict, unless it is a sanction. This is the so-called principle of *bellum iustum*.[8] However, a problem for these pundits is that the United Nations (UN) sanctioned and authorized war against Iraq. According to Lord Goldsmith (Peter Henry Goldsmith, the Attorney General of England and Wales), "all of these resolutions were adopted under Chapter VII of the UN Charter which allows the use of force for the express purpose of restoring international peace and security." Resolution 678 (1990) provided the underlying authority for the use of force to eject Iraq from Kuwait by "all necessary means" and to restore Kuwait's sovereignty, with the goal of reinstating international peace and security in the area. Lord Goldsmith opined that Resolution 687 (1991) "suspended but did not terminate" the authority to use force under Resolution 678, and imposed numerous obligations on Iraq. According to Goldsmith, a material breach of Resolution 687 revives the authority to use force. Resolution 1441 declared Iraq in "material breach" of its obligations under previous Security Council resolutions, gave it a final opportunity to comply with those obligations, and warned of "serious consequences" if it failed to comply fully. On September 12, 2001, President Bush announced the Bush doctrine of pre-emptive first strike, which the UN General Assembly and Security Council authorized by resolution. The issues surrounding principle of *justum bellos* are necessarily related to the legality of Western institution building in non-Western cultures and nation-states, especially when the impetus for reconstruction is military force and coercion, or hard power rather than soft power.[9]

---

[7] The Whitehouse, President George Bush, Three Years of Progress in the War on Terror, Fact Sheet, Sept. 11, 2004, http://www.whitehouse.gov/news/releases/2004/09/20040911.html. Jim Hoagland, Elections in Iraq and Afghanistan, June 20, 2004, Washington Post. Peter L. Bergen, Holy War, Inc., 196 (Free Press, 2001). Bruce Reidel, Al Qaeda Strikes Back, May/June 2007, Foreign Affairs.

[8] Hans Kelsen, (transl. Max Knight), The Pure Theory of Law, 321-22 (Regents of the Univ. of California, 1967).

[9] Ibrahim J. Gassama, International Law at a Grotian Moment: The Invasion of Iraq in Context, 18 Emory Int'l L. Rev. 1, 13-14, (spring 2004). Amy E. Eckert & Manooher Mofidi, Doctrine or Doctrinaire—The First Strike Doctrine and Preemptive Self-defense under International Law, 12 Tul. J. Int'l & Comp. L. 117, 119 (2004).

A problem of an American-led war against Iraq directly relates to issue of purposeful Western institution building. An issue still in dispute is whether the Bush Administration entered office with an original intent of institution building in Iraq and determined to effect a change in the governmental regime of Iraq. In 1998, The Project of the New American Century, an organization comprising prominent citizens, requested that President Clinton "enunciate a new strategy that would secure the interests of the U.S. and our friends and allies around the world. That strategy should aim, above all, at the removal of Saddam Hussein's regime from power." Some of those signatories became senior cabinet members in the Bush Administration, such as former U.S. Defense Secretary Donald Rumsfeld, and former U.S. Deputy Defense Secretary Paul Wolfowitz, whom also served as president of the World Bank until June 2007. In July 2004, according to former Defense Secretary Rumsfeld, "The United States didn't declare war on Iraq because of new evidence of banned weapons." According to Rumsfeld, "the U.S. declared war because it saw existing evidence of Iraqi arms programs in 'a dramatic new light' following the Sept. 11 terrorist attacks." Moreover, and troubling for many was the subsequent appointment of Wolfowitz to lead the World Bank. In terms of institution building by military impetus, war may well be what Carl von Clausewitz described over one hundred and seventy-five years ago as a "continuation of politics (*Politik*) by other means."[10]

Ugo Mettei outlines a second model of imposition by bargaining, such as acceptance of a legal model by a sort of subtle blackmail, which is describable as economic and political coercion rather than by military force and coercion. In order to gain access to international markets, nations change their laws according to Western standards, such as the cases of China, Japan, Egypt and other developing countries. This is the way international economic institutions and international non-governmental organizations (IGOs), such as the International Bank for Reconstruction and Development (IBRD or World Bank), International Monetary Fund (IMF), the General Agreement on Tariffs and Trade (GATT) and, now, the World Trade Organization (WTO), effect, or at least intend to effect, change in developing countries. In August 2006, Thomas J. Christensen, when testifying before the U.S.–China Economic and Security Review Commission, "discussed the notion of China as a responsible stakeholder in the global system."[11] In February 2007, Christensen, antithetically, observed that U.S. foreign policy should focus on urging China in the direction of being a responsible stakeholder. He did not explicitly state that China is not currently the responsible stakeholder we envision. Nonetheless, according to Christensen, "Our vision is a China that is more open, transparent, and democratic, and a China that will join us in actions that strengthen and support a global system that has provided peace, security, and prosperity to America, China, and the rest of the world." A problem for U.S. foreign policy, and its attendant institution building, is how to effectively encourage China to move in this direction.

G.A. Res. 1, U.N. GAOR, 56th Sess., U.N. Doc. A/56/L.1 (2001); U.N. SCOR, 4370th mtg. at 1, U.N. Doc. S/Res/1368 (2001).

[10] Iraq war not about new arms evidence: Rumsfeld, July 10, 2003, CBC News. Wolfowitz Nominated to Lead World Bank, CATO Instit., Mar. 17, 2005, http://www.cato.org/dispatch/03-17-05d.html#2. Peter S. Goodman, Ending Battle, Wolfowitz Resigns From World Bank, May 17, 2007. An Open Letter to President Clinton: "Remove Saddam from Power," in The Iraq War Reader 199 (Micah L. Sifry & Christopher Cerf eds., 2003). Antulio J. Echevarria, II, The Legacy of Clausewitz, JFQ, 76-77 (winter 1995-96).

[11] Thomas J. Christensen, Deputy Assistant Secretary for East Asian and Pacific Affairs, Remarks Before the U.S.–China Economic and Security Review Commission, Feb. 2, 2007, http://www.state.gov/p/eap/rls/rm/2007/79866.htm.

China may or may not offer a prime example of Western institution building by non-military means, such as imposition by bargaining, because "the civilization of modern industry first appeared in Western countries and then spread to non-Western countries," then "the modernization of non-Western countries is, first of all, a process of accepting the civilization of Western industrialization." Nonetheless, modern China is in the midst of economic and legal reforms. In China, the commencement of these reforms is, generally, attributable to the Deng Xiaoping era, when, in 1992, Deng Xiaoping visited Shenzhen, Guangdong Province, and officially declared China will adopt a socialist market economy, which many actually attribute as commencing modernization. They are economic and legal reforms that respectively date the Deng Xiaoping era and China's entry into the WTO. Past and present reforms are also subject to influence of both pre-accession and post-accession WTO membership. Moreover, because rules of accession for China would serve as a model for additional transition economies, especially following 1991 collapse of the former Soviet Union and Council for Mutual Economic Assistance (COMECON or CMEA), which was the economic and trading system of East European countries connected to the Soviet Union, Western developed countries, implicitly, created special conditions and rigorous accession terms for China. In terms of pre-accession China, although China had earlier commenced legal and economic reforms, these reforms were far-reaching, but incomplete.[12]

Finally, there is Ugo Mattei's third model, which is gravely distinguishable from the other two models, because it is fully consensual and is presented, "as diffusion by prestige, focusing on a deliberate process of institutional admiration that leads to the reception of law."[13] Fung Yu-lan (Feng Youlan, 1895-1990), in discussing the way of decrease (or retreat) and the way of increase (or advance), wrote, "If there are two such diametrically opposing patterns of life, it is obvious that there must be two ways of life no less opposing for him who may behold this, and in beholding, govern himself accordingly." Several means or forces are employable for effecting Western institution building. Most problematic is the force of military power and coercion, or simply hard power rather than soft power, which has especially presented a problem for the United States and its image in the international community. One source describes the Bush doctrine as pursuing a *pax-Americana* (American peace) global empire built by forcible means, where empire by consent is not an option. The problem of a methodology of force is that it frustrates rather than enhances the potential of Ugo Mattei's third model for institution building and transplanting law in intended recipient countries, which is a model that is fully consensual, and is presented, "as diffusion by prestige, focusing on a deliberate process of institutional admiration that leads to the reception of law." However, a genuine alternative to the methodology of force only births from a genuine understanding and tolerance of Sinicism, Islamism and other non-Western cultures and countries, because only then can a Western world engage in effective institution building. A model of institution building that bridges the gap between theory and application, by taking into account a broad range of political economy concerns, ranging from socio-economic to theological-political concerns, including the cosmos (*kosmos* or grown order) rather than *taxis*

---

[12] The Council for Mutual Economic Assistance, [Excerpted from Czechoslovakia: A Country Study, Glenn E. Curtis, ed., (Library of Congress, 1992).], http://www.shsu.edu/~his_ncp/CMEA.html. Nicholas R. Lardy, Integrating China into the Global Economy, 29-62 (Brookings Instit., 2002).

[13] For compilation of Belgium codes see: Les codes Larcier. Edition 2003, Tomes I-VII, (Bruxelles, Larcier, 2003). Louis Walinsky (ed.), Agrarian Reform as Unfinished Business, the selected papers of Wolf Ladejinsky (Oxford UP, 1977).

(or made order) of these non-Western spheres of humankind.[14] Consequently, Western institution building, regardless of methodology employed, presents a grave responsibility for Western cultures and countries seeking to build or rebuild non-Western cultures and countries.

7.3. Transplantation Model – Western Legal Borrowing

There are also the more orthodox Western models and taxonomies for transplanting and borrowing laws and legal systems. Western philosophers, scholars of law, sociology, anthropology and economics, generally, identify three core theories on legal borrowing that address the process of converging law and socioeconomic development. The three core theories on legal borrowing are, generally, evolutionary theory, cultural theory and utilitarian theory. These theories are not mutually exclusive, and therefore, in different areas may conceivably develop along different paths. These three generally described theories may converge in form and substance, and may lead to similar legal or juridical practices between countries, while other theories may even be more path dependent and slow to change.[15]

Evolutionary theory is distinguishable, because it predicts that law develops over time and in interaction with changes in a socio-economic environment. Classic proponents of evolutionary theory are Adam Smith, Henry Maine, Max Weber and Emile Durkheim. In particular, Adam Smith (1723-1790), a renowned Scottish political economist and moral philosopher, is perhaps best described as an economist and Deist, because he believed in a world governed by a benevolent system of natural law. Smith's God would not interfere after the event of creation, because Smith's God accordingly followed natural laws, such as the laws discovered by Isaac Newton (1642-1727). Adam Smith, in his classic *The Wealth of Nations* (*An Inquiry into the Nature and Causes of the Wealth of Nations*, 1776), offers a description of what could arguably be termed an earlier form of intelligent design. Smith's ideas arguably parallel Charles Darwin's *Origins of the Species* (1859), which was not intended to promote the idea of evolution rather "to debunk the concept of supernatural intelligence—the idea that the universe is the result of an idea."[16] Smith writes, "As every individual, therefore, endeavours as much as he can both to employ his capital in the support of domestic industry, and so to direct that industry that its produce may be of the greatest value; every individual necessarily labours to render the annual revenue of the society as great as he can. He generally, indeed, neither intends to promote the public interest, nor knows how much he is promoting it. By preferring the support of domestic to that of foreign industry, he intends only his own security; and by directing that industry in such a manner as its produce may be of the greatest value, he intends only his own gain, and he is in this, as in many other cases, led by an invisible hand to promote an end which was no part of his intention." Adam Smith's invisible hand, though addressing the chaos of economic affairs, most importantly,

[14] James Thuo Gathii, Humanizing The Pax-Americana Global Empire, vol. 4, no. 1 Wash. U. Global Stud. L. Rev. 121, 122 (2005), Book Review: Humanizing Our Global Order: Essays in Honor of Ivan Head, Edited by Obiora Chinedu Okafor & Obijiofor Aginam, Univ. of Toronto Press, 2003. F.A. Hayek, Law, Legislation and Liberty, vol. 1: 5, 36-37, 78-79 (Univ. of Chicago Press, 1973-79).

[15] Pistor & Wellons, Id.

also addresses historic sources of order, language, morals and other forces of society, which social theorists and others increasingly associate with the process of evolution.

Cultural theory is distinguishable because it, generally, suggests that legal evolution is a product of a combination of forces, especially culture. What is hailed as cultural theory is also associated with the theories of Montesquieu (or Charles-Louis de Sécondat, Baron de la Brède et de Montesquieu, 1689–1755). As a result, the concept of Asian values (*asiatische Werte*) that views cultural differences as the cause of Asia's path to economic success also represents this view. More generally, on the process of converging law and socio-economic development, cultural theory, which is associated with the theories of Montesquieu, provides, "Law and legal evolution are part of the idiosyncratic historical development of a country, and that they are determined by multiple factors, including culture, geography, climate, and religion. Although law is by no means static, legal evolution in each country is distinct and will produce vastly different outcomes. Far from converging over time, legal institutions remain different." Baron de Montesquieu, from the "nature of things," sought to deduce principles or laws that "express necessary relations." His most famous writing is *The Spirit of Laws* (*De l'esprit des lois*, 1748). Specifically, in *The Spirit of Laws*, he sought to deduce, and borrowing from the title of his book, *The Spirit of Laws,* or of the relation that the laws should have with the constitution of each government, the customs, the climate, religion, commerce, etc. Montesquieu further wrote, "In fine, they have relations to each other, as also to their origin, to the intent of the legislator, and to the order of things on which they are established; in all of which different lights they ought to be considered." In Book I, *Of Laws in General*, in *The Spirit of Laws,* he writes, "Laws, in their most general signification, are the necessary relations arising from the nature of things. In this sense all beings have their laws: the Deity His laws, the material world its laws, the intelligences superior to man their laws, the beasts their laws, man his laws." In the latter, Montesquieu inserted a footnote referencing "Deity" to Plutarch's *A Discourse to an Unlearned Prince*, wherein Montesquieu summarized Plutarch as follows, "Law is the king of mortal and immortal beings." [17] Plutarch (Greek scholar, Mestrius Plutarchus (c. 46-127)) wrote the compiled works entitled, *Morals* (*Moralia*), which included in volume IV the essay, *A Discourse to an Unlearned Prince*. The latter excerpt from Plutarch is in answer to the question, "Who then shall have the power to govern a prince?" Plutarch actually answers the question twofold: First, "The law, without doubt; which (as Pindar saith) is the king of mortal and immortal beings." Second, Plutarch further writes, "which is not written without in books nor engraven on wood or stone, but is a clear reason imprinted in the heart, always residing and watching therein, never suffering the mind to be without government." Montesquieu, not entirely a moral relativist, derived his laws of nature from the world itself, or how human beings actually lived rather than reason or God's commands. For Montesquieu, all that human legislatures need to do is to establish a code of natural law by examining the regularities that occur in the patterns of human living. Human legislatures ignored these laws of nature at their own and others' peril.

---

[16] Louis Menand, The Metaphysical Club A Story of Ideas in America (Farrar, Straus and Giroux, 2002). Adam Smith, The Wealth of Nations, (Bantam Dell, 2003). Charles Darwin, The Origin of Species, by Means of Natural Selection, (1859), (Barnes & Noble, 2004). Hayek, Id.

[17] J. Bronowski & Bruce Mazlish, The Western Intellectual Tradition: From Leonardo to Hegel 271 (Harper & Row 1962). Montesquieu, The Spirit of Laws, 3, In Great Books of the Western World (Robert Maynard Hutchins ed., 1952). Vol. IV, A Discourse to an Unlearned Prince, In Plutarch's Morals, Translated from the Greek by Several Hands (Corrected and Revised by William W. Goodwin), Vols. I-V (Little, Brown, & Co., 1878).

There is also the utilitarian theory that views law as an instrument for promoting economic development. The utilitarian theory assumes that legal change directly affects the behavior of economic agents, and thus, subsequently affects economic development. During the late eighteenth and early nineteenth centuries, Jeremy Bentham (founder of utilitarianism, 1748-1832) and his followers or second-generation utilitarians such as John Stuart Mill (1806-1873) formulated the doctrine of utilitarianism.[18] It was a philosophy distinguishable as one of the first rational and systematic attempts to address the social, economic and cultural impact of the Industrial Revolution in England. Utilitarians are also distinguishable as intellectual architects of the "great reform," addressing legal and social problems in England, at the close of the eighteenth century and beginning of the nineteenth century. What hails as Bentham's philosophy stems from the belief that human institutions ought to serve all elements of society, by providing for "the greatest happiness of the greatest number." Bentham for the purpose of defining this greatest happiness or good principle employed a "moral arithmetic," which evaluated each human action according to an actual formula that balanced units of pleasure with units of pain. In terms of Bentham's calculus, good supposedly resulted when pleasure as subjectively defined by each individual's enlightened self-interest predominated.

A major proponent of this theory is John Stuart Mill, a second-generation utilitarian. Mill, in *Utilitarianism* (1861), considered cultural and spiritual happiness to be of greater value than mere physical pleasure. In addition, Mill, in *On Liberty* (1859), presented the argument that utilitarianism requires that political arrangements satisfy the liberty principle, wherein each person must be guaranteed the greatest possible liberty that would not interfere with the liberty of others.[19] Consequently, each person could maximize his or her happiness. In terms of the art and science of political economy, Jeremy Bentham, in his classic *Manual of Political Economy* (1793-95), wrote, "According to the principle of utility in every branch of the art of legislation, the object or end in view should be the production of the maximum happiness in a given time in the community in question. In the instance of this branch of the art, the object or end in view should be the production of that maximum happiness, in so far as this more general end is promoted by the production wealth and the maximum of population." Bentham further observed, "Generally speaking, there is no one who knows what is for your interest, so well as yourself – no one who is disposed with so much ardour and constancy to pursue it." Statements such as the latter, in conjunction with Bentham dedicating a chapter in *Manual of Political Economy* to why it is unwise for government to interfere with economic life, especially trade, demonstrate that he explicitly, if not implicitly, followed the thoughts of Adam Smith. For instance, Bentham explicitly followed the thoughts of Adam Smith in his classic *The Wealth of Nations* (1776), when he wrote, "with respect to commerce, each individual is a better judge of his own interests than government can be for him." For these reasons, many detected in Bentham's writings, especially economic writings such as *Manual of Political Economy*, his first sustained treatment of political economy, and

---

[18] Patrick Bradley, Victorian Lessons: Education and Utilitarianism in Bentham, Mill, and Dickens, The Concord Review (1999). Jeremy Bentham, A Fragment of Government, 3 (J.H. Burns & H.L.A. Hart, eds.) (Cambridge UP, 1988). H.L.A. Hart, Positivism and the Separation of Law and Morals, Vol. 71, No. 4 Harv. L. Rev. 593, 612-21 (1958).

[19] John Stuart Mill, On Liberty and Utilitarianism, (Everyman's Library, 1906; rpt. Oxford UP, 1969).

Defence of Usury (1787), an underlying liberal theory and confirmed votary of *laissez-faire* economics.[20]

However, a troubling aspect of the utilitarianism of Jeremy Bentham, Mill, David Hume and others, and notwithstanding Bentham's calculus or "moral arithmetic," is that they did not leave us with an adequate descriptor of "utility" or the "greatest happiness principle." Mill, in *Utilitarianism* (1861), when describing utility wrote, "The creed which accepts as the foundation of morals, utility, or the greatest happiness principle, holds that actions are right in proportion as they tend to promote happiness, wrong as they tend to produce the reverse of happiness." William Stanley Jevons (1835-1882) also offers a definition of utility, or the coefficient of utility, and writes, "This function of utility is peculiar to each kind of object, and more or less to each individual. Thus, the appetite for dry bread is much more rapidly satisfied than that for wine, for clothes, for handsome furniture, for works of art, or, finally, for money. And every one has his own peculiar tastes in which he is nearly insatiable."[21] In addition, early utilitarianism (act-utilitarianism) evolves into a second-generation utilitarianism and new twentieth century forms, such as ideal utilitarianism (doing the optic act: act in accordance with rules of conduct). The problems of utilitarianism continued into the twentieth century, as many moral philosophers sought to modify it and harness its potential, while others simply dumped the theory. Prominent problems of utilitarianism have been: the difficulty of measuring and comparing utility; it is overly demanding; it fails to make typical moral distinctions between what is a positive obligation (what is wrong not to do) with what is permissible (what is not wrong to do); and seems to fail to take into account the diversity of the sources of obligation.[22]

A problem of the previously mentioned theories, being evolutionary theory, cultural theory and utilitarian theory, is that they are Western models and taxonomies, especially the evolutionary theory, and do not account for dissimilarities between Western concepts of authority and Sinic concepts of authority. In terms of China, these more orthodox models and theories of borrowing presents a dilemma, especially for a prospective Chinese neo-liberal coterie. In 1960, the Asian Development Bank (ADB) commissioned a thirty-five year study examining the role that legal systems played in six Asian economies: China, India, Japan, Republic of Korea, Malaysia, and Taipei. The ADB study concludes, "A key finding of this research project therefore is that law and legal institutions should not be viewed as technical tools that once adopted will produce the desired outcome . . . This finding cautions against the blind transplantation without due consideration for the relevant economic framework within which they shall operate. It also suggests that law reform projects should be assessed not in isolation, but within a broader context of economic policies." The reception of Western law

[20] J. Crimmins, Political Economy and Projectors: Bentham's Defence of Usury, The Philosophical Age Almanac 9: 58-72 (1999). Adam Smith, Id. Jeremy Bentham, Manual of Political Economy (1793-95). Jeremy Benthan, Manual of Political Economy (1993-95), 219-274, In Jeremy Bentham's Economic Writings, Vol. I, (W. Stark, ed.) (Burr Franklin, 1952).

[21] William Stanley Jevons, Brief Account of A General Mathematical Theory of Political Economy, Journal of the Royal Statistical Society, London, XXIX (June 1866), 282-87, (Section F of the British Association, 1862).

[22] Leonard P. Liggio & John V. Cody, Literature of Liberty: A Review of Contemporary Liberal Thought, (Institute for Humane Studies, 1980-1982). Hastings Rashdall, Theory of Good and Evil, 2 vols. (Clarendon Press, 1907). Jan Narveson, Morality and Utility (Johns Hopkins Press, 1967). Jonathan Harrison, Utilitarianism, Universalization, and Our Duty to Be Just, Proceedings of the Aristotelian Society, 53(1953). Richard Hensen, The Wrongness of Killing, Philosophical Review 80 (1971) (rpt. in James Rachels, ed., Understanding Moral Philosophy. Gilbert Harman, The Nature of Morality) (Oxford UP, 1977). Richard B. Brandt. A Theory of the Good and the Right, (Oxford UP, 1979).

by these countries took place in the second half of the nineteenth and the first half of the twentieth centuries. Although the contents of substantive economic laws and legal processes are determined initially by the source of these transplants, the influence of the original donor country becomes less important as countries begin to borrow from multiple sources. China also makes substantial use of laws and legal concepts of various countries with different legal systems, including civil law and common law systems. One can only assume that a Chinese neo-liberal coterie would propose the maintenance of a high degree of influence of original donor countries, which is typically Western culture and its legal tradition or common Western legal civilization. In this context, a proposed Chinese neo-liberalism coterie would, assumedly, propose an institutionalization of Western universalism and norms that are antithetic to a historicity of legal borrowing in Asiatic nation-states, as the previously mentioned ABD study suggests. Moreover, there remains the additional problem of the dynamics of the "transplant effect," which ultimately determines the level and degree of integration of law and legal processes into a given culture.[23]

7.4. Transplantation Model – Jurisprudence Model

Jurisprudence (*juris prudential*), generally, "encompasses the study of a legal system's scope, function, methodology, and guiding precepts."[24] Jurisprudence, as the science of law, admittedly, does not provide a perse model for transplanting and borrowing laws and legal systems. What jurisprudence offers is a tool of analyzing laws and legal systems, thus, indirectly providing models, methodologies and tools for assessing the effectiveness and efficiency of transplanted and borrowed laws and legal system. No doubt, jurisprudence is a tool equally addressing the issues of transplanting and borrowing norms, including social, economic and legal norms. Jurisprudence provides the tools for addressing and analyzing laws and legal systems, especially the legal institutions of other countries.

In terms of transplanting and borrowing laws and legal systems, one of the most important tools in the arsenal of Western jurisprudence is the theory of "law in action." The concept of "law in action" is actually attributable to a 1910 article written by American law scholar, Roscoe Pound (1870-1964). In the 1930s, the idea of the "law in action-law - law in text" dichotomy would further be explored by legal realist Karl Llewellyn, and then by other legal jurists and philosophers, including other legal realists. Renowned law scholars such as Pound, Oliver Wendell Holmes, Jr. (1841-1935), and others, are part of the turn of the nineteenth century American legal realism movement. The changes in American jurisprudence correspond with the changing politics and economics of an American society transitioning to a progressive era. Oliver Wendell Holmes, Jr., arguably, the paradigmatic American legal realist, is a primary contributor to the American legal realism movement. Oliver Wendell Holmes, Jr., in the *Path of the Law* (1897), wrote, "I look forward to a time when the part played by history in the explanation of dogma shall be very small, and instead of ingenious research we shall spend our energy on a study of the ends sought to be attained

[23] Pistor & Wellons, Id. Daniel Berkowitz, Katharina Pistor, and Jean-Francois Richard, Economic Development, Legality, and the Transplant Effect, CID Working Paper No. 39 (Mar. 2000), Center for International Development-Harv. Univ.

[24] Robert L. Hayman, Jr. & Nancy Levitt, eds., Jurisprudence Contemporary Readings, Problems, and Narratives, 5-6 (West Pub, 1995).

and the reasons for desiring them. As a step toward that ideal it seems to me that every lawyer ought to seek an understanding of economics." In America jurisprudence, many also associate law in action with the University of Wisconsin Law School, or the "Wisconsin Idea."[25] The novelty of law in action, as a legal theory, generally, is that it examines law not solely in the context of laws and statutes, rather how law applies in society. As a legal theory, it generally starts with observations about the behavior of institutions or real world phenomenon and then works backwards toward the legal philosophies guiding traditional jurisprudence, and employs a range of disciplines for this purpose, such as sociology, psychology, anthropology, history and other disciplines or sciences.

In Western jurisprudence, the distinctions between law in text and law in action parallel the similarities and dissimilarities between legal formalism and legal institutionalism. In particular, the notion of law in action stands in stark contrast to legal realism, especially American realism, because it more so reflects notions of legal formalism. Eugen Ehrlich, in *Fundamental Principles of the Sociology of Law* (*Grundlegung der Soziologie des Rechts*, 1913), concluded that John Austin (legal positivist, 1790-1859) and his followers are formalists, because they failed to concern themselves with living creations. According to Ehrlich, they were only interested in "the forms of the legal relations, not in their content, not in the germinative powers of the development of law, nor in its unifying regularity."[26] In Western jurisprudence, however, both legal realists, especially American realists, and legal instrumentalists, criticize legal formalism. In terms of Western jurisprudence, legal formalism is also reflective of legal positivism, because law making, especially in a democratic elected legislature, is the province of the legislature rather than judges. In particular, legal formalists argue for constraining the law-making powers of judges in interpreting legal text by their plain meanings, thereby intending to confine the judiciary to what the "law is," and not what law "ought to say."

For instance, in terms of the imperative legal positivism of John Austin, a proposition of law was true if it simply reported correctly the past commands of a political society.[27] Legal positivists may well hold to do otherwise, impinge or violates the separation of powers principle. However, there is, of course, the legal positivism of H.L.A. Hart (H.L.A. (Herbert) Hart, 1907-1992), whom seemingly compromises traditional notions of legal positivism, by seemingly rejecting, though only in part, Austin's traditional definition of legal positivism. Hart does so, though implicitly, because he essentially compromises John Austin's imperative legal positivism, when he addresses the problem of the virtue of commands. Hart, in the *Concept of Law* (1961), contends that the true grounds of law lie in the acceptance by the community as a whole of a fundamental master rule, being Hart's rule of recognition. This rule assigns to a particular person or groups the authority to make law. Therefore, rules of law are true not just in virtue of commands, but, more importantly, "in virtue of social conventions that represent the community's acceptance of a scheme of rules empowering

---

[25] Roscoe Pound, Law and Morals (Univ. of North Carolina Press, 1924, rev. ed. 1926). Karl N. Llewellyn, Jurisprudence: Realism in theory and practice, (1893, reprint Univ. of Chicago press, 1962). Karl N. Llewellyn, The Bramble Bush: On Our Law and Its Study (Oceana Pub, 1981). Oliver Wendell Holmes, Jr., The Path of the Law, 10 Harv. L. Rev. 457 (1897). Paul D. Carrington and Erika King, Law and the Wisconsin Idea, 47 J. Legal Educ. 297 (1997).

[26] Eugen Ehrlich, Fundamental Principles of the Sociology of Law (1913), (China Social Sciences Publishing House, Chengcheng Books, Ltd.: The President and Fellows of Harv. College, 1936).

[27] John Austin, The Province of Jurisprudence Determined (1832), Prometheus Books (2000). Ronald Dworkin, Laws Empire, 33-35 (Harv. UP, 1986).

such people or groups to create valid law." Hart still sees the separation of law and morals (*boni mores*) as essential to the meaning of legal positivism, because at the end of the day, the ideological underpinning of Hart still keeps faith with the insistence of the great Utilitarians (or Benthamites), Jeremy Bentham, John Austin and others, "on the separation of law as it is and law as it ought to be."

Hart still recognized the distinctions between rules and laws, especially the function of law in producing a social stability reflective of prevailing social norms. Hart presented the question, "What are rules and to what extent is law an affair of rules?" It is a question, though indirectly, searching for a definition of law. After contending there is not a familiar well understood general category of which law is a member, Hart proffers the following definition, if not explanation. He writes, "The most obvious candidate for use in this way in a definition of law is the general family of *rules of behavior*; yet the concept of a rule as we have seen is as perplexing as that of law itself, so that definitions of law that start by identifying laws as a species of rule usually advance our understanding of law no further." [28] As observed by Hart, in *The Concept of Law*, even skilled lawyers feel that, "though they know the law, there is much about law and its relations to other things that they cannot explain and do not fully understand." What distinguishes Hart's legal positivism from that of Austin's legal positivism is that Hart focused on social norms, or rules of behavior, at least to a greater degree than Austin. Hart is also distinguishable from Llewellyn, because for the legal realist Llewellyn the rules, social norms, or rules of behavior, were seemingly less important in the construct of a model legal system.

Legal formalism is also subject to criticism by the critical legal studies (CLS) movement, and most important, by Marxists. In the latter criticism, or from a Marxian perspective or analysis, law is indeterminate, while formalism ignores the reality of law serving as a tool of established power structures. In terms of Western transplantation theories, the problems are Marxism converging or diverging with Western jurisprudence, traditional Chinese jurisprudence converging or diverging with Western jurisprudence and traditional Chinese jurisprudence converging or diverging with Marxism. China and its laws and legal system present problems for Western jurisprudence, especially understanding Chinese jurisprudence. Western taxonomies generally measure the rule of law by the pairings of rule by man versus rule by law, policy-driven versus instrumental models and as thin versus thick theories of the rule of law. Western authority and experts employ the latter pairings to gauge China's progress in adopting a Western style of rule of law, rather than a Sinic-centric or culture-specific rule of law. Problematic for Western academics is the rule by law model that represents a prescriptive, normative and political view of what the relationship should be, thereby serving an instrument of government or mere instrument of policy.[29]

---

[28] H. L. A. Hart, The Concept of Law, (Oxford UP, 1961). H.L.A. Hart, Positivism and the Separation of Law and Morals, Id.

[29] Eric W. Orts, The Rule of Law in China, 34 Vand. J. Transant'l. L. 43, 93-94 (2001).

7.5. Transplantation Model-Modernization Theory

Although not manifesting a perse model of transplantation theory, the various Western theories of development for developing countries, though indirectly, address issues of transplanting law and economics. Modernization theory is also synonymous with development theory. The initial and major proponent of modernization theory is Walter W. Rostow, and then came others who would follow his theory, with some even formulating variant forms of social engineering. A primary concern of modernization theory is achieving sustainable development for developing countries. While there are several theoretical approaches to modernization theory, all of the modernization theory approaches emphasize social engineering, such as poorer societies emulating models of developed countries. In this respect, social engineering may entail, depending on the model of modernization theory, emulating economic models, political models, democracy models, legal systems, and even values, *ethos* and morals of Western developed countries.[30]

Prior to the Second World War (World War II, 1939-1945), economists and social scientists showed small concern for the economic development and industrialization of developing countries. However, in the era of post-Second World War, cold war (1945-1991) and decolonization, the attention of economists, other social scientists, government officials and the public shifts to the problem of these developing countries and former colonies. In international relations, during the administration of U.S. President Harry S. Truman (presidency, 1945-1953), the United States shifts its focus toward economic development and industrialization of developing countries under the Point Four Program. In the 1950s and 1960s, resources and federal funds were committed to developing and designing aid programs for these countries. The foreign policy implications were obvious, as aid programs serve to convince an emerging Third World to elect capitalism and democracy rather than communism or socialism. During the cold war, the former Soviet Union countered with a critique of U.S. foreign aid as being a tool of containment. In the environment of cold war policy, modernization theory eventually emerges. The United States, within this framework of U.S. foreign policy and cold war policy, financed the economic development and industrialization of Western Europe under the 1947 Marshall Plan or European Recovery Program (ERP), the economic development and industrialization of South Korea and Taiwan, and the reconstruction of Japan. The ensuing policy was a product of economists, social scientists and financial resources in the form of federal funding, being committed to understanding what was required to modernize "other" societies and develop benchmarks for assessing progress during the period of transformation.

Walter W. Rostow surfaced as the most prominent source on economic development. Rostow's theory was mostly distinguishable because of its stages theory of economic growth, which is from his classic *The Stages of Economic Growth: A Non-Communist Manifesto* (1960). Rostow's modernization theory was based on assumptions reflecting Western normative values, which resulted in his basic thesis that, "All societies can be placed in one of five categories, or stages of economic growth." He generally described these five categories

---

[30] Walter W. Rostow, The Stages of Economic Growth (Cambridge UP, 1960). Charles Kimber Pearce, Rostow, Kennedy, and the Rhetoric of Foreign Aid (Michigan State UP, 2001). For alternative modernization theory, see N. Smelser, Mechanisms of and Adjustments to Change, In T. Burns (ed.), Industrial Man (Penguin, 1969).

or stages of economic growth as follows. Characteristics of the first stage are traditional society, limited output, limited access to science and technology, and decentralized political power. The second stage represents the preconditions for take-off, which are new ideas favoring economic growth, higher levels of education, increased levels of entrepreneurship, more institutions capable of mobilizing capital, increases in investment, and a duality because of the persistent of traditional society. The third stage is a take-off stage, involving the commercialization of agriculture, and a growth in productivity. The fourth stage is the drive to maturity, as the economy begins to take its place in the international world, with increasing amounts of gross national product (GNP), about 10-15%, being allocated to investments, technology fostering transition to heavy industry, and ideas of a competitive capitalist market beginning to take hold. The fifth and final stage is mass consumption, with economic sectors specializing in durable consumer goods and services, and economic growth in the pursuit of profit maximization rather than centralized planning, which would inevitably influence social policy and government policy.

Most important, in the fifth stage, there is an evolution of societies and governments, and an increasing reflection of Western normative institutions and values. Driving the transformation from the first stage to the fifth stage are two separable, yet inseparable, key concepts -- evolutionary theory and functionalist theory. In terms of economic development, since human evolution is predetermined, then social change is mono-directional as it processes the transition from the first stage to the fifth stage, or from non-Western traditional society, to the model of modern Western society, and its attendant institutions and values. In comparison, functionalist theory, in effect, introduces liberalism or libertarianism to the formulation of modernization theory. Assuming economic development or industrialization presents the greater good (*summon bonum*) for all societies, it essentially offers economic liberalization in answer. Developing countries will adapt to the international world by adapting to economic liberalism, and its attendant institutions and values, and the governments of these countries will pursue liberal goals and policies. In terms of functionalist theory, to do otherwise is anti-social, and offends the stability and status quo of a more international order, which is dominated by Western developed countries. Modernization theory, and its reliance on both evolutionary theory and functionalist theory, reflects the thoughts of scholars from both the past and present. For instance, although there are many other scholars and their writings, there are the representative writings of Charles Robert Darwin (1809-1882), Talcott Parsons (1902-1979) and Comte (Auguste Comte or Isidore Marie Auguste François Xavier Comte, 1798-1857). Comte, known as the forerunner of modern functionalism, formulated the law of three stages, which was one of the first theories of social evolution, announcing that human development, or social progress, progresses from a theological stage to a metaphysical stage, and finally, to the positive stage. In addition, because Charles Darwin's theoretical approach to biological development stems from an evolutionary approach, social change is slow and incremental. Then there is Talcott Parsons and his four functional imperatives, which substantially contributed to the study of social evolution. Parsons divided evolution into four sub processes, comprising division, adaptation, previously excluded elements and generalization of values.[31]

---

[31] Darwin, Id. Auguste Comte, Positive Philosophy of Auguste Comte, Part I (1985) (Harriet Martineau, trans.) (Kessinger Pub, 2003). Talcott Parsons, Structure and Process in Modern Societies (Free Press, 1960).

For Walter W. Rostow, lack of capital formation was the primary problem for developing countries, especially those countries emerging from colonial rule. Rostow considered the goal of sustainable development possible, but still contingent on Washington providing needed funds as a catalyst for rapid economic growth. Rostow, and proponents of his theory, theorized that the latter would frustrate tendencies toward political unrest and other forms of agitation, such as political violence, nationalism, revolution, and guerrilla or partisan warfare (Spanish, literally *Guerra* or war), or those troublesome small or little wars. In the end, Rostow's theory, while aiding the expansion of U.S. foreign aid, actually, promoted a small degree of economic development and industrialization. The problem was that Rostow and those in power during the cold war era in Washington primarily focused on containing communism and socialism. Many deem that the theorizations of Rostow and others, including Washington diplomats, would have been more effective if focused on the promotion of economic development, industrialization and democracy. Developing countries, arguably, could have earlier been on the road to sustainable development, but for the cold war, Rostow, and his coterie, as leading proponents of both modernization theory and conjoining modernization with cold war containment policy, and Washington's policy of placing greater emphasis on projecting U.S. power abroad for containing communism and socialism.

What could have represented a classic example of Ugo Mettei's third model, which is fully consensual and presented as "diffusion by prestige, focusing on a deliberate process of institutional admiration that leads to the reception of law," resulted in the folly of policy errors, especially foreign policy driven by cold war policies and the balance of power. In the decades that ensued, in developing countries the world did witness a small degree of success in economic development and industrialization. What actually transpired was far from what could have transpired, in truly sustainable development for developing countries. The travesty of Western developed countries earlier failing to stay the course of economic development and democracy, may well be a delay in promoting the economic development and industrialization of many developing countries. During the late twentieth century, the world witnesses a series of economic or financial crises, from East Asian countries, to Latin American countries, which would signal a need to return - despite the complaints of the many antagonists to neo-liberalism - to the original agenda of liberalism and economic liberalism. In the new millennium, international economic institutions, such as the WTO, IMF and World Bank, are now constantly involved in the process of adapting to administrative failings and challenges of the past, thereby continuously evolving a more pragmatic neo-liberalism or economic liberalism. Although there have always been the antagonists of liberalism and economic liberalism, including modernization theory, what earlier occurred under the umbrella of cold war politics hardly substantiates economic liberalism as a failed Western ideal. Economic liberalism still offers one of the most viable means for promoting economic development, democracy and peace on a worldwide scale. Economic liberalism still serves as the most viable means, or perhaps more accurately, theoretical vehicle for transplanting laws, legal systems, economic models and normative norms. It may also present the most viable means for achieving an international perpetual peace or utopia.

7.6. TRANSPLANTATION MODEL- SOCIALIST MARKET LEGAL SYSTEM

There are many Western theories and models addressing this issue of transplanting and borrowing laws and legal systems. Nonetheless, despite the various Western theoretical approaches, in China, the problem of understanding legal transplantation is far from resolved. Adding fodder to the complexity of legal transplantation and borrowing are distinctive Chinese approaches or models for transplanting and borrowing laws or legal systems. There are also distinctive social, cultural and political economy concerns, regarding conditions for and desirability of transplantation and borrowing. Most problematic is the divergence between Chinese and Western theoretical approaches, especially as influenced by social, cultural and political economy forces.

In modern China, the problem of legal transplantation, because of one-party CCP rule and the need to legitimize a self-chosen rationale and Marxism as the official ideology, necessarily becomes an issue of putting in place what is termed a "socialist legal system." China is aware of the need to reform its legal system. China's major legislative goals are expressed threefold: "Continuing to revise laws that are not in conformity with China's obligations under the WTO rules; revising laws that are not conducive to enhancing the competitive power of Chinese enterprises in the international market; and improving laws offering protection to domestic enterprises and ensuring industrial safety."[32] Notwithstanding, reforms commencing in the 1980s, modern legal and economic reforms are also driven by accession to the WTO, as evidenced by China's major legislative goals. Improving China's socialist market economic system requires improving the country's legal system, because a well-established "socialist-market legal system" is naturally part of a well-established "socialist market economic system." Driving forces of modern legal reforms are earlier reforms commenced in the 1980s, accession to the WTO and the force of economic globalization. In 2002, Long Yongtu, Vice Minister, Ministry of Foreign Trade and Economic Cooperation, clearly enunciated China's position regarding the changing global economy. As announced by Long Yongtu, "Economic globalization is a major trend in the economic development in the world. To merge with the mainstream of the world economy and achieve greater development, China's economy must adapt itself to this trend. China's accession to the WTO is being done mainly to be part of the mainstream of the world economy in terms of our economic system and to create conditions for China to take part in economic globalization on a deeper and wider scope." One of the certainties regarding China is that it will commit "some" resources to "some" legal reforms for purposes of participating in global trade, or meeting its baseline WTO accession (or Protocol on Accession) requirements. There is a consensus on the need to reform China's legal system. The CCP, the ADB, and other international bodies, such as the WTO, recognize this need to establish sound legal mechanisms.

One Chinese source described the issue of legal transplantation in modern China as a process dating back to the 1980s and earlier modern reforms, which are rooted in legal

[32] Wang Baoshu, China's Accession to the WTO and the Building of a Socialist Market Economic Legal System, In China: Accession to the WTO & Economic Reform 331, 338 (Wang Mengkui ed., 2002). Long Yongtu, Negotiations on China's Accession to the WTO and the Market-Oriented Reform, In China: Accession to the

reforms from the late nineteenth century or late Qing.[33] In 1978, China governing party, the CCP, signaled a commitment to the goal of economic development and, arguably, economic globalization. The Third Plenary Session of the 11th Committee of the CCP adopted a policy of restoring the construction of a socialist legal system. During this session, the CCP announced a shift from a work priority of class struggles to economic construction. However, hailing the reforms initiated in 1978 is a circular way of avoiding the obvious, because traditional culture, in part, influences China's approach to transplantation. As previously mentioned, in China, there are different theoretical approaches to the problem of legal transplantation. Some legal academics and scholars approach the problem in terms of social theory. Others approach the problem by stressing the reconstruction of traditional Chinese culture. Then there are different theories such as the theory of legal culture, cultural approach and legal modernization theory. Notwithstanding other approaches, there are also the unwritten rules of a social and economic constitution driving relevant policy decisions, especially regarding the methodology and desirability of transplanting foreign laws and legal systems.

Chinese legal scholars interestingly when seeking to analyze the concept of legal transplantation employ Western theories and models or Western legal analytical tools. For instance, they employ the Western legal conceptualization of "law in text" (*wenben falv*) versus "law in action" (*xingwei falv*), and even rules on paper (*zhi mian gui ze*) and practical rules (*shi jian gui ze*). Legal academics or scholars theorizing legal transplantation in terms of social theory, generally, stress the analytical tool of "law in action" (*xingwei falv*) in doing so. One academic advocating the social theory approach is highly critical of legal transplantation, and perceives law as no more than rules made by legislatures. The latter produces the critical result of severing intrinsic links between the law and social life. The latter is problematic, because it minimizes, overlooks and denies the restrictions imposed by social life on the law. In terms of social theory, transplanting, legal transplantation or borrowing must premise on social life as the foundation of law, and not in isolation from social life. In addition, the latter theory in effect distinguishes between "law in text" (*wenben falv*) and "law in action" (*xingwei falv*). It is an inevitable result or effect, and must do so, because in Chinese judicial practice, generally, technical issues, such as civil code drafting rules, obscure theoretical problems.

For example, one scholar addressed the problem of legal reforms in the Tibet Autonomous Region (TAR), or Tibet, in terms of legal transplantation and the social theory approach. At issue was the difficult of prescribing to Tibetan citizens a legal notion of real estate. The problem is that lack of a legal meaning for the concept of real estate does not mean there is no land. In Tibet, land simply does not belong to anyone, which means they may use the land, but cannot own it. Real estate as a legal concept does not exist, and underlying this problem is the culture of local herdsmen. In pursuit of the social theory approach, it is observed that rule of law does not depend solely on law, but must take into consideration other factors, such as trust, morals and customs, including economics, though

WTO & Economic Reform, Id. Asian Development Bank, Asian Development Bank Publication, 1–4 (1999), http://www.adb.org/Documents/Others/Law_ADB/1&d_1999.pdf.

[33] Jiang Shigong, Introduction: Legal Transplantation in Contemporary China, Social Sciences in China (Zhongguo shehui kexue) (autumn 2004). Wang Xuedian, Historiography in China in the Last Fifty Years, 51, Social Sciences in China (Zhongguo shehui kexue) (autumn 2004). Jiang Shigong, The End of Transplantation, Social Sciences in China (Zhongguo shehui kexue) (autumn 2004).

termed as social economics and organizational change. However, in the analysis of transplantation and social theory, and law in action, the analysis takes a detour. After couching the issue of transplantation, as an issue of searching for what direction Chinese society should go, it is resolved that the key to developing the legal system is not transplantation, but "the development and transfer of China's society." The analysis turns from the social theory and law in action approaches to simply an argument grounded in Marxism, because development becomes imperative, as also the change in the mode of production, and organization and management of society. Once that change takes place, society requires "new laws to accommodate the needs of production and living, and new laws will emerge regardless of the existence or amount of foreign exchange of information, or the introduction and interpretation of foreign laws...Once the mode of production and living of a society has changed, the rules of the society or part of it will change, and legal reforms based on foreign exchange of information may achieve success."

As previously mentioned, legal formalism is subject to criticism by both the critical legal studies movement and Marxists. From a Marxian perspective, law is indeterminate, while formalism ignores the reality of law serving as a tool of established power structures. For this reason, China's political economy environment presents additional concerns, because CCP ideology influences social, economic and legal norms, resulting in either a positive or a negative influence on Chinese society. Notwithstanding internal and external wars, militarism, political culture, underdevelopment, poverty, flaws in constitutional design, and other forces, ideology has been a primary force in the construct of a Chinese legal system, including rule of law and constitutionalism. Due to the fact that Chinese institutions are value-laden and possess Confucian characteristics, culture may be the only force that equals, if not surpasses, the force of ideology. In this respect, the predominance of Confucianism is representative of all traditional schools of Chinese philosophical thought. Although they differ, "the major Asian religions and philosophies. . . share similar concepts about the origins and purpose of power." Chinese schools of philosophical thought include, among others, Confucianism, Neo-Confucianism, Legalism, Taoism, the Ying Yang School, Logicism, and Buddhism. Ideology and culture will influence the growth and direction of China's legal system, including constitutionalism, rule of law, and judicial review, because "economic transition is part of the transition in constitutional rules" and its "speed and the time path of the transition are determined by its driving mechanism." China's legal system, including rule of law and constitutionalism, reflects legal reform and economic development, as well as the forces of ideology and culture.[34]

Following the end of dynastic or imperial China, or the Chinese Revolution (1911), opposing camps of power offer different strategies and formulas for success and translate differently a struggle for a new nationalism. Those primarily vying for control were the Chinese communists and Jiang Jieshi's (Chiang Kai-shek) Nationalists (*Kuomintang*). These opposing military and political forces sought the similar goals of both control over a vast China and the eventual reunification of China, but under their own respective banners. From a Marxian perspective, modern debates concerning the Chinese Revolution (1911) mostly focus on whether it was nationalist or bourgeois in nature. For these critiques, the persistence of

---

[34] Ch'ien Mu, Id. David A. Funk, Traditional Chinese Jurisprudence: Justifying Li and Fa, 17 So. U.L. Rev. 1, 45–46 (1990). Pistor & Wellons, Id. Jeffrey Sachs et al., Economic Reforms and Constitutional Transition, http://ssrn.com/abstract=254110.

traditional culture frustrates an earlier modernization movement. From 1911 until 1949, the paradoxical interrelationships between traditional culture, Marxism and Western universalism crystallize. A Chinese model of Marxism was eventually adapted, Sinicized or localized to fit traditional culture, as occurred with Mao Zedong's (1893-1976) linking of the communist movement to a rural peasant class rather than orthodox Marxist dogma. Marxism and communist ideology took root in China because of the relegation of traditional culture to minimum importance, and other reasons. A society such as China where many consider monarchy as historically a part of the natural political order posed a strong barrier to Western constitutionalism and parliamentary government models of governance. Many societal forces contributed to China's transition to communism, the July 1, 1921 birth of CCP, and the CCP's views on constitutional theory and practice. The consequence in a post-1949 China, or post-WTO China, is the body politic of the CCP and one-party CCP rule.[35] The problem for modern China and legal formalism would be a Marxist critique of the legal system, which charges that it ignores the reality of law serving as a tool of established power structures, being in this case, the CCP and one-party rule.

In terms of Western legal theory, the previously mentioned social theories approaches and, admittedly, there may be other variant social theory approaches, are contradictory and conflicting. While one approach emphasizes social life or social norms as being the foundation of the law, the other emphasizes modern Chinese judicial principles, such as the power of judges to make law. The former approach stands in stark contrast to Western legal positivism, especially in the exalting of social norms over law, which challenges the primordial function of legal positivism's need to separate law from morals, or what law "is" from what law "ought" to say. In terms of Western legal theories, the latter approach, which stresses the reconstruction of traditional culture, more so, though oddly, resembles legal formalism and positivism. Moreover, assuming the reconstruction of traditional culture approach resembles legal formalism and positivism, such an approach may present additional problems because Marxism is traditionally critical of legal formalism. Assuming *arguendo*, the earlier mentioned social theory approaches are contradicting and conflicting, from a West centric perspective, Chinese law theories and China's legal system might present the worst of jurisprudential or juridical models. Conversely, the contradictions and conflicts thus far examined may lend to the surfacing of the particular idiosyncrasies of Chinese jurisprudence, or perhaps even China's particularism, as a distinctive product of traditional culture. Assuming traditional culture is persistent and systemic in modern China, at least in part, then Chinese legal jurisprudence, in both antiquity and modernity, may not be, as seemingly reasonably perceived from a West centric perspective, the worst of legal systems. Consequently, the social theory approaches to legal transplantation may bring into question issues of the need, efficacy and efficiency of Western theories of legal transplantation, especially the inherent assumptions of modernization theory, and its reliance on both evolutionary theory and functionalist theory.

The latter puts into play theories such as the theory of legal culture, cultural approach and legal modernization theory or legal modernization. Following the close of the infamous Great Cultural Revolution (*Wenhua Da Geming*, 1966-1976), the 1980s birth the theory of legal

---

[35] Guo Tao, Is China Now Out of the Danger of International Agreements?, Xiangdao (Guide), No. 6, Oct. 18, 1922 (People's Pub. House, 1954) 45-50. Zhu Zongzhen, Nature of the 1911 Revolution: A New Probe, Zhejiang Social Sciences (Zhejiang shehui kexue), no. 4, 2002. Zhou Enlai Tongyi Zhanxian Wenxuan (Zhou Enlai United Front Selected Works) 141. Mao Zedong Xuanji (Mao Zedong's Selected Works), Vol. 2, 628-629.

culture and intellectual fashion of blaming a failure in economic development on the absence of traditional culture, a problem reminiscent of the reform policy-revolution debate during the 1920s. However, by virtue of the theory of legal culture treating law as a cultural phenomenon, it would challenge Marxian analysis and its economic determinism, and necessitate the discarding and denial of its potential as a transplantation model.[36] The theory of legal culture, actually, evolves into a cultural approach and legal modernization theory or legal modernization. Following the previously mentioned classical modernization theory of Walter W. Rostow, in *The Stages of Economic Growth: A Non-Communist Manifesto* (1960), and its reliance on two key concepts -- evolutionary theory and functionalist theory -- for purpose of transplantation, drafting a model of legal modernization necessitates casting China as starting from a traditional stage and needing to transition to a modern stage, which represents the West and its institutions and normative norms. While cultural relativism or the cultural approach inhibits transplantation because of incommensurable cultural patterns and values, legal modernization (or legal modernization theory) enhances transplantation by prescribing an inevitable progression to the modern stage or transcendence of the traditional system by the modern one.

In terms of both classical modernization theory and legal modernization theory, as a theoretical assumption, developing countries in promoting economic development must borrow from Western laws and legal systems. In terms of classical modernization theory, such as that of Rostow and his stages theory of economic growth, there is an evolution of societies and governments, and an increasing reflection of Western normative institutions and values, because modernization theory demands conformity to Western and international standards. However, for China, there remains the problem of the cultural relative because it is difficult for legal modernization theory to take cultural patterns and values in the theory of legal culture, and place or transplant them into a requisite historical development pattern and values that allows for the genuine validation or validity of legal transplantation. Some attempt to correct this problem of the cultural relative, or imbalance in the societal rules or order, by shifting the ideological focus of transplantation from Marxism to the Weberian (Max Weber, 1864-1920) conception of formal rationality: not to protect ruling class interests rather protect rights and obligations of citizens. In the end, like the case of the Tibetan herdsmen, the analysis always, inevitably, turns from the theory of legal culture, cultural approach and legal modernization theory, though implicitly via the CCP's rhetoric, ideologies and actions, to simply an argument grounded in modern Marxism.

Then there are other legal academics advocating the distinguishable tool of "law in action," who subscribe to a theory that Chinese judicial practices are *de facto* legal transplantations. In the era of post-1979 legal reforms, when Chinese law is lacking in a subject matter or rule of law, then foreign law or international law sometimes serves as a sort of gap filler. This is typically the case of commercial laws or codes and the positing, though indirect positing, of the positive law of Western customs or customary law, and even non-state law. Eugen Ehrlich, in *Fundamental Principles of the Sociology of Law* (*Grundlegung der Soziologie des Rechts*, 1913), when discussing the theory of customary law, clearly sets forth a role of non-litigious custom in the development of law. While there is not a pre-1979 record in China's jurisprudential history of directly applying foreign law in domestic cases, in the post-1979 reform period, though a controversial subject, one can find cases of a national

[36] Jiang, The End of Transplantation, Id.

judicial practice of directly applying foreign law in domestic cases, such as "An Insurance Case Involving a Couple of Dead Lovers" (*Shengsi lianren de baoxian jiuge*, August 8, 2003).[37] The latter case involved a "health and peace life insurance policy" of the China Life Insurance Company, and issues of beneficiaries and payments of death benefits. Following a determination by the Taicang People's Court, Jiangsu Province, on April 7, 2003, and a subsequent appeal and disposition by the Second Civil Adjudication Division of the Intermediate People's Court of Suzhou, the relevant issues are resolved by reference to specific provisions from foreign laws; to wit: American Uniform Simultaneous Death Act. However, according to some legal academics, in distinguishing "law in action," the latter legal borrowing, unlike transplantation undertaken by a legislature, should be avoided because it is tantamount to judges creating law. Some legal academics deem the practice of judges creating law as contrary to Chinese judicial principles because it grants too much power to judges.

As for legal borrowing or transplantation undertaken by the legislature rather than judiciary, there are the post-1979 direct transplantations of foreign laws by the legislature, such as those cases involving foreigners and their issues of disputes. For example, there is the General Principles of the Civil Law of the People's Republic of China (*Zhonghua renmin gongheguo min fa tong ze*) and Law of the People's Republic of China on Economic Contracts Involving Foreign Interest (*Zhonghua renmin gongheguo she wai jingji he tong fa*).[38] In this respect, the laws enacted pursuant to legal reforms also contribute to the problem of legal transplantation. In matters pertaining to commercial and financial laws, China borrows from the principles of Anglo-American common law. The Chinese legal system characterizes a bifurcated system of foreign and domestic laws with divergent treatment, with legal reform often entailing an adoption of the principles of civil law, common law and international law. All of which compounds the difficulties and problems of a socialist market legal system or socialist market economic legal system. In addition, the problem with legal borrowing or transplantation by the legislature rather than judiciary is that it may inhibit the historical growth and evolutionary development of the laws and legal system, such as what occurs in Western constitutional or judicial models by gradual creation of judicial precedents on a case-by-case basis. In this respect, a socialist market legal system or socialist market economic legal system by primarily focusing on enacting new legal propositions or laws may problematically present a static rule of law model (rule by law or a policy-driven model) rather than one manifesting a living law model of the rule of law.

[37] Eugen Ehrlich, Id. Zhu Jingwen, Legal Transplantation in the Judicature: Employing Foreign Laws in China's Judicial Practice, Vol. 1, No. 1, Frontiers of Law in China, 112-120 (Jan. 2006), see http://www.cctv.com, "An Insurance Case Involving a Couple of Dead Lovers" (Shengsi lianren de baoxian jiuge, Aug. 8, 2003). Zhong Hua Ren Min Gong He Guo Min Fa Tong Ze (General Principles of Civil Law of the People's Republic of China) Adopted at the Fourth Session of the Sixth National People's Congress, promulgated by Order No. 37 of the President of the People's Republic of China on April 12, 1986, effective as of Jan. 1, 1987. Law of the People's Republic of China on Economic Contracts Involving Foreign Interest (Adopted at the Tenth Session of the Standing Committee of the Sixth National People's Congress, promulgated by Order No. 22 of the President of the People's Republic of China on Mar. 21, 1985).

[38] Zhong Hua Ren Min Gong He Guo Min Fa Tong Ze (General Principles of Civil Law of the People's Republic of China) Adopted at the Fourth Session of the Sixth National People's Congress, promulgated by Order No. 37 of the President of the People's Republic of China on April 12, 1986, effective as of Jan. 1, 1987. Law of the People's Republic of China on Economic Contracts Involving Foreign Interest (Adopted at the Tenth Session of the Standing Committee of the Sixth National People's Congress, promulgated by Order No. 22 of the President of the People's Republic of China on Mar. 21, 1985). Alice Erh-Soon Tay, "Asian Values" and the Rule of Law, http://dex1.tsd.unifi.it/jg/en/index.tm?surveys/rol/tay.htm.

China's legal system constituting a socialist market legal system or socialist market economic legal system is also problematic for other reasons. In terms of modern China, or Marxist, Leninist, communist or socialist rule, transplanting Western law and economics, and their respective theories and normative norms, does not occur in a vacuum because China is a communist country. As echoed by the words contained in the preamble of the Constitution of the People's Republic of China (*Zhonghua renmin gongheguo xianfa*, 1982 Constitution), it is a country, "Under the leadership of the Communist Party of China and the guidance of Marxism-Leninism, Mao Zedong Thought, Deng Xiaoping Theory, and the important thought of the Three Represents." The preamble further reads, "the Chinese people of all nationalities will continue to adhere to the people's democratic dictatorship, follow the socialist road, persist in reform and opening-up, steadily improve socialist institutions, develop a socialist market economy, advance socialist democracy, improve the socialist legal system and work hard and self-reliantly to modernize industry, agriculture, national defense and science and technology step by step, promote the co-ordinated development of the material, political and spiritual civilizations to turn China into a powerful and prosperous socialist country with a high level of culture and democracy."[39]

The problem of a socialist market economic legal system is that the problem of institution building, transplanting or borrowing legal and economic systems and normative norms, becomes contingent on the institutional analysis of a Marxian framework, or Marxist political economy. Chinese models of transplanting or borrowing legal norms and legal systems are constricted by the consequence of a Marxian framework, which always serves as a force driving institutional research and analysis, while also being hailed as the primordial explanatory system for institutional phenomena. For Marxist political economy, the impetus for development always originates in changing productive forces and relations of productions that satisfy material needs. The latter impetus for development is gravely different from the previously mentioned Western theories and models of development and transplantations, such as evolutionary theory, cultural theory, utilitarian theory, jurisprudence model, modernization theory and, in part, Ugo Mattei's model. There are also the inherent problems of a Marxian framework. A Marxian framework is problematic because it constricts available approaches to development and reform, such as the previously mentioned Western theories and models. A Marxian framework dictates that the economic structure (*Struktur*) of society constitutes the genuine basis on which legal and political superstructures (*Überbau*) must erect. In terms of Marxist political economy, it is from these superstructures that social consciousness corresponds. A Marxist framework views the basic structure of society as being economic or material, thereby largely determining the rest of social life.[40]

[39] Wang Baoshu, China's Accession to the WTO and the Building of a Socialist Market Economic Legal System, in China: Accession to the WTO and Economic Reform, 338 (Wang Mengku ed., Beijing: Foreign Language Press, 2002). Zhong Hua Ren Min Gong He Guo Xian Fa (Constitution of the People's Republic of China), Adopted at the Fifth Session of the Fifth National People's Congress on Dec. 4, 1982 and promulgated for implementation by the Proclamation of the National People's Congress on Dec. 4, 1982.

[40] Karl Marx, Das Kapital, (Gateway Editions, 1999). Niklas Luhmann, A Sociological Theory of Law (Elizabeth King & Martin Albrow, trans., 1985). Li Shenglong, The Overall Structure of the Institutional Analysis Theory of Marxism, Jingjixue dongtai, no. 5 (2003).

7.7. CONCLUSION

A problem of both economic liberalism and Marxism is that they challenge the importance of historical particularity, which creates additional problems because Chinese rights, in the sense of Chinese constitutionalism, are historically contingent. A core problem for both a proposed Chinese neo-liberal constitutional coterie, and Marxist coterie, when facing China's ontological base in tradition, is the construct of a legal system that will manifest a genuinely indigenous constitutional *ethos* for Chinese constitutionalism. John Rawls (1921-2002), in *Political Liberalism* (1993), addressed the ideas of an "overlapping consensus," or agreement on justice as fairness between citizens who hold different religious and philosophical views (or *conceptions of the good*), and the idea of public reason that constituted the common reason of all citizens.[41] More broadly, and in terms of China, the idea of an agreement on justice as fairness between persons holding different religious and philosophical viewpoints has an obvious relevancy. This is especially true, if one reasonably assumes that economic liberalism, Marxism and China's ontological base in tradition present different, if not, potentially conflicting societal foundational values. As a consequent, the ideas of Rawls becomes increasingly important, especially his contention that a society characterized by reasonable pluralism political stability is contingent on gaining the reasoned support of a citizenry who are committed to reasonable and conflicting doctrines. Moreover, in terms of Chinese law and economic reforms, especially a potentially, paradoxical interrelationship between social, economic and legal norms, there lies the crux of the problem.

[41] John Rawls, Political Liberalism, (Columbia UP, 1993).

Chapter 8

TRADE, FOREIGN AID AND SOFT POWER

8.1. POLITICAL ECONOMY OF TRADE

In 1989, the world witnessed East Asian regional economies, including the People's Republic of China (China), commence the pursuit of market-driven economic development via the vehicles of investment, trade and regional cooperation. It is economic dynamism, though China might object on nationalistic and ideological grounds, generally, considered accelerated by the world multilateral trading system and its international economic institutions, including Bretton Wood Institutions (BWIs); namely, the International Bank for Reconstruction and Development (IBRD or World Bank), International Monetary Fund (IMF), General Agreement on Tariffs and Trade (GATT) and then later, by the World Trade Organization (WTO). It is also a period corresponding to the end of cold war (1945-1991). Some view this earlier period of growth in Asian economies as a chain reaction commenced with a surge in the economic growth of Japan in the 1960s. In the 1970s, the dynamism of Japan's economy spreads to contiguous areas, such as Taiwan, South Korean and other newly industrializing economies (NIEs). In the 1980s, the contagion of economic growth would spread to ASEAN nations and China. A chain reaction would also eventually spread to the more remote contiguous areas of India and Pakistan.[1] Asian economies as a whole experienced an Asian real annual gross domestic product (GDP) that doubled the world's averages, reportedly 5.6 percent in the 1970s, 6.9 percent in the 1980s and 7.4 percent in the early 1990s (or 1990-1994).

Two years following the travesty of the Great Cultural Revolution (*Wenhua Da Geming*, 1966-1976), in 1978, China's polity, during the Third Plenary Session of the 11th Committee of the Chinese Communist Party (CCP), adopted a policy of restoring the construction of a socialist legal system and democracy, while also announcing a shift from a work priority of class struggles to economic construction. However, unlike the proposed reform and opening (*gaige kaifang*) of the economic infrastructure and its institutions, China's polity delays reform issues addressing the legal system and democracy, while prioritizing reforms focused on economic construction or economic reforms. In the following years, China's economic growth rates would surpass all others, including contiguous Asian areas such as Taiwan,

[1] Kakazu Hroshi, Growth Triangles in ASEAN, A new Approach to Regional Co-operation, APEC Discussion Paper (1997). ASEAN Secretariat, http://www.aseansec.org/.

South Korean and the new NIEs. China's average annual growth rate was reportedly 11.6 percent during the period from 1980 to 1994. In the same period, Japan experienced an average annual growth rate of only 2.7 percent. Despite its non-GATT-member status, because China would not become a WTO member until 2001, China in the 1980s had already emerged as a major player in the global economy. At the close of the infamous Great Cultural Revolution, China's trade grew dramatically faster than world trade. China's foreign trade rose from about $20 billion in the 1970s to about $475 billion in 2000 or, comparatively, from 0.6 percent of world trade in 1977 to 3.7 percent of world trade in 2000. In the early 1990s, the World Bank noted China's potential as an economic power. In terms of the Asian region, in the early 1990s, China accounted for 51 percent of the land area and 40 percent of the total population. In 1994, China's GDP was only 11 percent of Japan's GDP, but its purchasing power parity (PPP) was already larger than Japan's PPP.[2] In the early 1990s, the World Bank, in recognition of China's potential, predicted that in the early days of the new millennium China would take over the United States, as the largest economy in the world. Pre-accession WTO growth continues in post-WTO China.

Since initiating economic reform and an open-door policy some twenty-seven years ago, the Chinese economy has experienced high rates of growth. According to the United Nations (UN) Development Programme statistics, China experienced during the period from 1975 to 2003, a GDP per capital annual growth rate of 8.2 percent, and for the period from 1990 to 2003, a GDP per capital annual growth rate of 8.5 percent.[3] According to the 2006 WTO Trade Policy Review (TPR) Report by the Secretariat, which was prepared for the first TPR of China, following reforms commenced in 1978, the gradual opening of the economy to international trade and foreign direct investment (FDI), and allowing the emergence of a private sector alongside the public sector, especially in manufacturing, the Chinese economy grew by an average of over 9 percent per annum since 1978. From 1978 to 2005, GDP per capital increases from about $148 to $1,700. According to the TRP, a substantial portion of China's population living below the poverty line of $2 per day also experiences a drop from nearly 73 percent in 1990 to 32 percent in 2003. The TPR observes that since 2001, China's exports and investment driven growth results in a real GDP growth that averages close to 9 percent per year. In terms of China's pending social crises, such as growing income inequalities, uneven economic growth, and other pending domestic crises, the TPR reads, "China's proposals for its 11th Five Year Plan, which were approved in October 2005, emphasized the importance of a more balanced approach to development and the need to continue with these structural reforms." Finally, the TPR in its summary observations reads, "Proposals for the 11th Five Year Plan for National Economic and Social Development, approved in October 2005, aim to double GDP per capita by 2010 relative to 2000, while

[2] Chen Sixi, The Gradual Reform of the Electoral System in China, 94, 101, Social Sciences in China (Zhongguo shehui kexue) (spring 2004). Decision, Accession of the People's Republic of China, W/L/432 (Nov. 10, 2001). Jiang Xiaojun, China's Foreign Direct Investment: Its Contribution to Growth, Structural Upgrading and Competitiveness, 3-6 Social Sciences in China (Zhongguo shehui kexue), (summer 2003). Nicholas R. Lardy, Integrating China into the Global Economy (Bookings Inst., 2002).

[3] Human Development Report, Country Sheet China, Economic Performance, UN Development Programme, 2005. China's economy grows 9.9 percent in 2005, Jan. 26, 2006, People's Daily. Economy roars into New Year, Jan. 26, 2006, Shenzhen Daily. Carsten A. Holz, OECD — China Governance Project The Institutional Arrangements for the Production of Statistics, OECD Statistics Working Paper STD/DOC(2005) 1, 5-7 (Jan. 19, 2005).

paying attention to disparities in income distribution, energy efficiency and the environment, and the need to develop a harmonious society."[4]

Problematic are past reports of economic growth rates because they routinely contain embellished or reportedly higher rates of economic growth than real rates, by reflecting higher reported growth rates of 9 percent or more. According to Li Deshui, commissioner of the National Bureau of Statistics (NBS, *guojia tongjiju*), China's economy grew at an annual average growth rate of 9.6 percent from 1979 to 2004, at 10 percent in 2003, at 10.1 percent in 2004, and then at 9.9 percent in 2005.[5] Li reported that for 2005 the GDP was 18.23 trillion yuan ($2.26 trillion), reflecting value-added components of several industries. Li also reported that primary industry reached 2.27 trillion yuan (5.2 percent increase), secondary industry was 8.62 trillion yuan (11.4 percent increase) and tertiary industry was 7.34 trillion yuan (9.6 percent increase). Although challengeable on several grounds - theoretical and practical - Li also announced economic performance in 2005, "boosted the income per head of China's 1.3 billion citizens to $1,700, making the country richer than Morocco." Further, Li adds, "The data also means China, with output of 18.2 trillion yuan ($2.3 trillion), has overtaken France to become the world's fifth-largest economy and might also have leapfrogged fourth-placed Britain, depending on growth rates and currency changes in 2005." In 2006, China's GDP reportedly reaches $2.6847 trillion and per capita GDP surpasses $2000 for the first time, and many predict that by 2020 per capital GDP will reach $3000.

However, an IMF study observed that, in the long term, it is consumption rather than investment or even GDP serving as a better measure of economic welfare. A recent 2006 Organisation for Economic Co-operation and Development (OECD) study also found that within a national account framework, there are better measures of economic resources than GDP per capital, such as national product and net income. In terms of China, the earlier mentioned IMF study also observed the difficulty of operating in an environment of institutional deficiencies, which includes a weak legal framework, poor governance and economic data of dubious quality. A January 2006 article (*Shenzhen Daily*) reads, "Economists agreed that China had the wind in its sails." However, as early as 2003, Li Deshui acknowledged for the first time that China's economic estimates were flawed, and its research methods "did not always reflect the real situation," which necessitated that after about twenty years the NBS had to switch from the Soviet accounting system, and not standard international practices of readjusting quarterly and annual GDP growth estimates, to Western accounting standards. In terms of the reliability of China's statistics published by the NBS, one hopes that the "wind in its sails" is not from the "wind of falsification and embellishment" (*jiabao fukuafeng*).[6]

---

[4] World Trade Organization, Trade Policy Review Report by the Secretariat People's Republic of China, WT/TPR/G/161, 28 Feb. 2006.

[5] Zhonghua Renmin Gongheguo Guojia Tongjiju (People's Republic of China State Statistical Bureau or National Bureau of Statistics), http://www.stats.gov.cn. China's economy sees steady growth in 2005, Jan. 26, 2006, China Daily. Allen T. Cheng, Economic figures were flawed, top official says, Nov. 21, 2003, South China Morning Post. Holz, Id. What means to have a per capita GDP of US$2000?, Apr. 11, 2007, China Daily.

[6] Romina Boarini, Asa Johansson & and Marco Mira d'Ercole, Alternative Measures of Well-Being, OECD Social, Employment and Migration Working Papers No. 33 DELSA/ELSA/WD/SEM(2006)2, Feb, 17, 2006. Xu Dashan, Revised GDP for 2004 up by 16.8%, Oct. 21, 2005, China Daily. Economy roars into New Year, Jan. 26, 20006, Shenzhen Daily. Thomas G. Rawski, Economic Issues and the Future of China, (Univ. of Pittsburgh, 2003). Jiang Wei, Foreign trade continues growing, Jan. 12, 2006, China Daily. Jiang Zhuqing & Li Wengfang, Revision raises 2004 GDP for Beijing and Guangdong, Dec. 22, 2006, China Daily.

Nonetheless, from China, the picture for economic growth remains optimistic. In the new millennium, and as predicted by the World Bank during the 1990s, many in China are optimistic about taking over the United States as the largest economy in the world. In January 2005, Lin Yifu, president of the Global Young Chinese Business Leaders Forum (GYC) and director of the China Center for Economic Research at Peking University, announced, "China is expected to become the largest economic entity in the world by 2030."[7] Lin based his optimism on China's annual average growth rate of 9.7 percent. Lin predicted that the Chinese economy would maintain average growth rates between 7 to 10 percent in the next 20 to 30 years, or even longer. By 2030, he predicted that China's per capital income would equal 20 percent of U.S. per capital income. Given China's population of 1.3 billon is about five times larger than the U.S. population, China's economy will be as large as the U.S. economy. Chinese experts also predict, assuming the efficacy of Beijing's population control measures, China's population will peak at 1.5 billion in the mid-2030s. A controlled population growth to 1.5 billion in the mid-2030s, while arguably supporting the contention that China will become the largest economy, does not necessarily mean enhanced social welfare or security for its growing and aging population. Admittedly, if currency appreciated is accounted, China's economy would be 1.5 to 2 times that of the U.S. economy, thus, making China's economy the largest economic entity in the world. Lin predicts, by 2030, 100 Chinese companies will be members of the 500 largest businesses in the world and constitute 20 percent of the world's largest businesses.

Comparing China's economic growth rate to that of the United States is not a recent phenomenon, nor specifically related to China's high economic growth rates commencing in the late 1970s. The idea of a target growth rate comparable to that of the U.S. economy dates back much farther, it dates to the 1949 founding of modern China. A goal of attaining a growth rate comparable to that of the United States presents implicit policy concerns addressing domestic and international relations concerns, especially cold war concerns and the global balance of power. During the period from the 1949 founding of modern China and commencement of the U.S.-led Korean war (1951), according to the Tucker-Cohen thesis, then U.S. President Harry S. Truman (presidency, 1945-1953) and Secretary of State Dean Acehson (secretary, 1949-1953) were willing to establish normal diplomatic relations with China for purpose of preventing the CCP from leaning toward the former Soviet Union. However, it was a difficult task for the Truman administration to do so because of pro-Jiang (Jiang Jieshi or Chiang Kai-shek, 1887-1975) forces in the U.S. Congress, American public opinion and deliberate provocations by the CCP. As early as 1950, Mao Zedong and the Central Committee of the CPC (CPC) were well aware that the cross-strait issue (or Taipei-Beijing controversy) could only be resolved in China's favor by removal of U.S. intervention. The September 1954 Geneva Conference failed to offer any hope of resolving the Taiwan issue, both in the near future and in China's favor.[8]

---

[7] China to become the world's largest economic entity by 2030, Jan. 12, 2005, People's Daily. China's population to peak at 1.5b in 2030s, Jun. 23, 2006, China Daily.

[8] Warren I. Cohen, Was There a Lost Chance in China?, Vol. 12, No. 1, (winter 1997). Wang Lixin, Ideology and America's China Policy at the time of the Founding of New China: A Reexamination of Acheson and the Question of Recognition, Social Sciences in China (Zhongguo shehui kexue), 17-26 (autumn 2005). Mao Zedong, Guanyu huifu Zhongguo zai Lianheguo de he fa xiwei wenti (On Regaining China's Legitimate Seat in the UN) Sept. 30, 1956, in Selected Foreign Policy Works of Mao Zedong, (Central Party Literature Publishing House, 1933), 263-274.

In the following year, and while still dealing with the issue of how to bring about the removal of U.S intervention, specifically the removal of the United States Seventh Fleet from the Taiwan Strait, Mao Zedong resolved that China has two choices: "recover Taiwan as soon as possible" or "strengthen ourselves [China]."[9] In the fall of 1955, and frustrated by Sino-U.S. diplomatic talks, Mao decided on the course of catching up with the U.S. economy, in a short period. Mao told business leaders trying to develop industries, "It is our goal to catch up with and surpass the United States," and further, "We will not relax until the day we achieve our goal." The latter goal also served as one of the reasons for commencing the Great Leap Forward movement (*Dayuejin*, 1958-1962), which was the name given for China's Second Five Year Plan that was scheduled to run from 1958-1963, though *Dayuejin* is limited to the earlier years of this period. Two major events of this period are the Great Leap Forward and the Democratic "Rectification Campaign" (*Zhengfeng yundong*). In the latter, the CCP "endeavoured to set its ideology and organization straight under Mao Zedong." Both the Great Leap Forward and Democratic "Rectification Campaign" ended in failure, with the former, the Great Leap Forward, in the end producing a serious economic recession, especially in the agriculture sector.

A 1958 editorial appearing in the *People's Daily* predicted China would catch up with Great Britain in about fifteen years, and it would only take another 20 to 30 years to catch up with the United States. In 1958, at the Second Session of the Eighth National Congress of the CPC, Mao set a target date of seven years to catch up with Great Britain, and eight years to catch up with the United States. During the summer of 1958, Mao would revise these target goals with shorter periods. Mao proclaimed, "We don't need fifteen years to surpass Britain, nor seven years. Two or three years will be enough. We may make it in two years."[10] In November 2006, former World Bank chief James Wolfensohn warned Western countries of an economic future and altered balance of power dominated by China and India. Based on projections by investment bank Goldman Sachs, Wolfensohn predicted that within twenty-five years the combined GDP of China and India would exceed that of the G7 nations. China, from 2030 to 2040, would become the world's largest economy. He projected that by 2050, "China's current two trillion US dollar GDP was set to balloon to 48.6 trillion, while that of India, whose economy weighs in at under a trillion dollars, would hit 27 trillion." In the history of modern China, an economic growth goal of catching and then surpassing Western powers, such as the U.S. and Great Britain, are intertwined with Chinese policy, and manifest an influence on domestic and foreign policies.

The United States and other Western developed countries are concerned with China's economic growth rates, because they are affected by China's burgeoning economic growth.

---

[9] Mao Zedong, Zai Zibenzhuyi Gongshangye Shehuizhuyi Gaizao Wenti Zuotanhui shang de Jianghua (Speech at seminar on Socialist Transformation of Capitalist Industries and Commerce) Oct. 20, 1955, in Collection of Texts of Mao Zedong, (Central Party Literature Pub. House, Vol. 6, 500). Yang Kuisong, Reorientation of China's Foreign Policy and its causes: As seen from the two bombardments of Jinmen, 136-43, Social Sciences in China (Zhongguo shehui kexue) (summer 2003). Leonid A. Petrov, Turning Historians into Party Scholar-bureaucrats: North Korean Historiography in 1955-1958, East Asian History, Australian Nat'l Univ. (2006). Niu Jun, 1962: Eve of a "Left" Turn in China's Foreign Policy, 153-164, Social Sciences in China (Zhongguo shehui kexue) (summer 2003).

[10] Mao Zedong, Zai Di 15 Ci Zuigao Guowuhuiyi shang de Jianghua (Speech at the 15th Supreme State Conference), in Jianguo yilai Mao Zedong Wengao (Texts of Mao Zedong after founding of the PRC), Vol. 7, 381. Mao Zedong, Dui Beidaihe huiyi gongye lei wenjian de yijian (Comments on Industry related documents at the Beidaihe Conference) Sept. 2, 1958, in Texts of Mao Zedong after founding of the PRC, Vol. 7, 368. West must prepare for Chinese, Indian dominance: Wolfensoh, Nov. 26, 2006, Agence France Presse.

Since 1979, U.S.-China trade continues to grow. However, the U.S. economy has experienced a steadily growing U.S. trade deficit with China, from $30 billion in 1994 to $202 billion in 2005, and a deficit that rose by 15.4 percent to total $232.5 billion in 2006, which is largely due to a growth in U.S. imports from China relative to U.S. exports to China.[11] In January 1979, the United States and China established diplomatic relations and signed a bilateral agreement in July 1979, which followed a 1980 grant of most favored nations (MFN) treatment. Subsequently, from 1980 to 1990, U.S.-China total trade (exports plus imports) rose from about $5 billion to $20 billion and then, in 2005, to about $285 billion. Total U.S.-China trade rose from about $5 billion in 1980, to $285 billion in 2005. In 2006, China is the third largest U.S. trading partner, the second-largest source of imports and the fourth largest export market.

However, many issues continue to strain U.S.-China bilateral trade relations, such as a growing U.S. trade deficit, China's foreign currency policy, a lax protection of U.S. intellectual property rights (IPR), protectionism and other issues. For instance, as of June 2006, China's national composition of foreign exchange (Forex) reserves reached 941 billion yuan, ranking it as the world's highest and constituting about 35 percent of GDP.[12] On January 15, 2007, the People's Bank of China (PBOC) announces that the Forex reserve reaches record high of 1.0663 trillion U.S. dollars, PBOC statistics actually show the breaking of the one trillion U.S. dollar mark occurs in October 2006. This reflects a 30.22 percent increase from the close of 2005. During the first half of 2006, China actually became the world's largest foreign currency depositor. Notwithstanding issue of excessive Forex reserves, there is also the issue of how to dissolve the risk of U.S. dollar reserves in Forex reserves. In June 2006, U.S. dollar reserves account for about 70 percent of China's national Forex reserves. As of November 2005, China held about $250 billion of U.S. treasury bonds, which has implications for both Beijing and Washington in diplomacy and international trade policy, because of pressure from appreciation of the Chinese RMB (*Ren Min Bi*-currency of China or Chinese dollar, *Yuan*), the U.S. dollar would devalue. Although appreciation of the RMB should encourage or enhance purchasing power, it would also mean devaluation of Forex reserves, since the U.S. asset is a bull share of China's foreign reserves. In September 2006, Russia shifted a part of its Forex reserves from dollars to euros. For the United States, it is a problem of Middle East oil exporters, Russia, Asian countries and other countries, including China, diversifying their reserves out of the dollar.[13]

A rapidly growing Forex reserve benefits China in at least five respects: First, it greatly upgrades China's payment capacity and balance of income. Second, it greatly increases the potential for stabilizing exchange rate of the RMB. Third, a growing Forex reserve provides a solid basis for pushing forward the opening of China's capital account and the free change of RMB into foreign currency. Fourth, there is a resulting enhancement of the capacity of the national economy to resist risks and shocks, including external, political economy and macroeconomic forces. Fifth, and finally, a growing Forex reserve enhances China's impact on the international monetary market. Admittedly, many economists, including some in

---

[11] Martin Crutsinger, Trade deficit climbs to $763.6 billion, Feb. 13, 2007, AP.

[12] Are China's foreign exchange reserves accurate?, Aug. 28, 2006, People's Daily. Yan Qifa, Range of foreign reserve investment to be widened, Jan. 18, 2006, China Daily. China's foreign exchange reserve hit record high, Jan. 15 2007, Xinhua.

[13] China-U.S. Trade Issues, CRS Issue Brief for Congress, Order Code IB91121, Mar. 21, 2006. Russia Shifts Part of Its Forex Reserves from Dollars to Euros, Sept. 6, 2006, MosNews.

China, though representing a minority viewpoint, disagree that a growing Forex reserve is good for the development of the economy. In China, some economists urge diversification of the Forex reserve into oil, gold, silver and other rare metals as a hedge against risks, some argue that a 1 trillion-U.S. dollar Forex reserve is excessive as a guard against risks, and others argue that the problem is not so much the quantity of the Forex reserve, but the structure.[14]

The U.S. Trade Representative in a 2006 top-to-bottom review of China, while recognizing China's emergence as an international player in global trade, also recognized that U.S.-China bilateral trade relations pose continuing challenges. The U.S. Trade Representative found, "there is concern that the U.S.-China trade relationship lacks balance in opportunity, as well as equity and durability, with China's focus on export growth and developing domestic industries not being matched by a comparable focus on fulfilling market opening commitments and on the protection of intellectual property and internationally recognized labor rights." Additional concerns of the 2006 review are: "continued Chinese barriers to some U.S. exports; failure to protect intellectual property rights; failure to protect labor rights and enforce labor laws and standards; unreported and extensive government subsidies and preferences for its own industries; environmental concerns; spotty compliance with some international trade rules; and a large and growing imbalance in our bilateral trade flows, resulting in a trade deficit of almost $202 billion in 2005."[15] In April 2007, the U.S. Trade Representative also issues its National Trade Estimate Report on Foreign Trade Barriers or the 2007 National Trade Estimate (NTE) Report, which is annual report detailing foreign trade barriers to U.S. exports and investment and covers 63 major trading partners, including China. The 2007 NTE report addresses the same issues concerning China set forth in the 2006 top-to-bottom review such as China continuing to pursue problematic industrial policies that rely on trade distorting measures such as local content requirements, import and export restrictions, discriminatory regulations and prohibited subsidies. The 2007 NTE report also addresses China's inability to effectively enforce laws such as IPR laws, and other concerns such as agriculture and investment practices. The 2007 NTE report, generally, concludes that many of these shortcomings stem from excessive Chinese government intervention in the market through policy directives and the actions of individual officials, which are traceable to China's unfinished transition from a command economy to a free-market economy. According to U.S. Trade Representative Susan C. Schwab, "The report demonstrates that the Administration continues to use all enforcement tools at its disposal to ensure fair treatment in the global marketplace for U.S. workers and consumers."

Several forces are attributable to driving the earlier economic growth of East Asian economies, such as market-oriented growth policies, the Asian growth miracle, the "flying-geese formation" theory, "catch-up" theory and other forces or reasons. Western experts and authority, generally, summarize the pattern or policy of Chinese economic growth and development policies as reflecting a choice between two alternative patterns or policies:

---

[14] Forex reserve can be used to invest in foreign firms' share options, Nov. 1, 2006, People's Daily. Blessing or burden: 1 trillion-U.S. dollar reserves spark debate in China, Nov. 15, 2006, Xinhua. How to look at and what to do with China's US$1 trillion Forex Reserve?, Jan. 17, 2007, People's Daily.

[15] U.S.-China Trade Relations: Entering a New Phase of Greater Accountability and Enforcement Top-to-Bottom Review, United States Trade Representative, Feb. 2006. Bush Administration Submits Annual Trade Report to Congress, Office of the U.S. Trade Representative, Press Release, Apr. 2, 2007.

"big bang" approach or reforms and "gradualist" approach or gradual reforms.[16] While democracy, liberalization and privatization have been slow and incremental, China elected the gradualist approach and achieved a measure of economic success, as witnessed by its burgeoning economic growth. Many also deem China's policy of economic growth, and its "gradualist" approach to transition, as a prescription for future disasters because, "China's current stage of development, along with its rising market orientation and increasing integration with the world economy, may make the incremental and piecemeal approaches to reforms increasingly untenable and, in some cases, could even generate risks of their own." In addition, because, "there is much work to be done to make the economy resilient to large shocks, to ensure the sustainability of its growth, and to translate this growth into corresponding improvements in the economic welfare of its citizens," an "important lesson from the experiences of other countries is that periods of high growth can sometimes mask deep underlying problems."[17]

During the earlier reform years, China's economic reform has been characterized as schizophrenic in operation, as "capitalist free-trade enclaves were allowed in the southeastern provinces (far away from Beijing), and individual (or small groups of) villagers in some areas could establish and operate sizable industrial enterprises provided that these were formally registered as collectively-owned township and village enterprises (TVEs)." As policy experimentation rationalized future development policy, both economic growth and future economic development became contingent on whether past successes were: "(1) the result of China's economic experimentation that produced non-capitalist institutional innovations that were optimally suited to the country's particular economic circumstances, or (2) the result of China's institutional convergence and integration with the advanced WTO economies like France, Japan, and the United States." However, most seem to agree, including East Asian economies that market-oriented growth contributes to economic growth, which does not necessarily equate with being the primary force for economic growth. As the primary force for economic growth, market-oriented growth seems to be in competition with the previously mentioned forces. Market-oriented growth policies of East Asian economies may be an implicit recognition of the contributions of liberal economic policies. The latter still results in a search for an explicit rather than implicit recognition of the role of economic liberalism as primary force for economic growth. It is an issue of whether these Asian economies attribute liberal economic policies as either enhancing or hindering economic development. In terms of East Asia, difficulty sets in when searching for explicit recognition due to the East Asian financial crisis (1996-1997), because these economies totally, or partially, blame the BWIs and their neo-liberal policies for this crisis.

In order to explore issues of the complementary and paradoxical interrelationships of the various sources of order, such as economic, legal and social orders, it is necessary to first

---

[16] Saburo Okita, Approaching the 21st Century: Japan's Role, Tokyo: The Japan Times, 1990. Kaname Akamatus, A Historical Pattern of Economic Growth in Developing Countries, The Developing Economies, Preliminary Issue No.1, 1962, 3-25. Wing Thye Woo, A United Front for the Common Objective to Understand China's Economic Growth: A Case of Nonantagonistic Contradiction, Wu vs. Woo, Issues & Studies 39, no. 2 (June 2003), 1-23. Zhang Jun, Capital Formation, Industrialization and Economic Growth: Characteristics of China Structural Reform, Jinji yanjiu, no. 6 (2002).

[17] Gerard Roland, The Political Economy of Transition 37-38, William Davidson Instit., Working Paper No. 413, 2002. Dani Rodrik, Globalization is No Shortcut to Development, Beyond Transition, World Bank, July-Sept. 2001. Eswar S. Prasad & Raghuram G. Rajan, Modernizing China's Growth Paradigm, IMF Policy Discussion Paper, Mar. 2006.

ascertain the influence of economic liberalism and its attendant institutions, policies and normative norms. The latter is necessary, due to the yet to unfold consequences of China jointly pursuing, though deniable for nationalistic or ideological reasons, a socialist-polity polity and capitalist-economic policy. A China hailing Marxism as its official ideology, and continuing the process of finalizing the localization of Marxism (*Makesi zhuyi he Zhongguo shiji xiang jiehe*), presents a challenge to liberalism or economic liberalism, and its attendant institutions, policies, programs and goals, including normative norms. Marxist political economy remains problematic as a force driving institutional research and analysis, while China also hails Marxist political economy as the primordial explanatory system for institutional phenomena. In terms of a Western-inspired new dialectic vision of world order, while there are many international inter-governmental organizations (IGOs), the BWIs are the dominant international economic institutions. The issues of the benefits and consequences of economic liberalism, or even the Washington consensus or American consensus, which is a free market orthodoxy that emerged in the 1990s, are all-important. The latter also presents a challenge, because China commenced a surge in economic growth prior to WTO accession or during the pre-accession period. It becomes increasingly relevant whether China implicitly or explicitly recognizes liberal economic policies as enhancing its economic growth, or implicitly or explicitly rejects these contributions. For these reasons, it is necessary to explore the benefits of economic liberalism, the consequences of economic liberalism, and even the influence of these benefits and consequences on the United Nations (UN) Millennium Development Goals. China implicitly or explicitly recognizing economic liberalism as enhancing its economic growth, or hindering its economic growth, ultimately, serves as a measure of whether China, in the pursuit of economic growth, has actually Sinicized or localized Western normative economic liberalism in its direct application of the benefits of liberal economic policies and programs. The latter will ultimately influence the issues of the complementary and paradoxical interrelationships of various sources of order.

8.2. Liberalism and Millennium Development Goals

In September 2000, 189 member states (or countries) of the UN adopted a resolution called the Millennium Development Goals (MDGs),[18] whose primary objective was to reduce worldwide poverty in the next decade. The MDGs set targets for progress in eight areas, which are poverty and hunger; primary education; women's equality; child mortality; maternal health; disease; environment; and a global partnership for development; by a target date of 2015. A core problem for developing countries and non-market economies in transition, like China, are, historically, weak institutional capacities serving as a block to economic development. During the 2002 Financing for Development Conference in Monterrey, Mexico, former IMF Director Michel Camdessus noted that if the summit could only deliver one thing, it should be extending assistance to enhance institutional capacity in developing countries. Addressing this problem is the key to achieving the MDGs of reducing world poverty by half, by the MDG target date of 2015.

[18] United Nations Millennium Declaration: United Nations A/RES/55/2, General Assembly Distr.: General, 18 September 2000, Fifty-fifth session, Agenda item 60 (b), 00 55951, Resolution adopted by the General Assembly, [without reference to a Main Committee (A/55/L.2)], 55/2.

In 2004, in terms of progress on the MDGs, the IMF and the World Bank issued a joint report warning that plans outlined by the UN, and one of its year 2000 MDGs of four years ago to halve 1990 global poverty levels by the year 2015, will most likely not be met if current trade and aid policies continue. In 2004, the report observed that China and India accounted for about a third of the world's population, and with greater liberalization and having profited from economic globalization, both of these developing countries have made progress in reducing property. In China, the number of people living in "extreme" poverty was reduced from 40 percent in 1981 to 21 percent in 2001. Since 1982, China's GDP has risen by 500 percent. According to the IMF and World Bank, the 600 million Chinese living in "extreme" poverty in 1981 dropped to 200 million. In contrast, by 2004, some African countries, some Latin America countries and Russia (Russian Federation) had only slightly improved, and worsened in some cases. Countless development efforts have failed because developing countries, generally, lack institutions with the ability to sustain their economic policies.[19] Weak institutional capacities of developing economies are one of the major obstacles to economic development. One of the benefits of the economic liberalism and international economic institutions, including the BWIs, in terms of assisting rather than hindering economic development is recognition of the need for efficient and effective infrastructure investments that will strengthen institutional capacities in developing economies.

Former U.S. Deputy Defense Secretary Paul Dundes Wolfowitz, and now former president of the World Bank as of June 2007, began his appointment as World Bank president on June 1, 2005. The nomination of former U.S. Deputy Defense Secretary Paul Wolfowitz to lead the World Bank earlier sparked reactions around the world. The reactions ranged from official reserve to hostility, although there was some support for his appointment. The controversy surrounding his appointment was an association with the presidency of George W. Bush, and the Bush doctrine, a U.S. policy statement contained in *The National Security Strategy of the United States of America* (September 20, 2002).[20] The Bush doctrine is associated with and often characterized by many as modern American neo-conservatism, the 2003 Iraq War, and opposition to the 2003 Iraq War by some European countries and other countries. Paul Wolfowitz is also one of the signatories to the January 26, 1998 letter of the Project of the New American Century, which is an organization comprising prominent citizens, which earlier, on January 26, 1998, requested that then U.S. President William Jefferson Clinton (presidency from 1993 to 2001), "enunciate a new strategy that would secure the interests of the U.S. and our friends and allies around the world. That strategy should aim, above all, at the removal of Saddam Hussein's regime from power." According to Ian Vásquez, director of the Cato's Project on Global Economic Liberty, "The nomination of Paul Wolfowitz is a reminder that Washington has traditionally viewed the World Bank as an extension of the U.S. Treasury Department's international role; another tool in its foreign policy tool kit."[21] However, Wolfowitz as president of the World Bank did exhibit a more

[19] Carol Graham, Strengthening Institutional Capacity in Poor Countries: Shoring up Institutions, Policy Briefs, Brookings Instit., Apr. 2002. Jeremy Bransten, World: IMF, World Bank Say UN Poverty Reduction Plan At Risk, Apr. 16, 2004, Radio Free Europe.

[20] National Security Strategy of the United States of America, Sept. 2002, http://www.whitehouse.gov/nsc/nss.pdf.

[21] Peter S. Goodman, Ending Battle, Wolfowitz Resigns From World Bank, May 17, 2007. Peter S. Goodman, Bush to Pick Zoellick for World Bank, May 30, 2007, Wash. Post. Wolfowitz Nominated to Lead World Bank, Mar. 17, 2005, CATO. Letter to the Honorable William J. Clinton, Project for the New American Century, Jan. 28, 1998, http://www.newamericancentury.org/ iraqclintonletter.htm.

pragmatic rather than theoretical approach to achieving the MDGs. It is a pragmatic approach directly benefiting developing economies, in their quest for the benefits of economic liberalism and economic globalization.

According to the World Bank 2006 Global Development Finance Report, the year of 2005 was a landmark year in global development finance. The report observed that net private capital flows to developing countries reached a record high of $491 billion in 2005. In May 2006, as further evidence of the benefits directly flowing, and continuing to flow, to China, the World Bank announced a New Country Partnership Strategy (CPS) for China. The new CPS for China will cover the period from 2006 to 2010, and the World Bank Board, "endorsed its overall goals of helping to integrate China into the world economy, address poverty and inequality, manage resource scarcities and environmental challenges, strengthen the financial sector, and improve public and market institutions." According to former World Bank president Paul Wolfowitz, "The new Country Partnership Strategy recognizes clearly that helping China to strengthen its economy, manage its resources and environment, and improve governance, are important not only for the Chinese people but also for people all over the world." On June 1, 2006, the Annual World Bank Conference on Development Economics (ABCDE) concluded with a call for new analytical and evaluation tools to help decision-makers make infrastructure choices that deliver vital services such as energy, transportation and water, to facilitate growth and achieve the MDGs, while also remaining cost-effective and friendly to the environment. In observance of failed infrastructure investments in the past, former World Bank president Paul Wolfowitz announced the following new direction for infrastructure investments, "It must also focus on 'smart' growth, that is, growth that is economically sound, environmentally friendly, socially acceptable, locally desirable, and most important, growth that makes a difference in people's lives."[22]

International economic institutions, including the BWIs, such as the World Bank group, by exhibiting a more practical rather than theoretical approach to achieving the MDGs are assisting developing countries and LDCs in a variety of ways, ranging from assistance in poverty reduction to sustainable development. While countries such as China for nationalistic and ideological reasons oppose the many Western-inspired international economic institutions, including the BWIs, these countries both directly and indirectly benefit from economic liberalism and its resulting international economic institutions and attendant policies, goals and programs, especially assistance for poverty reduction and sustainable development. In the interim, China enjoys the benefits of economic liberalism, while linking the goals of building a *xiaokang* and harmonious socialist society to the MDGs,[23] which ideologically links with the two-stage development from *xiaokang* to *datong* and then a progression in Chinese Marxism between a socialist market society and world communism, or the attempt to finalize the localization of Marxism. Despite the policies, programs and target goals of Western conventionalism, such as liberal economic theories and the MDGs, China's polity may have adapted, Sinicized or localized the MDGs, or perhaps given them

[22] World Bank News, Changing the Face of Development Finance?, May 30, 2006. World Bank's New Partnership Strategy for China Focuses on Economic Integration, Poverty, and Sustainable Development, World Bank Press Release No: 2006/416/EAP, May 23, 2006. World Bank News, Making the Best Choices for Infrastructure, June 1, 2006.

[23] UNPD, Fully Constructing A Well-off China: A State Development Plan Integrating the Millennium Goals, Project No. RR/03/M02/A/PJ/99 (Dec. 2004).

distinctive Chinese characteristics reflecting the realities of a modern Chinese Marxist, communist or socialist society, as it continues to enjoy the benefits of economic liberalism.

8.3. LIBERALISM, POVERTY AND DEVELOPMENT

For China, notwithstanding burgeoning economic growth, there are the other direct and indirect benefits of liberal economic policies and institutions, such as the World Bank, IMF, GATT and WTO. China enjoys the direct benefits of the liberalization and facilitation of trade and investment (TILF), and FDI and foreign capital, in its pursuit of an export-based growth intended to conquer distant markets. Notwithstanding political motivations, in China, the political economy forces driving economic integration have been resource endowments and differing developmental levels (foreign capital and technology, and domestic land and labor) in pursuit of export-based growth.[24] China stands to benefit from the promotion of trade negotiation rounds in the WTO, especially the struggling Doha Development Agenda. Indeed, in terms of the world multilateral trading system, the promotion of free trade and investment, or TILF, benefits China.

China and other developing countries, including LDCs, also enjoy direct benefits from the assistance of these liberal economic policies and institutions, ranging from assistance in poverty reduction to sustainable development. Many World Bank activities directly support poverty reduction initiatives, with an added emphasis on rural development. The World Bank has substantially contributed to ongoing reforms in many areas, such as poverty reduction, rural development, environment, transportation, education, health, social protection, water issues, energy, financial reforms, enterprise reform and sector development. In May 2005, the World Bank-sponsored "Shanghai Conference on Scaling up Poverty Reduction" emphasized some success at poverty reduction. Following the latter conference, the World Bank supported the establishment of an International Poverty Center in China, and worked closely with China to identify and pilot innovative poverty reduction programs, such as the China Southwest, Qinba Mountain and Gansu and Inner Mongolia poverty reduction projects. On May 16, 2005, the International Poverty Reduction Center was officially established, and jointly supported by United Nations Development Programme (UNDP), China's Ministry of Commerce (MOFCOM) and the State Council Leading Group Office for Poverty Reduction and Development (LGOPR). According to Khalid Malik, UN Resident Coordinator and UNDP Resident Representative in China, "An independent, inclusive, creative and practically relevant Poverty Center will be an incredible resource to support China in building its harmonious *xiaokang* society."[25] Projects such as the China Southwest, Qinba Mountain and Gansu and Inner Mongolia poverty reduction projects have raised incomes, improved food

[24] M. Ulric Killion, Chinese Regionalism and the 2004 ASEAN-China Accord: The WTO and Legalized Trade Distortion, 31 NCJ Int'l L. & Com. Reg. 1 (2005). Robert F. Ash & Y.Y. Kueh, Economic Integration within Greater China: Trade and Investment Flows Between China, Hong Kong and Taiwan In Greater China: the Next Superpower?, 60 (David Shambaugh, ed.) (Oxford UP, 1995).

[25] World Bank, Shanghai Conference: Scaling Up Poverty Reduction: Lessons and Challenges from China, Indonesia, Korea and Malaysia, May 2004, http://siteresources.worldbank.org/INTKOREA/Resources/Special+Focus+Report.pdf. New Initiative Established to Alleviate Poverty, Beijing, May 16, 2005, Xinhua. UN Documents, General Assembly, Programme of Action for the Least Developed Countries for the 1990s, A/53/608/Add.5, Nov. 19, 1998. Zhonghua renmin gongheguo shangwu bu (People's Republic of China Ministry of Commerce, MOFCOM), http://english.mofcom.gov.cn/.

security and expanded access to basic services in the sixty-one poorest counties of China, and play an important role in attempting to foster rural developing and poverty reduction. China and other developing countries have received substantial assistance from the World Bank, in the form of loans for physical investments and grants. The extent of assistance to China is substantive, as evidenced by the fact that China's portfolio is one of the largest in the World Bank.

The World Bank, in accordance with the policy direction of China's 10th Five Year Plan, is assisting China by programs designed to improve its business environment, especially in transitioning to a market economy; addressing the needs of poor and disadvantage persons, including regions, through investment lending and grants; and facilitating an environmentally sustainable development process through investment lending and grants. China's 11th Five Year Plan, scheduled to take effect in 2006, reflects goals and policies similar to the 10th Five Year Plan. The development financing or infrastructure investments of the World Bank comprise low-interest loans, interest-free credit loans and grants. These loans and grants were provided to China through either the International Bank for Reconstruction and Development (IBRD) or The International Development Association (IDA), and in some cases, Britain's Department of International Development (DfID). The IBRD is one of the five institutions constituting the World Bank Group and provides IBRD loans to developing countries. Notwithstanding regional development banks, such as the Inter-American Development Bank, the other four institutions are the International Development Association, International Finance Corporation, Multilateral Investment Guarantees Agency and International Centre for Settlement of Investment Disputes.[26] The IDA constitutes a branch of the World Bank Group assisting the poorest developing countries in reducing poverty by providing interest-free loans (IDA loans) and grants (IDA grants) for programs aimed at boosting economic growth and improving living conditions. However, the IDA records now list China as a graduate from the IDA loan program, showing 1999 as the last fiscal year of IDA credit for China. There has also been a blending of the IBRD resources with grants from the DfID, which has also benefited China. While DfID's grant resources contributed to reduced costs of Work Bank assistance, they, more importantly, have helped China, because China has not been able to borrow from the Bank on more concessionary IDA terms since its July 1, 1999 graduation from the IDA loan program. These concessionary loans, generally, carry no interest and offer a much longer grace period and maturity than other forms of financing. Nonetheless, and notwithstanding assistance from other international economic institutions, and other IGOs, following the 1999 fiscal year of last IDA credit, China remained a substantive recipient of World Bank assistance. For instance, in 2003, according to the OECD Development Assistance Committee (DAC), in terms of official development assistance (ODA), China received, in terms of a net disbursement, an amount totaling $1,324.6 million.[27]

The World Bank accomplishes its objectives through a combination of loans for physical investments and grants, including technical assistance and non-financial services. In particular, lending addresses key government priorities in infrastructure, rural poverty reduction and natural resource management. From 1981 to June 30, 2006, World Bank commitments to China total about $40 billion (net of cancellations) for two hundred and

---

[26] World Bank, http://www.worldbank.org/.

[27] OECD, Development Assistance Committee 2005. World Bank, International Development Association, How IDA Resources are allocated, http://web.worldbank.org.

seventy-four (274) projects. In 1981, the World Bank made its first loan to China, which targets the support and development of Chinese universities. From the first project in 1981, the University Development Project with a total project cost of $200 million that was approved on June 23, 1981 and closed on June 30, 1986, to ongoing and pending projects in 2006, there are still about seventy-five (75) projects under implementation, making China's portfolio one of the largest in the Bank.[28] More accurately, China is the World Bank's largest IBRD borrower and the second largest recipient of IDA credits. World Bank lending to China, admittedly, accounts for a small share of China's resource flows, about 0.6 percent of GDP in the early 1990s, but what warrants understanding is that the World Bank, in exhibiting a more pragmatic rather than theoretical approach to poverty reduction and sustainable development, does not try to achieve its objectives mostly through lending or conditionality. Rather, by exhibiting a more pragmatic approach it relies mostly on persuasion and example, such as the dual track approach to building trust through lending while promoting policy dialogue through sector work, and relying on the demonstration effects of successful project experience in introducing new technologies, management skills and policy reforms. Nonetheless, by virtue of receiving a greater pro rata share of World Bank resources than others, China is still the lending borrower and recipient.

World Bank-supported projects can be found in almost all parts of China and in many sectors of the economy, with the portfolio concentrated in transportation (31 percent), urban development (25 percent), rural development (22 percent), energy (15 percent) and human development (6 percent). Transport projects focus on connecting the poorer inner provinces to the dynamic coast; urban projects focus on urban transport, sustainable water supply, and sanitation; and energy projects on meeting the economy's growing power needs. In fiscal year June 2004, the World Bank lent China about $1.2 billion for nine projects. For example, four of these projects are transport projects: Wuhan Urban Transport, Fourth Inland Waterways, Second National Railways and Hubei Shiman Highway. In fiscal years 2005-2006, World Bank lending to China is projected to range from $2.4 billion to $2.8 billion for up to 25 projects.[29] The grand total for World Bank Supported Projects in China for the period from 1981 to 2006 is approximately $39,900.51 million. However, this approximate grand total does not include partial guarantees for the following projects: 1994 Yangzhou Thermal Power of $90 million plus $30 million; 1995 Zhejiang Power Development $100 million, plus $50 million; and 1996 Ertan II Hydroelectric $100 million, plus $50 million. Following 1999, and cut off for IDA funding, China has thus far received from 2000 until 2006, or as of June 27, 2006, approximately $7,738.30 million (World Bank reported total of $7,202.80 million, plus the four new approved projects for $535.50 million approved on June 27, 2006) from the IRBD fund for World Bank projects. Commencing in 1981 and ending fiscal year 1999, China projects received a combination of IRBD and IDA funding, or singularly IRBD or IDA funds.

China continues to be a substantive recipient of economic development assistance from international economic institutions, and other IGOs. For instance, China was a recipient of the U.N. World Food Programme (WFP) from 1979 to 2005, which has been providing food aid to China, such as 43,450 tons of Canadian wheat (value of $7.2 million) delivered to China on

---

[28] World Bank, China Fuzhou Nantai Island Peri-Urban Development Project, Project ID: P003410. World Bank, Projects and Programs, China, 2006. China An Evaluation of World Bank Assistance (World Bank, 2005).

[29] World Bank, China-World Bank in China, 2006. World Bank, China - Country Brief, China, All Projects (updated 2006).

April 7, 2005 and earmarked for poverty alleviation projects in four of the poorest western provinces. China claims to have lifted millions of people out of "extreme" poverty over the past two decades, and in 2005 promised to spend heavily on easing politically volatile poverty in the poorer western provinces. However, despite an average growth rate of about 9 percent, China is recently experiencing a growth in the number of people living in poverty. In line with China's burgeoning economic growth, it is being asked to shoulder more responsibility by IGOs, such as the WFP, by directly addressing and managing some of its own problems and becoming a bigger donor instead of a recipient of aid. The largest donors to the WFP have been the United States (more than $1 million), the European Commission (over $200 million) and Japan (approximately $136 million). Moreover, according to Chen Jian, the director of agriculture for the remote north-western province of Gansu, which was a recipient of WFP aid, after WFP aid is phrased out in 2006, China will still need assistance from other international bodies and IGOs.[30] For instance, the biggest borrowing country of the Asian Development Bank (ADB) is China, and it is from the ADB that China received aid for preparing its 11th Five Year Plan. China ranks as the largest borrower from the ADB, with a cumulative total of about $14.9 billion by the end of 2005, followed in recent years by Indonesia, Pakistan and Viet Nam.

The primary contributors to the resources of these international economic institutions, and many IGOs, that have helped developing countries, such as China, are predominantly Western developed countries. As for the source of IDA resources, according to the World Bank, the largest source of IDA resources is new contributions made by donor countries. In 2006, these new contributions account for about $18 billion of approximately $33 billion in resources that will be made available to IDA borrowers during the three-year period of IDA14. The second largest source comes from internal resources, which includes repayments from graduated IDA borrowers, current IDA borrowers, investment income and other resources, including residual resources from past replenishments. In addition, there is another source of funds, stemming from transfers from IBRD net income. In terms of donor countries, the largest contributors to IDA14 and most recent replenishment of resources as of 2006, which account for about 60 percent of donor contributions, are the United States (12.95 percent), the United Kingdom (12.14 percent), Japan (11.75), Germany (7.96 percent), France (7.20 percent), Italy (3.80 percent) and Canada (3.75 percent). As of June 30, 2005, in terms of cumulative IDA subscriptions and contributions, and total donors contributing $124,061.32 million (99.77 percent), the leading contributing countries are the United States $28,691.78 million (23.07 percent), Japan $26,500.19 million (21.31 percent), United Kingdom $9,873.97 million (7.94 percent), Italy $5,170.58 million (4.16 percent), Germany $14,212.81 million (11.43 percent), France $8,693.72 million (6.99 percent) and Canada $5,299.80 million (4.26 percent).[31]

There are many antagonists of liberalism and economic liberalism, which includes China. Despite receiving substantial assistance in loans and grants, including technical assistance and

[30] World Food Programme, Organizational and Procedural Matters, Agenda Item 12, Executive Board Annual Session, Rome, 12–16 June 2006, GENERAL WFP/EB.A/2006/12. World Food Program phases out aid China, Mar. 13, 2005, Shanghai (AP). China no longer needs food aid, Dec. 13, 2004, BBC News. World Food Progamme, Funding WFP, 2006. Asian Development Bank, Funding and Lending, 2006, http://www.adb.org.

[31] World Bank, IDA, Table 1: Contributions to the Fourteenth Replenishment, 2006. World Bank, Cumulative IDA Subscriptions and Contributions as of June 30, 2005.

non-financial services, from international economic institutions, including the BWIs, China remains a reluctant economic globalist, multilateralist or "economic liberalist." For reasons of nationalism and ideology, China enjoys a growing empowerment as a developing country, while denying the enhancing force or influence of liberalism and economic liberalism on its growing empowerment.

8.4. LIBERALISM AND EMPOWERING DEVELOPING COUNTRIES

The consequences of liberalism or economic liberalism, and its policies, goals and programs affect issues of economic globalization and its attendant consequences, such as an earlier growing divide between developed and developing countries. In September 2003, during the fifth Ministerial Conference of WTO in Cancun, there is a collapse of much-needed trade negotiations, because the Cancun conference ended without a consensus. During this ministerial conference, the BWIs, and their development policies for developing countries and economies, served as one of many causes nearly bringing a collapse to the Doha Development Agenda. Former Chairperson Luis Ernesto Derbez attributed the lack of consensus to members remaining entrenched, in particular, on the "Singapore issues," which are issues of trade and investment, trade and competition policy, trade facilitation, and transparency of government procurement. These new or "Singapore issues," which are so named because they first entered the WTO agenda at the 1996 Singapore ministerial conference, were included in 2001 in the agenda of the Doha round of trade talks only after tense negotiations between the European Union (EU), which for years has been demanding a WTO treaty on foreign investment, and India, which has been leading the resistance to an expansion of the role of the WTO. A compromise then pushed a final decision to the Cancun WTO conference. According to the Doha ministerial declaration, which has now become the subject of different legal interpretations, negotiations were supposed to take place after the Fifth Session of the Ministerial Conference based on a decision to be taken, by explicit consensus, at that session on modalities of negotiations.[32] More important, what was, and is, of greater historical importance about the "Singapore issues" is the resulting division between developed and developing countries.

There are other examples of what may be a growing divide between developed and developing countries. In 2004, the WTO General Council's (GC) decision on the Doha Agenda work program, referred to as the "July package," which was agreed upon August 1, 2004, presents another example of this growing division. The "July package" was meant to restart trade negotiations following a failed 2003 Cancun summit. Developing countries took issue with the July framework negotiations, claiming that it deviated from traditional negotiations between developing and developed countries and is effectively a ministerial declaration that is not backed by any ministerial meeting. Representatives of developing countries feared that the "July package" might create an unwanted precedent, because only forty trade ministers were present, with some one hundred absent. They also feared that the GC improperly bypassed the ministerial conference by taking action at the July GC meeting,

[32] WTO News, Summary of 14 September 2003, Day 4: Conference ends without consensus. Mr. Ouedraogo, WTO Deputy Director-General (statement), Int'l Conf. on Financing for Development, Jan. 16, 2002, WTO news. C. Rammanohar Reddy, Decision time on Singapore issues at WTO, July. 28, 2003, The Hindu.

and charging that the GC meeting supplanted the need for a ministerial meeting. The gravest fear is that the GC may become the *de facto* supreme institution for WTO decision-making. The GC's decision was also being hailed by some developing countries as another major triumph for the major superpowers, particularly the United States.[33]

The WTO regime is addressing the concerns of developing countries in a more fair, just and democratic fashion, in answer to their quest for a "new" multilateralism rather than Hobbesian multilateralism. Developing countries have routinely viewed the problem of Western taxonomies, especially multilateralism, as one of a Hobbesian multilateral approach. In this respect, a Hobbesian moment is a reflection of people realizing that "the societal foundations of their lives are not as secure as they believe them to be," thus needing a "Leviathan" to make them secure, as opposed to suffering an ontological insecurity, and "strengthen[ing] their belief in their world, their ontology." During the post-Cancun period and the 2004 July GC meeting, the G20 group of developing nations has arisen as a possible key player for developing countries in trade relations. The G20 was thought to have broken a monopoly over trade negotiations held by the United States and EU. This equilibrium between trade powers in WTO trade round negotiations may be only temporary, however, because many developing countries are not included in the G20. Power politics and the marginalization of developing countries, admittedly, remains an ongoing concern of the WTO and Doha Development Agenda, though developing countries are witnessing increasing empowerment in the WTO regime. They are faring much better against a perceived imbalance of bargaining powers in WTO trade round negotiations, which have been, historically, perceived by developing countries as being dominated by the United States and the EU.[34]

The growing strength of developing countries and LDCs also demonstrate how far these countries have progressed from the earlier Singapore issues to the December 2005 WTO Hong Kong Ministerial Meeting. The WTO 2006 Annual Report observes, "Success in the marketplace has been well reflected in the strong and growing roles of developing countries not only in the Doha negotiations but in all facets of WTO activity... The growing role of developing countries in the WTO dispute settlement process is another indication of how developing countries are participating in the global system." According to Director General Pascal Lamy, the formation of powerful negotiating groups such as the G-90, G-33 and G-20 demonstrate that the WTO "is an organization in which all members can not only state their case, but can achieve meaningful objectives on their path towards development."[35]

Nonetheless, several factors have made the Doha Development agenda difficult to implement. As observed by U.S. Trade Representative Susan Schwab there would be no winners if the Doha Round of trade talks eventually collapsed. In July 2006, the Doha trade round talks were suspended after a dispute between the EU and United States over farm tariffs and subsidies, as the seven developed and industrialized countries, or the G7, failed to reach a consensus at the talks. Some argue the problem is its increasingly growing complexity, others argue that the agenda is too full. The Doha Development agenda is

---

[33] WTO General Council, Doha Work Programme: Decision Adopted by the General Council on 1 August 2004, WTO Doc. WT/L579 (Aug. 2, 2004). World Trade Organization, Day 5: Conference Ends Without Consensus. Walden Bello & Aileen Kwa, WTO: G 20 Leaders Succumb to Divide-and-Rule Tactics: The Story behind Washington's Triumph in Geneva, Aug. 10, 2004, Focus on the Global South.

[34] M. Ulric Killion, China's Foreign Currency Regime: The Kagan Thesis and Legalification of the WTO Agreement, 14 Minn. J. Global Trade 43 (winter 2004). Mike Vedby Rasmussen, '9-11': Globilisation, Security and World Order 15, Dansk Udenrigspolitisk Instit., Working Paper 2002/2.

[35] Annual Report 2006, World Trade Organization (2006).

focusing on opening markets for trade in services and trade facilitation, which are remnants of the "Singapore issues." However, it is especially the growing difficulty enhanced by the diversity of contracting parties, or negotiating parties. As earlier mentioned, developing countries and LDCs have become more active participants in these negotiations. Following the Uruguay round, the range of nations participating broadened, especially with the G20 that includes such powers as Brazil, China, India and South Africa. The latter nations are seeking to secure the interests of developing countries. There is also the G90 drawing together poorer developing countries and the G10, emphasizing a defense interest in agriculture. In addition, there are specific interest groups, such as Friends of Fish or Very Close Friends of Services.[36]

For developing countries, the primary concerns and consequences of multilateral trade have focused on trade in agriculture and textiles. It is a consequence dating back to the WTO Multi-fibre Agreement (MFA) ending and the Uruguay trade round (1986-1994). In 1986, the launch of the Uruguay Round of trade negotiations also symbolized the start of greater participation and effectiveness of developing countries in trade negotiations. During the Uruguay round, development strategies of developing economies began to shift toward an emphasis on exports. The major products and export concerns of these developing economies were agriculture and textiles, which were now being brought into the multilateral trade agenda. As for the developed countries, as a *quip quo pro*, they wanted more concessions on market access and trade rules, in exchange for concessions in agriculture and textiles. The Uruguay trade round has been characterized as simply a compromise of developing countries that accepted the Agreement on Trade-Related Aspects of Intellectual Property Rights (TRIPs, covering intellectual property) and some tariffs reductions of their own tariffs, in exchange for trade reforms in agriculture and textiles, especially the MFA. Adding to this complexity at Uruguay were growing divisions between developing countries on issues of both agriculture and textiles.[37] However, a sufficient identity of common interest allowed these developing countries to work together as a block. The display of this joint purpose at Uruguay may have resulted in their display of ability to block negotiations at the subsequently convened 1999 Seattle WTO ministerial meeting. However, the Uruguay round did lead to further liberalization in trade, especially by the reintegration of textiles and clothing into the multilateral world trading system.

There is also the unity and common cause of developing countries exhibited at the 2005 Hong Kong Ministry. This ministry demonstrated the extent to which the G20 gathering seeks to find common ground with the G90, in promoting the interest of developing countries. During the Hong Kong Ministerial Meeting, developing countries especially made substantial progress in agriculture. In terms of agriculture, the report of the negotiating chair, Crawford Falconer, referred to genuine and material progress having been made. In terms of export competition, the text of the agreement reads, "We agree to ensure the parallel elimination of all forms of export subsidies and disciplines on all export measures with equivalent effect to

[36] Top US trade envoy says no winners if global trade talks collapse, Aug. 29, 2006, Xinhua. Ken Haydon, After the WTO Hong Kong Ministerial Meeting: What is at Stake?, OECD Trade Policy Working Paper No. 27, OECD 2006.

[37] From Uruguay Round to Doha Developing Countries' Experiences with Trade Negotiations, CUTS-ARC Policy Brief, no.4/2002, at 1-2. WTO, Agreement on Trade-Related Aspects of Intellectual Property Rights (TRIPs), Annex 1C. H. E. Sok Siphana (speech), Globalization and Cambodia: History and Perceptible Trends, Globalization Conference: Cambodiana, June 27-28, 2001, http://www.moc.gov.kh/speeches/sok_siphana/globalization-and-cambodia.htm. Bernard M. Hoeman & Michel M. Kostecki, The Political Economy of the World Trading System, 105 (Oxford UP, 2001).

be completed by the end of 2013." For developing countries and LDCs, the Hong Kong Ministerial resulted in a greater degree of empowerment, greater sense of a democratic process, a perceived strengthened commitment to the development dimension of the Doha trade negotiation round and need for aid for trade."[38]

8.5. SINICIZING AND LOCALIZING LIBERALISM

In May 2006, Chinese Premier Wen Jiabao announced that UN reforms in the next stage should give priority to development goals for developing nations, and that UN reforms have made positive progress. Premier Wen Jiabao said China would firmly fulfill its commitment to the MDGs and continue its efforts to eliminate poverty. Wen Jiabao also stated that China would actively participate in the international effort to reduce world policy, and help more developing countries erase poverty and pursue economic development. Former UN Secretary-General Kofi Annan spoke highly of China's support for the MDGs and having provided long-term assistance for some African countries.

There are many examples of China's assistance, support and foreign aid, for some African countries. In May 2006, Nigerian Finance Minister Ngozi Okonjo-Iwuala announced that China would assist in the rehabilitation of the Nigeria railway system by an infrastructure investment or grant for $1 billion. Finance Minister Okonjo-Iwuala described the rehabilitation of the rail system as one of the infrastructure programs being embarked in line with an overall program of employment generation and poverty alleviation.[39] On February 2, 2005, Qi Jianwei, assistant inspector of the Department of Western Asian and African Affairs (MOFCOM), explained China's new pledge of tariff exemptions, commencing on January 1, 2005, for certain commodities from LDCs in Africa.[40] According to the MOFCOM, these tariff exemptions are intended to help least developed African countries promote their economic development. China's duty-free policy is designed to further expand Sino-African import and export trade, development investment cooperation, and expand bilateral cooperation in agriculture, infrastructure, and the development of natural resources and human resources. The duty-free policy covers 190 different types of favored commodities, which are covered by a policy formulated and based on commodities from 262 tax items that are actually imported from 29 LDCs in Africa. The duty-free policy (or zero tariffs) is for least-developed African countries that have established diplomatic relations with China. In February 2007, subsequent to a Beijing-hosted November 2006 China-Africa summit, and other high level contacts with African countries during the past four years, Hu Jintao visited eight African nations. All of this demonstrates that China with nearly $8 billion in

---

[38] Hong Kong 6th Ministerial, WT/MIN(05)/DEC, 22 December 2005, Doha Work Programme, Ministerial Declaration, Adopted on 18 December 2005. Ken Heydon, After the WTO Hong Kong Ministerial Meeting: What is at stake?, OECD Trade Policy Working Paper No. 27 (2006). Liu Weiling & Dan Yan, Last-minute deal breathes new life into trade talks, December 19, 2005, China Daily. Liu Weiling & Dan Yan, China to play bigger role in talks, Dec. 14, 2005, China Daily. Teddy Ng, Bo: WTO consensus worth celebrating, Dec. 20, 2005, China Daily. WTO, Understanding the WTO: The Organization, Least Developed Countries, http://www.wto.org/english/thewto_e/whatis_e/tif_e/org7_e.htm.

[39] UN reform should focus on development, Chinese premier, May 23, 2006, Xinhua. China offers 1 billion dollars for Nigeria's railway rehabilitation, Xinhua News, May 22, 2006. China offers tariff exemption for certain African commodities, February 3, 2005, People's Daily. Losing Libya, China Reform Monitor No. 614, Jan. 24, 2006. A New Attack against Taiwan, China Reform Monitor No. 602, Sept. 21, 2005.

investments already in place in resource-rich and governance-poor countries in the less-developed world, and Hu pledging billions more by 2010, intends to use its burgeoning economic growth in pursuance of geopolitical posturing or foreign policy goals.

In September 2005, China President Hu Jintao used his speech before the UN General Assembly to offer tariff-tree trade, debt relief and cheap loans to developing countries, and zero tariff treatment to certain products from LDCs that reject Taiwan's independence. China aid is routinely contingent on acceptance of the "one-China" policy and other geopolitical concerns, while also producing expected results, such as the cases of Libya and Senegal changing their diplomatic allegiance from Taipei to Beijing. As recent as August 2006, the African country of Chad severed its diplomatic relations with Taiwan, and switched its recognition and open official ties to Beijing. On August 6, 2006, Chinese Foreign Minister Li Zhaoxing and his Chadian counterpart Ahmad Allam-mi signed a joint communiqué to resume diplomatic ties between the two countries. In 1972, China and Chad established formal diplomatic links, which were severed in 1997, when Chad resumed diplomatic ties with Taiwan. Following Taiwan's 1971 expulsion from the United Nations, successive Taiwanese regimes have spent millions of dollars in economic aid to persuade countries, mostly in Africa and Latin America, to support its battle against Beijing for international recognition. As Beijing's economic influence grows, Taiwan is increasingly on the losing side of this battle for international recognition. As of August 2006, Chad is the seventh country to switch recognition to Beijing since Taiwanese leader Chen Shui-bian took office in 2000. In switching diplomatic allegiance, Chad follows the countries of Senegal, Libya, Macedonia, Commonwealth of Dominica, Vanuatu and Grenada. Only twenty-five (25) countries, which are countries in Africa, Latin America and the Pacific region, now recognize Taiwan. As of August 2006, after Chad resumed diplomatic ties with China, Chad became the 169th country that has diplomatic ties with Mainland China.[41]

Sub-Saharan Africa is fast becoming an investment destination. The World Bank Private Sector Development group finds that the continent of Africa attracted about $12 billion of FDI in 2004, constituting about 3 percent of the global total, with investment flows rising in 40 of the 53 African countries in the region. As of 2006, portfolio investments stand at about $3 billion, while continuing to rise.[42] China is also positioning itself to be a world player in the potential economic growth of Africa. The May 2006 public announcements of Chinese Premier Wen Jiabao regarding China's role in reducing world policy and supporting the MDGs, manifest, though implicitly, China's geopolitical posturing regarding Western economic liberalism. China's approach to world poverty reduction and support of the MDGs does present a development irony. There is also the issue of whether China's geopolitical posturing regarding Western economic liberalism, constitutes its attempt to Sinicize or localize Western economic liberalism and its international economic institutions and policies.

Direct benefits to China of economic liberalism are obvious, because China continues to benefit from Western economic liberalism, as seen in the recent case of the World Bank's New CPS for China. For fiscal years 2005-2006, World Bank lending to China is expected to

[40] Jacques de Lisle, Into Africa: China's Quest for Resources and Influence, E-notes, Feb. 2007, FPRI.

[41] Chad cuts diplomatic ties with Taiwan, Aug. 6, 2006, China Daily. China, Chad resume diplomatic ties, Aug. 6, 2006, Xinhua.

[42] World Bank, News & Broadcast, Seeing Africa as an Investment Destination, June 28, 2006.

range from $2.4 billion to $2.8 billion for up to 25 projects.[43] For this reason and others, there is an irony in China's approach to world poverty reduction and support of the MDGs, as evidenced by Wen Jiabo's May 2006 public announcement. China is a developing and non-market economy transitioning to a socialist market economy, and has the largest country portfolio of the World Bank. The irony also sets in with former UN Secretary-General Annan praising China for providing long-term assistance, in the form of infrastructure investments and grants, for some African countries. Whether China is motivated by geopolitical posturing, foreign policy (or international relations) concerns, or by genuine humanitarianism, the scenario of China, as a developing country and largest recipient of World Bank infrastructure investments, and assisting some African countries through infrastructure investments and grants, presents a certain irony. One reasonably suspects that China's primary motivation for extending assistance to African countries is more so geopolitical posturing or foreign policy strategy, rather than humanitarian assistance. The latter is a logical conclusion because of China's unique situation of being a developing country, being the largest recipient of World Bank infrastructure investments, tremendous domestic crises confronting China and other reasons. Even assuming *arguendo*, humanitarianism as a motivation, it is a secondary motivation, leaving us with a primary motivation such as geopolitical posturing or foreign policy strategy, an irony deserving the attention of developed and developing countries.

The tremendous domestic crises buttress geopolitical posturing or foreign policy strategy as primary motivation, especially the state of poverty in the mainland. In China, the number of people living in "extreme" poverty was reduced from 40 percent in 1981 to 21 percent in 2001, and since 1982, China's GDP has risen by 500 percent. While the 600 million Chinese living in "extreme" poverty in 1981 dropped to 200 million, both usage of the concept of "extreme" poverty, and optimism of the IMF and World Bank regarding poverty reduction, lends to a false impression of the state of poverty. This is especially true when half of China's 1.3 billion population may fit in the category of, simply, living in poverty, rather than "extreme" poverty. The number of people living on a dollar per day fell by 170 million, the adult illiteracy rate fell by more than one-half, "from 37% in 1978 to less than 5% in 2002," and "the infant mortality rate fell from 41 per 1,000 live births in 1978 to 30 in 2002." There has been progress in improving the dynamism of rural and urban economies, and substantial improvements in human development indicators, such as reduced illiteracy rates, decreased infant mortality rates, increased live birth rates and other improvements. However, the state of poverty is persistent. In 2003, the Chinese average per capita disposable income in urban areas was 8,472 yuan ($1,033) a year, while for farmers it was only 2,622 yuan ($319) a year. At the other end of the social strata, because there is no middle class in China, are the 5.67% that have an annual income of more than 200,000 yuan ($24,390), or the 2.14% with an average annual income of more than 500,000 yuan ($60,975).[44]

According to poverty guidelines of the World Bank, in terms of PPP and one USD equaling 3-5 RMB (yuan) and not 8.2 RMB (yuan), one USD per day is the minimum income

---

[43] World Bank, World Bank in China, Economic Achievements and Current Challenges, (Updated March 2005), http://www.worldbank.org.cn/English/Overview/overview_brief.htm#L1_0.

[44] Guo Kesha, China's Industrial Development Strategy and Policy Options in the New Era, 15-17 Social Sciences in China (Zhongguo shehui kexue) (Aug. 2004). Income gap between the poor and other groups widens, May 19, 2005, People's Daily. Pepe Escobar, The Great Wall of shopping, Jan 14, 2005, Asian Times. Fu Jing, Closing the gap between haves and have-nots, Dec. 17-18, 2005. Angang Hu & Yizhi Xiong, The Strategy of Knowledge-based Development: China's Long-run Future, 24-25, Social Sciences in China (Zhongguo shehui kexue) (winter 2003).

at the end of 1998, and there were 147 million poor rural persons, and in 2000, there were still 108 million poor rural persons. The problem is a persistently widening urban-rural gap in terms of income and social welfare. In 2000, for those living in urban areas, the disposable per capita income is 6,280 yuan, a gap that widened from 2.65: 1 in 1999 to 28.8: 1 in 2000, while further widening in 2003 to 3.23: 1. An additional problem is a population that peaks at 1.3 billion in January 2005 and is continuing to grow, while China's agriculture economy now employs about 50% of the labor force, which is the lowest average income group, comprising about 630 million persons or half of China's population. A population at the beginning of the Qin Dynasty that was only 100 million, and at the end of the Qing Dynasty grew to about 450 million, took only 100 years to peak at 1.3 billion. There are also the ongoing problems directly related to the prioritization of uncontrolled and uneven economic growth, such as growing income inequality, economically lagging western and northeast regions, unsustainable resource exploitation and other issues related to growing regional and global economic integration. The problem of uneven development and growth directly relates to both the problem of reducing poverty and assistance from the World Bank, other international economic institutions and BWIs, in the form of infrastructure investments. A World Bank report notes, "Market liberalization and other reforms associated with China's accession to the World Trade Organization (WTO) are delivering gains worth more than $40 billion a year to China's economy, and adding about $75 billion a year to real incomes worldwide." The World Bank report recommends that China make policy adjustments to balance the uneven distribution of benefits of these gains between the country's rural and urban regions.[45]

In the interim, the announced goals of Hu Jintao and Wen Jiabao to build a *xiaokang* society and harmonious socialist society, by the year 2020, is relegated to mere rhetoric, a *kong hua* (a slogan), old tricks in new conditions, or perhaps even the worst consequence of the progression in Chinese Marxism between a market socialist society and world communism. Adding irony to the state of poverty in China and political rhetoric of building a *xiaokang* society and harmonious socialist society, China's polity publicly and typically praises its ongoing economic growth. According to a May 2006 *Xinhua* news article, the Chinese economy grew by 10.3 percent in the first quarter, which is a tenth of a percentage point higher that earlier reported by the National Bureau of Statistics (NBS). The NBS reports that China's GDP in the first three months reached 4.339 trillion yuan ($542 billion), 7.7 billion yuan more than data released last month showed. The article further reports, "Of the total, primary industries scored 324.2 billion yuan in value added, 4.2 billion yuan more than the earlier data with year-on-year growth dropping by 0.1 percentage point to 4.5 percent. Secondary industries reaped 2.1614 trillion yuan, 0.1 billion yuan less previously reported with the growth unchanged at 12.5 percent; while tertiary industries reported 1.8534 trillion yuan in value added, 3.6 billion yuan more than earlier data revealed with the growth rate increasing by 0.2 percentage points to 8.9 percent."[46]

---

[45] China Statistical Yearbook, Annual Report of Chinese Rural Economic Development-Economic Green Book of 1997. Cai He, Social Situation of the Unemployed: A Noticeable Problem, Zhongguo dangzheng ganbu luntan, No. 5 (2002). Fu Jing, Measures urged to close income gap, Dec. 22, 2006. Bian Yi, Cheap labour cannot last, Dec. 8, 2005, China Daily. Pan Wei, Why are Chinese Farmers so poor?, Social Sciences in China (Zhongguo shehui kexue), 148-156 (autumn 2005). World Bank Study, Accession to WTO Delivers $40 Billion a Year to China's Economy but Gains Unevenly Shared, World Bank: News and Events, Feb. 21, 2005.

[46] China's GDP growth a tenth higher than preliminary statistics showed, May 24, 2006, Xinhua.

As regards tremendous domestic crises confronting China, especially the state of poverty, China essentially elected to make a value-laden choice to lend economic assistance to other developing countries rather than fully commit to pulling nearly half of its 1.3 billion population out of poverty. Whether a choice made consciously or unconsciously, implicitly or explicitly, by China, it is nonetheless a choice. The issue of choice only becomes confusing when seeking to discern, assuming discernability, simple poverty, from "extreme" poverty. In lending development assistance to developing countries, such as some developing African countries, the driving force is obviously the primary motivation of geopolitical posturing or foreign policy strategy.

In terms of geopolitical posturing or foreign policy strategy, China's motivation to lend assistance to developing African countries is driven and engaged, in part, through the mechanism of the CCP's "one-China policy." As recent as August 2006, China president Hu Jintao praised the west coastal African country of Benin for adhering to the "one-China policy," and announced that China "will increase mutually-beneficial cooperation with Benin in such fields as agriculture, infrastructure projects, telecommunications and energy." Since 1972, China has provided $200 million worth of aid to Benin, human resource training programs, helped to develop fisheries, agriculture and industry, and helped Benin to improve its infrastructure. China routinely makes its bilateral economic partnerships and bilateral diplomatic partnerships contingent on the acceptance of the ''one-China policy'' principle vis-à-vis Taiwan. As previously mentioned, at the close of 2005, Taiwan now has diplomatic ties with only 25 states, which are mostly Latin American and African nations. It is a trend turning in China's favor, such as the cases of Libya and Senegal. While Libya earlier agreed to extend diplomatic recognition to Taipei, according to a January 2006 report of Taiwan's official Central News Agency (CAN), China Foreign Minister Li Zhaoxing during a visit to Tripoli received different signals, as Li was given assurances by Libyan Foreign Minister Mohammed Abdel-Rahman Shalgam that Libya recognizes only one China. In October 2005, the African nation of Senegal also switched its diplomatic allegiance from Taipei to Beijing.[47]

In the international community, China appears adamant about other countries respecting its "one-China policy," but appearances may not be all that they seem. The mechanism of the CCP's "one-China policy" does not necessarily mean that it is the sole force behind the primary motivation of geopolitical posturing, because geopolitical posturing is also driven by a growing dependence on overseas resources and energy supplies, especially oil and natural gas, which also shapes military policy and ongoing military modernization.[48] For instance, in terms of a growing engagement with Africa, more than 30 percent of China's oil imports are from African states. China is also the largest consumer of copper and, since 2002, China-Africa trade has quadrupled. An opposition against Western normative economic liberalism drives China's mechanism of the "one-China policy" and fear of a dominance by Western developed countries and economies. Moreover, and most disconcerting, is that China is constantly lodging a complaint in the international community regarding the so-called "China threat," while formulating policy and goals pursuant to a perceived "Western threat." What is even more disconcerting is that an aversion to the dominance of Western neo-liberalism,

---

[47] Chinese president pledges to enhance cooperation with Benin, Aug. 29, 2006, Xinhua. Losing Libya, China Reform Monitor No. 614, Jan. 24, 2006. A New attack Against Taiwan, Id.

[48] 2005 U.S. Dept. of Defense Report, Id. Jeffrey A. Bader & Flynt L. Leverett, Oil, the Middle East and the Middle Kingdom, Aug. 16, 2005, Financial Times. China's Expanding Role in Africa: Implications for the United States, Center for Strategic and International Studies, (transcript: FNS), Feb. 8, 2007.

ultimately, worsens the crisis of poverty in China, while also rendering political rhetoric or ideology of building a better or "*xiaokang* (well-off) society in an all-round way" meaningless.

China in other regions of the world, including the Asian region, opposes neo-liberalism in the context of politics or geopolitics and economics or international economics. For instance, sales of Chinese military vehicles and weapons to some developing countries have aggravated conflicts, abetted violence and repressive rule. Under the veil of secrecy, China does not disclose assistance to regimes embroiled in internal conflicts and often shunned by the West. China has reportedly shipped hundreds of military trucks to Sudan and the Myanmar military, while also shipping rifles and grenades to Nepal's security forces. In Sudan, according to an August 2005 UN investigation, "China shipped more than 200 military trucks to Sudan, where large-scale violence in the Darfur region has claimed nearly 200,000 lives and forced more than 2 million people from their homes since 2003."

For China, the sale of illicit arms is a growing international business. As of 2006, arms sales are estimated to be in excess of $1 billion a year. However, "China rarely confirms sales of weapons and military equipment abroad, a secrecy that is compounding U.S. concerns about how Beijing is using its rapidly rising economic and diplomatic power abroad." In Myanmar (formerly Burma), China is supplying equipments to Myanmar's military junta, which has been involved in the "torture, killing and forced eviction of hundreds of thousands of civilians." According to reports from inside Myanmar, in April 2006, "Myanmar troops uprooted more than 11,000 ethnic minority civilians, often employing torture, killings and the burning of villages." In early 2006, China exported nearly 25,000 Chinese-made rifles and 18,000 grenades to Nepal's security forces. At the time, Nepal security forces were fighting thousands of anti-monarchy demonstrators with tear gas, rubber bullets and live ammunition. There is also a growing illicit trade in Chinese-made pistols in Australia, Malaysia, Thailand and South Africa. Amnesty International UK Director Kate Allen said, "In a bid to continue economic expansion and grab a slice of the lucrative global weapons market, China has shipped weapons into conflict zones and to countries that torture and repress their people. China's arms exports policy is reckless and dangerous, paying no heed to human rights. It [China] is the only major arms exporter that has not signed up to agreements preventing arms exports to human rights abusers. China's arms exports, estimated to be in excess of $1 billion a year, often involve the exchange of weapons for raw materials to fuel the country's rapid economic growth. But it is a trade shrouded in secrecy: Beijing does not publish any information about arms transfers abroad and hasn't submitted any data to the UN Register on Conventional Arms in the last eight years." In August 2006, Britain's House of Commons, Foreign Affairs Committee, also published a report condemning China for its ties to rogue regimes, tacit consent for corruption and unscrupulous business tactics. In the interim, former UN Secretary-General Annan hails China for outstanding achievement in addressing global challenges and securing world peace and development.[49]

The FY2000 National Defense Authorization Act (Section 1202) directs the U.S. Secretary of Defense to submit a report, "on the current and future military strategy of the People's Republic of China." Specifically, "The report shall address the current and probable

---

[49] Joshua Eisenman & Devin Stewart, China's New Rich and Global Responsibility, Sept. 29, 2006. Gillian Wong, Activists say Chinese arms fuel conflicts, June 11, 2006, AP. China highlights UN's "irreplaceable" role, May 20, 2006, Xinhua.

future course of military-technological development on the People's Liberation Army and the tenets and probable development of Chinese grand strategy, security strategy, and military strategy, and of the military organizations and operational concepts, through the next 20 years." The 2006 report of the U.S. Department of Defense addresses: "(1) China's grand strategy, security strategy, and military strategy; (2) developments in China's military doctrine and force structure, to include developments in advanced technologies which would enhance China's military capabilities; and, (3) the security situation in the Taiwan Strait."[50] Beijing is highly critical of the 2006 Department of Defense Report, and earlier reports submitted annually from 2000 to 2005. The 2006 report found that China's defense expenditures appear to be much higher than its government has acknowledged, coupled with a lack of transparency that understandably troubles its neighbors. According to the *China Daily*, while China's foreign ministry has yet to respond to the 2006 report, it contends that China's military spending of less than $40 billion in 2005 is only one-10th that of the U.S., and that Chinese officials dismiss U.S. warnings about its modernization, because Chinese military build-up serves both national security needs and need to protect its territory.

The 2006 Department of Defense Report bears special relevancy concerning the primary motivation of geopolitical posturing or foreign policy strategy. The 2006 Department of Defense Report, at relevant part, reads, "China's foreign policy is now global. It engages in key issues in almost all international security and economic institutions, including the UN and the WTO. Its decision to deploy peacekeepers to several African countries and to Haiti and its growing economic ties in Latin America reflect this new global role. Of more concern are China's economic and political links with states such as Iran, Sudan, Burma, Zimbabwe, Cuba, and Venezuela, which are objects of international efforts to influence in the direction of nuclear non-proliferation, political reform, stability, and/or human rights. China also continues to use its growing leverage to restrict Taiwan's international roles and convince Taiwan's remaining 25 diplomatic partners to shift diplomatic recognition to Beijing." The 2006 Report also observed that while China appears as an emerging power and willing to take on greater regional and international responsibilities, it actually fails to do so. Further, the 2006 Report reads, "On the other hand, China continues to dispute sovereignty claims in the South and East China Seas and is preparing for potential conflict over Taiwan. Chinese companies continue to play a negative role in the proliferation of advanced military capabilities, and continue to supply countries such as Iran with critical military technologies. Beijing has refused to join the Proliferation Security Initiative. China has not fully leveraged its close ties with Pyongyang to stem North Korean nuclear ambitions, and continues to maintain or strengthen political, economic, and military ties with Iran, Sudan, Burma, Zimbabwe, Cuba, and Venezuela, undercutting international efforts to influence those states."

Beijing strongly resents and disagrees with the 2006 Department of Defense Report. China Foreign Ministry spokesman Liu Jianchao characterizes the 2006 Report as an exaggeration of China's military strength and expenditures, which intends to spread the "China threat" theory. Liu describes China as a peace-loving country serving as an important force in promoting peace in the Asia Pacific and the world at large. Liu also said Taiwan is an inalienable part of China and urges the United States to stop selling weapons to Taiwan and sending the wrong signals to Taiwan secessionist forces. Ruan Zongze, of the China Institute

---

[50] Annual Report to Congress: Military Power of the People's Republic of China 2006, U.S. Dept. of Defense, May 23, 2006. US says surprised by China's rapid arms modernization, May 24, 2006, China Daily.

of International Studies, claims that the figures are incorrect, but offers no criticism of the lack of China's progress in improving military transparency. Ruan also criticizes the 2006 Report for conjuring up the "mainland threat" for purpose of pressuring Taipei to buy more weapons from the United States.[51] Chinese critics of the 2006 Report routinely fail to mention that China's arms exports, estimated to be in excess of $1 billion a year, often involve the exchange of weapons for raw materials to fuel the country's rapid economic growth. They also routinely fail to mention illicit sales of Chinese military vehicles and weapons to some developing countries have aggravated conflicts, abetted violence and repressive rule, in developing countries such as Sudan, Nepal and Myanmar (formerly Burma).

However, China's geopolitical strategies and pursuance of policies, goals and programs replicating the policies, goals and programs of economic liberalism and its international economic institutions, including the BWIs, have many drawbacks. Notwithstanding paradox of China's foreign aid policy, there are the difficult issues stemming from foreign aid delivery and the Dutch Disease phenomenon.

8.6. Dutch Disease, Foreign Aid and Soft Power

The issue of Chinese foreign aid, especially to Third World countries and LDCs, presents issues of the Dutch Disease phenomenon, a concept that made its first appearance in *The Economist* (1977). In 1959, the Netherlands discover a large reservoir of natural gas. By the year 1976, the newly discovered reservoir produced country revenues of about $2 billion and about $3.5 billion of savings in imports. However, in the late 1970s, the country witnessed about a 15 percent drop in gross corporate investments. Adding to this problem was a 16 percent drop in employment in the manufacturing sector; rise in total unemployment, though slight, from 1.1 percent to 5.1 percent; and a fall in the share of profits in national income from 16.8 percent in the 1960s to only 3.5 percent in the early 1970s. Discovery of this new reservoir of natural gas presents issues of the first oil crisis that was having a devastating effect on most Western developed economies, and why the Netherlands and its new reservoir of natural gas fares worst than others during this period. It was a process of deindustrialization of an existing manufacturing base attributable to an upward pressure (the newly discovered energy or natural gas) on both the Guilder and wage rate. One definition of Dutch Disease reads, "The deindustrialization of a nation's economy that occurs when the discovery of a natural resource raises the value of that nation's currency, making manufactured goods less competitive with other nations, increasing imports and decreasing exports."[52] Other sources such as W. M. Corden define Dutch Disease as, "the adverse effects on Dutch manufacturing of the natural gas discoveries of the nineteen sixties, essentially through the subsequent appreciation of the Dutch real exchange rate." Another source describes Dutch Disease as occurring, "when countries get large capital inflows, they tend to experience Dutch Disease effects to varying degrees because some sectors and industries tend to have their profitability increase as well as spending effects raise prices for their outputs,

[51] Pentagon paper shows 'Cold-War mentality,' May 25, 2006, China Daily.

[52] W. M. Corden, Booming Sector and Dutch Disease Economics: Survey and Consolidation, Vol. 36, No. 3, Oxford Economic Papers, 359-380 (Nov. 1984). The Economist, 82-83, Nov. 26, 1977. Sisira Jayasuriya, Paul Steele & Dushni Weerakoon, Aid, Cost Inflation and 'Dutch Disease': Effects and Implications, ADB Discussion Paper No. 39 (Nov. 10, 2004).

while others experience only the resulting cost increases." The concept of the Dutch Disease has also become widely used to describe those situations where a country experiences a good economic fortune, which later proves to have resulted in a net detrimental effect.

The primary concern of Dutch Disease theorists is developing models for responses, or potential compensation measures, to this phenomenom, whether or not it proves to be a temporary phenomenon. Many, generally, recognize Third World economics as presenting greater potential for the ill effects of Dutch Disease, because many developing countries and, especially, LDCs, historically, demonstrate a greater dependence on limited ranges of primary products. Because of a very limited range of primary products, product prices have proclivity to be highly volatile, thus, subject to large trade shocks. In the public discourse concerning Dutch Disease and economies of these volatile LDCs, numerous papers have addressed the issue of potential compensation measures, in response to large shifts in prices (or shocks to an economy). For instance, the richest countries have promised to double aid to the poorest countries, and most of these comprise African countries. However, there are many that deem this foreign aid as shocking, too much and even ineffective for various reasons.

Andrew Mwenda, a Uganda writer and radio host, perceives this aid to be, simply, too much, because, "Throwing money at African dictators cannot be a solution to ending poverty."[53] Mwenda contends that foreign aid is stalling the development of democracy in Africa, with leaders focusing on responding to donors rather than their own citizens. Many agree with this assessment of the consequence of foreign aid, such as George Ayittey, an economist, whom argues, "If Africa kept what it loses to corruption, weapons spending and capital flight and grew more for itself rather than importing food, the savings would equal what it gets in foreign aid." For Ayittey, when comparing the plight of African countries to Eastern Europe under communist rule, the primary problem is lack of democracy and good government (or governance) rather than simply lack of resources. Ayittey opines, "When the West was dealing with Eastern Europe, it didn't hand over money to communist governments. They funded groups like (Poland's) Solidarity. Let's find the African Solidarities and fund them." For these reasons, Ayittey proposes a development model focused on "supporting a free press, independent central banks, judiciaries and election commissions, and efficient and fair police and civil services." In theory, he does not deem African countries in need of aid, but since aid cannot be stopped, he suggests that African countries should be helped in a smart way. Former World Bank president Paul Wolfowitz expressed the same concerns at the 2007 International Conference on Improving Governance and Fighting Corruption. For the World Bank group, corruption and governance, though moral issues embracing a moral dimension, directly address development and poverty reduction issues. According to Paul Wolfowitz, "Poor governance, corruption or as my predecessor once said, 'A cancer on the development process and a cancer that is unfortunately the cause of a good deal of the poverty that we have seen and particularly in Africa.' Improvement in governance is the reason why we are seeing things begin to change." Tony Blair, the British Prime Minister, and his assembly of the international board, the Commission for Africa, share a similar viewpoint. In 2005, a report of the Commission for Africa acknowledges that Africa's poverty continues to worsen after decades of foreign aid

[53] Donna Bryson, Some question whether African aid helps, Jul. 10, 2006, AP. Paul Wolfowitz (speech), International Conference on Improving Governance and Fighting Corruption, Brussels, Mar. 14, 2007, WTO news.

and calls for aid that is more effective in the future, while also pressing African governments to fight corruption and engender greater responsiveness to its citizens.

The United States, as a leading donor of foreign aid, including food aid, is also struggling with the issues of effective and efficient delivery of foreign aid. In American politics, the debate concerning foreign aid has become a permanent fixture. For instance, during the post-East Asian financial crisis, there was the need for additional funding to bail out struggling East Asian economies. The late 1990s was a period of contrasting voices in the halls of the U.S. Congress, which reflected both partisan viewpoints and non-partisan viewpoints. The latter non-partisan viewpoints reflected that the issue of donor funding cut cross often-entrenched party lines, or Republicans versus Democrats. For instance, after suffering from a 1997 failure to gain Congressional approval for fast-track trade negotiating authority for the White House, a seemingly collective business community and the administration of then President Clinton (Clinton Administration, 1993-2001) rallied their efforts, instead, to focus on increasing fast-track funding for the IMF.[54] The Clinton Administration sought an $18 billion boost in the U.S. contribution for the IMF, as a means of helping to bail out troubled Asian economies, such as South Korea, Indonesia, Thailand and others. In 1997, the debate in the U.S. Congress concerning the fast-track funding of the IMF was, in part, sparked by a report in the *Financial Times* that the IMF is requesting $160 billion in new capital from member countries, a larger increase from that earlier agreed upon. According to Jim Saxton (R-NJ), then Chairmen of the Joint Economic Committee (JEC), "Such a heavy reliance on government money can pose significant risks to taxpayers, insulate IMF decision-making from market evaluation, and increase potential moral hazard problems. The large and growing risk to U.S. taxpayers requires a consideration of alternative funding sources. In addition, I do not believe that a huge IMF quota increase will be well received by the U.S. Congress." Those opposing fast-track funding, especially an $18 billion boost for the IMF, generally, perceived an opportunity to block or heavily condition funding for the IMF, World Bank and other international bodies. In the pre-East Asian financial crisis, the IMF relied on contributions from member nations and a loan facility called the General Arrangement to Borrow (GAB) to finance its assistance and bailouts. The IMF is, generally, recognized as the lender of last resort for countries, and also, not unlike the World Bank and other economic institutions, uses economic packages known as structural adjustment programs (SAPs), as in the case of over 90 countries, from Latin America, South Asia, to Africa countries. Given that the conditions for bailout loans for East Asian countries would resemble standard SAPs, many opposing the fast-track funding perceived a window of opportunity, vis à vis loan conditionality, to effectively address social welfare issues, such as labor rights, labor unions, minimum wage laws and other issues.

This does not mean that United States has ever failed to fund these key economic institutions. It is obvious that the United States was, and continues to be, the largest donor to the IMF, World Bank and other international bodies. In terms of the immediate post-East Asian financial crisis, the U.S. Congress, by House vote (a 243-180 vote) on September 25,

[54] William H. Miller, Uphill Battle for IMF funding, Industry Week, Mar. 1998. Press Advisory, U.S. Congress, Jim Saxton (R-NJ), Chairmen of the Joint Economic Committee, Alternative IMF Funding Examined By Saxton to Limit U.S. Taxpayer Risk, Dec. 16, 1997. UAW News Release, United Auto Workers International Executive Board Resolution on U.S. Contributions to the International Monetary Fund, Feb. 18, 1998. Labor Alerts, Campaign for Labor Rights, Oppose IMF "Fast Track Funding," Jan. 19, 1998. Fast-Track Measure Dies; IMF Funding In Question, Nov. 1, 1998, Nation's Business.

1998, rejected fast-track authority. Nonetheless, the United States continued, and continues, to fund the IMF and others. As for the post-East Asian financial crisis period, the IMF coffers had been nearly depleted, as the fund dealt with the financial crises in Asia, Latin America and Eastern Europe. In 1998, although the U.S. Congress had appropriated $17.9 billion, only about $3.4 billion had actually been installed in appropriations bills, thus, Congressional negotiations on setting restrictions on using the additional funds continued, and would be eventually resolved. The latter does not mean that the disputes and controversies concerning issues of foreign aid have been resolved. Rather, these disputes continue, while also evolving into new perspectives, presenting both old and new concerns and issues. For the United States, countries such as China and their aid donor policies are influencing the evolution of these concerns and issues.

In June 2006, a joint task force convened by the Brookings Institution and the Center for Strategic and International Studies (CSIS) released recommendations for reorganizing and reprioritizing U.S. foreign aid programs.[55] The Brookings-CSIS Task Force called for a comprehensive review of foreign aid, led by Congress but involving key non-governmental organizations (NGOs) and government agencies, with the Goldwater-Nichols Defense Reorganization Act of 1986 serving as its model. The Brookings-CSIS Task Force advocates a U.S. development mission that is on parity with U.S. defense and diplomacy, which could result in the creation of a Department for Global Development for bringing together more than fifty U.S. government units involved in aid delivery. The task force also noted that U.S. spending on foreign assistance has seen its greatest increase in forty years, an expansion that also produced a growing incoherence in policy and a fragmentation in organization. What was observed to be a critical problem was the threat to hard power assets, resulting in the United States needing to deploy its soft power more effectively and efficiently. The report is referring to what Joseph S. Nye, Jr. earlier phrased, or coined, as "soft power," during the early 1990s. As recent as 2003, Nye described "soft power" as, "the ability to get what you want by attracting and persuading others to adopt your goals. It differs from hard power, the ability to use the carrots and sticks of economic and military might to make others follow your will. Both hard and soft power is important in the war on terrorism, but attraction is much cheaper than coercion, and an asset that needs to be nourished." Nye opines that, "Soft power grows out of both U.S. culture and U.S. policies." When Nye first introduced the concept of soft power, the United States was not only the strongest nation in military and economic terms, but also in what Nye termed soft power. Soft power is, "the ability to get what you want through attraction rather than through coercion," which, "could be developed through relations with allies, economic assistance, and cultural exchanges." All of which could produce "a more favorable public opinion and credibility abroad."

In terms of the 2006 report of the joint task force, it is a critique centered on the United States failing to take fuller advantage of potential synergies, with these disparate efforts sometimes working at cross purposes. The task force essentially found that the United States punches well below its throw weight in the international community, which should be unmatched when measured in absolute aid dollars. For these reasons, U.S. foreign aid must

---

[55] Brookings-CSIS Task Force Releases New Recommendations on Transforming Foreign Aid, Brookings Inst., June 22, 2006. Joseph S. Nye Jr., Propaganda Isn't the Way: Soft Power, Jan. 10, 2003, Int'l Herald Tribune. Nye, Joseph S., Jr., Bound to Lead: The Changing Nature of American Power (Basic Books, 1991). Soft Power -The Means to Success in World Politics, Tysha Bohorquez reviews Joseph Nye Jr.'s book on the importance of soft power, UCLA Int'l Instit., Dec. 1, 2005.

move away from a one-size-fits-all approach and should be redirected by a unified framework fusing U.S. objectives supporting capable foreign powers and countering security, humanitarian and transnational threats with differentiation based on governance and economic capacities. As a result, U.S. aid programs must be customized to the capacity and need of beneficiary-countries, while also recognizing that beneficial-countries afflicted with poor governance routinely perform the worst in addressing human needs.

A classic example of the problems of efficient and effective delivery of United States foreign aid is the case of China and legal reforms. United States foreign operations appropriations for China primarily support democracy-related programs, such legal training, legal aid, criminal defense, labor rights, the development of NGOs in China, monitoring human rights conditions in China from outside China, and preserving Tibetan culture. United States funding has been substantive in the area of legal reforms. The U.S. Congress has approved substantive funding for such programs, reflecting a growth from $10 million in 2002, to $23 million in 2006. From 1999 to 2006, U.S. government funding for democracy-related programs in China was about $110 million.[56] Although the major recipients are Temple University (rule of law project), the International Republican Institute (village elections project) and the Asia Foundation (civil society project), many experts and authority suggest that U.S. congressional funding for legal reform efforts in China have produced limited benefits due to the lack of judicial independence, weak enforcement of laws, constraints on lawyers and political corruption. Perhaps what these experts fail to recognize is the underlying problem of the continuing influence of Marxism, China attempting to finalize the localization of Marxism, and China's reluctance to fully embrace economic liberalism due to nationalistic and ideological reasons, or perhaps simply an abhorrence of liberalism and neo-liberalism.

In the interim, China maintains that its foreign aid is not a threat to Africa, nor a threat to U.S. interests.[57] Chinese Premier Wen Jiabao contends that China's efforts, which are through the vehicle of foreign aid, to expand trade and energy ties in African and Latin American countries posed no threat to U.S. interests. According to Wen Jiabao, China's foreign policy is based on mutual benefit, and his country would not interfere in matters such as human rights. Wen states, "There is no way that someone could ever put the hat of neocolonialism on the head of China," and further, "China had given billions in aid to Africa and had sent thousands of medical and technical personnel to help with various projects." In 2005, after China became ineligible for food aid from the WFP, China extended effort to become the world's third-largest food aid donor (donating mostly wheat and wheat flour) in 2005, following the U.S. and EU. Nonetheless, China is, still, a recipient of various sources of neo-liberal aid, such as the World Bank, IMF and other international bodies.

The irony is that the substantial bulk of World and IMF funding comes from liberal (democratic) countries, or perhaps even some of the former neocolonialists referred to by Wen Jiabao, whose people have great concern about human rights violations. As one source observed, "Even people who are living in non-democratic countries and face torture and ill-treatment are indirectly financing the WB [World Bank] and IMF by paying taxes in their

[56] Thomas Lum, U.S.-Funded Assistance Programs in China, CRS Report for Congress, May 18, 2007. General Accounting Office, Foreign Assistance: U.S. Funding for Democracy-Related Programs, Feb. 2004.

[57] Premier Says China Is No Threat in Africa, June 19, 2006, Reuters. China emerges as major food donor, Jul. 21, 2006, China Daily. Aykut Erdogdu, Policy Memo: Human Rights in China, Heinz School Review, spring 2006.

own countries." The same source observed, "The economic interests of those non-democratic states may overshadow any attention paid to human rights violations." Problematic is that economic successes can potentially augment current practices of crimes against humanity in those countries, and perhaps even set a bad example for other states that are prone to human rights violations. Many consider China as an extreme example of this dilemma. Human rights groups are rightly concerned that China might obtain resources in Africa with little regard for the environment or the human rights records of the various African governments.

In February 2007, Chinese President Hu Jintao concluded visits to eight African countries, including Liberia, Sudan and Zambia. Hu has pledged or confirmed generous amounts of foreign aid. However, many developed countries and old donors, such as the IMF, World Bank, the Paris Club and London Club, perceive China aid to some developing countries as problematic.[58] There are growing concerns with China aid, which one sources described as threefold: First, Chinese aid is supporting oppressive regimes; i.e. Sudan and Zimbabwe. Second, China, by its lax concern for international environmental and labor standards, has been able to secure contracts for large projects, which typically would have been won by larger corporations from old donors. Third, China is increasingly saddling developing countries with debts they will be unable to pay. The issue of bad debts also concerns some African countries, because Sino-Africa policy is starting to resemble that of great powers from an earlier era. For instance, South African president Thabo Mbeki and others, such as Zambia politicians, are worried about Chinese investments creating a colonial relationship. In addition, some African countries worry about growing trade deficits, displacement of local industries by Chinese imports and Chinese competition for local businesses.

It is not intended to suggest that the Dutch Disease phenomenon is particularly a Chinese problem. Western developed countries, including the United States, may also have to address this issue, and perhaps even, historically, have been dealing with the same issues, but under distinctively different nomenclatures or labels. However, China's approach to foreign aid and loans presents problems warranting the attention of other countries, both developed and developing countries. In September 2006, both a statement from the G-7 group of developed countries and a recent U.S. Treasury report warn China against overloading developing and least-developed African countries, and other developing countries, with "high-priced loans" they cannot avoid to pay. The U.S. Treasury report described loans to the African countries of Ghana, Mozambique and Sudan as opportunistic loans. The G-7 group plans to address this problem with China through the vehicle of international diplomacy. According to the *Wall Street Journal*, Timothy Adams, U.S. Under Secretary for International Affairs, said, "There are some aggressive countries out there that are ramping up their export-credit agencies and looking to take advantage of countries with lightened balance sheets," and, "We want to send a strong signal that those kinds of behaviors will be frowned upon."[59] Conversely, Li Ruogu, chairman of China's Export-Import Bank, one of China's three policy banks, is quoted by the *Wall Street Journal* as stating these loans provide, "favorable social and economic returns" for these developing countries and will continue. In November 2006, former World Bank chief James Wolfensohn highlighted the recent and substantial investments of China and

[58] Lex Rieffel, Why Bad Loans Are Good For Africa, Feb. 13, 2007, Globalist. Jacques de Lisle, Id.

[59] Michael M. Phillips, G-7 to Warn China over Costly Loans to Poor Countries, Sept. 15, 2006, WSJ. China blasted for "opportunistic" African loans, China Reform Monitor No. 641, Oct. 2, 3006.

India in Africa, as a prime illustration of how these two emerging giants were exercising their increasing global influence. Wolfensohn contends, "the world has been put on notice that Africa is no longer the basket case that everybody had historically thought it was but is now front and centre in terms of development by India and China." The rise of these two powers is a phenomenon manifesting a return to form rather than a novelty, because these two countries "had accounted for 50 percent of global GDP from the 1500s until the industrial revolution reduced that to between five and seven percent." Beijing's November 2006 China-African summit, which attracts some 43 heads of African states, is noteworthy.

Notwithstanding Dutch Disease and China's geopolitical strategies as relate to the delivery of aid to other developing countries, in terms of China's foreign aid policy, especially reaching out to African countries, China presents an anomaly, as it remains one of the largest country portfolios of the World Bank, while struggling with tremendous domestic crises on the home front. There are still the many antagonists of economic liberalism and economic globalization, which may oddly include China's governing party, the CCP, and other developing countries, which have received substantial assistance from the various BWIs, and their liberal economic policies, goals and programs, ranging from assistance in poverty reduction to sustainable development. No doubt, China's reluctance to fully embrace economic liberalism and its policies, goals and programs are due to nationalistic and ideological reasons, or, perhaps simply an abhorrence of liberalism or neo-liberalism. Despite receiving substantial funds from the BWIs, since China begin initiating legal and economic reforms and an open door policy over twenty-seven years ago, China remains a reluctant economic globalist, multilateralist or neo-liberalist.

8.7. The Reluctant Neo-Liberalist

China may have, though mostly by default of Western institutions, Sinicized or localized Western normative economic liberalism, especially as an economic norm in its capacity to invoke norm change. This issue strongly resembles the ongoing debate concerning the linking or de-linking of international trade with international human rights. It is an issue that has long been a part of the discourse in free trade and fair trade, especially a controversial component of earlier Uruguay trade negotiation rounds addressing the framework of what would evolve into the WTO.

A problem for the U.S. may be the earlier de-linking of human rights from international trade during the U.S. Presidency of William Jefferson Clinton (1993-2001).[60] Admittedly, in terms of the economics of international trade (or international trade theory), it was arguably a sound de-linking. A contested issue, and debate continuing today, is the linking of trade and human rights, labor rights and other non-economic rights such as environmental standards. There are also the disciples of international economics that argue that trade should not be linked with social welfare rights.[61] There is also the historic problem of a failure of non-tariff

[60] Economic Casualties: How U.S. Foreign Policy Undermines Trade, Growth, and Liberty, (Solveig Singleton & Daniel T. Griswold, eds.). Ted Galen Carpenter, Eagle in the China Shop: The Economic Consequences of U.S. Global Meeting, 5-6, Cato Instit., 1999. Sam Vaknin, Analysis: The Jackson-Vanik debate, May 29, 2002, UPI.

[61] Jagdish Bhagwait, Free Trade Today 57, 67-80 (Princeton UP, 2002).

barriers or restrictions to change the conduct of so-called renegade countries,[62] which arguably presents a conflict or paradox between liberal economic theory and morality (*boni mores*), or the problem of the political morality of Western liberal economics. Some sources argue there should not be a logical connection between sanctions such as embargoes and liberty, which logically may hold true for arms embargoes. Adam Smith, in *The Wealth of Nations* (1776), describes how the development of commercial life in Europe "gradually introduced order and good government, and with them, the liberty and security of individuals." Likewise, French liberals Benjamin Constant and Alexis de Tocqueville emphasize how commerce creates a love of liberty.[63] For these viewpoints, trade sanctions are sanctioned as a "feel good," but ineffective approach for promoting social welfare rights such as human rights, because sanctions antagonize the governments of target countries, while, most dangerously, often radicalizing those in power.

There are opposing viewpoints, such as trade liberalization engendering a close link between increasing economic freedom and securing human rights. As opposed to radicalizing government, unlike sanctions or embargoes, trade liberalization weakens the power of government, thus, assumedly civilizing nations. One source observes, "The challenge for China is to get out of the way of the market and let it grow naturally along with civil society… The major impediment to China's freedom and long-run prosperity, of course, is the CCP. The crucial question is how to weaken the power of the CCP… China has been willing to experiment, but it has not yet provided the climate of freedom necessary for growing market-liberal institutions." While former China President Jiang Zemin did not shy away from criticizing presumed Western efforts to divide and Westernize China, the Hu Jintao administration has actively backed a campaign to criticize neo-liberalism and has cracked down on the expression of liberal opinion. Hu Jintao seems determined to address the problems facing China by strengthening CCP rule rather than adjusting the relationship between the party and society through greater openness.[64] A problem with de-linking of trade and social welfare rights are the reality of many developing countries, such as China, and their respective human rights records. Boycotts, strikes and other peaceful methods have not faired well in China, as evidenced by a record of egregious human rights and labor rights violations, including the growing number of public protests.[65]

The latter instances exemplify the problems of China and the liberal or Enlightenment project. For nationalistic and ideological reasons, China remains steadfast in its opposition to Western liberalism or economic liberalism. In terms of the conduct of China, and what a common Western legal civilization of the international community deems flagrant violations of international human rights, Western developed countries, such as the United States, are relying on soft power in seeking China's compliance with international norms. In the non-Western world, or the second world, the liberal project, admittedly, has not been a complete success, but neither has it been a complete failure. There are many successes attributable to economic liberalism and its international economic institutions. From the 1949 founding of

---

[62] Bernard M. Hoekman & Michel M. Kostecki, The Political Economy of the World Trading System the WTO and Beyond 21-22 (Oxford UP, 2001).

[63] Adam Smith, The Wealth of Nations (Bantam Dell, 2003). James A. Dorn, Trade and Human Rights: The Case of China, Vol. 16, No. 1, Cato Journal (spring/summer 1996).

[64] Joseph Fewsmith, China under Hu Jintao, China Leadership Monitor, Issue 14, spring 2005.

[65] Geoffrey York, Rising Tide of Labour Protest Has Chinese Leadership Worried, May 12, 2003, Globe & Mail. China Reform Monitor No. 616, Feb. 8, 2006.

modern China, to China's accession to the WTO, the world has witnessed China transition from isolationism, near autarky, excepting for its relations with the former Soviet Union and other communist regimes, to major world player, in terms of international trade and politics or diplomatic relations. Despite China's reluctance to fully embrace economic liberalism, and its attendant economic and political liberalization, the world witnessed China transition from the pursuit of concepts such as pure (or orthodox) Marxism, to the joint pursuit of a socialist-political polity and capitalist-economic policy. Notwithstanding the 1978 Third Plenary Session of the 11th Committee of the CCP announcing a shift from a work priority of class struggles to economic construction, the clearest evidence of the partial success of the liberal project has been China's earlier, though partial, abandonment of strategies and formulas for success based on a Soviet-style central planned economy, copying Stalinist industrialization, an agricultural collectivization system and other Soviet-style formulas for success.

In the end, China presents itself as a reluctant globalist, multilateralist or neo-liberalist. The world and the multilateral trading system is left with a paradox between a China of burgeoning economic growth, and a China remaining steadfast against the influence and force of economic liberalism, and its attendant policies, including liberal economic theories. In the interim, China's burgeoning economic growth is driven, in part, by resource endowments and differing developmental levels (foreign capital and technology, and domestic land and labor) in pursuit of export-based growth. In 2005, notwithstanding FDI from other countries, new U.S. FDI in China totaled about $4 billion.[66] As for total FDI, in 1980, China's FDI was only about $1 billion, Japan's FDI was about $3 billion and the Republic of Korea's (ROK) FDI was about $1.3 billion. In 2004, China's FDI rose to $560 billion, Japan's FDI was about $96 billion and the ROK's FDI was about $56 billion. Foreign investment, mostly FDI, has underwritten much of China's economic growth. A growing proportion of foreign funds, admittedly, were accumulated via the debt and equity offerings of Chinese firms in international capital markets and, though too lesser extent, in China's weak domestic capital markets. As of 2005, no Chinese firms were listed on the New York Stock Exchange, and the most cited reason was a reluctance to meet the requirements of the Sarbanes-Oxley Act of 2002, in particular, "the requirement that the CEO and the CFO certify the company's annual and quarterly reports."[67] The latter serves as a reminder of many issues, such as the "wind of falsification and embellishment" and China's need to switch from a Soviet accounting system, to Western accounting standards; and the explicit or implicit contributions of liberal economic policies and institutions to China's burgeoning economic growth. One can also add substantive financial funding and assistance from liberal economic institutions, such as the World Bank, IMF and WTO, as forces, in part, driving China's burgeoning economic growth. China should explicitly, if not implicitly, though it may deny for nationalistic and ideological reasons the importance of economic liberalism and its institutions, recognize economic liberalism as enhancing its economic growth. However, the perspective on the mainland may be quite different. As one Chinese academian, Wang Yuechuan, writes, "After a century of

[66] Ash & Kueh, Id. China boosts Int'l image with peaceful diplomacy, Jan. 11, 2006, China Daily. U.S. - China Economic and Security Review Commission Annual Report to Congress, 2005.

[67] Sarbanes-Oxley Act of 2002, (Public Company Accounting Reforms and Investor Protection Acts), Pub. L. No. 107-204, 116 Stat. 745.

the painful process of 'Westernization' in China, political and economic modernization is now being transformed into modernization with Chinese characteristics."[68]

8.8. CONCLUSION

China's economic growth model exemplifies an East Asian development model, dating back to the 1990s, of establishing a manufacturing crescent, the vocation of which was to reach out to the world and conquer distant markets or foreign markets.[69] However, there is a troubling paradox in China's global or geopolitical posturing. The paradox, or perhaps irony, lies in China's polity enjoying the benefits of Western-inspired liberal economic policies, programs and, especially, foreign aid assistance. Perhaps more paradoxical, or even more ironic, is China's adoption of foreign aid programs and assistance that intends to reach out to many Asian, African and Latin American countries. As previously mentioned, China's geopolitical posturing or foreign policy strategies are driven by its "one-China policy", and growing dependence on overseas resources and energy supplies, especially oil and natural gas, which are also motivations shaping China's military policy. China does so by emulating the very liberal economic models, goals, policies and programs that it opposes for nationalistic and ideological reasons. By so reaching out to many Asian, African and Latin American countries, China replicates the very liberal economic goals, programs and policies, including foreign assistance programs, which it deems, mostly attributable to nationalism and ideologism, the threat of Western powers and influence, especially, the United States or the ubiquitous "Western threat."

---

[68] Wang Yuechuan, Chinese Identity and Cultural Exports in the new Century, Guangdong shehui kexue, no. 3 (2004).

[69] François Gipouloux, Integration or Disintegration? The Spatial Effects of Foreign Direct Investment in China, China Perspectives, No. 17, May - June 1998.

Chapter 9

CHINA AND THE WESTERN THREAT

9.1. NONRECIPROCATING POLITICAL TYPOLOGY

The future directional path of legal and economic reforms in China is, essentially, reducible to issues of whether Western universalism, and its legal and economic theories and models, present a viable alternative or admixture to traditional culture and Marxism. The complementary or paradoxical interrelationships between competing sources of order either inhibit or enhance the prospects for Chinese neo-liberalism (*xin ziyou zhuyi*) and a potential Chinese neo-liberal (*xin ziyou* or *xin ziyou pai*) coterie. Complementary and paradoxical sources of order only exacerbate the issue of a critical acceptance of Western universalism, and its legal and economic theories and models, because China's paradoxical sources of order of traditional culture and Marxism, actually, neither fully prescribe Western legal and economic theories and models, nor fully proscribe them. The latter consequence or truism stems from a Chinese polity jointly pursuing a socialist-political polity and capitalist-economic policy, and constituting a reluctant globalist, multilateralist or neo-liberalist. In the real world, it is, admittedly, difficult to ascertain where and how a Chinese neo-liberal coterie would fit in modern China's social-political environment, especially a social-political environment attempting to finalize the localization of Marxism to the realities of traditional culture and society (*Makesi zhuyi he Zhongguo shiji xiang jiehe*). The most useful analytical tools for measuring social-political environments are typologies, which are highly regarded analytical tools, because from the labels of typology one can often measure the highs and lows, the good and bad, and even what is successful versus unsuccessful. Typology is, generally, definable as the doctrine of the study of types or prefigurative symbols such as scriptural literature, the systematic classification or study of types, simply symbolism, or as assigning labels to objects or ideas under scrutiny.[1] For China's modern social-political environment, the tool of political typology may or may not offer assistance in genuine understanding, especially concerning the prospects of a Chinese neo-liberal coterie. A political typology enjoying a long history of usage rather than short usage or new usage has greater proclivity to aid an analysis of a social-political environment.

---

[1] Robert G. Pielke, Political Typology: A Suggestion Clarification, Reason Papers No. 7, 33-52 (spring 1981). Max Weber, Methodology of the Social Sciences, (Shils & Finch, trans.) (Free Press, 1949).

Notwithstanding a traditional culture and society spanning a history of 5,000 years or more, a relatively new post-1949 China presents a social-political environment of relatively short usages of political typologies. In terms of ethical reasoning, a short usage is problematic because a political typology may require explanations regarding meanings or agreed-upon meanings, which often produce morals-loaded and culture-loaded meanings, terms and concepts. A typical political typology may comprise labels such as leftist versus right rightist, liberal versus conservative, Marxists versus libertarians (or liberals), or even teleological thinkers versus deontological thinkers, and a host of other presumed social-political and value-laden antonymous combinations. An assigned typology's accuracy, especially political typology, is largely contingent on whether an assigned usage simply makes sense for a particular community. In terms of China and its social-political environment, and problematic for Marxist rules of order, addressing issues of political typology necessitates addressing issues linked to the particularism of China and its ontological base in tradition. Ronald Dorkin addresses, though indirectly, the same issue, which is the problem and search for validity in terms of communal integration.[2] The problem and prospects of a proposed Chinese neo-liberal coterie is no less a problem and search for validity in terms of communal integration. For modern China, there are the problems of resolving the conflicts or paradoxical relationships between a genuine validity reflective of its ontological base in tradition and a Western-inspired normative validity, and between traditional culture and modern Marxism. As in Tao Yuan-ming's ideal life in *Tao huayuan* and the struggle between traditional Confucianism (learn and use theory) and Taoism (return to nature thesis), a seemingly historic problem inherited from antiquity and continuing in the new millennium is traditional culture going against the conventionalism of an era. However, the greater issue may lie in the struggle of modern Marxism against Western liberalism or economic liberalism, a struggle seen and reflected in the paradox between a "China threat" and "Western threat."

One must, admittedly, question how liberalism or economic liberalism can portend Western universal values for modern reforms, if the social-political environment of China, and its attendant cultural relative political typology, native language, culture, ideology, thought system and appropriate lexicons, positions liberalism or neo-liberalism farther left of center or extremely far left of conventionalism than even the "new left" or radicals. China still perceives liberalism, and its intended consequence of Western democracy, as a threat to internal security.[3] Problems for liberalism, economic liberalism and other pro-democracy forces are external, political economy or macroeconomic forces. China presents an anomaly in terms of international relations and trade relations. Problematic for China are September 11, 2001 or 9/11, and the economics of terrorism that ensured; geopolitical changes in world politics; pro-democracy movements; War in Iraq; North Korea and nuclear proliferation on the Korean peninsula; Iran and nuclear proliferation; United Nations (UN) Security Council Resolution 1701 (Adopted by the Security Council at its 5511th meeting, on 11 August 2006) and resulting August 14, 2006 cease-fire in the Israel-Lebanon conflict or Israeli-Hezbollah (Hizbollah or Party of God) conflict; and other external forces. China perceives these

---

[2] Ronald M. Dworkin, Liberal Community, 77 Calif. L. Rev. 479, 480 (1989).

[3] M. Ulric Killion, China Internet Tax: Issues of Particularism, Liberalization, and Integration, vol. 11 MSU-DCL J. Int'l L. J. (summer 2003). Al Santoli, (ed.), China Reform Monitor No. 490, Apr. 1, 2003.

external, political economy or macroeconomic forces as a threat to internal security, whether true or not, which are threats that affect on-going legal and economic reforms.[4]

From the perspective of some developed countries, one of the issues of tenuous Sinic-West relations is reducible to the core problem of the "China threat," a phrase often found in both Western media and literature, and routinely denied by China through its media and literature. However, a key problem often overlooked in Sinic-West relations has, historically, been the "Western threat." There are ample historical antecedents substantiating a "Western threat," though it may be describable in other terms, such as "fear of the barbarian" in antiquity; an earlier fear of *pax Mongolia* (or Mongol peace); fear of Western powers, especially military powers (Sino-British Opium Wars, 1839–1842 and 1856–1860, and Unequal Treaties, *Bu pingdeng Tiaoyue*); fear of foreigners; fear of desinicization; and even the fear of *pax Americana* or American peace. China, admittedly, does not speak of a "Western threat" rather addresses as one of the crucial sources of tensions in Sinic-West relations, the "China threat." There are many in Western and developed countries that hold steadfast to a fear of the "China threat," from ordinary citizens, politicians, scholars, entrepreneurs and others. Depending on one's perspective, political preferences, relative political typology or perhaps even culture relative political typology, it is a "Western threat" or "China threat" driving Sinic-West relations toward tenuous rather than optimality.

Many Chinese sources attribute the Sinic-West divide to the problem of the "China threat." According to Zhao Chuang, general-director of Department of Foreign Economic Cooperation of Ministry of Commerce of China, in 2005, foreign capital and foreign direct investment (FDI) in China was $60.5 billion and Chinese oversea investments were about $7 billion.[5] Zhao adds that the ratio between the latter two types of investment is not only lower than the average level of developed countries, which is between 1:1.2 to 1:1.4, but also lower than the average of other developing countries, which is about 1:0.19. In 2006, during the East Asia Investment Forum at Weihai, in Shandong Province, Zhao Chuang was attempting to demonstrate that while Chinese overseas investments are experiencing high growth rates, China is not yet a world power in terms of foreign investment, thus China does not pose a threat to any country or enterprises in the world. Zhao Chuang and others such as Cai Wu, minister of the Information Office of the State Council, implicitly, contend that the problem of Sinic-West relations is the dubious and Western-preceived "China threat" and not anything attributable to China.

Some Chinese sources describe the "China threat" as a historic progression of four stages or waves that eventually births the political typology of the "China threat." A first stage or wave of this historical progression occurs during the period, "when China took effective measures to keep social order in the face of great political changes of Eastern Europe and the collapse of Soviet Union." Second, during the mid-1990s, there is the second stage or wave, when the pivotal event in history is the Taiwan-strait crisis and some Western countries overreacting to China's actions to safeguard its national unification agenda. During the third stage or wave are the September 11, 2001, or 9/11, terrorist attacks, which results in U.S.

[4] Patrick Lenain et al., The Economic Consequences of Terrorism (OECD, Econ. Dep't, Working Paper No. 334 (2002).

[5] Why is China always haunted by the "China threat"? Aug. 2, 2006, People's Daily. Who believes the new "China threat theory"?, July 8, 2006, People's Daily. Stronger China poses no threat to other nations, July 5, 2006, People's Daily. Qin Jize, "China threat" remarks criticized, Dec. 23, 2005, China Daily. Cai: China no threat to others, Apr. 20, 2007, China Daily.

politicians, during the early days of the U.S. presidency of George W. Bush, overstating the political rhetoric of China as an enemy. In March 2005, there is the fourth stage or wave, when some western countries, taking China's military power as a lead-in and core matter, weave a complex "China threat," which runs the gamut, from military affairs, politics, economics, energy, environment, culture, technology, geopolitics, stability of Taiwan Strait, to regional security. From the Chinese perspective, many deem the root cause of the "China threat" as being attributable to all shapes, forms and varieties such as democracy, human rights, Chinese textile dumping, low labor costs, energy demands, food supplies and others variants of the threat, because developed countries have always been suspicious and cautious of China's burgeoning economic growth and society. Many also deem the party ideology of building a harmonious socialist society and harmonious socialist world, as an adequate defense to the proponents of the "China threat," which should belie fears of developed and developing countries of the "China threat."[6]

A problem for China's governing polity is an increasing sensitivity to external, political economy, or macroeconomic forces, which results in China often sending mixed signals to the international community. All of which acts to the detriment of China's aspiration to be a world power player or leader in the international community. The issue of China's mixed signals affects many international relations concerns, ranging from geopolitical posturing, Asian regional peace and security, international trade, foreign aid and a host of other concerns. These mixed signals, in part, stem from what many in China, implicitly, by virtue of nationalism and ideologism (or ideology) perceive as external threats, which manifest the promotion and usage of the nonreciprocating political typology -- the "Western threat."

9.2. Western Threat – Communist North Korea

As of May 2006, the Islamic Republic of Iran (Iran) was threatening to withdraw from the Treaty on the Non-Proliferation of Nuclear Weapons (NPT). Iran's threat serves as reminder to the international community of the 2003 withdrawal of Democratic People's Republic of Korea (DPRK or North Korea) from the NPT, and China's effort and participation in diplomatic talks with Kim Jong Il. Concerning the North Korean nuclear threat and nuclear proliferation on the Korean peninsula or regional nuclear proliferation, since 2004, the United States has sought to resolve this issue through bilateral rather than multilateral talks, which have centered on China's growing regional geopolitical power. In 2005, the issue of a North Korean nuclear threat seemed far from resolution and remained unresolved in 2006. Many suggest China is employing the six-nation talks addressing the North Korean nuclear issue for purposes of redefining strategic positions of the United States, Japan and South Korea on the Korean Peninsula.[7] In 2005, during the period when talks had yet to resume, many perceive China's initial response as a reluctance to bring North Korea

---

[6] 'China threat' fear countered by culture, May 29, 2006, China Daily. China promotes its culture overseas to dissolve "China threat," May 28, 2006, Xinhua. China not a threat to world energy security, June 1, 2006, People's Daily.

[7] Treaty on the Non-Proliferation of Nuclear Weapons, http://www.un.org/Depts/dda/WMD/treaty/. Victor Davis Hanson, The Global Shift, June 10, 2005, National Review online, http://www.victorhanson.com/articles/hanson061005.html. Upcoming six-nation talks in jeopardy, Feb. 21, 2005, Asian news.it, http://www.asianews.it/view.php?l=en&art=1489.

back to the negotiation table. One source reported, "Until concrete evidence is produced China –the main go-between in the six-nation talks– has declined making any comment." No doubt, China is capable of reining in Kim Jong Il, if it elects to do so. One source opined that China actually derives a psychological satisfaction from watching Pyongyang's nuclear roguery stymie the U.S. and Japan.

In 2005, Pyongyang, following withdrawal from the NPT, announces that North Korea actually possesses nuclear weapons. In September 2005, Pyongyang agreed to give up its nuclear program in exchange for U.S. aid and security assurances, but negotiations stalled in November 2005, because of Pyongyang's anger over U.S.-imposed sanctions for alleged currency counterfeiting and money laundering. In May 2006, negotiations had yet to resume, and South Korean Foreign Minister Ban Ki-moon and Russian Foreign Minister Sergey Lavrov meet for purpose of discussing the restart of the stalled six-party talks. As of November 2005, North Korea still refuses to return to the negotiating table because of American sanctions on the Macao-based bank, Banco Delta Asia, for allegedly distributing counterfeit U.S. dollars and laundering money for Pyongyang. As of July 2006, after promptings from the United States, the People's Bank of China (PBOC), which is China's leading lender, also froze all of its North Korean accounts suspected of connections with North Korea's alleged counterfeiting activities. In 2005, Beijing froze about $24 million of Pyongyang's cash in the Banc Delta Asia, and as of July 2006, Beijing had frozen North Korean assets held in the Macao branch of the PBOC. However, as of August 2006, North Korea has evaded these sanctions by opening new accounts in 23 other banks in 10 countries, which includes countries such as Vietnam, Mongolia, Russia, and other Asian and European countries that the U.S. suspects are used to handle money for illicit arms trade and other illegal activities. By September 2006, and indicative of a growing problem for Pyongyang, according to Stuart Levey, the U.S. Treasury Department Undersecretary for Terrorism and Financial Intelligence, banks in Singapore, Vietnam, China, Hong Kong and Mongolia have discontinued the handling of North Korean banking business.[8]

According to the 2006 U.S. Pentagon annual report on Chinese military power, "China has not fully leveraged its close ties with Pyongyang to stem North Korean nuclear ambitions." In June 2006, after a prolonged hiatus in six-party nuclear disarmament talks with Pyongyang, the U.S., Japan and South Korea are facing a new concern, Pyongyang's accelerated preparations for testing a missile that has the potential to strike the United States, which is the Taepodong-2 long-range missile.[9] The most recent crisis involving North Korean was the July 5, 2006 launch, though failed after 42 seconds, of the Taepong-2 missile. Problematic is that a working version of the Taepong-2 missile could possibly reach the United States and other areas in the Asian region, such as Japan and South Korea, which are within range of Pyongyang's missiles. On July 5, 2006, North Korea also fired six shorter-range missiles that dropped in the Sea of Japan. This is the second time that North Korea and its nuclear-weapons program has alarmed the world and threatened regional peace and security. In August 1998, Pyongyang also launched a Taedong-1 missile over Japan that eventually fell into the Pacific Ocean. In 1998, the UN Security Council responded with a press statement, which was problematic for the U.S. and Japan, because it was far from being

[8] N. Korea said evading bank sanctions, Tokyo, Aug. 19, 2006, UPI. John Brinsley, N. Korea Opened Vietnam Bank Accounts, Intelligence Report Says, Aug. 20, 2006, Bloomberg. Jennifer Veale, North Korea's Mounting Trouble, July 30, 2006, Time magazine. Asia Security Monitor No. 171, Sept. 13, 2006.

[9] China Reform Monitor No. 629, June 6, 2006. U.S.: North Korea preparing missile test, June 16, 2006, AP.

a binding UN Security Council resolution or even a chair statement that expressed concerns regarding Pyongyang's nuclear roguery. In 1998, it was China strenuously objecting to any discussions concerning Pyongyang's nuclear-weapons program in the Security Council.

In October 2002, North Korea confirmed suspicions of the reactivation of its nuclear weapons program, while also causing another international crisis by expelling International Atomic Energy Agency (IAEA) inspectors and declaring that it would withdraw from the NPT. In the past, the U.S. has imposed sanctions, mostly economic sanctions, in response to Pyongyang-invoked international crises. Generally, these economic sanctions have been imposed for four elemental reasons: "(1) North Korea poses a threat to U.S. national security, as determined by the President and renewed annually under the terms of the Trading with the Enemy Act and National Emergencies Act; (2) North Korea is designated by the Secretary of State as a state sponsor or supporter of international terrorism, pursuant to the Export Administration Act of 1979; (3) North Korea is a Marxist-Leninist state, with a Communist government, and stated as such in the Export-Import Bank Act of 1945, and further restricted under the Foreign Assistance Act of 1961; and (4) North Korea has been found by the State Department to have engaged in proliferation of weapons of mass destruction - to date only missile proliferation - pursuant to the Arms Export Control Act, Export Administration Act of 1979, and Iran Proliferation Act of 2000."[10]

On July 5, 2006, in response to Pyongyang's missile launches, an emergency UN Security Council session convenes, and while China and Russia could not defend the North Koreans, they still oppose an imposition of sanctions. Article 41 of the UN Charter allows the Security Council to impose sanctions against nations which pose a threat to international peace and security, such as arms embargoes, travel sanctions, financial restrictions, civil aviation restrictions and import/export bans of certain commodities, which may also include down-grading or suspension of diplomatic ties. China and Russia maintain that only diplomacy would halt the isolated regime's nuclear and rocket development programs.[11] The U.S. and Britain support Japan in the circulation of a resolution that seeks to ban any country from transferring funds, material and technology that Pyongyang could use in missile and weapons of mass destruction (WMD) programs. Japan is also seeking to impose sanctions outside of the proposed resolutions and threats of sanctions. According to Shinzo Abe, then Japan's Chief Cabinet Secretary, "Japan will take any kind of sanctions we can," including economic and financial sanctions. The latter presents the prospect that both the U.S. and Japan could conceivably impose economic sanctions, with or without a UN Security Council resolution.

Notwithstanding a possible UN resolution forthcoming in the future, in 2004, Japan revised its Foreign Exchange and Foreign Trade Law, which now permits its government to intervene by halting track and block cash remittances to North Korea or any other country. In 2004, Japan revised the Foreign Exchange and Foreign Trade Law to allow its government to halt trade and block cash remittances to North Korea, or any country, without a UN resolution. In 2004, Japan also enacted a new law authorizing its government to ban the docking of North Korean ships or ships that have visited North Korea at Japanese ports, such as the Mangyongbyon-92 ferry. On July 5, 2006, immediately following Pyongyang's missile

[10] Congressional Research Service, Report for Congress, North Korea: Economic Sanctions, Jan. 24, 2007.

[11] Edith M. Lederer, China, Russia resist North Korea sanctions, July 5, 2006, AP. Hisane Masaki, N Korea's missiles met by Japanese sanctions, July 6, 2006, Asian Times Online. Joseph Coleman, Analysis: N. Korea calling for attention, July 5, 2006, AP.

launches, Japan did ban the docking of the Mangyongbyon-92, which shuttles between Wonson (North Korea) and Niigata (Japan) and serves as the main direct link between North Korea and Japan. For North Korea, the economic consequences may be critical because until 2002, Japan was North Korea's second-largest trading partner, lagging only behind China. It was trade, in part, facilitated by a large ethnic-Korean community in Japan. However, and reflecting growing tensions between Japan and North Korea, as of 2006, two-way trade continues to shrink, with Japan now lagging behind China, South Korea and Thailand as trading partners with North Korea. Although not major trading partners, Russia and India are also trading partners with North Korea. According to Shinzo Abe, "Japan also plans to bring up the issue at the Group of Eight (G8) summit to be held in St Petersburg later this month." In terms of international diplomacy, some hope that the August 2006 meeting of the G8 would force the hands of both China and Russia, because China and Russia are more likely to be able to facilitate a stall on concrete resolutions against both Pyongyang and Tehran after the August G8 meeting. In July 2006, the Security Council is also struggling with the issue of Iran and nuclear proliferation, and Tehran's 2006-resumed development of its uranium enrichment program.

China and Russia favor a weak Security Council statement such as a presidential statement without any threat of sanctions, but thirteen delegations favored a resolution with threat of sanctions. The proposed resolution of the thirteen delegations would have condemned Pyongyang's role as the world's leading proliferator of ballistic missiles and related technology, and also demand that Pyongyang immediately cease the development, testing, deployment and proliferation of ballistic missiles, and reconfirm its moratorium on missile launching. Further, the proposed resolution would have urged Pyongyang to return to the six-party talks without preconditions and stop its nuclear-related activities, especially plutonium reprocessing and uranium enrichment. Since both China and Russia hold veto power in the UN Security Council, a strong resolution with threat of sanctions is improbable, at least in the near future. As for Pyongyang, as a self-proclaimed nuclear weapons state, it announced that the threat of sanctions would be tantamount to a declaration of war. In weeks before the July 5, 2006 launch, the U.S. and Japan warn Pyongyang that the planned Taepodong-2 launch would constitute a violation of Pyongyang's 1999 self-imposed moratorium on ballistic mille tests, the 2002 agreement between Japan and North Korea, and an agreement stemming from the 2005 six-party nuclear talks. However, Pyongyang contends that its moratorium on ballistic missile tests was no longer applicable because it is not longer involved in direct talks with Washington.

China's position is both clear and ambiguous. China and Russia will use their veto power to defeat a resolution with actual or real sanctions. China's UN Ambassador Wang Guangya, although expressing regret and concern over North Korea's missile launches, was far more ambiguous regarding what council action would actually be acceptable to Beijing, while also stressing the importance of constructive actions for maintaining peace in North Asia. Wang said, "I think that in 1998 similar circumstances that the Security Council issued some sort of comments or statements. We'll see." The only clarify offered by China is a clear intent to veto any resolutions threatening sanctions against both Pyongyang and Tehran. As observed by Takashi Shiraishi, an East Asian affairs expert at Japan's National Graduate Institute for Policy Studies, "China is likely to oppose any imposition of sanctions on North Korea over this problem, so I think the process will ultimately be inconclusive."

Admittedly, many view China as encouraging reforms in North Korea. In 2005, there was $2 billion in bilateral trade between China and North Korea. China is Pyongyang's largest benefactor and provides about 70 percent of North Korea's annual food and energy needs. There is a historical relationship between Beijing and Pyongyang. King Jong Il routinely seeks China's guidance and encouragement, while also frequently visiting Mainland China for purpose of touring special economic zones and meeting with Chinese leaders. According to Daniel Sneider, associate director for research at Stanford's Asia-Pacific Research Center, "China is clearly the paradigm for North Korea right now" and "We've been watching the senior North Korean leadership traipsing in and out of China on a regular basis." However, the role of China in its geopolitical posturing is not a benign one, as U.S. officials even accuse Beijing of being complicit in the counterfeiting allegation, "by allowing banks in Macau to accept counterfeit U.S. dollars from North Korea and put them into international circulation."[12] A problem is that Pyongyang and Kim Jung Il, because of support from countries such as China and Russia, remain defiant. On July 5, 2006, following the adverse reaction of the international community to its nuclear-weapon programs, North Korea threatened to test-fire more missiles, while warning of even stronger action if other countries attempt to pressure North Korea.[13] As of August 2006, amid new reports that Pyongyang might be preparing a nuclear test, a pro-North Korea newspaper published in Japan reports, "We cannot say for sure there will be no nuclear test by North Korea to strengthen its self-defense, if the Bush administration steps up the hard-line stance in military and other areas." Pyongyang carrying out a nuclear test poses such a grave threat to the peace and security of Japan, Northeast Asia and the international community that South Korea and China have agreed to continue cooperation to prevent a nuclear test.

One source rightly observes that Beijing, and not Washington, has the power to decide the fate of North Korea.[14] Beijing continues to support Pyongyang and resist calls from Washington and Tokyo for tough responses when Pyongyang breaks its word. No doubt, China benefits from North Korea's behavior and using Pyongyang as a proxy, when seeking to probe vulnerabilities of the United States, South Korean and Japan. The question awaiting an answer is when will Beijing pull the plug on Kim Jong Il? In September 2006, according to Choe Su Hon, Deputy Foreign Minister of the DPRK, Pyongyang rejected further talks on its nuclear program. In October 2006, North Korea also announced that it will conduct a nuclear test in the face of a threat of a nuclear war by the United States, a declaration that provokes alarm and condemnation from leaders around the world.[15]

However, in January 2007, North Korea finally agrees to resume six-nation talks that are aimed at winding up Pyongyang's nuclear arms program, which offers hope, though small, based on the history of negotiations. The result was the "North Korea-Denuclearization Action Plan," which was announced on February 17, 2007. One source opines the new action

[12] Ester Pan, North Korea's Capitalist Experiment, Council on Foreign Relations, June 8, 2006.

[13] Kwang-Tae Kim, N. Korea vows to continue missile launches, July 6, 2006, AP. Korea: N Korea might try nuclear test, Aug. 19, 2006, Taipei Times. Burt Herman, S. Korea, China fight N. Korea nuke test, Aug. 25, 2006, AP.

[14] Niall Ferguson: When will China pull the plug on North Korea?, July 10, 2006, L.A. Times. DPRK rejects further talks on nuclear program due to U.S. breakdown, Sept. 27, 2006, Xinhua. North Korea says it will stage nuke test, Oct. 3, 2006, AP. George Jahn, Experts: Nuke test holds radiation risk, Oct. 3, 2006, AP. North Korea agrees to resume talks, Jan. 19, 2007, Reuters.

[15] James Laney & Jason Shaplen, How to Deal with North Korea, Feb. 21, 2007 update to Mar/Apr. 2003 essay, Foreign Affairs.

plan will result in either an ephemeral diplomatic victory or a genuine breakthrough on the cold war's (1945-1991) last frontier. Some critics of the new action plan assail the Bush administration for giving Pyongyang too little, too late, and at too great a cost, while others accuse the Bush Administration of rewarding the Kim Jong Il regime's misdeeds with an accord full of loopholes.[16] Moreover, as of March 18, 2007, there is a pending resolution over the issue of U.S. financial sanctions that have frozen some $25 million in North Korean funds, in the Banco Delta Asia. According to North Korean nuclear envoy Kim Kye Gwan, upon release of the $25 million in frozen funds North Korea will stop its nuclear activity. In March 2007, the U.S. actually lifts the freeze on the assets held at the Macao Bank, while Pyongyang stalls on shutting down its nuclear reactors. All of which, including the "North Korea-Denuclearization Action Plan," is, problematically, contingent on Pyongyang, especially Kim Jong Il, staying faithful to these agreements, and not break its word, as it broke past agreements such as Pyongyang's 1999 self-imposed moratorium on ballistic mille tests, the 2002 agreement between Japan and North Korea and the agreement stemming from the 2005 six-party nuclear talks.

9.3. Western Threat –Islamic Republic of Iran

Adding to the problem of North Korea is the dispute concerning Iran and nuclear proliferation. Iran is a signatory state of the NPT and in 2006 resumed development of its uranium enrichment program. Iran's problem is that a diplomat accredited to the IAEA said the level of enriched uranium alleged in its possession is higher than the low-enriched material used to generate power and heading toward weapons-grade level. The IAEA is the international center of cooperation in the nuclear field, which was originally set up in 1957 as the "Atoms for Peace" organization and housed within the United Nations family. The IAES works worldwide to promote safe, secure and peaceful nuclear technologies. The NPT establishes a safeguards system that is under the responsibility of the IAEA, which also plays a central role under the NPT in transferring technology for peaceful purposes.[17] As for the NPT, its primary pillars are non-proliferation, disarmament and the right to peacefully use nuclear technology.

Iran contends that it resumed the uranium enrichment program for purpose of a civilian nuclear energy program and claims the right to peaceful uses of nuclear energy based on NPT Article III, Paragraph 3, and Article IV. In May 2006, Iran was threatening to withdraw from the NPT, which serves as reminder to the international community of the 2003 withdrawal of North Korea. Tehran, and unlike Pyongyang, maintains that its nuclear program will produce or generate electricity and claims a right to the peaceful use of nuclear energy under the NPT. Iran President Mahmoud Ahmadinejad announced that Tehran would not hesitate to reconsider its NPT membership, which is a threat of withdrawal from the NPT. Iran's parliament announced, notwithstanding a peaceful or diplomatic solution, they would have no

---

[16] Report: U.S., N. Korea resolve bank issue, Mar. 18, 2007, AP. Macau 'unblocks' N Korea funds, Apr. 10, 2007, BBC. US presses NKorea to start reactor shutdown by deadline, Apr. 12, 2007, AFP. North Korea-Denuclearization Action Plan, U.S. Department of State, Feb. 13, 2007, http://www.state.gov/r/pa/prs/ps/2007/february/80479.htm.

[17] Ali Akbar Dareini, Iran rejects incentives to halt enrichment, May 14, 2006, AP. International Atomic Energy Agency, http://www.iaea.org/About/index.html.

choice but to call on the government to retract its signature of the Additional Protocol and to place on its agenda an examination of Article 10 of the NPT, which specifically covers the procedure for leaving the treaty. Article 10, Paragraph 1, reads, "Each Party shall in exercising its national sovereignty have the right to withdraw from the Treaty if it decides that extraordinary events, related to the subject matter of this Treaty, have jeopardized the supreme interests of its country."

Washington and its allies, Britain, France and non-permanent Security Council member Germany, are pressuring the UN Security Counsel to suspend Tehran's uranium enrichment program. In 2006, they are seeking Security Council approval for a UN resolution that would threaten possible further measures if Tehran does not suspend uranium enrichment, which is a process that can produce fuel for nuclear reactors to generate electricity or potentially make atomic weapons. In May 2006, U.S. President George Bush President said, "An armed Iran will be a threat to peace. It will be a threat to peace in the Middle East, it will create a sense of blackmail, [and] it will encourage other nations to feel like they need to have a nuclear weapon. And so it's essential that we succeed diplomatically." These Western nations seek to invoke Chapter VII, Articles 39-51, of the UN Charter, which allows economic sanctions or military actions for purpose of forcing Tehran's compliance. Conversely, Russia and China have veto power as two permanent Security Council members and oppose invocation of Chapter VII, and possible economic sanctions and military action. Both Russia and China complained about a section of the draft resolution that requires countries to stop selling technology to Tehran that could help its nuclear program, which they characterized as sanctions by another name. Article 41 of the UN Charter does provide for economic and other kinds of non-military measures for maintaining or restoring international peace and security. Chapter VII, Article 41, reads, "The Security Council may decide what measures not involving the use of armed force are to be employed to give effect to its decisions, and it may call upon the Members of the United Nations to apply such measures. These may include complete or partial interruption of economic relations and of rail, sea, air, postal, telegraphic, radio, and other means of communication, and the severance of diplomatic relations." Accordingly, sanctions deliverable as economic and nonmilitary measures are allowable specific countermeasures to violations of international law, and such coercive measures are employable in connection with international peace and security.

In May 2006, the United States, when seeking Russia's support for a UN Security Council resolution, even agreed to invoke only Article 41 of Chapter VII and not the whole chapter. By doing so, the proposed language of the draft does not include language of an immediate threat of military force. According to European diplomats, "The American agreement has improved the chances that the Russians will go along with the resolution."[18] There appears to an implicit understanding that the same considerations and conciliatory efforts would not improve the chances that China will go along with the resolution. However, the latter strategy, in part, prevails, because on June 1, 2006, the six key players, being the United States, Britain, France, Germany, Russia, and China, agree to jointly offer Iran a new choice of incentives (or rewards) for giving up suspect nuclear activities, or punishment for

---

[18] Ali Akbar Dareini, Iran renews threat to exit nuclear treaty, May 7, 2006, AP. Iran threat to quit atomic treaty, May 7, 2006, BBC. Criticism of UN Iran draft mounts, May 6, 2006, BBC. Steven R. Weisman, U.S. Accepts Draft on Iran That Omits Use of Force, May 31, 2006, N.Y. Times. Six world powers agree on Iran incentives, June 1, 2006, AP. Parisa Hafezi, Iran sees some positive signs in atomic proposal, June 6, 2006, Reuters. Qin Jize, Beijing urges talks on Iran nuclear issues, Jan. 18, 2005, China Daily.

refusing to do so. They are incentives are helping Iran to develop a nuclear power plant and other economic benefits, and would be on the table for a proposed new round of bargaining with Tehran, while also representing a major policy shift for the United States. In 1980, Washington broke ties with Tehran, and by virtue of agreeing to join ongoing talks under certain conditions, it would be the first major public negotiation in more than a quarter century between these countries. For nearly twenty years, Iran covered up sensitive nuclear fuel research and development from the UN, until an Iranian exile group blew the whistle. Iran then impeded probes by the UN atomic energy agency, which pointed to military links with Iran's nuclear development project. As of June 2006, the European powers have been negotiating with Tehran for nearly three years and, since 2005, trying to resume talks.

Problematic is that both Russia and China are Tehran's trading partners. In 2006, the U.S. is urging Russia to reconsider its commitment under an arms-contract with Iran for the purchase of Tor-M1 surface-to-air missiles. Russian Defense Minister Sergei Ivanov maintains, notwithstanding some major event, an intention by Russia to fulfill this contract. In terms of trade and nuclear industry, Russian nuclear industry is also anticipating work on two new nuclear power plant projects. Vladimir Pavlov, of the Russia's Nuclear Power Plants Organization, which is a subsidiary of the Atom Stroi Export Company that is building Iran's Bushehr nuclear power plant, announced, "Russia's nuclear industrial units are equipped with the most advanced technologies in manufacturing nuclear power plants." In May 2006, Vladimir Pavlov announces completion of 90 percent of operations at the Bushehr plant's first unit. In May 2006, both Russia and China advised Tehran that they would oppose economic sanctions and military action. Iran's confidence runs high. In May 2006, Iran Foreign Minister Manouchehr Mottaki announces, "no sanctions or anything like that will be on the agenda of the Security Council."[19] A potential problem is a motivation by Russia of the pursuit of profit or market profitability and perhaps near term stability, rather than international human rights and regional security concerns in the Middle East. The latter are pressing concerns for the United States, EU countries, Israeli and other countries. In February 27, 2005, Iran and Russia signed a nuclear fuel deal at the guarded Bushehr nuclear facility in southern Iran, which would start the delivery of atomic fuel shipments for a Moscow-built nuclear reactor in Iran. Gholamreza Aghazadeh, the Iranian Vice President, and Alexander Rumyantsev, the Russian Federal Atomic Energy Agency chief, signed the agreement after touring Iran's $800 million complex. The deal requires the return of spent fuel to Siberian storage units after about a decade of use. Russia and others were assuming that the latter condition would effectively belie concerns of the United States that Iran would use the fuels to make nuclear weapons.[20]

While Russia has the $1 billion deal for the Bushehr project in southwestern Iran, China also enjoys an open field when searching for energy deals such as the 2004 $50 billion deal to develop the Yadavaran gas field and annually buy 10 million tons of Iranian liquefied natural gas for 25 years. In terms of geopolitics, China and Russia are forming a block to U.S. presence in Central Asia, primarily through the vehicle of the Shanghai Cooperation Organization (SCO), which now includes Kazakhstan, Kyrgyzstan, Uzbekistan and Tajikista. Although Russia and China originally established SCO for purpose of combating ethnic separatism in Central Asia, SCO evolved into what is more accurately described as a regional

---

[19] Russia Reform Monitor No. 1382, May 28, 2006. Russia Reform Monitor No. 1375, May 4, 2006.

[20] Official: Iran nuke deal close, Feb.8, 2005, Reuters. Russia, Iran sign nuclear fuel deal, Feb.28, 2005, Reuters.

security organization. Many describe SCO as a mini-North Atlantic Treaty Organization or an anti-NATO gathering intending to turn back U.S. influence in the energy rich Islamic territories of the former Soviet Union, a description substantiated by the invitation to Iran to attend SCO meetings. Donald Rumfeld observed, "It strikes me as passing strange that one would want to bring into an organization that says it's against terrorism ... the leading terrorist nation in the world: Iran." In addition, in terms of oil resources, Iran has the world's second largest reserves of petroleum, which is estimated at 132 billion barrels or about 11.1 percent of the world's known reservoirs, and the second largest reserve of natural gas or about 971 trillion cubic feet (or 27.5 trillion cubic meters), or 15.3 percent of known reservoirs.[21]

By June 5, 2006, a package put together by the United States, Russia, China and the EU3 (Britain, France and Germany) offers economic and diplomatic incentives, if Tehran relinquishes domestic enrichment, which can generate power as well as make weapons-grade uranium for warheads. The offer also contains the threat of UN sanctions if Tehran remains defiant. The immediate response is following Monday morning trading, when stocks tumbled as crude futures raced higher on Iran's threat to cut oil imports. Iran's top leader, Supreme Leader Ayatollah Ali Khamenei, and not ultra conservative President Mahmoud Ahmadinejad, warns that energy shipments from the Gulf region are subject to disruption should Iran come under attack from the United States. The Sunday warning unnerved a Monday morning energy market that was already concerned about the threat of another hurricane season devastating Gulf Coast refineries. A barrel of light crude reportedly jumped from $1.02 to $73.35 on the New York Mercantile Exchange. As for using oil as a weapon, Iran is the world's fourth-largest oil exporter and the second-largest producer in the Organization of Petroleum Exporting Countries (OPEC).

However, a potential Iranian threat of using oil as a weapon may be more bark than bite because Iran's energy future is growing dimmer. According to the National Iranian Oil Company (NIOC), by 2010, Iran's oil production could fall short of earlier planned projections, by as much as half a million barrels per day. Gholam Hossein Nozari, director of NICO, announced, "We are not close to the 5.0 million bpd target of the fourth [five-year, from 2005 to 2010] plan." Nozari attributes Iran's production problems to lackluster investment in aging oil fields, because "more than 80 percent of the current total oil output is being provided from aged oil fields that need serious investment to increase production."[22] Despite oil production estimated at about 3.9 million barrels daily, Tehran still needs additional investments in the oil industry. According to Mohsen Yahyavi, deputy chairman of the energy committee of Iran's parliament or *majles*, the oil industry needs some $100 billion investment over the next two decades. Yahyavi stated, "Oil, gas, and petrochemical projects need huge investment and we will seek domestic and international investments."[23] In terms of the geopolitics of oil, "More than 70% of the increase in oil demand comes from developing countries (notably China and India), which see average annual demand growth of 2.5%."[24] Many predict that the oil supply, which a small number of Middle East producers increasingly

---

[21] Michael T Klare, New moves on the tripolar chessboard, June 17, 2006, Asian Times.

[22] George Jahn, Envoy to show Iranians anti-uranium deal, June 5, 2006, AP. Christopher Wang, Stocks slide on Iran supply threats, June 5, 2006, AP. Ali Akbar Dareini, Iran says incentives proposal needs study, June 6, 2006, AP. Iran Democracy Monitor No. 20, Sept. 1, 2006. Problems on the oil front, Aug. 29, 2006, Agence France Presse.

[23] Iran Democracy Monitor, No. 30, Dec. 2006. Tehran Mehr, Dec. 9, 2006.

[24] Fatih Birol, (testimony), U.S. Senate Committee on Energy and Natural Resources Oil Market Outlook and Policy Implications, Jan. 10, 2006, http://energy.senate.gov/public/_files/Birol.doc.

dominate, will peak within a decade. Countries such as Iran and Iraq have the potential to expand oil production, while Saudi Arabia remains the largest producer. A critical concern is whether non-OECD countries will make investments in increasing oil production. Non-OECD countries may choose to deliberately develop their production capacities slowly and non-responsively to an increasing global oil demand. The latter would be the consequence of either capital shortages that prohibit oil producers from investing in expanding capacities or a slower growth in OPEC oil production that drives up global oil prices.

Iran receives a new package of incentives, and pursuant to UN Resolution 1696, should respond by August 31, 2006. On August 22, 2006, and then again on August 29, 2006, Iran responds by announcing that it will neither stop uranium enrichment activity or even temporarily suspend its uranium enrichment, nor forfeit the right to do independent research into nuclear technology. In August 2006, Iran responds with its second military exercise, which signals a readiness to fight, and on August 26, 2006, Iran President Mahmoud Ahmadinejad announces to the world that the Iranian people would use force to protect its disputed nuclear program. In response to Iran's earlier August 22, 2006 twenty-one page formal response to the incentives package, Russia Defense Minister Sergei Ivanov stated, "It is at least premature and unsound to speak of sanctions" against Iran. On August 25, 2006, Russian Foreign Ministry spokesman Mikhail Kamynin indicated, "Russia will continue with the idea of seeking a political, negotiated settlement concerning Iran's nuclear program." Extreme sanctions, such as a trade ban or freezing assets, remain problematic due to likely opposition by Russia, China and others, especially because of badly needed oil imports from Iran, and other traditional economic and strategic ties with Tehran. There have been suggestions of less harsh sanctions, such as travel restrictions on Iran officials or ban on use of dual-use technology, which are less harsh or relatively low-level sanctions more likely to attract Russian and Chinese support for sanctions against Iran.[25]

Washington considered rallying its allies to impose sanctions of their own, which are independent of the UN Security Council. Given the probability of a block by China and Russia, when seeking sanctions against Iran for failure to suspend its nuclear program, the United States has threatened parallel sanctions that are outside the purview of the UN Security Counsel. John Bolton, former U.S. Ambassador to the UN, stated, "The question of what to do about Iran is certainly not confined to the Security Council," and further, "You can envision sanctions being imposed outside of the Security Council as the United States has unilaterally imposed sanctions on Iraq pursuing to its own statutes ... Other governments can do the same." What primarily concerns the United States, as observed by Gregory Schulte, U.S. permanent representative to the IAEA, is that a peaceful nuclear program does not need enrichment. For this reason, the U.S. considers Iran's nuclear enrichment as part of a military nuclear program. In addition, the IAEA report only buttressed suspicions Iran is engaging in activities that are only consistent with a weapons program. Conversely, Ruan Zongze, Deputy Director of the Chinese Institute of International Studies, characterized the problem as a U.S. Greater Middle East Initiative, which is employing a strategic initiative to gain control in the Middle East region, thereby forcing the region to be dependent on the United States and become part of its wider hegemony. It is a greater U.S. Middle East initiative, supposedly,

[25] Russia deems sanctions on Iran "premature", Aug. 25, 2006, Xinhua. U.S. envoy suggests unilateral action against Iran, Aug. 29, 2006, Xinhua. Iranian president pledges to maintain nuke program with force, Aug. 27, 2006, Xinhua. Nasser Karimi, Iran's president defies U.N. on deadline, Aug. 31, 2006, AP.

linked to Iran being the second largest oil exporter in OPEC, producing 3.8 million barrels daily and having control over the Straits of Hormuz, which is an instrumental thoroughfare for oil transport in the Gulf region.[26]

Diplomacy may or may not resolve the issue of Tehran and nuclear weapons and Tehran may or may not withdraw from the NPT. One suspects that all of the major international players, including China and Russia, cannot see any benefits derived from Tehran's withdrawal, especially in the promotion of international peace and security. However, and indicative of problems in the international community, the proposed solutions to the issue of Iran and nuclear weapons appear divisible along the lines of liberal countries and illiberal countries, and perhaps even developed countries and developing countries. Complicating the issues are countries such, as China, who perceive the potential solutions to the Tehran and nuclear weapons crisis as a threat to their internal security. Couching the controversy, admittedly, in terms of a crisis may be premature. Notwithstanding that Iran may not be able to produce nuclear weapons in about 10 years according to the Central Intelligence Agency (CIA), and some - French and Israeli experts - argue a shorter period of about 1 to 3 years, its membership in the NPT is critical to international peace and security, as does its withdrawal from the NPT also potentially threaten international peace and security, especially in the Middle East region. Estimates on when Iran will be able to produce nuclear weapons are many, ranging from 1 to 3 years (French/Israeli estimates), to 5 years (U.S. pentagon estimate), to 10 years (CIA estimate). In October 2005, President Mahmoud Ahmadinejad notably declares that the Jewish state should be "wiped off the map." In April 2006, Iran Rear Admiral Mohammad Ebrahim Dehqani announced, "If America gets up to mischief, Israel will be our first target to hit."[27] Iran's recent threat to Israel, conjoined with potential withdrawal from the NPT, only serves to exasperate the threat to international peace and security. For instance, on May 23, 2006, during the Washington meetings between President Bush and new Israeli Prime Minister Ehud Olmert, Iran conducts a public test of its "Shahab-3" medium-range missile, which is a partial success. In the interim, and in response to both the Iran nuclear crisis and earlier announcements by President Mahmoud Ahmadinejad regarding the Jewish state, Israel starts to accelerate its strategic response to Iran's nuclear advances by stepping up its efforts to develop long-range cruise missiles suitable for striking the Islamic Republic's nuclear facilities, as well as improving its Arrow theater missile defense system.[28]

The Iranian President Mahmoud Ahmadinejad is also problematic because the effective head of Iran's political establishment is not the president rather the Iran's Supreme Leader or the religious leader selected by an Assembly of Experts. In terms of religious authority, Iran's new president Ahmadinejad, unlike both of his predecessors Ali Akbar Hashemi Rafsanjani (president, 1989-1997) and Mohammad Khatami (president, 1997-2005), is not a cleric rather a military man. This presents possibility of Iran President Mahmoud Ahmadinejad holding a power base of his own distinct constituency, which he may be able to marshal in the event of

---

[26] U.S. official urges UNSC to sanction Iran by deadline, Aug. 29, 2006, Xinhua. Nasser Karimi & George Jahn, Iran defies U.N.; sanctions possible, Aug. 31, 2006, AP. US-Iran power play rocks the Middle East, Aug. 29, 2006, People's Daily.

[27] U.S. intelligence on Iran called sketchy New CIA leader to confront gaping holes in knowledge, May 7, 2006, N.Y. Times. Pentagon sees Iran with bomb in 5 years: report, Aug. 31, 2006, Reuters. Iran army retracts Israel threat, May 4, 2006, http://www.dailytelegraph.news.com.au/story/0,20281,19026255-5001028,00.html.

[28] Missile Defense Briefing Report No. 202.

an internal power struggle. Ilan Berman writes, "Since taking office in August 2005, however, the 50-year-old Ahmadinejad has done much to demonstrate his radical credentials. He has ratcheted up the Islamic Republic's hostile rhetoric toward Israel and the United States. His government has systematically rolled back domestic freedoms and deepened its control over Iranian society. And, under his direction, the Islamic Republic has accelerated its very public march toward an atomic capability." As of September 28, 2006, after talks with European negotiators fail to reach an agreement, President Ahmond Ahmadinejag rejected demands that Tehran suspend its uranium enrichment activities, while proclaiming that Tehran was determined to pursue nuclear energy for peaceful purposes.[29]

The geopolitical posturing of China regarding Tehran and nuclear weapons presents a paradox. The hard power (or military power) of the United States is based in part on its soft power (or economic power), or what Joseph S. Nye, Jr. coined as "soft power," during the early 1990s, an "ability to get what you want through attraction rather than through coercion."[30] For Nye, it is soft power that "could be developed through relations with allies, economic assistance, and cultural exchanges." All of which could produce "a more favorable public opinion and credibility abroad." Despite aspirations of multipolarity against the lone unipolarity power, it is an economic power that will not soon wane, resulting in a hard power that will continue for a substantial period. In addition, a paradox arises from the growing economic interdependence of the United States and China. Wang Jisi, dean of the School of International Studies at Peking University and director of the Institute of International Strategic Studies at the Central Party School of the Communist Party of China, observed the, "United States is a global leader in economics, education, culture, technology, and science. China, therefore, must maintain a close relationship with the United States if its modernization efforts are to succeed. Indeed, a cooperative partnership with Washington is of primary importance to Beijing, where economic prosperity and social stability are now top concerns."[31] Wang recognizes that a decline of U.S. soft power will reduce its hard power, which paradoxically reduces China's hard power and soft power. For China, adhering to Wang's thoughts would represent an unexpected policy shift in the fate of a China bent on challenging the economic powers of the United States. It is a problem only made worst when countries, such as China, continue to view the United States as pursuing a *pax Americana* or American hegemony.

In terms of the UN Security Council, Russia and China appearing to form a voting block against liberal-country members, the Western countries, of the permanent Security Council, such as the United States, Britain, France and non-permanent member Germany, presents potentially dangerous precedent. The issues of East Asian and Korean regional peace and security also pitted Russia and China against the same liberal countries and members of the Security Council. As of August 2006, and evidencing the growing tensions on the Korean peninsula caused by Pyongyang, as a defensive move against Pyongyang's mounting missile threat, the United States, at Kadena Air Base, in Okinawa, Japan commenced the deployment

[29] Ilan Berman, Understanding Ahmadinejad, June 2006, no. 1. Ahmadinejad: Iran won't halt uranium enrichment even for a day, Sept. 28, 2006, AP. Ted Galen Carpenter, Iran's Nuclear Program: America's Policy Options, Policy Analysis no. 578, Cato Instit., Sept. 18, 2006.

[30] Nye, Joseph S., Jr., Bound to Lead: The Changing Nature of American Power (Basic Books, 1991).

[31] Wang Jisi, China's Search for Stability with America, Sept/Oct 2005, Foreign Affairs.

of the Patriot Advanced Capability-3 (PAC-3) theater missile defense system.[32] In the international crises of the Middle East, Iran and the Israeli-Hezbollah peace, China's need to import oil from Iran and Russia helping Iran build a nuclear reactor substantiates that China and Russia are forming a potential voting block against the same Security Council members. This block is developing as collusion between Russia and China to routinely oppose UN Security Council resolutions proposed by liberal-country members, generally, seeking tough sanctions such as the use of force and economic sanctions. Problematic is collusion by China and Russia to oppose tough sanctions against illiberal countries or non-Western developing countries. The Chinese delegation, though Nationalist government, when convening with participants at the San Francisco Conference of 1945 for purpose of drafting the UN Charter is a far cry from the present UN participation, actions and geopolitics of China. In May 1945, one of three new proposals put forward by the Chinese delegation was that in response to events threatening world peace, the Security Council has the right to take emergency measures.[33]

The collusion between China and Russia is problematic for other reasons, especially in terms of Iran and nuclear proliferation, because in the second world rather than first world the perception is that Iran, Russia and China stand jointly against the United States. Many consider Iranian's stance, in conjunction with the support of Russia and China, as presenting the possible seeds of the start of the next world war or third world war. Ilan Berman analyzes Iran's March 2007 two-week seizure of British sailors and marines in the Persian Gulf as a "flagrant piece of political theater."[34] The goal was to signal their resolve to deepen the nuclear program crisis, and signal a readiness and willingness to fight for Iran's nuclear program. Bernan perceives Iran's recent actions as a wake up call to the EU "troka" or France, German and Britain, who from 2003 to 2005 fail to revive diplomatic dialogue effectively addressing Iran's nuclear program. He characterizes the March 23, 2007 hostage taking as signaling the bankruptcy of diplomacy, but contends that Washington can assist the EU countries in adapting to new realities concerning Iran. In answer, Berman proposes focusing on trade relations, because Germany, France and Italy account for about 30 percent of the commercial goods that Iran annually imports, while France, Italy and the Netherlands consume about $10 billion annually in Iranian exports, mostly oil and petrochemical products. Berman, essentially, is suggesting that extreme measures such as asset freezes, reductions in FDI and bilateral trade embargoes could be effective in compelling Iran toward good global citizenship.

On September 14-15, 2006, Larry M. Wortzel, chairman of the U.S.-China Economic and Security Review Commission, when giving testimony before the Commission on China's Proliferation Record and Role in Resolving North Korea Nuclear Crisis, discussed the strategic partnership between China and Iran, and Tehran's nuclear ambitions as an international crisis.[35] Wortzel noted that two forces drive China's obstructionism. First, there

---

[32] Asia Security Monitor No. 169, Aug. 21, 2006. John Mendolsa, Iran, Russia and China to stand jointly against US? Iran refuses to scale back its nuclear program – Russia and China quietly backs, Aug. 22, 2006, India Daily.

[33] Jin Guangyao, The Nationalist Government and the Creation of the United Nations, Zhongguo shehui kexue (Social Sciences in China), (Aug. 2004) 37-50. Zhongguo daibiaotuan huiyi jielun (Conference Conclusion of the Chinese Delegation), 6th Sess., May 2, 1945, in Wellington Koo Papers, Box 85.

[34] Ilan Berman, Iran gives Europe a wake-up call, Apr. 18, 2007, Baltimore Sun.

[35] Testimony before the U.S.-China Economic & Security Review Commission, Hearing on "China's Proliferation to North Korea and Iran, and Its Role in Addressing the Nuclear and Missile Situations in Both Nations," Sept.

are China's growing energy needs such as oil and petroleum products, and a runaway economy. Estimates project China's oil consumption will reach 7.4 million barrels daily in 2006 -- a half-a-million barrel per day increase over 2005 levels. By 2020, according to some estimates, Beijing's energy deficit could top eight million barrels per day. Tehran is an indispensable energy partner for China. In 2004, these two countries address their mutual interest by execution of two accords, which estimates hold to be worth about $100 billion over the next twenty-five years, and grant Chinese firms extensive rights to develop Iranian oil and natural gas reserves. There were also other deals between the two countries that boosted their energy partnership, which some value as now worth about $120 billion or more. As Tehran became China's single largest oil supplier, Beijing reciprocated by assisting Tehran in diplomatically and economically engaging other foreign powers. The second force driving cooperation between these two countries is mutual opposition to American primacy in the international community, as Beijing has openly declared a commitment to a multi-polar world in a post-cold war era, a diluted American influence in world affairs and the pursuit of partner nations equally antagonistic to the United States. As observed by Matthew Bunn, Harvard University's Managing the Atom Project, what distinguishes Iran from North Korea is that, "Iran is a state with vast oil and gas resources and a web of commercial and political relations with a large number of important states."

A critical concern is Tehran granting Chinese firms extensive rights to develop Iranian oil and natural gas reserves. Following the April 2007 meeting of the Gas Exporting Countries Forum (GECF) or OPEC-style cartel ("gas OPEC"), in Doha, Qatar, the supply of the global gas market is becoming an increasingly growing force in geopolitics. The 2001 founding of GECF is for purpose of maintaining stability or security of the global gas supply. The April 2007 meeting of GECF is important because there are 22 countries in attendance, which boast more than 70 percent of global gas reserves. In 2005, estimates show world gas consumption at about 2.75 trillion cubic meters, and about 6.9 percent of this consumption is for natural gas (LNG). According to estimates from the International Energy Agency, world demand for LNG will increase from about 246 billion cubic meters in 2007 to about 476 billion cubic meters by 2010.[36] On April 6, 2007, Viktor Khristenko, Russian Minister of Industry and Energy, announces, "The OPEC was a reaction to the appearance of the global oil market. However, a global gas market will form no earlier than 10-15 years from now, and an organization of gas exporters will hardly emerge before that." Leaders supporting formation of a "gas OPEC" are many, mostly illiberal countries, such as Iranian supreme leader Ayatollah Sayyed Ali Khamenei and Venezuelan President Hugo Chavez, with others such as Russian President Vladimir Putin, Qatari Emir Sheikh Hamad bin Khalifa AL-Thani and Algerian President Abdelaziz Bouteflika voicing interest or support. Many Western countries and some non-Western countries such as Egypt oppose the formation of an OPEC-style cartel or "gas OPEC" for gas exporting countries, which intends to control the essential sources of global energy.

Finally, in the cases of North Korea, Iran and other illiberal or non-Western countries, the problem of a China-Russia collusive veto block may be an issue of international diplomacy

14, 2006. U.S.-China Economic & Security Review Commission, http://www.uscc.gov/. Iran shrugs off U.N. nuclear pressure, Mar. 9, 2007, AP.

[36] "What political game does "Gas OPEC" play?, Apr. 12, 2007, People's Daily. Egypt opposed to "gas OPEC", Apr. 9, 2007, Xinhua. "Gas OPEC" not to be formed within 15 years, says Russian official, Apr. 7, 2007, Xinhua.

and negotiations, which may or may not entail considerations of the culture relative, or the problem of a "second world" perception, whether rational or irrational, of the "Western threat." For many illiberal countries or non-Western countries seeking to challenge U.S. primacy in the international community, a primary problem are liberal autocracies, which are regimes led by leaders, though un-elected, that still respect their citizens rights and uphold the rule of law are rare and exceptional body politics.[37] Consequently, the problem of a "second world" perception of a "Western threat" more realistically tends toward the issue of political labels or political typology of illiberal nation-states (or illiberal democracies) casting against liberal nation-states (or liberal democracies).

9.4. Western Threat –The Vatican

China perceives many external, political economy and macroeconomic forces as a threat to its internal security, and from the July 1, 1997 takeover of Hong Kong, the Beijing-Taipei controversy or cross-strait relations, to U.S. proposed resolutions to the U.N. Human Rights Commission (UNHRC) condemning its human rights record, China routinely casts criticisms of its policies and practices as interference with its internal affairs. An extreme example of China's geopolitical strategies and reaction to the slightest criticism of its policies is its strained diplomatic relations with the Vatican (State of the Vatican City, *Stato della Città del Vaticano* or Holy See), especially concerning China's "one-China" policy and the Vatican's diplomatic relationship with Taiwan. Beijing is adamant about that the Vatican City ceasing to recognize Taiwan, while the Apostolic Nuncio (or Papal Nuncio) currently residing in Taiwan is, in fact, the Vatican's envoy to China. According to Cardinal Angelo Sodano, Secretary of State of the Vatican, in order to move the nunciature (or diplomatic mission of the Holy See) from Taiwan to Beijing, Beijing must first establish diplomatic ties with the Vatican. China is gravely concerned about interference with its internal affairs and counts as example the "Western threat" of the Vatican directing the activities of the Chinese Catholic Church. On May 12, 2005, Benedict XVI, during his first address to the Vatican's diplomatic body, focuses on nations that the Holy See does not have diplomatic relations with, which many interpret as addressing the issue of poor Beijing-Vatican relations.[38] Notwithstanding persecution of Catholics, imprisonment of Bishops and priests and denial of religious freedoms, China continues to worsen a strained diplomatic relationship by the consecration of bishops. Admittedly, on June 28, 2005, there is the consecration, supposedly, with the approval of the Holy See, of party-appointed bishop Joseph Xing Wenzhi, who is the successor of both the patriotic bishop of Shanghai, Aloysius Jin Luxian, and the underground Catholic Church Bishop, Joseph Fan Zhongliang. However, Beijing, through the Office for Religious Affairs, denies Vatican approval in the nomination of Joseph Xing Wenzhi, rather maintains that the nomination of Joseph Xing Wenzhi is a Chinese affair and not privy to approval by the Vatican. There are apparently many cases where the Vatican and Beijing have reached agreements over the nominations of bishops, but Beijing maintains secrecy

[37] Fareed Zakaria, The Future of Freedom: Illiberal Democracy at Home and Abroad (Norton, 2003).

[38] Catholic Encyclopedia (1914), http://www.catholicity.com/encyclopedia/. Catholic World Report, Aug/Sept. 2005. GoodNews, May 12, 2005, http://www.catholic.or.kr.

regarding these joint efforts. In addition, Chairman of the Patriotic Association Liu Bainian has also criticized the Holy See for maintaining ties with Taiwan.[39]

In May 2006, Vatican spokesman Joaquin Navarro-Valls criticized China for ordaining two Catholic bishops. In response, Chinese Foreign Ministry spokesperson Liu Jianchao said, "The Vatican must terminate its so-called diplomatic links with Taiwan, and it should not interfere in China's internal affairs, including any intervention under the pretext of religious affairs." Lu Xinhua, Commissioner of the Ministry of Foreign Affairs in Hong Kong, expressed the same sentiments and while announcing that China does not have a timetable for forging diplomatic ties with the Vatican, "reiterated China's long-lasting stance towards a normal relationship with Vatican: the latter must sever ties with Taiwan, persist in the one-China policy and should not interfere in China's internal affairs." China is gravely concerned that Vatican City is now the only European Union country that has a formal diplomatic relationship with Taiwan. While China promotes its role as a new key player in the international community, its actions more often, than not, speak of a reluctant world player, which China may be doing so either unknowingly or purposefully, in response to the "Western threat." China as a rising power is anxious about possible Western imposed values backed by Western, especially United States, collective intervention.[40]

9.5. Western Threat –Regional Economic Integration

The post-cold war era is one of growing global economic tensions rather than cultural or ideological tensions. These global economic tensions evolved from fear that at the close of the cold war, the United States would not be able to resolve its trade disputes with Europe and Japan. In the advent of the United States retreating into economic isolationism because of these unresolved disputes, there was fear of the formation of three major tracing blocs based on the dollar, yen and deutschmark, respectively, the United States, Japan and Germany.[41] The creation of the North American Free Trade Agreement (NAFTA) only heightened these fears. The foreign diplomacy (or international relations) and international trade policy of many developing countries, including China, would be driven, and continues to be driven, by a fear of being excluded from a regional trade agreement, such as a yen bloc, as well as from the European Community and a dollar bloc in the Americas. The most common form of regional trade agreements, preferential trade agreements, customs unions and free trade areas are the euphemistically referred to as free trade areas (FTAs).

As of May 2006, the United States' FTAs, along with the European Union's (EU) FTAs, are described by one source as, "the most far reaching in terms of achieving substantial change — or legal grounds for it — in other countries' social and economic policies by setting U.S.-friendly standards for investor privileges, environmental protection, workers'

---

[39] National Catholic Reporter, July 15, 2005. America, July 18, 2005. Adista, July, 16, 2005, 12. Catholic World Report, Aug/Sept. 2005, 25. Zenit, Sept. 30, 2005.

[40] No timetable for diplomatic ties with Vatican, May 11, 2006, China Daily. Zhang Yunling, Whither the World Order? 9-12, in Zhang Yunling & Guo Weihong, (eds), China US Japan and Russia in a Changing World (Beijing: Social Sciences Documentation Publishing House, 2000). Vatican's criticism on China's bishops ordination "unfounded," FM spokesman, May 7, 2006, People's Daily.

[41] Tim Harcourt, APEC's Labor Agenda: Negotiating The Future, 4-5 (2000). Paul Bowles, APEC: Progress Based on the Wrong Model?, Canadian Business Economics 48, 57 (fall 1997). Lincoln Wright, APEC—Australia's Pragmatic Asia Policy?, JPRI Working Paper No. 8: Apr. 1995.

rights, intellectual property rights, deregulation of service industries and privatisation in general, wherever they are signed." From the more comprehensive FTAs to the least comprehensive, these FTAs follow "a blueprint pattern, with the strongest 'to date' serving as a model for the next one(s)." Prior to 2000, the United States had successfully negotiated only three comprehensive FTAs, which were with Canada, Israel and Mexico. Conversely, in the post-2000 period, the United States has successfully negotiated FTAs with Australia, Bahrain, Chile, Jordan, Oman, Morocco, Singapore, South Korea, Peru and the six Central American parties to CAFTA (Costa Rica, Dominican Republic, El Salvador, Guatemala, Honduras and Nicaragua). The United States is presently negotiating FTAs with another dozen or so countries, such as South Korea, Panama, Thailand, the United Arab Emirates, Colombia and Ecuador (as part of the Andean process), and the five parties to the US-SACU talks (Botswana, Lesotho, Namibia, South Africa and Swaziland). As of 2006, there are also thirty-four countries involved in the Free Trade Area of the Americas (FTAA) process with the United States. In 2006, Washington is also reportedly considering for FTA talks, the countries of Malaysia, Algeria, Egypt, Tunisia, Saudi Arabia and Qatar.[42]

The earlier mentioned fear of the formation of three major tracing blocs based on the dollar, yen and deutschmark, only enhances with the growing trend of regionalism and proliferation of FTAs. There are increasing numbers of FTAs. From 1990 to 1994, the number of FTAs substantially jumped, with twenty-nine new FTAs reported to the WTO. From 1995-1999, the number of FTAs grew by an additional sixty-four agreements, twenty-eight involving transition economies. After 2000, FTAs between developing countries (South-South agreements), and not FTAs between developed countries (North-North agreements) or FTAs between developed and developing countries (North-South agreements), constituted a larger percentage of the new FTAs reported to the WTO. In a three-year period (2000-2002), there was a fifty-five percent growth in the number of new FTAs. The WTO estimates that there will be over 300 such regional trade arrangements by 2007.[43] It was fear further enhanced by deepening European integration or the EC-92 that led to a fear of a fortress Europe and the U.S. decision to form a preferential trade agreement with Canada, and the subsequent FTAs that followed in a seemingly blueprint pattern.[44] Western powers, such as the U.S. and EU, commenced the race to form FTAs and led the race by employing Western liberal economic models or theories. The threat to the "other" world, the "Western threat," is obvious, because, as of 2006, most United States FTAs and new FTA initiatives have involved Western Hemisphere countries. One of the most important FTA initiatives, are the United States negotiations for a Free Trade Area of the Americas (FTAA). The United States has already successfully negotiated FTAs with Canada and Mexico, Chile, the five members of the Central American Common Market (CACM) or *Mercado Común Centroamericano* (MCCA) and the Dominican Republic, as well as new trade talks with

---

[42] Free Trade Area of the Americas, About the FTAA, http://www.ftaa-alca.org/alca_e.asp. US FTAs, Bilateral.org, http://www.bilaterals.org/rubrique.php3?id_rubrique=55.

[43] Andrew L. Stoler, Preferential Trade Agreements and the Role and Goals of the World Trade Organization 2-3 (2004) (on file at the Institute for International Business, Economics & Law, Univ. of Adelaide). WTO, World Trade Report 47 (2003), http://www.wto.org/english/res_e/booksp_e/anrep_e/world_trade_report_2003_e.pdf. World Trade Report 2003, Table IB.9, 47, World Trade Organization, Geneva, 2003. WTO: Regional Trade Agreements: Facts and Figures, http://www.wto.org/english/tratop_e/region_e/regfac_e.htm.

[44] Maurice Schiff, Small Is Beautiful: Preferential Trade Agreements and the Impact of Country Size, Market Share, Efficiency, and Trade Policy, World Bank, Working Paper 1688, Oct. 1966.

Panama and some Andean Community countries. The latter promotes hopes for a larger hemispheric agreement, which will cover about 40 percent of total U.S. merchandise trade.[45]

China's response to the fear of formation of three major tracing blocs based on the dollar, yen and deutschmark; a fortress Europe and the EC-92, and the U.S. decision to form a free trade agreement with Canada; and the growing trend of regionalism and proliferation of FTAs was to join the global trade race to form FTAs. However, in the move for bilateral free trade agreements, China challenged, and continues to challenge, Western liberalism, economic liberalism and liberal economic models or theories. China pursued, and continues to pursue unorthodox rather then orthodox models of regionalism. In terms of the orthodoxy of liberal economics, regionalism based on the European Union model and its formal institutionalization and progression from FTA to economic union or those comprising developed economies and developing economies, such as the North American Free Trade Agreement (NAFTA), are successful models of integration. In these instances, the economic benefits of integration far outweighed the incidental economic costs of any secondary political considerations that may have motivated integration.[46] Conversely, China now proposes a model of regional integration that is primarily motivated by political or geopolitical considerations. From policies such as focusing on Association of Southeast Asian Nations (ASEAN) becoming China's first FTA partner, export-based growth (the unorthodox) rather than import-based growth (the orthodox), and moving for bilateral free trade agreements with developing and least developed countries (LDCs) (the unorthodox) rather than North-South FTAs (the orthodox), Chinese regionalism presents a distinctive blueprint pattern of regionalism primarily motivated by political or geopolitical considerations rather than economics. As China more pursues the unorthodox rather than orthodox liberal economic models or theories, China may someday find itself in a race to the bottom. What the rest of the world has to worry about is how China's inevitable economic train wreck, as associated with the normal growing pains of any rapidly developing economy, though not ending the Chinese economic miracle, will affect them. One source observes, "A weakly led and politically insecure China, roiled by unfulfilled nationalist aspirations, might prove an unpredictable actor on the world stage." In the interim, in the move for bilateral FTAs, China is demonstrating a distinctive Chinese model for regionalism (*quyu zhuyi*), if not a "new regionalism" (*xin quyu zhuyi*), which challenges Western liberalism, economic liberalism, liberal economic models or theories, multilateral trade and the goals and aspirations embodied in the World Trade Organization (WTO).

In terms of China's political environment, and its perceived external threats or even the "Western Threat," the challenges to Western liberalism, economic liberalism and liberal economic models are obvious. However, most problematic and disconcerting, is that China's

---

45 News Releases, The United States Should Pursue Fewer but Larger Free Trade Agreements, Institute for International Economics, May 7, 2004. The Central American Common Market (CACM) or Mercado Común Centroamericano (MCCA) is an economic trade organization founded on Dec. 13, 1960, comprising five Central American nations: Guatemala, El Salvador, Honduras, Nicaragua, and Costa Rica. The Columbia Electronic Encyclopedia (6th ed. 2006).

46 M. Ulric Killion, Chinese Regionalism and the 2004 ASEAN-China Accord: The WTO and Legalized Trade Distortion, 31 NCJ Int'l L. & Com. Reg. 1 (2005). Bela Balassa, The Theory of Economic Integration (1961). Regionalism and World Order (Andrew Gamble & Anthony Payne eds., 1966). OECD, Regional Integration Agreement, OECD Publication, Jan. 1, 2001. Sheng Lijun, China-ASEAN Free Trade Area: Origins, Developments and Strategic Motivations, ISEAS Working Paper: International Politics & Security Issues Series No. 1(2003), 13. Jim Jubak, Why China's train wreck will hit us, too, July, 28, 2006, Jubak's Journal. A Dragon out of Puff, June 13, 2002, The Economist.

blueprint pattern of new regionalism challenges the economic efficiency and effectiveness of China's regional integration strategies, by employing this new regionalism for purposes of diluting U.S. strategic unilateralism in the East Asian region. With the United States preoccupied with war in Afghanistan, Iraq, the Israeli-Lebanon or Israeli-Hezbollah (or Hizbollah) peace, the Middle East and especially threat of Iran becoming a nuclear power, China is steadily gaining as an international player in East Asia. In doing so, China is also pulling long time U.S. allies into its embrace. China's geopolitical posturing has resulted in a growing influence extending across East Asia, the Southeast Asia-Pacific region, the Philippines and Australia. One source observed, "Some specialists predict that Beijing will eventually develop a position of dominance with the countries of Southeast Asia similar to the US relationship with Latin American states -- a first among equals, the nation whose voice invariably carries the day as much because of its disproportionate size and power as the strength of its argument."[47] In the final analysis, China's new regionalism, which is primarily motivated by political or geopolitical rather than economic considerations, by design is intended to challenge Western powers (the hard power) and influence (the soft power). Moreover, in terms of Western models of regionalism, it is China, more so than any other developing country or economy, which "demonstrates the potency of nationalism and embodies possible alternatives to Western conceptions of democracy and capitalism." Consequently, "China is a reminder that history is not close to an end and in that sense it issues a cultural, political, and if one will, ideological challenge to those who entertain especially expansive and dialectic visions of world order," especially Western dialectic visions of world order.[48]

9.6. Western Threat –Neo-Imperialism

The Age of Imperialism commences in the 1860s and becomes known as the new imperialism or neo-imperialism. By definition, imperialism is a policy of extending control over foreign countries for purpose of acquisition and maintenance of empires. A feat accomplished by territorial conquest or indirectly through the forces of diplomacy and economics. It is a concept birthed mostly by European countries colonizing other countries. In terms of the United States, there is the charge of the newly evolved concepts of modern imperialism, modern Western imperialism and even a *pax Americana* or American hegemony. It is a growing problem of the international reality that the United States as the lone superpower possesses in abundance both hard and soft power, a charge based on America and its powers -- political, economic and military powers. America's ability to exert influence in the international community and pursue an interventionist policy has resulted in accusations of America seeking to build an American empire or *pax-Americana*. The concepts of modern imperialism, modern Western imperialism and *pax-Americana* or American empire are associated with the continuation of foreign policy interests that were earlier associated with colonial expansion. It is a charge mostly made by antagonists of liberalism, neo-liberalism and economic globalization, and counts as supporters many

[47] Tyler Marshall, China poised to dominate influence in Asia, Aug. 13, 2006, Boston Globe.

[48] M. Ulric Killion, Three Represents and China's Constitution: Presaging Cultural Relativisitic Asian Regionalism, 13 Currents Int'l Trade L.J. 23 (summer 2004).

developing countries and former colonial countries. For China, there is the "Western threat" definable by political typology, political economy and international relations lexicons, such as the words (or characters) *xin diguo zhuyi* (neo-imperialist) and *xin zhimin zhuyi* (neo-colonist).

China's describes a new threat to internal security as U.S. neo-imperialism, a name that its polity may see fit to borrow in reference to neo-liberalism. In response to the "China threat," defense of aid to African countries, and while admitting that exchanges between China and African countries are elements of soft power, Chinese Premier Wen Jiabao announced, "No one can claim China is practicing neocolonialism in Africa." One Chinese source commented that from the 1840s or the post-Sino British Opium Wars period, "China suffered under colonial aggression, and thus has many common grievances with African countries."[49] Beijing characterizes Chinese sovereignty of this earlier period as semi-colonial, and by doing so, invokes norms of solidarity with other developing and post-colonial countries. In February 2007, President Hu Jintao, when visiting several African countries, invoked the histories binding China and African countries, while stressing that China, unlike other foreign aid donors and trading partners, has never invaded Africa countries nor colonized them: what he characterizes as colonial aggression and oppression by foreign powers.

While doing so, China is strategically employing the tools of aid, loans and zero-tariffs in the pursuit of soft power and remaining adamant about its altruistic or humanitarian goals, and steadfastly, though contradictory, opposing the path to liberalism and neo-liberalism, and increasingly associating the "Western threat" with neo-liberalism and neo-imperialism. China's geopolitical strategies are experiencing some success, such as Sino-Africa policy and increasing bilateral trade relations, an increasing acceptance of the "one-China policy" by African countries, increasing access to Africa and Middle East natural resources, and a growing number of China's partners, now including some African countries, in mutual opposition to American primacy. In April 2007, a clear example occurs when a U.S. delegation, when visiting some African countries for purpose of announcing intention to establish a new Africa command (AFRICOM), resembling the Pacific Command and Central Command, hear expressions of fear about a new U.S. military command on the African continent by groups from countries such as Nigeria, South Africa, Kenya, Ethiopia, Ghana and Senegal.[50] No doubt, China's Sino-Africa policy, as many increasingly recognize, is mercantilist and strategic rather than market-based and altruistic or humanitarian. Despite China's mercantilist and imperialist proclivities in the pursuit of soft power, a badge of neo-imperialism standing alone, whether true or not, poses a strong rhetorical and ideological barrier to the successful transplantation of Western legal and economic theories and models, a crisis only made worst by China's continuing attempt to finalize the localization of Marxism.

One of the many articles critiquing the U.S.-led war against Iraq reads, "Overwhelming force is counterproductive when applied against popular resistance because it inevitably increases the very resolve of popular resistance it aims to awe into submission." Despite such geopolitical gestations, it is the historicism of Western imperialism, including a perceived

---

49 Who are the "neo-colonialists" in Africa?, June 26, 2006, People's Daily. China has 'no selfish interests' in Africa, June 21, 2006, China Daily. China and African countries boost soft power through cultural exchanges, June 19, 2006, Xinhua. Dai Bingran, Reconsideration on Sovereignty, Ouzhou yanjiu, no. 5 (2003).

50 Jacques de Lisle, Into Africa: China's Quest for Resources and Influence, E-notes, Feb. 2007, FPRI. New U.S. command prompts fears in Africa, Apr. 23, 2007, AP.

modern imperialism of the United States, whether true or not, which serves as one of many sources of contention driving Sinic-West relations toward tenuous rather than optimality. Liberalism, economic liberalism and economic globalization becomes increasingly problematic for many developing countries such as China, because many developing countries perceive neo-liberalism and economic globalization as often bearing a striking resemblance to historical imperialism and colonialism. These countries often perceive neo-liberalism and economic globalization as creatively manifesting adverse consequences for their countries under the guise of benign intervention or commercial relations, which strikingly resembles earlier historical imperialism and colonialism. These countries often perceive, whether true or not, strategies of economic, technological and cultural domination as either accompanying or serving as alternatives to the acquisition of land.[51]

From the prospective of the "other" world, U.S. primacy in the international community, and even perhaps the "Western threat," is especially challengeable on moral grounds, because in the post-World War II period, the United States and its allies have been constantly engaged in war, such as the U.S.-led wars in North Korea (1951), Vietnam (1961) and Grenada (1983), which were followed by Libya, Panama, the Gulf War, Kosovo, Afghanistan and now Iraq. Vassilis K. Fouska and Bulent Gokay opine that the United States is now pointing its sword toward Iran and North Korea, and "the flames of war ignited by the U.S. are spreading across the world." They argue that the new American imperialists use rhetoric such as "maintaining peace" and "democracy and freedom" to disguise themselves, and in a post-9/11 world, a war on terror replaces war on communism as a new "neo-imperialistic" phase in U.S. foreign policy.[52] For these reasons, and others, the identification of neo-liberalism with neo-imperialism, and perceiving a threat of Western powers and influence, especially, the United States, or the ubiquitous "Western threat," whether rational or irrational, frustrate aspirations for a Chinese neo-liberal coterie.

9.7. CONCLUSION

The denial of the prospects of liberalism and economic liberalism is, in part, an issue of political labeling or the culture relative political typology, and reflective of modern China's social-political environment and its nationalism and ideologism. For Karl Marx, the illusion of idealism that communist can carry into the revolutionary camp is ideologism (or ideology), because ideas make history.[53] Depending on one's perspective, political preferences or cultural relative political typology, it is a "Western threat" or "China threat" driving Sinic-West relations toward tenuous rather than optimality, which creates problems for the invocation of Western rules, norms, *ethos* and values for modern Chinese society. We (the West), as liberal proponents of Western universalism and its legal and economic theories and models, and the "China Threat," versus they (the Sinic), as illiberal proponents of finalizing the localization of Marxism and the "Western Threat," present a serious *impasse* in resolving

[51] John Carlos Rowe, Literary Culture and U.S. Imperialism: From Revolution to World War II, (Oxford UP, 2002). Henry C.K. Liu, The War may end the age of the Superpower, Commentary, Apr. 5, 2003, Online Asia Times.

[52] Vassilis K. Fouskas & Bulent Gokay, The New American Imperialism: Bush's War on Terror and Blood for Oil (Praeger Security Int'l General Interest, 2005). US: Possibility of world war never too far away, Aug. 29, 2006, People's Daily.

[53] "Hegelianism", Encyclopædia Britannica Online, academic edition (2007).

paradoxical interrelationships between competing legal and economic orders. For both the West and East, this serves as a reminder of the dangers of nationalism and ideologism in the promotion and usage of nonreciprocating political typologies such the "China threat" and "Western threat."

Chapter 10

POLITICAL ECONOMY OF LEGAL ORDER

10.1. POST-WTO CHINA AND REFORMS

During the late nineteenth century, China struggled with the then current debate of reformist policy versus dynastic or imperial rule, and during the post-Qing period, the debate evolves to the reformist policy versus revolution debate. After the 1949 founding of the People's Republic of China (China), while a post-1949 China continues to struggle with the issues of reform policy and revolution, the 1949 victory of the Chinese communists and the Communist Party necessitates casting the issues in terms of the new label or political typology of economic construction. During the historical debates concerning how to modernize or Westernize China, from the late-Qing to post-1949 China, traditional culture Chinese (primarily traditional Confucianism) suffers relegation, though for various reasons, to minimum importance. Traditional culture or "old" culturalism suffers displacement, as in the act of moving something from its natural environment, for various reasons, from Sun Yat-sen seeking to overthrown Manchu rule of the late Qing, to Mao Zedong and other Chinese communists advocating class revolution. During the debates concerning dynastic or imperial rule, reform, revolution and economic construction, the issues of legal reform, like "old" culturalism, equally suffered relegation to minimum importance. It would not be until the eve of the infamous Great Cultural Revolution (*Wenhua Da Geming*, 1966-1976) that China's polity seriously turned its attention to the modernization of its legal system or legal reforms, in conjunction with economic construction or economic reforms.

In the early days of post-1949 China, strategies and formulas for success varied and were experimental, ranging from a Soviet-style central planned economy, copying Stalinist industrialization, an agricultural collectivization system, the Great Leap Forward movement (*Dayuejin*, 1958-1962), the Democratic "Rectification Campaign" (*Zhengfeng yundong*),[1] to other programs and campaigns. However, earlier strategies and programs of economic construction virtually came to a halt with the onset of the Great Cultural Revolution. During the eve of the Great Cultural Revolution, as of 1978, achieving economic goals would be the measure of the success or failure of policies and, supposedly, individual leadership. Two

---

[1] Williams Harms, China's Great Leap Forward, Univ of Chicago Chronicle, Vol. 15, No. 13, Mar. 14, 1996. Lu Wei, Institutional Constraints, Economics Imbalance and Fiscal Policy – On China's Transitional Economy Since 1998, 3-5, Social Sciences in China (Zhongguo shehui kexue) (Aug. 2004). Janos Kornai, Economics of Shortage, (North-Holland, Amsterdam, 1980) 4-15.

years following the travesty of the Great Cultural Revolution, in 1978, China's polity, during the Third Plenary Session of the 11th Committee of the Communist Party Congress (CPC), adopted a policy of restoring the construction of a socialist legal system and democracy, while also announcing a shift from a work priority of class struggles to economic construction.[2] However, unlike the proposed reform and opening (*gaige kaifang*) of the economic infrastructure and its institutions, the CCP delays the reform of China's legal system, and greater political liberalization and democracy, as China's polity prioritized reforms focused on economic construction or economic reforms. The significance of reforms in light of China's entry into the World Trade Organization (WTO) is the influence of WTO membership on both past and present reforms, or during the pre-accession and post-accession periods, especially implementation of the rule of law.[3]

The issues of China's legal system and rule of rule comprised a large part of the debate, which surrounded China's December 11, 2001 accession to the WTO. The United States and other countries intensify their criticism of China's legal system and rule of law when scrutinizing China's application for WTO membership. For China, accession represents a prescription for broad systemic reforms in the areas of transparency (*toumingdu*), fairness (*gongping*) and independent judicial review (*duli sifa shencha*). Post-WTO China has expended considerable effort in striving to comply with WTO standards and rules, as pertains to its legal system and rule of law. For China, a commitment to rule of law, and its attendant independent judicial review, derives from its acceptance of key provisions in the protocol on accession, such as Articles 2(A)3 and 2(D). In addition, there is the amended Agreement on Implementation of Article VI of the General Agreement on Tariffs and Trade 1994, at Article 13, on Judicial Review, which requires, "Each Member whose national legislation contains provisions on anti-dumping measures shall maintain judicial, arbitral or administrative tribunals or procedures for the purpose, *inter alia*, of the prompt review of administrative actions relating to final determinations and reviews of determinations within the meaning of Article 11. Such tribunals or procedures shall be independent of the authorities responsible for the determination or review in question." An earlier WTO Appellate Body Report also confirms that WTO members must establish sound legal mechanisms for implementing their obligations under the WTO Agreement. Implementation of rule of law and its attendant independent judicial review is necessary, in terms of Western legal norms, to legal reform and economic development.[4] China's polity also recognizes an obligation and need to reform its legal system. For China, a well-established socialist market economic system requires a well-established socialist market legal system or socialist market economic legal system.

---

[2] Chen Sixi, The Gradual Reform of the Electoral System in China, 94, 101, Social Sciences in China (Zhongguo shehui kexue) (spring 2004).

[3] Protocol on the Accession of the People's Republic of China, WT/l/432, Nov. 10, 2001, available at http://docsonline.wto.org [hereinafter Protocol on Accession]. Marrakesh Agreement Establishing the World Trade Organization, Apr. 15, 1994, Legal Instruments - Results of the Uruguay Round, 1867 U.N.T.S. 154, 33 I.L.M. 1144 (1994).

[4] India - Patent Protection for Pharmaceutical and Agricultural Chemical Products, Report of the Appellate Body, WT/DS50/AB/R, 19 Dec. 1997, e.g., at paras. 57-58. Asian Development Bank, Law and Development at the Asian Development Bank: A Summary of the Law-Related Development Activities of the Asian Development Bank, ADB Publication, Vol. 54, 4-5 (1998). Wang Baoshu, China's Accession to the WTO and the Building of a Socialist Market Economic Legal System, In China: Accession to the WTO and Economic Reform, 338 (Wang Mengku ed., Beijing: Foreign Language Press, 2002). Asian Development Bank, ADB Publication 1–4 (1999), http://www.adb.org/Documents/Others/Law_ADB/1&d_1999.pdf.

Many recognize that legal reforms are needed, in order to sustain economic growth and prosperity. The directional growth and development of Chinese constitutionalism, rule of law and independent judicial review has national, interregional and international implications that affect the growth and prosperity of both China and the world's economy. The CCP, the Asian Development Bank (ADB) and other international bodies, such as the WTO, recognize this need to establish sound legal mechanisms. Eric W. Orts observed, "Some independent judicial authority appears to be evolving gradually, especially in the area of business law." However, Orts also rightly observes, "The Chinese legal system followed the Marxist thought that the Communist Party should have 'absolute control' over the 'organs of the state.'" As a practical consequence, given a priority of sustaining economic growth and prosperity, modern legal reforms have focused on compliance, though minimum, with the standards imposed by the WTO protocol on accession and the Trade Review Mechanism (TRM) or Trade Policy Review Mechanism (TPRM). Post-WTO reforms have focused on improving China's socialist market economic legal system, implementing WTO rules and enacting laws that, generally, tally with the WTO rules.[5] A critical component and measurement of modern legal reforms will be China's adoption, Sinicization or localization of the rule of law, as measured by Western ideal rule of law rather than Marxist legal theory or socialist jurisprudence.

A problem is that the pursuit of establishing a socialist market legal system or socialist market economic legal system directly links with the problem of the CCP attempting to finalize the localization of Marxism to the realities of traditional culture and society (*Makesi zhuyi he Zhongguo shiji xiang jiehe*). The historical attempt of the early Chinese communists and now, the CCP, to finalize the localization of Marxism also presents issues of the problems associated with localizing Marxist legal theory or socialist jurisprudence, and presents a ubiquitous challenge to both the Western ideal rule of law model, and what remains of traditional Chinese jurisprudence. Many experts and authority while hailing and praising China's progress in legal and economic reforms, seem willing to deny that Marxism, post-Marxism and neo-classical Marxism are still the subjects of theoretical discourses within and without the halls of both Chinese academia and Western academia. Policies and actions of China's polity, the CCP, effectually manifest problematic modern legal reforms that are primarily driving the pursuit of minimum WTO compliance and Marxist ideals rather than domestic needs of its citizens. Despite minimum compliance with the WTO rules, the latter presents issues of China's model of constitutional government and whether China's model rises to the level of a constitutional state or rule of law state where citizens are protected from the arbitrary exercise of governmental powers, while also enjoying legally based civil liberties and freedoms that can be enforced pursuant to the rule of law.

[5] Eric W. Orts, The Rule of Law in China, Eric Orts, Vol. 34 Vand. J. Transnat'l L. 43 (2002). Jerome Alan Cohen, Tiananmen and the Rule of Law, in The Broken Mirror: China after Tiananmen 323-328 (George Hicks, ed., St. James Pr., 1990). Jiang Wei, China's WTO achievements recognized, Dec. 15, 2005, China Daily. Agreement establishing the Trade Policy Review Mechanism (Annex 3 of the Marrakesh Agreement Establishing the WTO) [hereinafter TPRM]. The Transitional Review Mechanism is unique to China and is required by Article 18 of the Protocol on Accession. Id. Song Linfei, China's Accession to the WTO and the Building of a Socialist Market Economic Legal System 331-364, In China: Accession to the WTO and Economic Reform (Wang Mengku ed., Beijing: Foreign Language Press, 2002). Chi Fulin, China The New Stage of Reform (Beijing: Foreign Language Press, 2004).

10.2. Western Rule of Law

The rule of law, though variously described, "is neither a rule nor a law." In terms of Western jurisprudence, the rule of law is, generally, definable as "a doctrine of political morality which concentrates on the role of law in securing the correct balance of rights and powers between individuals and the state in free and civilized societies."[6] In terms of the Western Enlightenment, and its subsequent interpretations, the potential for democracy, liberty and freedom are contingent on a state embracing the rule of law or the state of legality. The latter liberal or Enlightenment ideals of democracy, liberty and freedom, as presumed greater social goods, can only develop to the extent that law guarantees the rights of citizens, such as civil rights and political freedoms. The road to justice, ultimately, depends on the ability of citizens of a state to speak freely and publicly about any experiences of injustice.

For instance, in Germany, a state of legality is a *Rechtsstaat* (literally, a law-based state or a constitutional state), where the rule of law restrains the exercise of state power or government power. The concept of *Rechtsstaat* (constitutional state) first appeared in the German context in Robert von Mohl's book, which is entitled *German Police Science after the Principles of the Right State* (*Die deutsche Polizeiwissenschaft nach den Grundsätzen des Rechtsstaates*, 1832-1834), in contrast to the term "autocratic police state" (*aristokratischen*). A *Rechtsstaat* (state of legality) is also characteristic of other Western legal systems, such as Anglo-American jurisprudence or rule of law and French *État de droit.* Donald P Kommers observed that Germany provides a model constitution for the world because its courts have exclusive power to invalidate laws on constitutional grounds. In the constitutional state or rule of law state, such as a *Rechtsstatt*, citizens are protected from the arbitrary exercise of government powers or authority, while also enjoying legally based civil liberties and freedoms that can be enforced pursuant to the rule of law, in a court of law.[7] A country can hardly be described as a liberal democracy, if it fails the test of being a constitutional state or state of legality, such as a *Rechtsstaat.* For this reason, a *Rechtsstaat* is also describable as rule of law, limited government, substantive due process, reasonableness, equal protection, and full and fair hearing, which is equally true of Anglo-American rule of law and French *État de droit.*

There have, admittedly, been problems in defining the rule of law. In a globalizing multicultural world, it is the problem of constitutionalism and democratic transition. In a post-cold war (1945-1991) era of ensuing globalization, the world is witnessing the phenomenon of "conceptual stretching."[8] In non-Western and developing countries such as China, there is a proclivity to employ Western notions of democracy and constitutionalism in description of a diverse range of social and political phenomena, including differing theoretical approaches

---

[6] Alex Carroll, Constitutional and Administrative Law 18 (Law Press 2002). Martin Kriele, Human Rights and the Separation of Powers, in Fa Zhi (The Rule of Law), (Josef Thesing & Winfried Jung, ed.) (Beijing: Fashi Chubanshe, 2005). Jiang Shigong, The End of Legal Transplantation, Social Sciences in China (Zhongguo shehui kexue), 159 (Aug. 2004).

[7] L. Heuschling, État de droit, Rechstaat, Rule of law, (Paris: Dalloz, 2002). Michel Rosenfeld, The Rule of Law and the Legitimacy of Constitutional Democracy, 74 S. Cal. L. Rev. 1307, 1308-09, (2001). Ulrich Karpen, Conditions of 'Rechstaat' Efficiency Particularly in Developing and Newly Industrialising Countries, in Fa Zhi (The Rule of Law), (Josef Thesing & Winfried Jung, eds.), (Beijing: Fashi Chubanshe, 2005). Susan Newman, Comparing Courts, Wash. U. Sch. of L. Magazine 8-9 (spring 2002).

[8] Giovanni Sartori, Concept Misformation in Comparative Politics, American Political Science Review, LXIV, 1033, 1041 (1970).

and models. The multifarious nature of rule of law has lent to different meanings in different concepts and in different legal systems, because there seems not to be a consensus on what the rule of law means, nor what it stands against. The rule of law has also been described as having both a descriptive and prescriptive content because, as true of the conceptualizations of liberty and equality, descriptive meanings of the rule of law are contingent on assigned prescriptive meanings. For this reason, in terms of the rule of law of more complex contemporary polities, one should anticipate vigorous disagreements concerning the relevant prescriptive standards at stake. Consequently, the rule of law has come to mean different things for different legal traditions, such as Anglo-American rule of law, German *Rechtsstaat* and French *État de droit.*

For example, the American appellate review structure, and its activism and powers of constitutional review, generally, characterize a judicial pyramid structure in the placements of power, adjudication and review. American courts will generally focus on the legal rights of parties, because as observed by Chief Justice Marhsall, in *Marbury vs. Madsion* (1803), a primary task of the American courts has always been "to say what the law is."[9] A distinguishing feature of American courts is the authority to rule on the constitutionality of a law, while also fashioning appropriate legal relief for parties. It is a model reflecting the clearest example of a judicial model that fully promotes legal accountability rather than political accountability. There are also other Western models, such as the revision model of Germany's Federal Constitutional Court (*Bundesverfassungsgericht*), and the cassation models of France's Court of Cassation (*Cour de cassation*) and Italy's Constitutional Court (*Corte costituzionale*) that sits atop the Supreme Court of Cassation (*Suprema Corte di Cassazione*), which sits atop the hierarchy of ordinary courts, with the final word on statutory interpretation. William J. Nardini describes Italy's Constitutional Court as often rendering "informal declarations of unconstitutionality," which reflects a denounce-decline-demand decision-making model. The Constitutional Court after denouncing a law, one that fails to live up to constitutional principles, often declines to annul it, while demanding, though implicitly, that the legislature enact corrective legislation. The latter resembles the practice of the Austrian Federal Constitutional Court (*Verfassungsgerichtshof*) that, though distinguishable, delays implementation of a decision for a year, in order to allow the legislature time to enact corrective legislation. In terms of actual constitutional authority, pursuant to Italy's Constitution (*Costituzione della Repubblica Italiana*, 1948), the Constitutional Court has the power of "negative legislation" or the power to render judgments that accept a constitutional challenge (*sentenze di accoglimento*). The Constitutional Court, alternatively, can decline a constitutional challenge (*sentenze di rigetto*).

The efficiencies of the rule of law-civil law systems versus rule of law-common law systems, admittedly, have been debated. During the late 1990s, a group of economists conducting cross-country research concerning legal rules and economic growth concluded, "countries whose legal systems originated in the English common law have enjoyed superior per capita income growth compared with civil law countries, whose law is based on European codes, especially those countries whose law is based on the Napoleonic codes and hence on

[9] Marbury v. Madison, 5 U.S. (1 Cranch) 137, 177 (1803). William J. Nardini, Passive Activism and the Limits of Judicial Self-Restraint: Lessons for America from the Italian Constitutional Court, Vol. 30, Seton Hall L. Rev. 1 (2000). Austrian constitutional tribunal (Bundes-Undes-Verfassungsgesetz) (Constitution) (B-VG) Austria, art. 139, para. 5.

French law [*Code civil des français*]."[10] Many would disagreement with this conclusion and, instead, hail the superiority of civil law systems. The civil law-common law dichotomy has been the subject of debate for a substantial period. For instance, on the European continent, Germanists or Germanist jurists and legal historians, such as Otto Gierke (Otto Friedrich von Gierke, 1841-1921), searched for guidance from sources of Roman law, from the juristic science of the Roman *pontifices* in prehistoric times, the *Law of the Twelve Tables* (*Lex Duodecim Tabularum*, published 451-450 B.C.), the *Code of Justinian* (*Corpus Juris Civilis*, compiled AD 529 to AD 565), to later students of Roman law and written commentaries on praetor's edicts of Roman jurisconsults. They did so for purpose of interpreting the development and meaning of German law, as did studies of the antecedents to German law influence Herr von Gierke's views on *Rechtsstaat* and the federal nature of medieval states, which led him to become an early opponent of civil law systems.

However, for countries sharing the commonality of shared-universal values in the sense of the Platonic idea or Aristotelian form and its progeny of a Western legal tradition or common Western legal civilization, there is the commonality of the Enlightenment and its subsequent interpretations, especially the high ideal of a liberal democracy. In addition, the different Western models of constitutional review or judicial review, such as appeals, revision and cassation, despite their diverging and distinctive histories and procedural structures, eventually converge to a three-tier structure resembling a pyramid structure. It is now a tacit assumption that, though there may be inherent problems in both rule of law systems, rule of law systems are superior to non-rule of law systems, because rule of law systems promote democracy, and greater predictability and stability. There is also the commonality of pursuing a more liberal international economic order based on a market system, sound money and the rule of law. Perhaps as a matter of public choice theory, though primarily concerned with economic analysis of political rather than market choice, individuals generally choose to have government rather than not have government or return to the state of nature, by surrendering a portion of their individual liberties as a necessary part of the social contract with others similarly situated. Individuals consent to government under a constitutional state or rule of law state, because they are better off under a body of laws.[11]

The legally based civil liberties and freedoms that are enforced and protected by a state of legality, law-based state or constitutional state pursuant to the rule of law, are guaranteed through the mechanism of Montesquieu's (or Charles-Louis de Sécondat, Baron de la Brède et de Montesquieu, 1689–1755) separation of powers, which is from his most famous writing, *The Spirit of Laws* (*De l'esprit des lois*, 1748).[12] The institution of Western constitutionalism,

---

[10] Kenneth W. Dam, The Law-Growth Nexus 5 (Brookings Inst. Press, 2006). Fritz Schulz, History of Roman Legal Science, (Oxford UP, 1967). Barry Nicholas, An Introduction to Roman law, (Oxford UP, 1992). Sobei Mogi, Otto von Geike, his political teachings and jurisprudence, (P.S. King & Son, 1932).

[11] Gerard Alexander, Institutionalized Uncertainty, The Rule of Law, and The Sources of Democratic Stability, Comparative Political Studies, Vol. 35, No. 10, 1145-1170 (2002). Kenneth Arrow, Social Choice and Individual Values (1963), (Yale UP, 1970). Iain McLean, Public Choice: An Introduction (Blackwell Pub, 1987). Jeffrey L. Harrison, Law and Economics 291-99 (West Group, 2000). James A. Dorn (Statement), U.S.-China Economic and Security Review Commission, China's Financial System and Monetary Policies: The Impact on U.S. Exchange Rates, Capital Markets, and Interest Rates (109th Congress, 2nd Sess, Aug. 22, 2006).

[12] M. Ulric Killion, China's Amended Constitution: Quest for Liberty and Independent Judicial Review, Wash. U. Global Stud. L. Rev., Vol. 4, No. 1, 43 (2005). Montesquieu, The Spirit of Laws, In Great Books of the Western World 3 (Robert Maynard Hutchins ed., 1952). Jeffrey Sachs et al., Economic Reforms and Constitutional Transition, at 15 (Oct. 2000), http://ssrn.com/abstract=254110. Charles F. Hobson, The Great

such as U.S. constitutionalism, evolves around the interrelated legal concepts of popular sovereignty, separation of powers and independent judicial review. Rule of law is important for independent judicial review, because independent judicial review evolves from the rule of law and exhibits characteristics distinctive of Western legal norms and history. In terms of judicial review, many hail the U.S. Supreme Court's decision in *Marbury vs. Madison*, as establishing the "leading precedent" of independent judicial review. However, the notion itself actually predates Chief Justice Marshall's 1803 decision in *Marbury*. "It was employed by the *parlements* of the Ancien Régime to justify their refusal to record acts contrary to the basic laws of the kingdom. Abbé Sieyés also invoked it, declaring in 1795 that either the constitution is binding or it is a nullity. The same idea was later proposed by Carré de Malberg, establishing a link between the possibility of review on the one hand and the separation of constituent and constituted powers on the other." During the pre-Reformation period, earlier Christian institutions also evolved the concept of a separation of powers in an earlier ongoing struggle between the Papacy and secular rule, as in the case of the Holy Roman Empire.[13]

Thomas Hobbes (1588-1679), whom is considered by many, such as Pierre Manet, as the father of classical liberalism and the founding and paradigmatic liberal, would contribute to modern philosophy his materialist philosophy of the seventeenth century, including the evolution of his rationality of absolute power into democratic power sharing. Hobbes's materialist philosophy, though inadvertently, also evolved into the seemingly dissimilar idea of a separation of powers. Moreover, just as the notion of judicial review preceded Marshall's pronouncement in *Marbury*, there were others, such as Niccoló Machiavelli (1469-1527) that preceded Baron de Montesquieu. Some contend that Machiavelli anticipated Montesquieu, and his separation of the powers of government, in his enthusiasm for a mixed government. Machiavelli, in his *Discourses on the First Decade of Titus Livius* (*Discorsi sopra la prima deca di Tito Livio*, 1513–21), wrote, "In fact, when there is combined under the same constitution a prince, nobility, and the power of the people, then these three powers will watch and keep each other reciprocally in check." Western jurisprudence, and its institutions of constitutionalism and judicial review, stem from several origins, including the Enlightenment thinkers. An important distinguishing feature of Western jurisprudence jurisprudence is that it emanates from philosophical ideals, fear of oppressive government and the need to limit the exercise of popular democracy. For instance, the U.S. Constitution bore its roots in the fear of a monarch and the need to limit the exercise of popular democracy, which paralleled a fear of Nazi rule under the Weimar Republic when writers drafted a post-World War II German Constitution.[14]

Chief Justice: John Marshall and the Rule of Law 47 (1996). Michel Troper, The Logic of Justification of Judicial Review, 1 Int'l J. Const. L. 99, 103 (2003). Raymond Carre De Malberg, La Loi, Expression De La Volonté Générale (Law, An Expression of the General Will, 1931) 126 (Economica eds., 1984).

13 James Kurth, The Fate of the West in the Age of Globalization: Triumph or Twilight?, Vol. 1, No. 10, FPRI newsletter (2000).

14 Thomas Hobbes, Leviathan (1651) 85 (M. Oakeshot, ed, Oxford 1946). Pierre Manet, An Intellectual History of Liberalism (Princeton UP, 1996). Niccoló Macchiavelli, The Discourses of Niccolo Machiavelli (1513–21) (W. Clark ed., Leslie J. Walker trans., Routledge & Kegan Paul, 1950). Donald P. Kommers, Book Review, 9 E. Eur. Const. Rev. No. 1/2 (2000), (reviewing Andras Sajó, Limiting Government: An Introduction to Constitutionalism, 1999).

10.3. The 1982 Constitution and Constitutionalism

Notwithstanding rule of law, a country's constitution, while serving as an important force in the governance of a polity, also serves as an importance force for compelling a positive, discursive model of judicial review. In 1997, China's polity, the CCP, through its National People's Congress (NPC), announced that China would be governed by rule of law. In 1999, the concept of rule of law was added to the 1982 Constitution of the People's Republic of China (*Zhonghua renmin gongheguo xianfa*, 1982 Constitution). As of 2007, the 1982 Constitution has undergone four constitutional amendments—on April 12, 1988, March 29, 1993, March 15, 1999, and March 14, 2004. However, it is the third constitutional amendment (*xiugai xianfa*) or the 1999 constitutional amendment to the 1982 Constitution that declares China would practice rule of law and upgrade the private sector from complement of the socialist economy to an important component of the country's socialist market economy.[15] The third amendment to the 1982 Constitution (Approved on March 15, 1999, by the 9th NPC at its 2nd Session) made the following change to the original text in the Preamble: "The basic task of the nation is to concentrate its efforts on socialist modernization by following the road of building socialism with Chinese characteristics. Under the leadership of the Communist Party of China and the guidance of Marxism-Leninism, Mao Zedong Thought and Deng Xiaoping Theory, the Chinese people of all nationalities will continue to adhere to the people's democratic dictatorship, follow the socialist road, persist in reform and opening-up, steadily improve socialist institutions, develop a socialist market economy, advance socialist democracy, improve the socialist legal system and work hard and self-reliantly to modernize industry, agriculture, national defense and science and technology step by step to turn China into a powerful and prosperous socialist country with a high level of culture and democracy." In addition, an amendment to Article 5, the first section, of the 1982 Constitution, reads, "The People's Republic of China practices ruling the country in accordance with the law and building a socialist country of law."

Constitutionalism is defined as "Government in which power is distributed and limited by a system of laws that must be obeyed by the rulers."[16] Notwithstanding the *de facto* power of the CCP, pursuant to the 1982 Constitution, the NPC is the highest organ of state power. It is the national legislature and the supreme organ of state power. The NPC's standing body is the Standing Committee of the National People's Congress (NPCSC). The NPC exercises typical legislative functions, such as, enact and amend basic laws, elect Procurator-General, plan for national economy and social development, declare war, amend constitution, and other powers.[17] However, the powers of the NPC are distinguishable in two respects. The NPC also

---

[15] Zhong Hua Ren Min Gong He Guo Xian Fa (Constitution of the People's Republic of China), Adopted at the Fifth Session of the Fifth National People's Congress on Dec. 4, 1982 and promulgated for implementation by the Proclamation of the National People's Congress on Dec. 4, 1982, [Xianfa [Const.] (1982) (P.R.C.).]. Zhong Hua Ren Min Gong He Gou Xian Fa Xiu Zheng An (Amendment to the Constitution of the People's Republic of China), Adopted at the First Session of the Seventh National People's Congress on Apr. 12, 1988 and promulgated for implementation by the Proclamation No. 8 of the National People's Congress on Apr. 12, 1988, [Xianfa Xiu Zheng An [CONST. AMEND.]. Xianfa Xiu Zheng An [CONST. AMEND.] arts. 3-11 (Mar. 29, 1993) (P.R.C.). Xianfa Xiu Zheng An [CONST. AMEND.] arts. 12-17 (Mar. 15, 1999) (P.R.C.).

[16] Webster's II New College Dictionary, 242 (3rd. ed. 2001).

[17] M. Ulric Killion, Post-WTO China and Independent Judicial Review, 26 Hous. J. Int'l L. 507 (2004). Xianfa [Const.] (1982) (P.R.C.), Chapter III, Articles 57, 58, 61,62, 62(2), 67(1) and 67(4). Zhonghua renmin gongheguo shangwu bu (People's Republic of China Ministry of Commerce, MOFCOM), http://english.mofcom.gov.cn/.

has the power to enforce the Constitution, and through the NPCSC has the power of judicial review. The NPC meets once a year, which results in its State Councilors and Ministers in charge of ministries or commissions, such as China's Ministry of Commerce (MOFCOM), having more powers than expressly delegated in the 1982 Constitution. The brief annual session of the NPC is filled with numerous items of business, including examination of the government's work and budgetary review. In comparison, the NPCSC meets bi-monthly, while mainly focusing on lawmaking issues. The NPC and its Standing Committee, the NPCSC, seldom have the time to conduct constitutional overviews and investigations of constitutional violations, especially the many suggestions and comments from individuals.[18]

The 1982 Constitution marginalizes the power of the judiciary. One must read Articles 5, 67(1), 67(4), and 127, in conjunction with the earlier discussed constitutional division of governmental power to understand how the judiciary is rendered constitutionally weak and marginalized. The preamble of 1982 Constitution reads, "this Constitution, in legal form . . . it is the fundamental law of the state and has supreme authority. The people of all nationalities, all state organs, the armed forces, all political parties and public organizations and all enterprises and institutions in the country must take the Constitution as the basic stand of conduct, and they have the duty to uphold the dignity of the Constitution and ensure its implementation." Further, amended Article 5 reads, "the People's Republic of China governs the country according to law and makes it a socialist country ruled by law." Article 127 of the 1982 Constitution provides that the Supreme Court or Supreme People's court (*Zuigao Renmin Fayuan*) is the highest judicial organ. Some Western experts and authority, admittedly, hail the 1982 Constitution, which uses the 1952 Constitution as a framework, as possessing a workable set of institutions capable of moving China toward democracy: "a series of four levels of people's congresses from the local to national level exercising popular sovereignty."[19] However, these explicit constitutional provisions reduced a potential for a Western rule of law rubric, to a non-Western rule of law rubric; reduced a potential constitutional, rule of law and legal accountability, to political accountability; and left China's judicial system without a positive discursive machinery for judicial review: Neither constitutional review or a constitutional court, nor decentralized (or diffused) or centralized (or concentrated) constitutional review.

Upon further examination of the 1982 Constitution, the weaknesses of the judiciary and legal system become more obvious. The sole power to interpret the constitution and laws of China, or legislative interpretation power (*lifa jieshi quanli*), does vest with the NPCSC.[20] Further, there is the promulgation of China's new legislative procedure law, the 2000 Legislation Law of the People's Republic of China (*Zhonghua Renmin Gonghe Guo Lifa Fa* or *Lifa Fa*), which seeks to better define roles of lawmakers and procedures, and attempts to establish legal hierarchy between the constitution, laws, administrative regulations and orders, at both national and local levels.[21] In addition, notwithstanding conflicting national and local laws, the State Council has administrative interpretation power (*xingzheng jieshi quanli*),

---

[18] China set up new Agency to see to Constitution Application, June 21, 2004, Xinhua. Meng Yan, New Agency to see too Constitution application, June 21, 2004, China Daily.

[19] Andrew J. Nathan, China's Transition 73 (1997).

[20] Xianfa [Const.] (1982) (P.R.C.), Chapter III, Articles 67(1) and 67(4).

[21] Legislation Law of the People's Republic of China (Zhonghua Renmin Gongheguo Lifa Fa), (Adopted at the Third Session of the Ninth National People's Congress on Mar. 15, 2000, promulgated by Order No. 31 of the President of the People's Republic of China on Mar. 15, 2000, and effective as of July 1, 2000).

which is the constitutional power to interpret all administrative regulations, while agencies such as the Ministries and Commissions have administrative interpretation powers over departmental rules and regulations. Consequently, in practice, the constitutional alignment of governmental power places the NPC in greater power over both the Supreme People's Court and State Council Ministries and Commissions. Although the State Council, the highest executive organ, is not in actual practice, or power, subordinate to the NPC, the Supreme People's Court, the highest judicial organ, is in constitutional text and practice, or power, actually subordinate to both the NPC and State Council in judicial interpretation powers. Moreover, the Supreme People's Court has judicial interpretation power (*sifa jieshi quanli*), but it is limited delegated power to interpret laws and regulations of China arising from actual cases, which is not the same power constitutionally vested with the NPCSC to interpret the constitution and laws of China (*lifa jieshi quanli*).[22] A distinction between interpreting laws arising from actual cases, as opposed to interpreting a constitution is a fine line. Two earlier Letters of Reply ("Reply") from the Supreme People's Court show this fine line of demarcation. In a 1955 Reply, the Supreme People's Court writes that it is not appropriate to cite the Constitution as a basis for a decision. Further, in a 1986 Reply, the Supreme People's Court writes that courts should not cite opinions or Replies.

The process of amending China's constitution is also problematic. Article 62(1) of the 1982 Constitution, as opposed to judicial decision, other existing conventional practices, or other existing non-conventional practices, governs the process of amending constitution. The 1982 Constitution grants the NPC authority to amend the constitution, and its simplicity in language and constitutional grant of authority speaks to a flexible rather than rigid process for amendment.[23] The 1982 Constitution reads, "The National People's Congress exercises the following functions and powers . . . to amend the constitution [*xiugai xianfa*]." The power to amend the constitution wholly vests with the NPC, and all past amendments (*xiuzhengan)* to the 1982 Constitution were enacted by the Seventh NPC, Eight NPC and Ninth NPC. However, despite a frequency in constitutional amendments, and, no doubt, constitutions may need to be revised and amended, in terms of Western constitutionalism, a constitution should provide rigorous procedures for its amendment. According to Andras Sajo, "[A] viable constitution -- that is, one that guarantees and respects the ideal of constitutionalism -- will make sure that it does not promise more than it can deliver; that it confines itself mainly to the protection of negative liberties; and that it organizes the branches of government in a way that limits state power without interfering with the effective exercise of popular government."[24] In China, there is a dangerous precedent of constitutionalizing party ideologies by a flexible

---

[22] Xianfa [Const.] (1982) (P.R.C.), Chapter III, The Structure of the State, Section 1, The National People's Congress, Articles 67(1) and 67(4). 1955 Letter of Reply: Letter of Reply Concerning the Inappropriateness of Citing Constitution as a Basis for Convictions and Sentencing in Criminal Judgments; 1986 Letter of Reply: Reply Concerning How People's Courts Are to Cite Legally Normative Documents When Producing Legal Documents.

[23] Dag Anckar & Lauri Karvonen, Constitutional Amendment Methods in the Democracies of the World, Paper delivered at the XIIIth Nordic Political Science Congress, Aalborg, Denmark, Aug.15-17, 2002. Xianfa [Const.] arts. 62(1) and 67(1)-(2) (P.R.C.) (1982). Xianfa Xiu Zheng An [CONST. AMEND.] arts. 1-2 (Apr. 12, 1988) (P.R.C.). Xianfa Xiu Zheng An [CONST. AMEND.] arts. 3-11 (Mar. 29, 1993) (P.R.C.). Xianfa Xiu Zheng An [CONST. AMEND.] arts. 12-17 (Mar. 15, 1999) (P.R.C.)

[24] Donald P. Kommers, Limiting Government-An Introduction to Constitutionalism by Andras Sajor, East European Constitutional Review, Vol. 9, No. 1/2, (winter/spring 2000), (Comments on Limiting Government – An Introduction to Constitutionalism, by Andras Sajor). Balance between consistency, adaptability, Oct. 30, 2003, China Daily. Human rights, private property fixed as pillars, Dec. 23, 2003, China Daily.

rather than rigid constitutional amendment process. For instance, the March 2004 amendment to 1982 Constitution incorporated Jiang Zemin's "The theory of the Three Represents" (Three Represents, *San Ge Daibiao*) into the preamble of the 1982 Constitution, as one of the guiding principles of the nation, "together with the heritage and further development of Marxism, Leninism, Mao Zedong Thought and Deng Xiaoping Theory." The latter exhibits a marked proclivity of China's polity, the CPC and NPC, to constitutionalize party ideology. In terms of normative versus semantic constitutionalism, party ideology may take over or supplant a constitution, or a constitution may emerge that affirms or demands compliance to party ideology. Modern Chinese constitutionalism is shrouded and obscured by CCP ideology. Indeed, there is an inherent danger that the CCP will write its entire ideology into the constitution.[25] In terms of Western constitutional norms, constitutionalizing party ideology remains a questionable practice, especially a flexible amendment process frequently incorporating ideology. It equally demonstrates the historical struggle of party ideologies against the force and paradoxical sources of legal orders, such as traditional culture (and its jurisprudence) and models of Western constitutionalism (and its rule of law).

The latter also presents issues of the significance of constitutionalizing ideologies, such as the theory of the "Three Represents," while still leaving the problem of ascertaining the true significance of the CCP announced goals such as building a *xiaokang* or moderately well-off society and a harmonious socialist society. Moreover, the practice of constitutionalizing party ideologies, such as the "Three Represents," may produce additional problems for China's polity, the CCP, and Chinese society, especially the goals of building a *xiaokang* and harmonious socialist society. In terms of orthodox Western constitutional theory and practice, China's practice of constitutionalizing party ideology presents an unorthodox constitutional practice, which may present grave consequences in the future, especially concerning issues of governance, legitimacy and building a genuine *xiaokang* and harmonious society.

In terms of the unorthodox constitutional practice of constitutionalizing party ideologies, Anne F. Thurston demonstrates the gist of this problem of unconventionalism, by a simple, yet poignant, question, "Are the names of your leaders mentioned in your constitution?"[26] Despite China's non-orthodox and non-Western approach to constitutional theory and practice, and the many controversies surrounding Jiang Zemin's proposed constitutional amendments, both the CPC and the NPC would incorporate Jiang Zemin's theory of the "Three Represents," respectively, into the CPC constitution and the 1982 Constitution. On November 14, 2002, the Party's Sixteenth CPC, by unanimous agreement, amended the Constitution of the CPC by inclusion of Jiangs theory of the "Three Represents." Thereafter, on March 14, 2004, the NPC amended the 1982 Constitution by incorporating the theory of "Three Represents" into the preamble, as one of the guiding principles of the nation *together with* the heritage and further development of Marxism, Leninism, Mao Zedong Thought, and Deng Xiaoping Theory.[27] For modern China (or post-1949 China), there is the CCP's historical quadruplet of ideologies, namely, Marxism, Leninist Principles, Mao Zedong

[25] Killion, China's Amended Constitution, Id.

[26] Anne F. Thurston, Memory and Mourning: China Ten Years after Tiananmen, SAIS Review - Volume 19, Number 2, Summer-Fall 1999, 61-79.

[27] Full Text of Resolution on Amendment to CPC Constitution, Nov. 15, 2002, China Daily. Barbara Foley, Id. Human Rights, Private Property Fixed as Pillars, Dec. 23, 2003, China Daily. Jiang Faces Reform Attacks From Within, Aug. 28, 2002, CNN.

Thought, and Deng Xiaoping Theory. In modern China, this quadruplet of ideologies is associated by common properties manifesting ultimate goal of preserving one-party communist-led or socialist-led rule. The quadruplet of ideologies became the quintuplet (or combination of five of a kind) of ideologies with the inclusion of Jiang Zemin's "Three Represents" Theory. On March 14, 2004, the last ideology added to the 1982 Constitution and quadruplet of ideologies by constitutional amendment was Jiang Zemin's controversial "Theory of Three Represents," which was incorporated into the preamble of the constitution. The preamble of the 1982 Constitution at relevant part reads, "Under the leadership of the Communist Party of China and the guidance of Marxism-Leninism, Mao Zedong Thought, Deng Xiaoping Theory, and the important thought of the "Three Represents," the Chinese people of all nationalities will continue to adhere to the people's democratic dictatorship, follow the socialist road, persist in reform and opening-up, steadily improve socialist institutions, develop a socialist market economy, advance socialist democracy, improve the socialist legal system and work hard and self-reliantly to modernize industry, agriculture, national defense and science and technology step by step, promote the co-ordinated development of the material, political and spiritual civilizations to turn China into a powerful and prosperous socialist country with a high level of culture and democracy."

However, unlike the "Three Represents," the CCP's announced goals of building a *xiaokang* society and a harmonious socialist society are not constitutionalized in the 1982 Constitution. The CCP's announced goals of building a *xiaokang* society and harmonious socialist society, by virtue of the explicit constitutionalization of Jiang's theory of the "Three Represents," admittedly, could arguably, though the faintest of arguments, constitute their implicit incorporation into the 1982 China constitution. In other words, these goals are hardly of constitutional import. In addition, the explicit or implicit constitutionalizing of ideologies still leaves in tact the problems of writing ideologies into national constitutions. Ideologies are dangerous in and of themselves. It is a danger only enhanced when ideology is constitutionalized. Notwithstanding the dangers of ideologies, especially one-party CCP rule, there is a specific danger presenting the potential for a constitutional crisis. "In China, there is an inherent danger of a flexible constitutional amendment process that allows for the frequent constitutionalization of political ideology. Because the 1982 Constitution manifests a history of constitutionalizing official party ideology, China runs the risk of becoming victim to political and ideological forces as ideology supplants the 1982 Constitution, the 1982 Constitution emerges as no more than an affirmation of official party ideology and a demand for conformity to it."[28] More specifically, in terms of modern Chinese rules of order, the latter presents problems for the written and unwritten rules that govern Chinese society, while equally challenging the genuine intent or purpose of China's polity, in announcing the goals of building a *xiaokang* and harmonious socialist society. The latter also still leaves pending the unanswered question of the true significance of these goals. The world is still left to speculate whether the goals of building a *xiaokang* and harmonious socialist society are a fact, fiction, slogan, ideology, political rhetoric or, simply, old tricks in new conditions. For the CCP, all of this enhances problems of governance, legitimacy and building a *xiaokang* society and harmonious socialist society.

---

[28] Killion, China's Amended Constitution, Id. Suna Kili, Problems of the Application of Contemporary Constitutions, in Modern Constitution, 117, 131–32 (Thomas Fleiner-Gerster ed., 1988).

Ideology has been a force in Chinese constitutionalism, and culture may be the only force that equals, if not surpasses, the force of ideology, because Chinese institutions, including constitutionalism, are value-laden institutions possessing Confucian characteristics.[29] Ideology will influence the growth and direction of Chinese constitutionalism, and its attendant rule of law and judicial review, because "economic transition is part of the transition in constitutional rules," and its "speed and the time paths are determined by its driving mechanism."[30] The driving mechanisms are arguably internal and external wars, militarism, political culture, underdevelopment, poverty, flaws in constitutional design, ideology and other forces. Constitutionalism will reflect legal and economic reforms, and equally so, the force of ideology. The effect of constitutionalizing ideology has yet to be determined, especially its effect on defining Chinese constitutionalism, and its attendant rule of law and judicial review. Efficacy of a constitution is contingent upon constitutional provisions reflecting "not only sound political theory but also the values and historical experiences of the people whom the constitution will govern."

Then there are the issues of a proposed Chinese neo-liberal coterie and "neo-liberal constitutionalists." Assuming a political position farther left than even the "new left," in the social-political environment, there is little prospect for the citizenry or polity to reflect on the tenets of liberalism or economic liberalism. Assuming the political position of liberalism in China is akin to radicalism, if not anarchy, in terms of China's polity, the CCP, and its attendant cultural relative political typology, native language, culture, ideology, thought system and appropriate lexicons, an attempt to transplant liberalism in China's political, legal and economic systems will not fair well. A concomitant issue is the role of traditional culture in the selection and construct of social, economic, political and legal institutions. Another question is the extent to which a proposed Chinese neo-liberalism embodies Western classical liberalism or economic liberalism. During a February 21, 2003 symposium of Chinese neo-liberals, an American-based Chinese neo-liberal coterie, comprising Chinese born dissidents from the Tiananmen Square tragedy of 1989 era, urged that the Chinese people must be persuaded that rule of law (*fa zhi*) and neo-liberal constitutionalism will address their needs. The participants uniquely refer to themselves as "neo-liberal constitutionalists" that fully embrace Chinese neo-liberalism as the proper course for reforms and the future of China.[31] Given a contention that the "new elite" will foster Western liberal norms, one reasonably assumes a Chinese neo-liberal coterie would borrow notions of rule of law and economic liberalism from Western universalism and norms. Universalism is, "the assumption that there are irreducible features of human life and experience that exist beyond the constitutive effects of local cultural conditions... a hegemonic view of existence by which the experiences, values and expectations of a dominant culture are held to be true for all humanity."[32] In answer to question of where does China go now, the invocation of neo-liberalism in Mainland China, in answer to this question is problematic for other reasons.

---

[29] Qian, Mu (Ch'ien Mu), Traditional Government in Imperial China A Critical Analysis, 121, Chu-tu Hsueh and George O. Totten (trans.) (Chinese Univ of Hong Kong, 1982).

[30] Katharina Pistor & Philip A. Wellons, eds., The Role of Law and Legal Institutions in Asian Economic Development 1960-1995, (Oxford UP, 1998). Jeffrey Sachs, Wing Thye Woo, & Xiaokai Yang, Economic Reforms and Constitutional Transition, Inframarginal Economics (Oct. 2000).

[31] Richard Gunde, Distinguished Chinese Political Activists Discuss Constitutionalism & Political Reform, Feb. 2003, UCLA Asian Instit., http://www.isop.ucla.edu/article.asp?parentid=3243.

[32] Bill Ashcroft, Gareth Griffiths, & Helen Tiffen, Key Concepts in Post Colonial Studies, (London: Routledge, 1988), 235.

A Chinese concept of neo-liberal constitutionalism is expressed by the words (or characters) *xin ziyou lixian zhi*. In particular, the concept of constitutionalism is embodied in the words (or characters) *lixian, lixian zhi* or *jianli xianfa*, which are concepts from the late-Qing that literally mean "building up the constitution."[33] For modern China, and its attendant cultural relative political typology, native language, culture, ideology, thought system and appropriate lexicons, a Western conceptualization and its attendant native language, culture, ideology, thought system and appropriate lexicon, of constitutionalism, including neo-liberal constitutionalism, will not share the same value-laden meaning, nor influence. In 2006, the Pew Global Attitudes Project conducted a public opinion poll of 15 countries, including China. Polling results show that 80 percent of Chinese citizens were satisfied with the direction of China or the way things are going in China. The latter, though problematic, especially for a proposed "neo-liberal constitutionalist" coterie, lends credence to an earlier observation of the late eminent Chinese scholar Jiang Tingfu. In 1935, Jiang opined, "If the People do not want a share in government, no constitution can present them with any political power."[34] The value-laden ideals of Western constitutionalism and its underlying theories of democracy and liberty, espoused by such Enlightenment thinkers as John Locke and Jacque Rousseau -- "that government was held in trust instead of by ordained right and that the monarch was a mere agent of society with 'no will, no power but that of law' -- were conceptions 'alien' in the traditional Chinese social structure of hierarchical relationships and patriarchal values' and the Chinese vestiture of authority not in the people, but in the state.[35]

Problematic is a modern Chinese society still "suffused with hierarchical relationships and patriarchal values where authority was traditionally vested in the state and not the people." The Western concepts of liberty (old liberty) and economic liberalism (new liberty) are also value-laden concepts, thus, presenting a paradox for Chinese conceptualizations of liberty expressed by the words (or characters) *ziyou* (old liberty) and *xin ziyou* (new liberty). For instance, Chinese liberty (*ziyou*), and demonstrative of problems in value pluralism, is characteristically, "something we do, not something I do." Admittedly, the Pew Global Attitudes project only interviewed 2,180 people between the ages of 18 and 60, and polling was skewed towards urban areas in China, with interviews being mostly conducted in the urban areas or cities of Beijing, Shanghai, Guangzhou, Xinxiang, Jinzhong and Luzhou. Moreover, taking this survey at face value may only speak to the powers of nationalism, ideology and Marxism rather than the success of modern reforms, especially the 1978 promised reforms of political liberalization and democracy. Chinese constitutionalism is still developing, but the forces of nationalism, ideology and Marxism, and perhaps a "new" culturalism rather than "old" culturalism, and other forces, impedes its growth towards a Western model of constitutionalism, as opposed to a variant thereof, such as an economic-specific or culture-specific model.[36]

---

[33] Randle Edwards, Symposium on China and Constitutionalism: Introduction, J. of Asian Law, vol. 9, no. 1 (fall 1995), (Conversely, constitutionalism has been defined as "xianfazhuyi, lit[erally], the ideology of the constitution."). Survey: 80% Chinese satisfied with direction of China, June 14, 2006, China Daily.

[34] Jiang Tingfu, GMD and Members of GMD, Review of Independence, No. 176, 14 (1935).

[35] Killion, China's Amended Constitution, Id.

[36] Ricard A. Rosen, Constitutional Process, Constitutionalism, and the Eritrean Experience, Vol. 24, No.2 N.C. J. Int'l L. & Com. Reg. 263, 273 (winter 1999). Rett R. Ludwikowski, Constitution Making in the Countries of Former Soviet Dominance: Current Development, 23 Ga. J. Int'l & Comp. L. 155, 158 (1993). Heinz Klug, Model and Anti-Model: The United States Constitution and the Rise of the World Constitutionalism, 2000 Wis. L. Rev. 597, 604-13 (2000).

10.4. Judicial System and Reforms

In February 2005, China announced that it will "speed up" judicial reforms, and address issues, such as judicial review, the jury system, court organization, supervision and other related issues. According to Hu Yunteng, Deputy Director of the Research Office of the Supreme People's Court, the primary concerns are the study of defects under the current adjudication supervision system. Chinese law experts, generally, perceive the adjudication supervision procedure as manifesting three defects: First, the court and procuratorate can commence reviews, while litigants experience difficulty seeking a review or initiating an appeal. Second, the court's "free jurisdiction" is too large, or perhaps better stated, the court has too much discretion concerning reviews. Thirdly, the unlimited number and time for application for review leads to disorder and lower efficiency in handling law cases, therefore, producing verdicts deemed "marathon lawsuits" and "the turning-over of sesame seed cake." These defects are perceived as threatening the foundation for rule of law because they affect the rendering of judicial judgments, public confidence and the goal of achieving social stability or social relations.[37]

Reforms also address the issues of a trial by jurors. As of May 1, 2005, the *Decision on Perfecting the People's Juror System* passed by the 10th NPCSC was effective. The new jury system addresses issues surrounding the People's jurymen, who take part in trials and supposedly have the same rights as judges. The NPCSC in fashioning the People's jurymen system adopts a design proposal of the Supreme People's Court. Under the new system, preliminary elections of people's jurymen will take place during the months of January and February. In March and April, these jurymen or court personnel will receive intensive training. After completion of their training, the Standing Committees of County People's Congresses will appoint them, by placing them at their designated respective posts by May 1. Previously, the courts designate rotating jurors that will participate in trials, but, after May 1, 2005, there will be random extractions of jurymen for trials.

There is also the issue of court supervision of law cases. In China, the judicial committee is the highest judicial organ or organization within the court system. The basic duty of the judicial committee is to "summarize judicial experiences, discuss major or difficult cases and other problems related to judicial work." Under the Chinese system, as described by some Chinese law experts, "The judge does not make judgment, while the judicial officer does not try cases." Consequently, "It is the collegiate bench that tries some cases, but it is the judicial committee that makes the final decision." Generally, the three major defects of this system, in particular, the judicial committee, are the following: First, the organizational form of the court and its judicial committee is administrative-oriented. Members of the judicial committee are routinely presidents of law courts or tribunals, and the recruitment of experienced judges is not a priority. Second, the operational form manifests a conference-style, where the deliberations of a meeting room supplant legal tribunals and lend small value to legal proceedings. Third, there is a mystic surrounding a resolution, because the judicial committee routinely neither stamps approval by signatures of members and reasons for judgment, nor commits its verdict to writing.

---

[37] China is speeding up judicial reform, Feb. 19, 2005, People's Daily. Fu Yulin, Comparative Research on Judicial Hierarchy, 39-51 Social Sciences in China (Zhongguo shehui kexue) (spring 2003).

In China, the path of legal reforms is legal change responding in an ad hoc fashion to socio-economic change.[38] In response to social and economic conditions, the polity, the CCP, implements policy change and then the CCP, acting through its NPC, NPCSC and other agents of power, enacts legislation implementing these changes. A problem with China's legal system is that the post-enactment of social and economic changes, prompting policy change, have typically gone beyond the scope of the law. This then requires the State Council to implement regulations in response to new challenges. China's legal system and constitutionalism are distinctive because of their unique interrelationship, if not subservience, to China's polity, the CCP, NPC, NPCSC, the State Council and other agents of power, and policies prioritizing economic growth. Ongoing legal and economic reforms emphasize defining new international markets and rules of international trade rather than enhancing civil-political rights of individualized civil individuals. The pursuit of WTO compliance, though minimum compliance, rather than domestic needs of its citizens is one of the primary forces driving modern legal and economic reforms. Post-WTO reforms have focused on improving China's socialist market economic legal system, by implementing WTO rules and enacting laws that generally tally, though minimal compliance, with the WTO rules. China's history of prioritized economic growth, a changing world of international markets and globalization required a development policy focused on how laws are defining markets and how this affects international transactions, rather than focusing on the civil-political rights of its citizens. The problem for Western experts and authority is that Chinese rule of law remains at one remove from Western rule of law, with its ontological base in traditional culture still heavily burdened by the influence of Marxist, Leninist, communist or socialist ideology, now lending to a seemingly descriptive rule of law model or the antithesis of Western ideal rule of law. The issue of failed civil-political rights will eventually affect economic growth and economic development. A problem of a nexus between civil-political rights and economic development is a possible correlation of individual civil-political rights with legal safeguards for "other" individuals. The advent of a nexus between ongoing legal and economic reforms, and failed civil-political rights, prospectively could negatively influence and project a poor global image of Chinese legal safeguards for "other" individualized civil individuals, such as foreign importers, foreign exporters, transnational corporations and "other" individuals or legal persons.

There are also many law cases serving as a measure of Chinese constitutionalism, rule of law and independent judicial review. These cases also serve as a test of modern legal reforms, while also serving as a challenge to one-party CCP rule and its exclusivity in executive powers of government. Many hail, though a controversial subject, a July 24, 2001 Reply as China's Marbury vs. Madison (*Marbury*). The constitutional measure of China's *Marbury* is its progeny.

---

[38] M. Ulric Killion, Post-WTO China: Quest for human rights safeguards in sexual harassment against working women, 12 Tul. J. Int'l & Comp. L. 201 (2004). Fan Gang & Xin Chunying, The Role of Law and Legal Institutions in Asian Economic Development: The Case of China, Patterns of Change in the Legal System and Socio-Economy 11 (Harv. Inst. for Int'l Dev., Development Discussion Paper No. 664, Nov. 1998), http://www.hiid.harvard.edu/pub/pdfs/664.pdf.

10.5. China's Marbury vs. Madison

A July 24, 2001 Reply is arguably an implicit adoption by the Supreme People's Court of the principles of constitutionalism embodied in *Marbury vs. Madison*, and reads (English Translation) as follows.

> "Announcement of the Supreme People's Court. (Zui gao renmin fayuan guanyu yi qinfan xingming quan de shouduan qinfan xianfa baohu de gongmin shou jiaoyu de jiben quanli shi fou ying chengdan minshi zeren de pifu The reply of the Supreme People's Court Concerning Whether Civil Liability Arises When the Constitutionally-Protected Fundamental Right of Citizens to Receive Education Is Violated by Means of Violating Rights in a Person's Name) was adopted at the 1,183rd Session of the Judicial Committee of the Supreme People's Court on June 28, 2001. It is hereby promulgated. It shall come into effect as from August 13, 2001. July 24, 2001. The Reply of the Supreme People's Court Concerning Whether Civil Liability Arises When the Constitutionally-Protected Fundamental Right of Citizens to Receive Education Is Violated by Means of Violating Rights in a Person's Name, To the Shandong Provincial Higher People's Court: We have received your court's Request for Instructions Concerning the Dispute Involving Rights in a Person's Name Between Qi Yuling and Chen Xiaoqi, Chen Kezheng, the Jining Municipality School of Commerce of Shandong Province, the Tengzhou Municipality No. 8 High School of Shandong Province and the Tengzhou Municipal Education Commission of Shandong Province. After study, we hold, on the basis of the facts in this case, that Chen Xiaoqi and others have violated the fundamental right to receive education enjoyed by Qi Yuling in accordance with the provisions of the Constitution by means of violating rights in a person's name. This has produced the result of actual damages. Commensurate civil liability arises. Reply is hereby given."[39]

The Reply and its reliance on the constitution are antithetical to the court's long practice of refusing to rely on the constitution, and it is here the controversy begins. Although the language seems innocuous, its subsequent interpretation causes a stir. The genesis of the controversy is an article written by Huang Songyou, Chief Judge of the First Civil Division of the Supreme People's Court, entitled "Making the Constitution Justiciable and its Significance". He analyzes the reasons the Supreme People's Court will not cite directly to the Constitution. A 1955 Reply states that it is not appropriate to cite the Constitution as a basis for decision.[40] A 1986 Reply of the Supreme People's Court also provides that courts should not cite opinions and replies. An interpretation given to the Replies forbid a direct citing of the Constitution. He does however note that the 1955 Reply and 1986 Reply are equally subject to an interpretation of being only recommendations, as opposed to mandates, and further distinguishes them on other grounds. Judge Huang argues that the Reply establishes a precedent for the justiciability of the constitution, in that the constitution may now enter judicial proceedings just as with any other laws or regulations, and may serve as a legal basis for judgment. He sees far-reaching implications arising from this Reply. First, the

---

[39] Adopted at the 1,183rd Session of the Judicial Committee of the Supreme People's Court on June 28, 2001, Fa Shi [2001] No. 25. China Legal Change, http://www.chinalegalchange.com/freebref.htm.

[40] Huang Songyou, Chief Judge of the First Civil Division of the Supreme People's Court, Making the Constitution Justiciable and its Significance, People's Court Daily, Aug. 13, 2001. 1955 Letter of Reply: Letter of Reply Concerning the Inappropriateness of Citing Constitution as a Basis for Convictions and Sentencing in Criminal Judgments. 1986 Letter of Reply: Reply Concerning How People's Courts Are to Cite Legally Normative Documents When Producing Legal Documents.

Reply establishes a precedent for court protection of fundamental rights of citizens stipulated in the Constitution. It is in this distinction that Judge Huang argues that the Reply creates a landmark decision in China's legal system. The fundamental rights of citizens, if so stipulated in the Constitution, are now subject to protection, irrespective of a conversion of such rights under ordinary legal norms. He is addressing the judicial norm of converting fundamental rights into ordinary laws and regulations. Secondly, Judge Huang argues that the Reply implicitly creates a precedent for justiciability of the Constitution. Thirdly, the Court uses a civil method to regress violations of fundamental rights, as opposed to criminal or administrative law remedies. However, contrary to the contentions of Judge Huang, these cases seem rare and typically involve disputes best characterized as involving nominal societal interests, as opposed to challenging governmental acts undertaken by China's polity, the CCP. A true test of independent judicial review, or constitutional law, is judicial activism, or judicial interpretations, calling for social engineering, which occasionally represent intrusions into legislative and executive matters.

10.6. Progeny of China's Marbury-BMW Case

There are cases that shock the conscience of justice, mostly due to China's model of judicial review, such as what is referred to as the *BMW case*.[41] On October 16th, 2003, Su Xiuwen, while driving a new BMW, killed Liu Zhongxia, in Harbin, Heilongjiang Province, China. Before the accident, it is reported that, "Su admitted cursing Dai and hitting him with her purse after his tractor scraped her BMW. She said she was upset by the accident and thought the car was in reverse when it sped into the crowd. She also said she had learned to drive only recently and could not find the brakes." Dai Yiquan, 46, the widower of the deceased Liu Zhongxie, is a poor farmer. The handling of this incident drew suspicions locally and nationally. As for the cause of suspicions, locally and nationally, "Newspaper reports noted that police never opened a manslaughter investigation, that no witnesses were called to testify in Su's trial and that statements taken from them were not read in court. Police would not say whether technicians examined Su's car or whether investigators tried to verify her claims of limited driving experience." The North-East China (or Dongbei) case only appeared more troubling, when it was reported that the BMW, which struck Liu Zhongxia and caused her death, also injured several bystanders before crashing into a tree. In 2003, the BMW case war heard and resolved in local court. On December 20, 2003, a local court in Heilongjiang Province, after ruling the case a "traffic disturbance," sentenced Su to a suspended sentence. Problematic of this decision and showing of leniency, is that the decision in the *BMW case* displays many of the problems of the Chinese legal system. First, in China, the *BMW case* represents the growing divide between the rich and the poor, and urban and rural. For instance, Su Xiuwen was married to Guan Mingbo, a wealthy businessman. In comparison, the victims Dai Yiquan and his deceased wife, Liu Zhongxia, were members of the poor strata of Chinese society. Second, the public was under the impression that little, if any, investigation was undertaken in what should have been, at a minimum, a case of manslaughter. It was a poor impression also owing to a failure to investigate all facts,

[41] Philip P. Pan, The Unquiet Death of a Chinese Peasant—Lenient Treatment for Driver in 'BMW Case' Ignites Media Frenzy, Wide Discussion of Wealth and Justice, Jan. 16, 2004, Washington Post.

witnesses, and summon evidence before the court. Third, assuming the guilt of Su, the resulting verdict of a suspended sentence was perceived in China as one that "shocks the conscience" of justice.

The case of Su Xiuwen speaks to a problem of justice, be it civil or criminal justice, in modern Chinese society, especially in terms of China's model of judicial review. According to Yang Xiaohuai, a defense lawyer in Beijing, the "basic problem was the lack of an independent judiciary, which undermines trust in the legal system. ' In China, there is a phenomenon,' he said. 'Power is greater than the law, money is greater than the law and connections are greater than the law.'" In addition, the growing public distrust resulting from the *BMW case*, as evidenced by the flooding of the Internet by Chinese citizens, or netizens, over this case, speaks to an issue of not only independent judicial review, but also the need for popular sovereignty. One suspects that the *BMW case* may also, eventually, demonstrate the *de facto* power of China's polity in that, in response to public outcry over the verdict, party officials ordered an investigation into the handling of the case. While a post-verdict or judgment investigation in the *BMW case* may lead to a just result in this particular case, it does little for the development of independent judicial review. Indeed, there is a growing fear that the CCP and its instruments of power, such as the NPC, NPCSC, and Judicial committee of the Supreme People's Court, will increasingly interfere with the disposition of judicial cases, much to the dismay of those who favor independent judicial review. For example, and as reported by the Washington Post, in December 2003, China's highest court ordered the execution of an alleged gangster after a similar outcry on the Internet against a decision to grant him a reprieve based on evidence he had confessed under torture. Several months earlier, outrage on the Internet over the death of a college student in police custody led the party to abolish a regulation allowing police to detain people without proper identification.

10.7. PROGENY OF CHINA'S MARBURY-SEEDS CASE

In China, conflicting legislation, or the conflicts between national and local laws, often occurs. Many Chinese law experts deem the problem as a potential hindrance to development of a socialist market economy. For instance, there is the renowned "*Seeds case*." The case involved Li Huijuan, a judge in Luoyang Intermediate People's Court, in Central China's Henan Province.[42] In 2003, Li Huijuan addressed a conflict between a national law on seeds and a provincial regulation (or local law) on seeds issued by the Henan People's Congress. In the course of a civil case, Li Hujian had to the address legal issue of entitlement to compensation for the alleged failure to honor a corn seed contract. Li was virtually fired after challenging the authority of the local people's congress.

Judge Li Huijuan considered the 2003 case a ruling on a mundane case about seed prices.[43] However, following her ruling, the Luoyang Middle Court's discipline committee contacted her, because Henan Province officials complained that the ruling contained a serious political error. In the conflict between national law and local law (or provincial law), Judge Li ruled the local law was invalid. By doing so, she made Chinese legal history, which set in motion a national debate concerning judicial independence (or independent judicial

[42] New NPC body to address law conflicts, June 19, 2006, China Daily.
[43] Jim Yardley, A young judge tests China's legal system, Nov. 28, 2005, N.Y. Times.

review) in a relatively closed Chinese political system. Problematic is that in China the judge is not the final arbiter of law, rather China's polity. According to the *New York Times*, "What Li had considered judicial common sense, the People's Congress of Henan Province considered a judicial revolt. And their initial response was to try to crush it. Li, who had less than three years on the bench, feared her career might be finished." Judge Li said, "An order by those in power has forced local leaders, none of whom dared to stand on principle, to sacrifice me." Further, Judge Li said, "I'm just an ordinary person, a female judge who tried to protect the law. Who is going to protect my rights?" The issue of whether the ruling Communist Party truly intends to allow an independent judiciary remains pending. Judge Li, with a Master's Degree in law, gave her carefully worded verdict in October, 2003, saying the clause in the local regulation, which contradicts the national seed law, is "automatically invalid, because the local regulation is lower than the national law in the legal hierarchy." The source of Judge Li's problem was that the Henan Provincial People's Congress Standing Committee later issued a notice claiming Li's ruling was an "illegal review of the local regulation in nature and encroached on the functions of the legislative body."

In January 2003, Judge Li was named presiding judge over a three-judge panel hearing a dispute between two local companies over the price of seeds. The legal dispute revolved around a conflict between national and local law. The local law required seed prices to be set by the state, while the national law favored prevailing market rates. Judge Li ruled based on the national law and never anticipated the trouble that ensued, especially from the politics of this case and the parochial interests of two companies fighting over thousands of dollars. For instance, during deliberations on the case, a city official forwarded a letter from one company to Li's supervisor, which included a written instruction for the court, "Please pay attention." In anticipation of controversy concerning this case, Judge Li had submitted a draft ruling to the court director, who had, in turn, forwarded it to a trial committee, and everyone signed off on the ruling. In June 2003, the opposing parties were informed of the ruling. However, by October 2003, word of the case had reached the Henan Province People's Congress, which is the top legislative body in the province. The legal affairs office of the Henan Province People's Congress interpreted the ruling as a challenge to the lawmaking authority of the People's Congress. The ruling was oddly attributed solely to Judge Li and described by local officials as a serious breach of law. Mao Yinduan, head of the legal office, said, "The authority of the National People's Congress system is not to be challenged." Mao further added, "The judge in this case was very young and had little experience. She had every right to choose which law to use. But courts have no right in a verdict to say which law is invalid." China's legislative procedure law (*Lifa Fa*) states that local laws that conflict with national laws should be abolished. Judge Li thought including this point in her opinion was within her judicial purview. It was not Judge Li's intention to challenge the political system, nor, apparently, that of had her director or the trial committee. Nonetheless, Judge Li, and not the court officials who had approved the decision, faced the possibility of serious punishment. Li had stumbled upon a fundamental contradiction in the Chinese system, because, generally, judges are supposed to refer conflicts in law for review by the NPCSC, and then follow the decision made by the NPCSC. However, such referrals are rare, and when they do occur, the Standing Committee rarely shows interest in these conflicts. As a result, judges are becoming accustomed to assuming this role, and resolving the dispute by simply leaving the conflicting law untouched or unresolved.

10.8. Progeny of China's Marbury-Sun Zhigang's Case

A case involving the death of Sun Zhigang, a 27-year-old graphic designer from Hubei Province, is considered to be an important constitutional decision, if not constitutional development. In March 2005, Sun Zhigang, was mistaken as a vagrant, and subsequently detained in Guangzhou, Guangdong Province. Sun Zhigang did not have in his possession his temporary residency card or identification card. The tragedy of this story is that after his arrest, several days later he was found death. Authorities report that inmates at a repatriation center beat Sun Zhigang to death. After his reported death, in June 2006, an attending nurse at this repatriation center was sentenced to death for his leading role in Sun's death. One inmate held responsible for his death was given a suspended death sentence, while another ten inmates received sentences of up to life imprisonment. In addition, another six persons, comprising a policeman, two doctors, two nurses, and a person in charge of the center, received sentences of two to three years for neglect of duties. This case brought attention to the problems of law and millions of immigrates, who live and work outside of their province. Subsequently, the State Council rescinded the 1982 *Regulation on the Detention and Deportation of Vagrants and Beggars in Cities*, which granted local police authority the power to detain people who could not produce local residency permits.[44]

The conflict of law or legislation problem stems from the 2000 *Lifa Fa*, which provides that only national laws apply in settling issues concerning a person's political rights and personal freedom. In March of 2000, China promulgated the new legislative procedure law (or *Lifa Fa*), which sought to better define roles of lawmakers and procedures, and attempts to establish a legal hierarchy between the constitution, laws, administrative regulations and orders, at both national and local levels.[45] The new legislative procedure law (*Lifa Fa*) also had the affect of prohibiting expansion of judicial review powers of the Supreme People's Court, and its lower courts. The history of the legislative procedure law dates back to early 1993. The legislative procedure law was intended to streamline China's law making process by setting forth a clear line between legislative powers of the NPC and NPCSC, and, of course, between laws and administrative regulations.[46] An original intent of the NPC in drafting this law was to curb irregular practices in law making, such as authority being exceeded, and problems of overlapping and conflicts between laws and regulations. One could say that the problem of conflicts of laws between national laws and local laws were not the primary driving force for promulgating the legislative procedure law, rather a clear exposition and consolidation of the powers of the CCP, through its NPC and NPCSC. In terms of judicial power, legislative procedure law maintains that the NPC, NPCSC, and the Supreme People's Court continue to enjoy the power to interpret law when necessary. However, in light of the 1982 China constitution, and its explicit grant of authority to the NPCSC to interpret the constitution and laws of China, *lifa jieshi quanli*, the NPC confirmed that the Supreme People's Court is to be limited in its judicial interpretation power, *sifa jieshi*

---

[44] New NPC body to address law conflicts, June 18, 2006, China Daily.

[45] Legislation Law of the People's Republic of China (Zhonghua Renmin Gongheguo Lifa Fa), (Adopted at the Third Session of the Ninth National People's Congress on Mar. 15, 2000, promulgated by Order No. 31 of the President of the People's Republic of China on Mar. 15, 2000, and effective as of July 1, 2000).

[46] M. Ulric Killion, Quest For Legal Safeguards for Foreign Exporters Under China's Anti-Dumping Regime, 29 N.C. J. Int'l L. & Com. Reg. 417 (2004).

quanli, which is the limited power to interpret laws and regulations of China arising from actual cases.

In the case of Sun Zhigang, local government was widely criticized in the media for exceeding this authority or national law. In response to this public controversy and in order to correct a constitutional oversight, in May 2006, the NPCSC set up a new agency within its legislative affairs commission. The job of this new agency will be to review whether legislation, government and judicial decisions accord with the stipulations of the 1982 Constitution. In terms of Chinese judicial review, the *Lifa Fa* stipulates that individuals have the right to request the NPCSC to review conflicting legislation, which is the conflict between national law and local law. By striking the offending regulation, the NPCSC did not have to review the legislation. Xu Zhiyong, of the Law Department at Beijing Post and Telecommunications University, observed that this resulted in the NPCSC not "having to review the legislation in accordance with law and somewhat eased the increasing pressure on the top legislature to honor its constitutional duty to safeguard legislative unity throughout the country." He further added that the latter result was praised as a good result, although "it ended in a typical Chinese way," because after all social progress takes time.

Problematic is ascertaining what Xu Zhiyong means by his contention that this dispute was resolved with a good result and in a Chinese way. As earlier mentioned, the problem of a Chinese way is a path of development describable as legal change responding in an *ad hoc* fashion to socio-economic change. In actual practice or the Chinese way, in response to social and economic conditions, the polity implements policy change and the NPC then enacts legislation implementing these changes. A problem with China's legal system, or the Chinese way, is that the post-enactment of social and economic changes, prompting policy change, have typically gone beyond the scope of the new law (or legislation). This then requires the State Council to implement regulations in response to new challenges. No doubt, China's legal system and constitutionalism are distinctive because of their unique interrelationship, if not subservience, to China's polity, CCP, NPC and policies of economic development, especially the Chinese way of directing emphasis toward defining new international markets and rules of international trade rather enhancing civil-political rights.[47]

10.9. Progeny of China's Marbury-Sex Harassment Cases

There is also the case of China's first sex harassment (*xing sao rao*) case. Before borrowing the legal concept of *xing sao rao*, sexual harassment was simply referred to as *shua liu mang* (to play the hoodlum), which refers to the natural tendency of making bodily contact or showing body language. The first sexual harassment case, admittedly, may not be a progeny of China's *Marbury*, but, by virtue that it was decided during the same year, and the issues involved, it presents a historical precedent for Chinese jurisprudence. In China's first sexual harassment case, the plaintiff, Ms. Tong, was unsuccessful because of insufficient evidence and lack of a sexual harassment law.[48] When this case was decided, it was generally

[47] Killion, Post-WTO China: Quest for human rights safeguards in sexual harassment, Id. Fan & Xin, Id.

[48] Woman Loses First Case of Sexual Harassment, Dec. 24, 2001, China Daily, http://www1.chinadaily.com.cn/en/doc/2001-12/24/content_99244.htm. Zheng Ming, China's First Sexual Harassment Lawsuit, Mar. 2002, China Today, 18. You Yi Nu Xing Bu Zai Chen Mo, Nan Jing Se Lao Zong Shou Xing Zai Ci Bao Guang [Another Woman Is Not Silent Any Longer, Nanjing "Pornographic GM"

deemed difficult to prove sexual harassment because of vague domestic laws, lack of a sexual harassment law, and lack of adequate constitutional safeguards. In addition, opinions diverge regarding the effectiveness of domestic laws and whether the 1982 Constitution could serve as an adequate safeguard against sexual harassment in the workplace. China's first sexual harassment case, actually, enjoys its own progeny. However, the progeny of Ms. Tong's case has not been a flood of similar lawsuits; rather, the result has been an increasing awareness of sexism, if not chauvinism. Ms. Tong's case has only minimally influenced the subsequent level of judicial activity when measured by the number of case filings. Subsequently to Ms. Tong's, there are four sexual harassment cases filed in Mainland China. On July 5, 2002, Ms. He, a Wuhan teacher, filed the first sexual harassment case in Hubei Province against her school's office assistant director. On September 29, 2002, Ms. Mei in Yunnan Province filed China's third sexual harassment case against her supervisor. In April 2003, a twenty-five-year-old, Lei Reman, filed the first sexual harassment case in Beijing against her supervisor. In addition, in April 2003, a Nanjing saleswoman, with the alias Fei Fei, won a lawsuit alleging sexual harassment against her company's manager.[49] As of 2005, and according to *Xinhua* news, since 2001, there have been ten cases of sexual harassment brought before the courts and only one case has been proved.[50]

Before accession to the WTO in December 2001, China introduced a host of legislation directly and indirectly affecting women's rights, such as, though not exhaustive, the Criminal Law of the People's Republic of China, Marriage Law of the People's Republic of China, Labor Law of the People's Republic of China, General Principles of Civil Law of the People's Republic of China and Law of the People's Republic of China on the Protection of Rights and Interests of Women. In China, women seeking legal safeguards, generally, based their cause of action on one of the following laws: General Principles of Civil Law of the People's Republic of China, Criminal Law of the People's Republic of China, or Law of the People's Republic of China on the Protection of Rights and Interests of Women. However, these laws proved problematic because: domestic laws only indirectly addressed sexual harassment, by penalizing insults to dignity and reputation; the language is vague and general,

Exposed Again], May 2, 2002, People's Net, http://news.tom.com/Archive/1006/2003/5/2-21165.html. Jing Cheng Shou Li Xing Sao Rao An Fu Chu Shui Mian, Nu Hai Ju Zuo Chen Mo Gao Yang [First Sexual Harassment Case in Beijing Comes to Surface, Girl Refuses to be the Silent Lamb], Apr. 4, 2003, Chinese Businessman Net—Chinese Businessman Reports, http://news.tom.com/Archive/1006/2003/4/4-5243.html. Gan Su Ri Bao Guan Yu Xing Sao Rao Wen Ti De Diao Cha [Gansu Daily Reports Investigation about Sexual Harassment], Apr. 18, 2003, Everyday Gansu—Gansu Daily, http://news.tom/com/Archive/1002/2003/4/18-41802.html.

[49] Legal Push to Boost Women's Rights, June 24, 2003, S.P.R.C. Morning Post. Hu Bei Yi Nu Jiao Shi Bu Kan Shang Si Xing Sao Rao Nu Shang Fa Ting Suo Pei Yi Wan Yuan [A Female Teacher of Wu Han City Recently Filed a Lawsuit in Jianghan District Court Claiming Ten Thousand Yuan in Damages Because She Cannot Stand Superior's Sexual Harassing Behavior], July 05, 2002, Chinese news net, http://news.tom.com/Archive/1002/2002/7/5-31113.html. Hu Bei Yi Nu Jiao Shi Bu Kan Shang Si Xing Sao Rao Nu Shang Fa Ting Suo Pei Yi Wan Yuan [A Female Teacher of Wu Han City Recently Filed a Lawsuit in Jianghan District Court Claiming Ten Thousand Yuan in Damages Because She Cannot Stand Superior's Sexual Harassing Behavior], July 5, 2002, Chinese news net, http://news.tom.com/Archive/1002/2002/7/5-31113.html. Shang Si Yan Yu Tiao Dou Dong Shou Dong Jiao Yun Nan Shou Li "Xing Sao Rao" An Kai Shen [Superior with Language Teases and Touches Everywhere on the Body, Yunnan's First "Sexual Harassment," Case Goes to Trial], Sept. 9, 2002, China news net, http://news.tom.com/Archive/1006/1127/2002/9/29-73396.html. First Sex Harassment Case for Beijing Woman Awaits Verdict After an Uphill Battle to Bring Her Grievances to Court, July 21, 2001, S.P.R.C. Morning Post. Gu Minkang, A Preliminary Study of Civil Liability for Sexual Harassment, Shidai faxue, No. 3 (2004).

[50] China to outlaw sexual harassment, BBC news, June 26, 2005, Xinhua.

thus increasing the burden of proof; domestic laws do not define what constitutes sexual harassment, which further enhances the burden of proof; and domestic laws did not directly address sexual harassment in the workplace.[51]

An amendment to the Law on the Protection of the Rights and Interests of Women (LPRIW) was included in the 2005 legislative agenda. On August 29, 2005, the NPC passed amendments to the LPRIW, which "prohibits sexual harassment of women," and empowers women to "lodge complaints" with relevant organizations. On December 1, 2005, the amendments to the LPRIW became effective. The LPRIW was also amended by the addition of a clause, "granting men and women equal status is a basic state policy of the country. The state will adopt necessary measures to gradually improve various systems to guarantee the rights and interests of women and remove all sorts of discrimination against women." In addition, the amendments also purport to address issues of political rights, employment, birth insurance and domestic violence. As for the efficacy of the new law, it remains to be determined. In the past, vagary of language, lack of sexual harassment definition and other drafting details may have been the product of intentional design in the drafting process. In terms of China and legislative drafting, Teemu Ruskola employs the term "aspirationalism," to explain the phenomenon of under-enforced laws and laws purposefully drafted in seemingly vague and general terms.[52]

10.10. The Conflict of Laws

Although the 1982 Constitution and legislative procedure law, or *Lifa Fa*, stipulates and provides that local regulations should not contradict national laws, the previously mentioned *Seeds case* still triggered controversy over whether China should establish a judicial review mechanism. Wang Zhenmin, vice-director of the Law School at Tsinghua University, said a multi-layer law making mechanism causes the conflicts in legislation. Although the 1982 Constitution states that the NPC and its Standing Committee, the NPCSC, exercise the power of lawmaking, the State Council, local people's congresses and administrative departments at both central and local levels are equally entitled to make regulations within their jurisdictional areas. A frequent occurrence in China is one issue being governed by two, or even more, different regulations, and sometimes regulations with substantially different stipulations. Wang Zhenmin observed, "Beneath the conflict of legislation lies the conflict of interests of different departments and local administrations and, in a word, power distribution." Wang recommended that the legislature should consider establishing a Constitutional Committee or Constitutional Court that would guard against constitutional violations and undertake a function similar to the judicial review of common law legal systems. It is tacitly assumed that

---

[51]. Zhong Hua Ren Min Gong He Guo Xing Fa [Criminal Law of the P.R.C.] (adopted 1979, revised 1997). Zhong Hua Ren Min Gong He Guo Hun Yin Fa [Marriage Law of the P.R.C. (adopted 1980, amended 2001). Zhong Hua Ren Min Gong He Guo Lao Dong Fa [Labor Law of the P.R.C.] (adopted 1994). Zhong Hua Ren Min Gong He Guo Min Fa Tong Ze [General Principles of Civil Law of the P.R.C.] (adopted 1986). Zhong Hua Ren Min Gong He Guo Fu Nu Quan Yi Bao Zhang Fa [Law of the P.R.C. on the Protection of Rights and Interests of Women] (approved 1992). Sexual Harassment Thorny Issue for Lawmakers, Jul. 1, 2003, China Daily.

[52] China to enact first anti-sexual harassment law, Mar. 4, 2005, China Daily. China Outlaws Sexual Harassment, Aug. 29, 2005, Xinhua. Teemu Ruskola, Note, Law, Sexual Morality, and Gender Equality in Qing and Communist China, 103 Yale L.J. 2531, 2531-32 (1994).

Wang was recommending the Anglo-American rule of law-common law system, and not the continental rule of law-civil law systems, nor its older continental common law system. A common law system described by some jurists such as Roscoe Pound, Eugen Erhlich and others, as a case law legal system that presupposes what is termed the "free finding of law."

In China, before the Law on Legislative Procedures was enacted in 2000, there were vague procedures for the review of laws. The Law on Legislative Procedures empowers citizens, administrative and judicial bodies to submit written requests to the NPCSC for final review of conflicting legislation. This law serves as a means of supervising implementation of the 1982 Constitution and laws, during a period when a judicial review mechanism has not yet been established in China. In the previously mentioned case involving Judge Li Huijuan, in November 2003, four mainland lawyers sent a written proposal to the NPCSC suggesting the top legislative body should review the validity of the local regulation and issue a prompt rectification of administrative regulations and local legislation, which conflict with the 1982 Constitution and laws of China. As of 2006, no progress has been made in Li's case. Wang Zhenmin also recommended that this new agency established by the NPCSC should conduct its legislative review in a transparent fashion. Further Wang suggested, "They should conclude each case with a formal written judgment supported by adequate reasons, instead of solving the problem behind close doors."

However, the new agency established by the NPCSC offers more promises than deeds. The NPCSC has established a new agency, as a division under the Legal Affairs Commission of the NPCSC, which is designated to review whether legislation or government decisions tally with the 1982 Constitution.[53] As of 2006, this new agency comprises a small staff of about 10 to 15 persons. A primary goal of this new agency is safeguarding legislative unity and consolidating the NPC's constitutional supervision, while also creating a division for examining administrative regulations, local laws and judicial interpretations. The agency will be primarily carrying out its intended function through the collection of information on constitutional violations from the public, including suggestions and comments from individuals. Under the *Lifa Fa*, the NPC and its standing committee, the NPCSC, have the power to make national law, and the State Council has the power make administrative laws and regulations. As for local government, people's congresses and their standing committees of provinces, municipalities and autonomous regions have the right to create local laws, local regulations and regional laws. The problem is the conflict between these local laws and regulations, and the power of the NPCSC to enact laws.

Mei Ying Gechlik, in a 2005 study of Chinese legal reforms that focused on Shanghai's legal reforms, rightly perceives that one of the essential needed reforms of the legal system is a transparent and independent mechanism for judicial review.[54] A core problem for China -- and Chinese constitutionalism -- is the lack of positive discursive machinery for judicial review.[55] The 1982 Constitution does not vest the judicial organ of its government with the judicial independence shared by courts in the United States, but neither do the constitutions of some Western countries. In Western countries, the responsibility of constitutional interpretation will generally vest with the judicial bodies of its respective countries. In the

[53] China set up new Agency to see to Constitution Application, June 21, 2004, Xinhua. Meng Yan, New Agency to see too Constitution application, June 21, 2004, China Daily.

[54] Mei Ying Gechlik (formerly, Veron Hung), Judicial Reform in China: Lessons from Shanghai, 19 Colum. J. Asian L. 97 (spring/fall 2005).

[55] Killion, Post-WTO China and Independent Judicial Review, Id.

West, generally, models for constitutional review, or constitutional courts, are models of either a centralized (or concentrated) or a decentralized (or diffused) constitutional review. The 1982 Constitution reveals a lack of any real semblance of constitutional authority in its judiciary. Its judicial model subscribes to neither a decentralized nor a centralized constitutional review. For China and proposed legal reforms, the lack of both a decentralized and centralized constitutional review mechanism, including a constitutional court, is problematic.

The lack of an independent mechanism for judicial review is especially problematic, and only compounds the problems in those cases of uncertainty and conflicts of laws, because judges must seek advice from their court leaders. The latter procedure is also problematic, because it only enhances the problem by giving rise to increasing opportunities for inter-court and intra-court influence and interference. In 2004, in answer to this need for an independent mechanism for judicial review, the NPCSC established a constitution review body. As observed by Mei Ying Gechlik, "details about this body, especially surrounding its power and authority to operate with a high degree of transparency and independence, remain unclear." Accordingly, "The constitutional review body referred to in this article is probably the much less august Office of Filing and Review of Regulations" (*Fagui bei'an shencha shi*) that was established in May 2004 under the Legal System Working Committee (*Fazhi gongzuo weiyuanhui*) of the NPCSC. More particularly, in December 2005, the NPCSC "adopted two sets of rules to prescribe procedures on legislative review to be followed by the Office of Filing and Review of Regulations." First, the NPSCS amended the *Xingzheng fagui, difangxing fagui, zizhi tiaoli he danxing tiaoli, jingji tequ fagui bei'an shencha gongzuo chengxu* [Working Procedures on Filing and Review of Administrative Regulations, Local Rules, Rules of Autonomous Regions and Individual Rules, and Regulations of Special Economic Zones]. Second, the NPSCS passed the *Sifa jieshi bei'an shencha gongzuo chengxu* [Working Procedures on Filing and Review of Judicial Interpretations].[56]

10.11. LOCALIZING MARXIST LEGAL THEORY

The previously mentioned laws, regulations and law cases serve as a measure of modern legal reforms. A problem is that these laws, regulations and law cases equally present plausible different perspectives regarding the success or failure of ongoing legal and economic reforms. In a post-1949 China, individual civil litigants pursuing legal rights in a court of law demonstrate a degree of success in modern legal reforms. These law cases evidence the substantive changes made to China's legal system. These cases equally substantiate the many new laws continuously being enacted by the NPC such as the earlier mentioned 2005 LPRIW, as well as many regulations being enacted by various administrative bodies such as the 2002 Provisions of the Supreme People's Court on Several Issues Concerning the Application of Anti-Dumping Administrative Cases, [*Zhonghua renmin gongheguo zuigao renmin fayuan gonggao (Zui Gao Renmin Fayuan Guanyu Chengli Fanqingxiao Xingzheng Anjian Yingyong Falv Ruogan Wenti De Guiding*), and 2001 Anti-Dumping Regulation of the People's Republic of China (*Zhonghua renmin gongheguo*

[56] Mei Ying Gechlik, Id., Jiao Hongchang, Wei xian wei fa shencha de zhongyao jinzhan [Jiao Hongchang, Important Development of Constitutional and Legislative Review], Dec. 26, 2005, Fazhi Ribao (Legal Daily).

fanqingxiao tiaoli).[57] The 2005 study of Chinese legal reforms conducted by Mei Ying Gechlik illustrates these substantive improvements. Her study, by focusing on Shanghai's legal reforms, highlights the vast improvements in Shanghai's legal system and demonstrates that Shanghai could possibly serve as the archetypal path to legal reforms.

There is another perspective, however, conversely demonstrating a degree of failure in modern legal reforms. Modern legal reforms follow a pattern similar to economic reforms. It is a problem of policy experimentation rationalized by CCP policy. As policy experimentation rationalized future development policy, both economic growth and future economic development became contingent on whether past successes were: "(1) the result of China's economic experimentation that produced non-capitalist institutional innovations that were optimally suited to the country's particular economic circumstances, or (2) the result of China's institutional convergence and integration with the advanced WTO economies like France, Japan, and the United States." The issue of legal institutional convergence versus divergence is also heavily influenced by policy experimentation. In terms of legal reforms and legal experimentation, the 2006 WTO Trade Policy Review Mechanism documents that since the mid-1980s the NPC continues to authorize the State Council to issue interim provisions that become laws only after being tested, and there is also the routine implementation of policies on a trial basis.[58] China's legal experimentation, like its economic experimentation, inevitably produces non-capitalist institutional innovations that are, supposedly, optimally suited to China's particular circumstances; i.e. the localization of Marxism (*Makesi zhuyi he Zhongguo shiji xiang jiehe*), or the adapting, Sinicizing or localizing the orthodoxy of Marxism to the realities of traditional culture and society. In addition, legal reforms are hardly uniform, in that the success or failure of ongoing legal reforms are contingent on resource availability, court personnel, training and qualifications of judges, training and qualifications of lawyers, transparency of new laws and administrative regulations, and many other factors, which are also affected by the problems of the historic urban-rural arrangement or disparity in developmental goals. Depending on one's perspective, political preferences, nationality or even self-proclaimed ideology, ongoing legal reforms may be deemed a success or failure, or even partly a success or partly a failure. Measuring the state of modern legal reforms is reminiscent of continuing Western debates concerning whether or not there is rule of law in China.

There is also the litany of flaws, though not necessarily design oriented, in China's model of constitutional government. Western experts and authority rightly search for a state of legality or constitutional state, resembling models of a Western constitutional state, such as Anglo-American rule of law, German *Rechtsstaat*, and French *État de droit*. Models of a state also described as rule of law, limited government, substantive due process, reasonableness,

---

[57] Killion, Quest for Legal Safeguards for Foreign Exporters Under China's Anti-Dumping Regime, Id. Zhonghua renmin gongheguo fanqingxiao tiaoli [Anti-Dumping Regulation of the People's Republic of China], State Council of China, Nov. 26, 2001, art. 53. Zhonghua renmin gongheguo zuigao renmin fayuan gonggao (Zui Gao Renmin Fayuan Guanyu Chengli Fanqingxiao Xingzheng Anjian Yingyong Falv Ruogan Wenti De Guiding) [Provisions of the Supreme People's Court on Several Issues Concerning the Application of Anti-Dumping Administrative Cases], The Supreme People's Court, Nov. 2, 2002.

[58] Wing Thye Woo, A United Front for the Common Objective to Understand China's Economic Growth: A Case of Nonantagonistic Contradiction, Wu vs. Woo, Issues & Studies 39, no. 2 (June 2003), 1-23. WTO, Trade Policy Review Report by the Secretariat People's Republic of China, Trade Policy Review Body, WT/TPR/S/161, 28 February 2006.

equal protection, and full and fair hearings. The flaws in Chinese constitutionalism, including rule of law, are primarily problems of constitutional practice rather than flaws in constitutional design, which presents issues of a constitutionalism in text-constitutionalism in action dichotomy. In terms of constitutional practice, the problems are substantive and many, ranging from the historical incorporation of party ideologies, to the CCP's views on constitutional theory and practice, and other flaws. For instance, China's democratic centralism and socialist democracy lack separation of powers and constitutional review. This absence challenges the enforceability and effectiveness of constitutional provisions, such as the 2004 constitutional amendments, which supposedly address liberty, human rights and property rights. China's constitutional practices, and not constitutional provisions, are gravely distinguishable from Western constitutions in both theory and practice. One apparent distinction of the 1982 Constitution is that its constitutional provisions do not necessarily vest Chinese citizens with a cognizable legal right of action. In order for a provision in the 1982 Constitution to be enforceable in a court of law, the provision must first be reduced to an ordinary legal norm through the judicial process of converting fundamental rights into ordinary laws and regulations. It is by this means only that a person's cognizable legal rights vest. A problem with Chinese legal norms is that, given China's governmental structure and the *de facto* power held by the CCP, safeguarding liberty becomes an issue of safeguarding social rights. The justiciability of social rights provisions in the 1982 Constitution is, ultimately, contingent upon China's CCP rather than the judiciary.

In terms of a constitutionalism in text-constitutionalism in action dichotomy, the U.S. Country Reports on China routinely find, "The Constitution and laws provide for fundamental human rights; however, these protections often are ignored in practice."[59] For instance, the 1982 Constitution prohibits gender-based offenses in article 48, which calls for equality of women. The 1982 Constitution also addresses the plight of women in other articles: Article 33 stipulates that all citizens are equal before the law; Article 35 guarantees freedom of association; Article 49 provides the State must protect marriage, family, and mother and child; and Article 33 of the 1982 Constitution holds, "All citizens of the People's Republic of China are equal before the law, [*Zhonghua Renmin Gongheguo Gongmn Zai Falu Mianqian Yilu Pingdeng*]." These constitutional stipulations demonstrate that the problem of China's constitution is not one of flaws in design, rather the 1982 Constitution and its prescriptions for equality and their respective applications demonstrate the distinction between constitutionalism in text, and constitutionalism in action. The exercise of extra-constitutionalism by China's polity, the CCP, and resulting disparity between constitutionalism in text and constitutionalism in action, admittedly, may be attributable to the process of ongoing legal and economic reforms. Many constitutional theorists agree that constitutional judicial review is not the sole discursive engine for crafting political values and solutions. At moments of crisis, or what Stephen Krasner termed a punctuated equilibrium, an entire people may be mobilized to civic action. "In normal times, the people may be content with representation and constitutional judicial review, while they largely focus on private affairs; while at times of what Bruce Ackerman calls constitutional politics the level of civic action may become extraordinary." For instance, Bruce Ackerman identified three republics in American history, "before and after the civil war and in the modern regulatory social

[59] Country Reports on Human Rights Practices for 2000, S. Rep. No. 107-32, at 737 (1st Sess. 2001). Country Reports on Human Rights Practices for 2002, S. Rep. No. 108-30, at 749 (1st Sess. 2003).

welfare state initiated in the 1930s by the New Deal."[60] There are parallel examples, such as an earlier mobilization in the South Korean constitutional politics of reform, and Japanese politics of resistance to corruption. Assuming legal reforms, in China, are undergoing a process resembling political experimentation in economic reforms, the rationale of political experimentation only, inevitably, delays the formation of a flexible market system, sound dollar and the rule of law, including protecting citizens from the arbitrary exercise of government power and guaranteeing legally based civil liberties and freedoms.

The constitutionalism in text-constitutionalism in action dichotomy presents a real problem, especially concerning the plight of Chinese citizens. Conversely, in China, many contend that government actions are often challenged, which is an increasing phenomenon due to institutional changes associated with reforms.[61] There are several cases hailed as challenging executive authority, including political rather than legal accountability. Some of the cases and issues challenging government action have been described as: Investigations by People's Congresses; hearing into prices; administrative examination and approval; expulsion of discipline-violating college students; judicialization of constitutional law; detention and sending back home of indigent migrants, pre-marriage physical check-ups; impeachment of judges; discrimination against hepatitis B patients; emergency measures in the face of SARs and bird flu; land acquisition; urban demolition and resettlement; illegally prolonged detention; labor security; judgments on the Liu Yong case and the BMW case; and combating corruption and building a clean government. The problem of the plight of the average citizen is that the problem of a persistent state of extra-constitutionalism in practice also produces distinctive juridical practices, such as distinctive appellate procedures. As earlier mentioned, while Anglo-American rule of law, German *Rechtsstaat* and French *État de droit* are distinctive, they still converge around a commonality of the Enlightenment and its subsequent interpretations, especially the high ideal of a liberal democracy. This commonality also results in a convergence of juridical practices, including appellate procedures, which reflects a convergence of constitutionalism in action and constitutionalism in text of these country-samplings of Western jurisprudence. For example, the Western juridical practice of appeals, generally, represents a judicial pyramid structure in their placements of power, adjudication and review. While earlier Western models of appellate review structures diverge because of distinctive histories and procedural structures, they, despite their differences, eventually converge to a three-tier structure resembling a pyramid structure. Representative of the various Western models of appellate review are Anglo-American rule of law and its appellate court model, German *Rechtsstaat* and its revision model (political revision) such as Germany's Federal Constitutional Court (*Bundesverfassungsgericht*), and French *État de droit* and its cassation model (courts of cassation) such as France's *Cour de cassation*.

China's appellate review model or structure is in stark contrast to Western models, because it is a pole-shaped two-tier structure rather than pyramid-shaped three-tier structure.

[60] Michael C. Davis, The Emerging Global Scenario and the East Asian Perspective on Human Rights, (CCA-AI Conference on Human Rights in 2000), http://www.wscfap.org/pages/praxis/p20011_s.htm. Stephen D. Krasner, Approaches to the State, Alternative Conceptions and Historical Dynamics, Comparative Politics, Vol. 26/2, 1984, 223-245. Bruce Ackerman, We The People (Belknap Press, 1991).

[61] Shen Kui, Normative Basis for the Changes of China's Public Law, 28-40 Social Sciences in China (Zhongguo shehui kexue) (winter 2004). Fu Yulin, Comparative Research on Judicial Hierarchy, 39-51 Social Sciences in China (Zhongguo shehui kexue) (spring 2003). Charles Platto, Civil Appeal Procedures Worldwide (West Pub, 1992). Reference Materials of Court Organization Law and Procedure Law, Vol.1, 254 (China's People's UP, 1954).

The establishment of a two-tier structure is attributable to the 1954 founding of modern China, the political economy of the 1950s, official CCP ideology and policy about the role of law and legal issues in modern Chinese society and culture. Although, before 1954, there is a three-tier structure in place that includes a one-tier system for small unappealable cases, the 1954 Court Organization Law and Procedure Law create the present two-tier structure. As previously mentioned, during the early days of post-1949 China, strategies and formulas for success varied and were experimental, ranging from a Soviet-style central planned economy, to copying Stalinist industrialization, and other programs and campaigns, which include copying the judicial model and appellate review structure of the former Soviet Union and its People's Courts. Despite modern legal and economic reforms, the two-tier structure still operates in China and produces the result of each court of first instance being able to act as a court of final instance, from the intermediate to higher courts, and firmly embeds the juridical practice of extra-constitutionalism in practice through trial supervision procedures. From the perspective of the CCP, extra-constitutionalism in practice and trial supervision procedures manifest an appellate review structure that enhances and supports policies, goals and actions of the CCP, because the two-tier model intensifies extra-procedural control, while also creating requisite scaled political effects of correcting errors. The two-tier model is mostly a product of a political economy environment that demands appellate procedure to conform to the policies, actions and goals of the CCP, rather than appellate procedures gradually creating judicial precedents on a case-by-case basis.

Recent laws, regulations and law cases also present issues of the law in text (*wenben falv*)-law in action (*xingwei falv*) dichotomy, and the rules on paper (*zhi mian gui ze*)-practical rules (*shi jian gui ze*) dichotomy. Although these concepts are grounded in Western legal conceptualizations that were borrowed or transplanted from Western legal theorizations, Chinese juridical practice and theorizations have given them distinctive Chinese characteristics. Admittedly, The transplantation of economic laws are usually less controversial than constitutional, administrative and other domestic laws, because economic laws address issues of efficiency, stability and predictability in the marketplace, especially global market, and do not pose an immediate threat, whether true or not, to a non-Western society or culture. However, the problem with the Chinese judiciary's ability to safeguard liberty, including the norms of economic equality prescribed by the WTO standards, such as the non-discrimination norm of most-favored-nations (GATT, Art. I, MFN clause) treatment requiring equal treatment to economic transactions,[62] arises from the fact that liberty in terms of Western constitutionalism constitutes negative liberty rather than positive liberty, such as the case of the pursuit of a behavior laid down by one-party CCP rule and a self-chosen rationale principle.

Independent judicial review addresses issues of substantive due process rather than procedural due process or "an opportunity to be heard . . . at a meaningful time and in a meaningful manner." Substantive due process constitutes individual liberty and poses a threat to the CCP, because it address both the government's power and the protection of fundamental rights, as opposed to the procedural due process safeguard of a right to be heard.[63] One can occasionally witness the successful pleading of rights in a court of law based

---

[62] Helen Yu & Alison Guernsey, What is the Rule of Law?, Univ. of Iowa Center for Int'l Finance and Development (2006).

[63] J.S. McClelland, A History of Western Political Thought 264 (Routledge, 1996). John H. Jackson, The Jurisprudence of GATT & WTO-Insights on Treaty Law and Economic Relations 57–58 (2002). Richardson

upon supposed constitutional norms, as evidenced by Judge Huang's article, the July 24th, 2001 Reply, or China's *Marbury*, and some of the previously mentioned cases, such as the sexual harassment cases. However, it is equally true that there are cases that shock the conscience of justice, such as the *BMW case*, the Death of Sun Zhigang, the *Seeds case* and other law cases and abuses of government power, such as post-Tiananmen Square Tragedy of 1989 prosecutions and persecutions; crackdowns against Falungong; and continuing crackdowns against pro-democracy, cyber-democracy, teledemocracy and many others. These law cases equally demonstrate that the law cases of successful private litigants are rare, typically involve disputes of nominal societal interests and rarely challenge the government's actions. A litmus test of independent judicial review is still whether there is judicial activism or judicial interpretations that call for social engineering. In addition, the distinctions between constitutionalism in text and constitutionalism in action, law in text (*wenben falv*) and law in action (*xingwei falv*) and rules on paper (*zhi mian gui ze*) and practical rules (*shi jian gui ze*) are driven by the forces of ideology, one-party CCP rule and the influence of Marxism, Leninism, communism or socialism, or Mao's socialism. Indeed, one-party CCP rule is the greatest barrier to fully implementing a state of legality or constitutional state, including rule of law.

Problematic in describing the rule of law in the context of Chinese jurisprudence, are the Western methodologies and tools for doing so, because the requisite "correct balance" is routinely defined in terms of Western taxonomies. As a result of the latter "correct balance" being definable in terms of Western taxonomies, Western experts and authority tend to define law in terms of rule by man versus rule by law, policy-driven versus instrumental models of rule of law, and even based on thin versus thick theories of rule of law. Western authority employs the later West-centric theories, or pairings, in gauging China's progress in adopting rule of law. A potential problem is that these pairings are measuring China's legal system and rule of law against Western models and Western rule of law, as opposed to a Sinic-centered or culture-specific rule of law. In China, legal transplantation of Western law and its attendant norms face the challenge of an emergence of law under particular social and historical conditions.

In terms of China's polity, any genuine consideration of constitutionalism, rule of law and judicial review must take into consideration China's historical particularities, because efficacy of a constitution is contingent upon constitutional provisions reflecting "not only sound political theory but also the values and historical experiences of the people whom the constitution will govern."[64] It is a matter of *auslegungsmaxime* (general rules of interpretation), because constitutional values contribute to proper understanding of constitutional provisions. In addition, it must be borne in mind that a tendency of Third World countries to copy constitutional structures, regardless of the particularity of circumstances (historical particularities), attributed to the failures of constitutions in the Third World. For instance, the latter consequences have been attributed to the recent failures of developing

v. Belcher, 404 U.S. 78 (1971). Fuentes v. Shevin, 407 U.S. 67, 80 (1972). Armstrong v. Manzo, 380 U.S. 545, 552 (1965).

[64] Ricard A. Rosen, Constitutional Process, Constitutionalism, and the Eritrean Experience, Vol. 24, No.2 N.C. J. Int'l. L. & Com. Reg. 263, 273, (winter 1999). Hiroshi Nishihara, The Significance of Constitutional Values, Waseda Univ, Tokyo/Japan (2001). Rett R. Ludwikowski, Constitution Making in the Countries of Former Soviet Dominance: Current Development, 23 Ga. J. Int'l & Comp. L. 155, 158 (1993). John S. Dryzek, Constitutionalism and its Alternatives, Prepared for presentation at the Social and Political Theory Program Workshop on "Democratic Theory: The Canberra Papers," Mar. 27, 2002.

countries attempting to adopt a model of world constitutionalism, the United States constitutional model or a liberal constitutional political economy design, such as the failures in Russia, British ex-colonies in Africa and other countries, intending to promote a Western market system. Economic-specific and culture-specific constitutions are arguably a discernible trend of post-cold war constitution-writing countries. For China, in terms of constitutionalism, rule of law and judicial review, one aspect of the historical particularities that ought to be considered is a distinctive jurisprudence emanating from traditional culture or China's ontological base in tradition.

Modern China does have a legal system, and has had a legal system since antiquity. For instance, in terms of rule of law or a constitutional state, and its attendant judicial review, Liu Nanping traced the Chinese history of following legal precedents in light of three periods, before 1912, 1912 to 1949, and after the 1949 founding of modern China.[65] During the history of dynastic China, there is a long history of using decided cases as legal precedent. Before 1912, and as early as the Western Zhou (771 B.C. to the 11th Century), the practice of trying cases by legal precedence without prior enactment of statutes existed. The practice of case law precedence also existed in the dynasties subsequent to the Zhou. For example, the practice was referred to as *tingxingshi* in the Qin Dynasty (221 B.C.-206 B.C.), *jueshibi* in the Han Dynasty (206 B.C.-220 A.D.), *xuyiqianju* in the Tang Dynasty (618 A.D.-907 A.D.) and *yilicongshi* in the Song Dynasty (960 A.D.-1297 A.D.). The terms *jueshibi*, *xuyiqianju* and *yilicongshi* refer to the practice of following previously decided cases. From 1912 to 1949, during the period of the Republic of China (R.O.C.), one also finds a Western style of legal precedence. Decided cases and interpretations of particular provisions by the court served as legal precedents in the judicial process. In addition, the Supreme Court had its own reporter referred to as The Collection of Decided Cases of the *Dali Yuan* and its reported decisions enjoyed a Western style of legal precedence.

There is also rule of law in modern China. However, as observed by Michael W. Dowdle, "While the general consensus is that there is no real rule of law in China, we actually have a great deal of difficulty explaining why." The problems are obvious. Western models and theories, such as the earlier mentioned pairings, used to analyze China's legal system and rule of law either expand or constrict genuine understanding of China's legal system and rule of law, because Western approaches, and theorizations, may be bound by a conceptualization of rule of law as a West-centric concept, Western social good or presumed social good,[66] and even as the continuing problem of the universal versus the particular. All of which challenges a Western critique of China's rule of law, especially Western methodologies, taxonomies, terms and concepts employed for doing so. For instance, and typical of the inherent problems, developing the rule of law in China in the normative and political sense may be divorced from a theory of democracy.

In modern China's native language (Mandarin or *Putonghua*), or appropriate legal lexicons, the word (or characters) *yifazhiguo*, *fazhiguo* and, especially, *fazhi* are variously rendered as "rule of law," "rule by law" and "according to law." From antiquity, there are

[65] Nanping Liu, "Legal Precedents" with Chinese Characteristics: Published Cases in the Gazette of the Supreme People's Court, 5 J. Chinese L. 107 (1991).

[66] Michael W. Dowdle, Heretical Laments: China and the Fallacies of "Rule of Law," Cultural Dynamics, (Nov. 1999), 287. William P. Alford, Exporting "The Pursuit of Happiness", 113 Harv. L. Rev. 1677, 1682 (2000). K. Tribe, Introduction to Neumann, Law and Socialist Political Theory, Economy and Society 10 (1981), 316–333.

also different and distinct meanings, though not as clear-cut as modern legal lexicons, such as Xu Shen (Han scholar, AD 58-147), in the *Analytical Dictionary of Chinese Language* (*Shuo Wen Jie Zi*, AD 100), and his describing a judicial judgment by linking normative value judgments to judicial procedure. The various renderings are attributable to the meanings of these terms varying with different speakers and usages. Therefore, it becomes important to examine what is actually happening under China's rule of law rubric. China's rule of law rubric may refer to a system where law becomes a tool of governance or what is commonly referred to as rule by law. In this instance, the rubric becomes what is, generally, referred to as rule by law, which is a policy-driven model of rule of law or a descriptive, positive and instrumental view of the relationship. Conversely, China's rule of law rubric may refer to a system in which government is held equally accountable for its actions and incorporates respect for internationally recognized human rights under the rule of law. As an antithesis to rule by law, this rule of law rubric presents the classic Western model of the rule of law or a prescriptive, normative and political view of what the relationship should be. Problematic for China is evidence of various usages of law or its legal system in crackdowns against those labeled political dissidents, such as post-Tiananmen Square Tragedy of 1989 prosecutions and persecutions; crackdowns against Falungong; and continuing crackdowns against pro-democracy, cyber-democracy, teledemocracy and many others. All of which problematically indicates that Chinese officials are using law or rule of law, in the former sense, as a tool of governance or what is commonly referred to as rule by law.[67]

There is also the often-overlooked influence of Marxism on ongoing legal reforms, because both ideology and culture influences the growth and direction of China's legal system, including constitutionalism, rule of law and judicial review. The often-overlooked and primordial influence on modern legal reforms is Marxism, or the ongoing process of attempting to finalize its adaptation, Sinicizaton or localization (*difang hua*). The primordial influence of Marxism, Leninism, communism, socialism, or even Mao's socialism, on modern Chinese legal reforms, ultimately, presents issues of reconstructing Chinese Marxist legal theory or a Chinese Marxist legal system. This is not only a difficult task, but also equally the gist of the problem of modern legal reforms. China presents itself to the international community as a socialist-political polity jointly pursuing a capitalist-economic policy, and here lies an elemental problem of modern reforms.

Many Western experts and authority recognize a distinctive Marxist legal theory or socialist jurisprudence, and widely representative of this group are Janet Campbell, Franz Neuman and even the authoritarian, proto-fascist theories developed by Carl Schmitt. For instance, Janet Campbell, in *An Analysis of Law in the Marxist Tradition* (2003), attempts to show how a socialist society could be a truly free society, or even perhaps, though implicitly, a Marxian utopia or perpetual peace. In an analysis of Marxist legal theory, Campbell draws from the historical development of legal theory grounded in Marxist political economy from an earlier development of law in the former Soviet Union and its People's Courts. For Campbell, although a system of regulation in socialism may not be on par with Western ideal rule of law, it still presents a viable alternative that does not ignore the regulatory needs of

[67] Yang Yi, Methodology for Contemporary Chinese Scholarly Research: An Overview, 60-68, Social Sciences in China (Zhongguo shehui kexue) (spring 2006). James V. Feinerman, The Rule of Law with Chinese Socialist Characteristics, 96 Current History 278, 280 (1997). Eric W. Orts, The Rule of Law in China, 34 Vand. J. Transnat'l L. 43, 93-94 (2001). Dangerous Meditation-China's Campaign Against Falungong, Jan. 2002, HRW.

society, which is also compatible with the Marxist critique of the legal order. Campbell does recognize the viability of a distinctive Marxist legal theory or socialist jurisprudence.[68]

Others also advance a Marxist legal theory or socialist jurisprudence. Following the close of cold war and cold war polarization, there is the current resurgent of interest in the legal scholarship of Franz Neumann, a legal and political theorist.[69] His earlier contributions to legal scholarship suffered a period of disfavor because of earlier cold war polarization, in both ideology and international relations. During the 1940s and 1950s, Neumann's social democratic program and proposed policy reforms suffered increasing marginalization. The latter was due to his defense, though misinterpreting rule of law, of a socialist version of the rule of law (or libertarian socialist account of the rule of law) and individual rights. His viewpoints were deemed too liberal for most orthodox Marxists, in particular, Marxist-Leninist political parties. His viewpoints also included a socialist critique of contradictory aspects of liberalism, including the co-existence of economic libertarianism and political authoritarianism, and hence appeared even too left-wing for rightist. It was a viewpoint situated between Marxism and liberal democracy, and between authoritarian state socialism (as led by Stalin's Soviet Union) and free-market capitalism (dominated by U.S. strategic interests and McCarthyite purges of un-American leftist). Some contend that Neumann was ahead of his times because his views espoused a third way between unregulated capitalism and state socialism.

There is also the authoritarian, proto-fascist theory developed by Carl Schmitt, whom is also, interestingly, a former Nazi jurist prosecuted during the Nuremberg International Military Tribunal in 1947. Since 1985, and post-humously, there is also a growing interest in the scholarship of Schmitt that is largely attributable to a re-emergence of a radical right as a distinctive political force, especially on the European continent, which finds its outlet in extreme nationalistic expressions such as ethnic cleansing against perceived, though irrational, threats. Schmitt attacked what he perceived as critical contradictions and the problematic nature of plausible but false neutrality of the liberal constitutional state. He attacked liberalism's claim to accord pluralistic and non-judgmental tolerance to all substantive accounts of what constitutes the common good, which, in practice, implicitly undermined citizens' efforts to organize their lives according to well defined communal values that diverge from liberalism's own commitment to market-oriented individualism.[70] Schmitt foresaw untenable positions stemming from a liberal state's application of such substantive neutrality, which was a problematic commitment to universal values of pre-political individual rights and a non-ideological proceduralism. The untenable positions were between a natural law commitment to the subordination of positive law to higher natural rights and opposing the position of Hans Kelsen's positivism; and further, between an authoritarian imposition of the truth of its individualistic values that threaten to displace opposing perspectives and a denial of possibility of an absolute truth to competing political ideologies. He also perceived the problem of liberalism as presenting a structural incoherence,

[68] Janet Campbell, An Analysis of Law in the Marxist Tradition (Mellen, 2003).

[69] Michael Salter, Neo-Fascist Legal Theory on Trial: An Interpretation of Carl Schmitt's Defence at Nuremberg from the Perspective of Franz Neumann's Critical Theory of Law, Res Publica 5: 161–194 (1999). M. Jay, The Dialectical Imagination: A History of the Frankfurt School and the Institute of Social Research 1923–1950 (Little Brown, 1973). Tribe, Id.

[70] Carl Schmitt., The Crisis of Parliamentary Democracy, (E. Kennedy, trans.) (MIT UP, 1985). D. Dyzenhaus, Legality and Legitimacy: Carl Schmitt, Hans Kelsen and Hermann Heller (Clarendon, 1997).

which results in state paralysis when state action was needed in the face of enemies. For Schmitt, threats to the state required the mobilization of a unified homogeneous state, "which is centered around a sovereign's personal vision of its people's unique historical destiny." He feared that liberal constitutionalism leaves a state defenseless against effective colonization by privately funded special interest groups, "whose pervasive impact creates widespread popular disillusion with respect to both liberal parliamentary institutions and the wider democratic political process." Schmitt deems liberals as overemphasizing legality, when attempting to avoid political decisions in their quest for a precisely organized system of legal rules.[71] A critical component of Schmitt's theory is a sovereignty that does not lie in a system of principles, rather the power to make exceptions to customary legalities for purpose of addressing emergencies, because a primary function of the sovereignty is to preserve order.

Schmitt's critique of liberal constitutionalism depends upon a series of dramatic inversions of the assumptions of liberal ideology, including "the relationship between *abstractly universal* and impersonal general legal principles characteristic of Enlightenment rationalism (such as the rule of law), and the essentially *particularistic* and *concrete* character of full blooded contestation between starkly incompatible ideologies." For Schimitt, while "liberalism claims to *subordinate* sovereign political power to a supposedly closed system of self-sufficient legal norms, the 'separation of powers' and ideologically-neutral constitutional procedures expressive of reason," he would subordinate all legal-constitutional authority to an essentially particularistic form of untamable sovereign power, which effectively denies the very possibility of any such overarching neutrality. Schmitt also advanced the reversal of "liberalism's prioritization of the relationship between mundane constitutional norms and the 'exceptional state.'" Schmitt does so, "by interpreting the power to identify the latter as *constitutive* for the authority of the former." For Schmitt, liberalism promotes political-cultural pluralism and open-ended discursive deliberation between competing perspectives on the goals of public policy rather than decisive and pre-emptory sovereign action that is unhindered by constitutional limitations, which is needed to enforce the absolute value that a sovereign power promotes as a substantive principle of homogeneity. Indeed, his inversions are authoritarian, especially, when reducing principles of constitutionality to a secondary expression of sovereign power, which is independently constituted by non-rational brute force and an unaccountable decision. The latter establishes the fundamental nature of the legal order of a liberal state, and therefore cannot be held accountable to the content of merely derivative constitutional norms. Schmitt's decisionism effectually reduces legal authority, which is regulated by rule of law to an instrumental form of sovereign power.

As one source observed, "Regardless of our historical and political distance to Carl Schmitt, his writings continue to pose serious questions for any discussion of liberalism and parliamentary democracy, especially at a time when both in the United States and in the European Union the interpretation of constitutional law is undergoing considerable change."[72]There is also the continuing inherent danger of ideals grounded in proto-fascist theories, such as those of Schmitt, because, "For as long as civil libertarian appeals to preserve democratic values of accountability, transparency and openness to maximum participation in the exercise of public and private power fail to gain and sustain majority

[71] David Gordon, Review of Carl Schmitt: Politics and Theory, by Paul Edward Gottfried, N.Y. : Greenwood Press 1990, The Review of Austrian Economics, Vol. 6, No. 1, 117-20 (1992).

[72] Christian J. Emden, Review of Jan-Werner Miller, A Dangerous Mind: Carl Schmitt in Post-War European Thought, H-Net Reviews, Jun. 2005, http://www.h-net.msu.edu/reviews/showrev.cgi?path=298891122323542.

support amongst those both exercising and subject to such power, then a distinctly fascistic reconstruction of our existing governmental, institutional and social system remains an ever-present possibility." For instance, a Nazi regime was able to rely upon strong support from both practitioner and academic branches of the legal profession, and from support within and without the legal profession. The greatest danger lies in the potential re-emergence of the same or different version of Fascism. For this reason, "it is conceivable that many of the arguments used to greatest effect by the Nazi jurist Carl Schmitt to ridicule and undermine support for a civil and human rights-based form of liberal parliamentary democracy will resurface, and then gain increasing support, in 'radical' and would-be avant-garde circles."

Nonetheless, and still problematic, Karl Marx deemed law to be superfluous in a socialist utopia and law in a capitalist society as merely a tool of the elite bourgeoisie. For Marx, law did play a role in the transition from capitalism to communism. However, it is a limited role, because Marx and Friedrich Engels, as economic determinists, perceived law in a capitalist society as being a tool of the elite bourgeoisie. Driving forces of social, political and economic life were the contradictions in material and economic life. Such contradictions arise from a conflict between the social forces of production and the relations of production -- the class and property relations of society -- within which these productive forces have developed. Marx, in *A Contribution to the Critique of Political Economy* (*Grundrisse der Kritik der politischen Ökonomie/Rohentwurf*, 1859), opined that law is just another ideological form through which men become conscious of this conflict and fight it out.[73] A primary force shaping law are necessarily the economic relations and changing economic circumstances, leaving legal systems (or institutions) as one of many areas of class struggle that must be fought out. Law, like other social phenomena, is subject to the Marx and Engel's dialectical materialist analysis, which examined the interaction between the economic base of society and the ideological superstructure.

Engels, in *Ludwig Feuerbach and the End of German Classical Philosophy* (*Ludwig Feuerbach und der Ausgang der klassischen deutschen Philosophie*, 1886), compared the French Civil Code (*Code civil des français*) and Roman law with English and Prussian law.[74] Engels, in the wake of the 1789 Revolution, wrote, "If the state and public law are determined by economic relations, so, too, is private law, which indeed in essence only sanctions the existing economic relations between individuals which are normal in the given circumstances. The form in which this happens can, however, vary considerably. It is possible, as happened in England, in harmony with the whole national development, to retain in the main the forms of the old feudal laws while giving them a bourgeois content...However, after a great revolution it was also possible for such a classic law code of bourgeois society as the French *Code Civil* to be worked out on the basis of Roman Law. If, therefore, bourgeois legal rules merely express the economic life conditions of society in legal form, then they do so well or ill according to circumstances." The latter is the materialist conception that generally guides Marxists in the role that law plays in a Marxist or communist society, as equally true in the preceding formation of social and economic life.

In terms of a search for a Marxian utopia or perpetual peace, Marx essentially perceived the abolishing of the old state apparatus and its replacement by a more egalitarian and

---

[73] Karl Marx, in the preface to A Contribution to the Critique of Political Economy (1859). Karl Marx, A Contribution to the Critique of Political Economy, Moscow" (Moscow: Progress, 1977). Paul Phillips, Marx and Engels on Law and Laws, Martin (Oxford UP, 1980).

[74] Engels, Ludwig Feuerbach and the End of German Classical Philosophy (1886) (Moscow: Progress, 1978).

democratic state. The latter would occur when the working class took power and commenced building socialism, which is the first stage of the transition from socialism to communism, or perhaps the new CCP-ideology presenting a nexus between the progression in antiquity from *xiaokang* to *datong*, and an ideological and corresponding progression in Chinese Marxism between a socialist market society and world communism. For Marx and Engels, the state would wither away when communism was achieved. This is the point in society when the productive forces of man had developed and had been rationally planned to a state, when scarcity and inequality was eliminated, including the struggle for individual existence. In this Marxian utopia, there will no longer be private, nor conflicting ownership of the productive forces; the social inequality of capitalism is overcome; and the majority of working people have become accustomed to administering their own affairs and those of society without the need for legal and physical coercion. It is a socialist society described by Janet Campbell, as a truly a free society, and by Franz Neumann as a libertarian socialist account of the rule of law, while also, arguably, being advanced by the problematic authoritarian, proto-fascist theories developed by Carl Schmitt. Perhaps, more accurately, China represents a socialist-political polity truly manifesting the continuing search for a Marxian utopia or perpetual peace, by attempting to finalize the localization of Marxism.

If China's polity, the CCP, is attempting to finalize the localization of Marxism, then modern reforms must be constructed in terms of the institutional analysis of a Marxian framework or Marxist political economy. A primary concern of Marxist political economy is the subject of the relations of production. In modern China, as a starting point and theory of analysis, Marxist political economy continues to serve as a theoretical tool and framework in the fundamental analysis of economic institutions, and corresponding political and legal institutions.[75] It is institutional economics serving as a theoretical system in the analysis of social, economic, political and legal institutions, and many other philosophical forms. Although Marxist institutional analysis can be said to comprise two critical theories or levels of theories, the most important critical theory is the elemental institutional analysis forthcoming from the basis premises that productive forces determine production relations, economic foundation decides superstructures (or society's institutions and ideas) and a core segment that covers the social division of labor. The problems become increasingly obvious, when one considers Marxist political economy theories as driving institutional research and institutional analysis, and being hailed as the force providing an explanatory system for institutional phenomena.[76] The consequences are obvious in terms of ongoing modern legal and economic reforms, including the need for greater political liberalization.

In terms of the institutional analysis of a Marxian framework or Marxist political economy, critical components of Marxian analysis or economic determinism are the economic base (*Struktur*) of society and the superstructure (*Überbau*), with the latter comprising the social, political, legal and religious institutions, including other philosophical forms.[77] For China, and on-going legal and economic reforms, and the paradoxical

[75] Li Shenglong, The Overall Structure of the Institutional Analysis Theory of Marxism, Jingjixue dongtai, no. 5 (2003). Sun Hui, Marx's Ontology and Its Significance in Our Times, 29-38, Social Sciences in China (Zhongguo shehui kexue) (spring 2003).

[76] Zou Shipeng, Localization of Marxism in China and the Construction of China's Modernity, 12-21, Social Sciences in China (Zhongguo shehui kexue) (summer 2005). Jiang Shigong, Towards a Jurisprudence of Legislators, 61-72, Social Sciences in China (Zhongguo shehui kexue) (summer 2005).

[77] Niklas Luhmann, A Sociological Theory of Law (Transl: Elizabeth King & Martin Albrow), (China Social Sciences Publishing House, Chengcheng Books: The President and Fellows of Harv. College, 1985).

interrelationships between competing sources of order, the latter presents problematic phenomenon of the economic base being the fundamental causal force in Marx's materialistic conception of history. Marx sets forth a clear exposition of his materialistic concept of history in the preface to the *A Contribution to Critique of Political Economy* (*Grundrisse der Kritik der politischen Ökonomie/Rohentwurf*, 1859). For China, and on-going legal and economic reforms, and the paradoxical interrelationships between competing sources of order, the latter presents problematic phenomenon of the economic base being the fundamental and exclusive causal force in Marx's materialistic conception of history. Marx when setting forth a clear exposition of his materialistic concept of history in the preface to *A Contribution to Critique of Political Economy* writes, "In the social production which men carry on they enter into definite relations that are indispensable and independent of their will; these relations of production correspond to a definite stage of development of their material powers of production. The sum total of these relations of production constitutes the economic structure of society--the real foundation, on which rise legal and political superstructures and to which correspond definite forms of social consciousness. The mode of production in material life determines the general character of the social, political and spiritual processes of life."

For Karl Marx, although the superstructure is an important factor, the economic base is the fundamental and exclusive causal influence because, as seen in Marx's classic *The German Ideology* (*Die deutsche Ideologie*, 1845-1846), the economic base is the fundamental and exclusive causal force in his materialistic conception of history.[78]Admittedly, there is a controversy regarding how to define the superstructure, which evolves into the controversy of how to measure its attendant influence on politics, religions, laws, other institutions and other philosophical forms comprising the superstructure. Orthodox Marxism, by virtue of the classic publications of Marx in *The German Ideology*, and Marx and Engels in the preface to *A Contribution to Critique of Political Economy* (*Grundrisse der Kritik der politischen Ökonomie/Rohentwurf*, 1859), maintains that the superstructure, such as the political, legal, religious and other philosophical forms, has no causal influence. For instance, Alex Callinicos, in *Making History: Agency, Structure and Change in Social Theory* (1987), argues that the economic base is an all-encompassing casual influence, constituting both the forces and relations of production. There is also Gerald Allan Cohen, in *Karl Marx's Theory of History: A Defence* (2000), whom limits the role of the economic base to the relations of production. Cohen also recognizes that the issue of the influence of the superstructure is a controversial topic. Some, perhaps representing a minority viewpoint or even unorthodox Marxists, even argue that the superstructure serves as a superficial cause rather than fundamental cause in Marx's materialistic conception of history. For instance, Callinicos intimates that Marx recognizes a historical superficial influence, if not casual influence, of the superstructure in early Western civilization, such as the influence of politics in ancient Greece and Rome, and even Catholicism during the Middle ages. However, and antithetically, by

[78] Karl Marx, The German Ideology, Critique of Modern German Philosophy According to Its Representatives Feuerbach, B. Bauer and Stirner, and of German Socialism According to Its Various Prophets, Part I: Feuerbach, Opposition of the Materialist and Idealist Outlook, D. Proletarians and Communism, Individuals, Class, and Community, in Karl Marx & Frederick Engels, Collected Works, Vol. 5, http://www.marxists.org/archive/marx/works/cw/. Karl Marx, (1859), Id. Alex Callinicos, Making History: Agency, Structure and Change in Social Theory 173-75 (Polity Press, 1987). Gerald Allan Cohen, Karl Marx's Theory of History: A Defence 216-17 (Clarendon, 2000).

virtue of Marx's materialistic conception of history, the superstructure of neither politics, nor religious, could ever rise to the same level or prominence in modern society.

Nonetheless, an elemental problem of Marxian analysis is that, notwithstanding a superficial influence on the superstructure, the economic base gives rise to the superstructure, thereby presenting the phenomenom of the base conditioning the superstructure, or the politics, religions and laws or rule of law, once it comes into existence.[79] Moreover, even assuming a superficial influence of the superstructure, an advocacy of a superficial role of the superstructure, in essence, challenges Marx's materialistic conception of history. In terms of Marx's materialistic conception of history, any role assigned to the superstructure, such as even a superficial influence, ultimately, challenges the economic base as the fundamental and exclusive causal influence, thereby rendering Marx's theory of history as a false doctrinaire. A continuing problem of Marxism, and as observed by Alex Callinicos, in *The Revolutionary ideas of Karl Marx* (1983), the economic base conditions the superstructure by limiting its development, which, most important, includes limiting the development of constitutionalism, rule of law and independent judicial review.

A Chinese Marxist legal theory and rule of law also struggle with the requisite of being a living law, which reflects a development of law - development of legal propositions dichotomy, and a tacit assumption that legal propositions are rooted in the past. A body of laws must be a living law and subject to change, because a complete presentation of all legal relations in a code is a difficult task. A distinguishable characteristic of Western judicial models, such as appeals, revision and cassation, is that they address living law. This is not the same as modern China's legislative practices, or a path of legal reforms, presenting a model of legal change responding in an ad hoc fashion to socio-economic change, which pursuant to Marxian political economy seeks to imprison the law of time or its citizens, and denies a continuity between past and present legal histories. A body of laws must be a living law that also experiences a natural evolution and development of law, and not merely ad hoc enactments of laws or the development of legal propositions.

Eugen Ehrlich, in *Fundamental Principles of the Sociology of Law* (*Grundlegung der Soziologie des Rechts*, 1913), writes, an "attempt to imprison the law of a time or of a people within the sections of a code is about as reasonable as to attempt to confine a stream within a pond. The water that is put in the pond is no long a living stream but a stagnant pool, and but little water can be put in the pond... It could not be otherwise."[80] Despite legal positivism and its attendant command theory and progeny, legal propositions do not present a complete picture of the state of the law, neither what the law actually is, nor what it actually should be. A problem of a Marxian political economy is economic determinism, which heavily weighs against a body of law or rule of law, and any other legal system or institution, being reflective of a living law, especially a legal system or institution primarily focused on enacting legal propositions, though impossible to cover all legal relations, and not a natural evolution and development of law. Harold J. Berman writes, it is "a uniquely Western belief: that a body of law, a system of law, contains, and should contain, a built-in mechanism for organic change and that it survives, and should survive, by development, by growth." It is the problematic consequence of the economic base (*Struktur*) of society defining and confining the

[79] Alex Callinicos, The Revolutionary ideas of Karl Marx 97 (Bookmarks, 1983).

[80] Eugen Ehrlich, Fundamental Principles of the Sociology of Law, (China Social Sciences Publishing House, Chengcheng Books: The President and Fellows of Harv. College, 1936). Harold Berman, The Origins of Historical Jurisprudence: Coke, Selden, Hale, 103 Yale L.J. 1651 (1994).

development of the superstructure (*Überbau*); namely, constitutionalism, rule of law, independent judicial review and other philosophical forms of society.

10.12. Conclusion

A problem for those proponents advocating an increasing role of the superstructure as a causal influence rather than superficial influence, if any influence, is that such advocacy, essentially, renders Marx's materialistic conception of history as a problematic doctrinaire, false prophecy, false history and failing promise of a future Marxian utopia or perpetual peace. The worst consequence for China, and its polity, the CCP, and its citizenry is that it may render the final attempt to localize modern Marxism or the final localization of Marxism (*Makesi zhuyi he Zhongguo shiji xiang jiehe*) as, simply, meaningless, especially for Marxist legal theory or socialist jurisprudence serving as the path for modern legal reforms. Rather than an path to modern legal reforms promoting a variant of the Western model of a state of legality or constitutional state, such as Anglo-American rule of law, German *Rechtsstaat* and French *État de droit*. As Niklas Luhmann succinctly observes, "The various legal propositions as such, the legal institutions divorced from their presuppositions, have no information to convey," because if there is a unifying regularity in the phenomenom of legal life, it can only be found in the fact that legal life is conditioned upon the social and economic constitution and not the fundamental and exclusive causal influence of economic determinism. Borrowing from the words of Xu Zhangrun, when translating a thesis of the late eminent scholar Liang Shuming (1893-1988), "He [Liang Shuming] wished to find a way out of the holistic crisis for his homeland, to establish a home for the mind by creating a new life for the Chinese people and Chinese society where *Physis* [nature] could hopefully accommodate *Nomos* [law] compatibly and competently; where the transcendent source of meaning and humane feeling, founded upon a new basis, could be reintegrated and reflected into rules of law as a whole."[81] For these reasons, rule of law can only be the result of an evolution of legal systems and not the starting point, as the CCP attempts to do so by, simply, enacting new legal propositions or laws.[82]

---

[81] Xu Zhangrun, Western Law in China: Transplantation of Transformation, Social Sciences in China (Zhongguo shehui kexue) (autumn 2004). Liang Shuming, The First Road that will not work for us Politically, Vol. 5 (1930).

[82] Fareed Zakaria, The Future of Freedom: Illiberal Democracy at Home and Abroad, (Norton, 2003). Freed Zakaria's thesis concludes, historically, rule of law and a liberal market economy precede liberal democracy and suffrage, because rule of law can only be the result of an evolution of legal systems, and not the starting point.

Chapter 11

CULTURE AND HISTORICAL JURISPRUDENCE

11.1. CHINESE NEO-LIBERAL COTERIE

The critical issues of a proposed Chinese neo-liberal coterie and neo-liberal constitutionalists directly relate to issues of legal and economic reforms, transplanting or borrowing legal and economic systems or institutions, merging liberalism and economic liberalism with traditional Chinese culture (primarily traditional Confucianism), and blending a distinctively different Chinese jurisprudence with Western jurisprudence. Modern China is experiencing the same difficulty in its attempt to finalize the localization of Marxism to the realities of traditional culture and society (*Makesi zhuyi he Zhongguo shiji xiang jiehe*) because Marxism, as a Western theorization or philosophy, is rooted in classical German philosophy, French socialism and British political economy. Western liberalism's underpinning philosophical foundation also attributes to problems of its transplant or integration into China's legal system. From Hugo Grotius (1583-1645) to H.L.A. (Herbert) Hart (1907-1992), and other jurists and philosophers, one consistently discovers an inherent coercive proclivity in liberal democratic constitutionalism. Although there are several branches and sub branches of jurisprudence, especially in American jurisprudence, such as legal realism, sociological jurisprudence, critical legal studies, postmodernism and others, for purposes of contemplating jurisprudence for a proposed Chinese neo-liberal coterie or even neo-liberal constitutionalists, focus is directed towards three general Western philosophies of law, which are historical jurisprudence, legal positivism and natural law theory. Natural law theory is distinguishable as embodying rules and concepts of moral (*boni mores*) principles, which are derived from reason and conscience. Positivism or legal positivism represents a body of rules laid down and enforced by a sovereign, because while most positivists do not deny that law ought to serve moral ends, the ends of justice, they argue that what law is, is a political instrument, a body of rules manifesting the policies of the legitimately constituted political authorities. For legal positivist, only after it is established what law is may one ask, "what it ought to be." However, the latter viewpoints of most positivists are those of modern positivists, which may or may not be reconcilable with classical positivism. As for naturalists, they, generally, believe that one cannot know what the law is "unless one considers at the same time what it ought to be." For naturalists, legal norms, implicitly, have a moral and political purpose.[1]

Historic issues of morals and politics are especially keen for China and its ontological base in traditional culture.[2] One questions what significance a proposed Chinese neo-liberal coterie, especially neo-liberal constitutionalists, would, actually, attribute to China's historical particularity, because a failure to attribute any role to historical particularity leaves one thinking that attributes of culture, communal integration or in-place societal *ethos* play a minimum role in modern legal reforms. Nonetheless, as always the case of moral and political dilemma surrounding the integration of legal systems, the issue ultimately resolves to one of choice for modern China and its socio-econo-legal order, because a *sine qua non* of a successful resolve of these competing institutions is conflict. A problem for a proposed Chinese neo-liberal coterie may be a denial of the dynamics of culture. For modern legal reforms, many would prescribe a minimal role of culture and historical particularity. While modern Marxists hail economic determinism, cultural determinism prescribes, "The conviction that the accumulated knowledge, the organized beliefs, and the way of life prescribed by a culture determine not only all other aspects of human cognition and social behavior but also the dynamics of the culture itself. Such a conviction sees culture as an autonomous cultural system." Cultural determinism posits that cultural values, and not economic determinism, ultimately condition modes of cultural relationships, such as social, political and legal relations. For China, cultural determinism prophesizes entrenched institutional or foundational values, such as social, political and legal norms, reflective of a persistent and systemic traditional culture. In the philosophy of law (jurisprudence or *juris prudential*) parlance, the latter translates into an ontological base in traditional culture. *Juris prudential* encompasses, "the study of a legal system's scope, function, methodology, and guiding precepts." Law and the evolution of legal systems are part of the idiosyncratic historicity of a country, and are products of multiple factors, especially culture. The conception of social order as historically contingent and evolving, which conceptually embodies China's ontological base in tradition, may also explain this phenomenon. In modern China, an ontological base in tradition prophesizes distinctively Sinic infrastructures, such as social, political and legal institutions, which perhaps constitutes a blend of both non-Western and Western models and taxonomies, if not simply distinctive Chinese models and taxonomies.[3]

For these reasons, a proposed Chinese neo-liberal coterie would have to ignore the advent of the institutional dynamics of traditional culture, which involves what many deem to be Asian values (*asiatische Werte*). While the phrase Asian values is attributable to several sources, the earliest source is an article appearing in the *Economist* (1995), which reads, "The rise of Japan and the East Asian tigers has caused many people to reinterpret the economic impact of Confucianism".[4] In the late 1990s, many East Asian government leaders, such as

[1] Harold Berman, The Origins of Historical Jurisprudence: Coke, Selden, Hale, 103 Yale L.J. 1651 (1994).

[2] A. Charles Muller, Essence, Function and Interpenetration Early Chinese Origins and Manifestations, Vol. 7 Bulletin of Tokyo Gakuen Univ. (1999), http://www.human.toyogakuenu.ac.jp/~acmuller/articles/tiyung-earlyorigins.htm.

[3] Robert L. Hayman, Jr. & Nancy Levitt, Jurisprudence Contemporary Readings, Problems, and Narratives, 5-6 (West Pub, 1995). Klaus Krippendorff, Dictionary of Cybernetics (2007), http://pespmc1.vmb.ac.be/ASC/CULTUR_DETER.html.

[4] The Economist, Jan. 21, 1995: 39. Seok-Hyeon Kim, A Critical Review of Asian Value and Asian Model, Nov. 1999.

Lee Kuan Yew, former senior minister of Singapore, and Mahathir Modhamad, former prime minister of Malaysia, generally, recognized and articulated rhetoric of a role of traditional Confucianism in economic development, by specific reference to the phraseology of Asian values. The rhetoric of Asian values represented the critical acknowledgement by many East Asian leaders of the force of traditional culture in modern reforms and other issues of governance, such as development and, implicitly, constitutionalism. The latter relevancy is obvious, because a consideration of constitutional *ethos* for constitutionalism necessitates consideration of traditional culture. A proposed Chinese neo-liberal coterie predicts an extension of legal borrowing to a concept of cultural borrowing, because a proposed Chinese neo-liberal coterie must deny in its search for validity in terms of communal integration that traditional Confucianism is systemic and persistent in modern China.

There are two aspects to the problem of a proposed Chinese neo-liberal coterie and traditional culture. First, the historicity of Western culture and its Western universalism is distinctively different from the historicity of traditional Chinese culture and a historical particularity grounded in 5,000 years or more of Chinese civilization. In comparison, grounding a Western culture, in the limiting sense of classical liberalism, is an intellectual history of eighteenth century Europe. Classical liberalism is a political philosophy with intellectual roots in Renaissance humanism that gains considerable momentum as a cultural movement after the Reformation. Classical liberal thinkers, for purpose of challenging presuppositions of Medieval Europe, contend that each human being is a repository of certain God-ordained inalienable rights, which are rights that classical liberalism normatively seeks to safeguard. Second, in a discourse concerning Chinese constitutionalism, especially constitutional *ethos*, the concept of neo-liberalism arguably deserves minimal attention, because its origins are a response of Western developed countries to the East Asian financial crisis (1978-79), Mexico's financial crisis and other financial crises during the 1990s, including the Argentine financial crisis (1930s) and birth of dependency theory (*dependencia* or *dependencia* school). Notwithstanding origins of classical liberalism, the origins of neo-liberalism make its roots suspect as a viable source of *ethos* rather than indigenous values evolving from an ontological base in tradition, which as a fundamental constitutional precept are requisite for constitutionalism. The problem remaining for Western classical liberalism, economic liberalism and constitutionalism, is that they are European-American concepts of relatively recent provenance, especially when compared to the provenance and history of traditional Chinese culture.[5]

11.2. Constitutions, Democracy and Liberty

One tacitly assumes a proposed Chinese neo-liberal coterie would urge a constitutional convention that adopts a discursive model of constitutionalism that mirrors American constitutionalism and a separation of powers and independent judiciary that mirrors the United States' model of government. Such a movement would essentially urge a constitutionalism that is seemingly over-simplistic and fails to recognize the real inner-

[5] Ronald Dworkin, Liberal Community, 77 Calif. L. Rev. 479, 480 (1989). Hanna Fenichel Pitkin, The Idea of a Constitution, 37 J. Legal Educ. 167 (1987). Wm. Theodore De Bray, The Constitutional Tradition in China, 9 J. Chin L. 7 (spring 1995).

workings of Western constitutionalism. In Western jurisprudence, models of constitutions diverge on issues of constitutional review versus constitutional courts, and centralized (or concentrated) constitutional review versus decentralized (or diffused) constitutional review and other variations. A reality of world constitutionalism is constitution-writing nation states adopting variants attributable to many social forces, such as cultural and economic forces, and count as examples: American judicial review model (based on *Marbury vs. Madison*, 1803); new (British) Commonwealth model (Mauritius) that cannot be classified either under the American or the European model; Austrian (continental-constitutional review) model (based on Hans Kelsen's Model of 1920, involving the interconnection of the principle of the supremacy of the constitution and the principle of the supremacy of the parliament); mixed (American continental) model with the elements of both a centralized (or concentrated) and decentralized (or diffused) system; Constitutional courts; High courts or their special departments; French (continental) model (based on the model of the French Constitutional Council-*Conseil Constitutionnel*, 1958); Systems without constitutional and judicial review; and International judicial institutions with certain functions of constitutional review, such as the European Court of Human Rights in Strasbourg and the African Court of Human Rights.[6]

Notwithstanding a commonality grounded in the theories and philosophies of the intellectual European Enlightenment thinkers, there are contrasting models of constitutions and constitutionalism. The independent judicial review and activism of the United States judiciary is actually atypical to Western jurisprudence, and count as examples Israel, New Zealand, the United Kingdom (or Great Britain) and Sweden, which do not have constitutionally-granted independent judiciaries.[7] Liberal democracies such as Great Britain, actually, have not had a written constitution for a substantial period. Great Britain and its parliamentary supremacy do not have constitutional provisions on both separation of powers and independent judicial review (constitutional review). Moreover, despite such dissimilarities, democracy in Great Britain is no less than that of the United States. An assumed urging for a model of constitutionalism that exactly mirrors American constitutionalism also seemingly fails to recognize the shortcomings of the U.S. judicial model, which is a judicial model subject to criticism because of its failings in many respects, such as the charge of excess in liberty. The U.S. model of constitutionalism is more accurately describable as a republican form of government and not a full embodiment of democracy, in the purest sense of democracy.

The original political lexicon for democracy dates to two words from the Ancient Greek language: First *demarchy*, then *democracy*. When constructing a political lexicon that represents the ideal of government by the people, ancient Greece culture would have to conjoin the word *demos* (for the people) with one of two available verbs for power, being *Kratos* (or the verb *kratein*) and *archein*. While *archein* is already in usage by compound words such as monarchy, oligarchy and anarchy, the verb *kratein* is problematic because it seemingly denotes brute force rather than government by rule. In addition, in ancient Greece, the root or verb *archein* and resulting noun of *demarch* (or *demarchy*) to express rule by the

---

[6] Francisco Ramos, The Establishment of Constitutional Courts: A Study of 128 Democratic Constitutions, Review of Law & Economics, vol. 2, no. 1, art. 6 (2006), http://www.bepress.com/rle/vol2/iss1/art6. Arne Mavčič, Tables of comparative constitutional review, http://www.concourts.net/.

[7] Peter H. Russell, Toward a General Theory of Judicial Independence, in Judicial Independence in the Age of Democracy, 1, 22 (Peter H. Russell & David M. O'Brien eds., 2001). Lord Irvine of Lairg, Sovereignty in Comparative Perspective: Constitutionalism in Britain and America, 76 N. Y. Law Rev. 1, 16 (Apr. 2001).

people could not be used, at least in Athens, because the term *demarch* was already used to describe the office of the head of a local group (or district), the *deme*.[8] The lexicon of democracy rather than *demarchy*, eventually, comes to represent government by the people, and during a modern era, democracy further evolves into the distinctions between direct and indirect democracy or republican form of government. For instance, the U.S. model and its constitution provides for indirect democracy or republican form of government rather than direct democracy.[9] Given promptings for a U.S. model of constitutionalism, one reasonably assumes a Chinese neo-liberal coterie would hardly be concerned with the task of discerning between direct and indirect democracy for modern China.

From Ancient Greek, there are also the interrelated and original meanings for political (*politikon*), citizen (*politees*) and city-state (*polis*). These concepts, including democracy, address issues of human association and coexistence and, ultimately, pursue what Aristotle (384-322 BC) deems the good of the *polis* or justice, because "the good of political science is justice, in other words, the common interest."[10] As observed by Ludwig von Mises (1881-1973), "nobody has ever contested that the idea of liberty was created in the cities of ancient Greece." The latter lexicons from ancient Greece and their original meanings also bear a strong resemblance to concepts from traditional Chinese culture. Aristotle, in *The Politics* (*Politica*), parallels the ideals of Confucius or the traditionalist school, when he expands the idea of human coexistence from family to clan rather than the city-state. Hegel (Georg Wilhelm Friedrich Hegel, 1770-1831) also pursues a similar idea, when pursuing the ideal of ethical entities stemming from coexistence, such as the family, civil society and state. However, during the time of Aristotle, the concept of "civil society" was non-existent, and individuals coexist as simply individuals and as citizens of a *polis*. If Confucius or the traditionalist school is distinguishable, it will be by virtue of an advocacy of natural ethical relations based on the family to the ethical relations of the city–state, because Aristotle deems ethics of life in the *polis* as the ultimate virtue commanding all others, since the *polis* was prior in nature to both the individual and the family. Most important, there are the similarities, especially concerning the political lexicon of democracy, presenting a possible resolution of paradoxical interrelated sources of order.

Given these potential similarities between traditional culture and early Western culture or ancient Greece, one questions whether a Chinese neo-liberal coterie or neo-liberal constitutionalists would consider traditional culture, and its traditional government, traditional political theory and traditional jurisprudence, as historic sources of democracy. There are traces of history in traditional culture that evidence vestiges of democratic government. In China, democracy in its purest form or direct government by all the people concerned remains an impractical idea, which also holds true for early colonial and modern America. There are similarities between representation in modern Western democratic governments, and traditional culture and traditional government. In Chinese antiquity, a group or class of

---

[8] F. A. Hayek, Law, Legislation and Liberty, Vol. III: 38-41 (Univ. of Chicago Press, 1973-79),

[9] Bookchin, Murray, New Perspective in Libertarian Thought, Vol. 1, No. 5 Comment Apr. 15, 1980, http://dwardmac.pitzer.edu/anarchist_archives/bookchin/commentv1_5.html. Abrams, Elliott, (ed.) Democracy: How Direct? Views from the Founding era and Polling era, (Altamira Pr; 2002).

[10] Deng Anqing, Tracing the Origin of the Concept of Ethics in the West: An Existentialist Interpretation of Aristotle's Concept of Ethics, Social Sciences in China (Zhongguo shehui kexue) 34-43 (spring 2006). Richard M. Ebeling, (ed.), Money, Method, and the Market Process: Essays by Ludwig von Mises (Kluwer Academic Pub, 1990). Aristotle, The Politics, In Selected Works of Aristotle 29-30 (Yan Yi, ed.) (Beijing: Renmin Univ. of China Press, 1999).

people, such as intellectuals who served as representatives of a majoritarian interest, usually conducted actual governing. For modern China, the same holds true by analogy, though tenuous analogy due to the lack of popular sovereignty in the election of National People's Congress (NPC) members, because communists even advocate that government should be conducted exclusively a by group or class of people, or proletariat class.[11] While democracy in its purest form remains an ideal, the high ideal of representative democracy is, and was, a reality in both modern Western democratic governments and traditional Chinese government. Traditional culture and its traditional political theory required scholars prepare for government service by thorough study of the work of sages and by diligently practicing traditional Confucian principles. These scholars entered officialdom through the traditional civil service examination (*keju*). In this context, pursuant to traditional political theory, the opinions of scholars are assumedly representative of well though-out intelligent opinions of the general populace.

There are other similarities between traditional Chinese government and U.S. constitutionalism. Under a democratic form of government such as the U.S. Constitution, there is an equally compelling philosophical struggle between man and law, which shares an academic kinship to scholarly discourses grounded in the debate between Confucianism and legalism (or school of *Fajia*, the legalists or realists). One can draw a correlative argument in similarity when one collimates the U.S. judicial selection process with traditional Chinese culture and traditional political theory. The U.S. judiciary selection process for appointment of justices to the U.S. Supreme Court exhibits a proclivity towards selection of the sort of wise and benevolent man sought after under the principles of traditional culture. Girardeau A. Spann, when describing a socialized U.S. judiciary, writes, "Judges, of course, are not selected at random. However, the judicial selection procedures that we customarily utilize may exacerbate matters by effectively making judges more majoritarian than if they were selected at random. For reasons of checks and balances, federal judges are selected through a process that is intentionally political. They are appointed by the most majoritarian official in the government and confirmed by the upper house of the legislature after public hearings in which their political preferences are thoroughly explored. Although judicial temperament and legal competence play some role in the appointment and confirmation process, the acceptability of a candidate's political inclinations is likely to be dispositive at both stages . . . The political nature of our judicial selection procedures has the effect of reducing the range of attitudes that will be reflected in our judicial population. Only mainstream political preferences will survive the appointment and confirmation process."[12]

In antiquity, there is also evidence of sovereignty. Given the vast size of China, historically, it has been a practical impossibility to vest political power and authority in the hands of one person. Political power and authority had to vest with a collective rule of a large number of persons rather than the practical constraints of a single ruler struggling to maintain control over a vast China. No doubt, a typical Westerner would find the concept of a sharing of government powers in a Chinese dynasty difficult to fathom. For Westerners and their conventionalism and language, the notion of an emperor, or the Emperor (*Huangdi*), is difficult to reconcile with the sharing of government powers or Montesquieu's (*De l'esprit*

---

[11] Jiang Jinsong, The National People's Congress of China (Beijing: Foreign Language Press, 2002).

[12] Girardeau A. Spann, Race Against the Court, The Supreme Court and Minorities in Contemporary America, 21 (N.Y. UP, 1993).

des lois, 1748) separation of the powers of government principle. Most Westerners are simply content to subscribe to theories describing dynastic rule as feudalistic, autocratic and statist. While the Chinese are not concerned with sovereignty per se, nor is it a critical issue in dynastic history, practical realities necessitate power sharing. Since the Han Dynasty (206 B.C. to A.D. 220), there has never been a pure monarchy, because due to practical realities all of the power of government could not vest in one man alone. Notwithstanding exceptions such as the Qin (221-207 B.C.) and Qing (1644-1911) Dynasties, it was not government formed by aristocrats, the military or capitalists; rather it is government by the literati. From the Han to Ming Dynasties, all of the essential power of dynastic government lay in the hands of intellectuals.

The organizational structures of dynastic governments also contribute to this sharing of government powers. Qian Mu (*Ch'ien Mu*, 1895-1990), in *Traditional Government in Imperial China: A Critical Analysis* (1982), found that despite the contributions of the Qin dynasty in establishing a central administration for the empire, it was during the Han Dynasty that new forms of government achieved permanence and stability.[13] For this reason, Han institutions best illustrate patterns of traditional government. During the Han, there is a typical division of the cabinet and administrative staffs and both the Emperor and Chancellor, the highest administrative official, had a secretariat. The Emperor also had six Masters (*Liu shang*), who had different functions, five of them administrate the daily private life of the Emperor and one, the Master of Writing (*Shang shu*), was the secretary for the imperial palace. Further, the secretariat of the Chancellor comprises thirteen bureaus (*Ts'ao*), ranging from the West Bureau, East Bureau, Bureau of Households or Revenue, Bureau of Memorials, Bureau of Plaints or Litigation, Bureau of Regulations or Standards, Bureau of the Commandant or Military Transportation, Bureau of Bandit Suppression or Control, Bureau of Decisions or Criminal Executions, Bureau of Weapons or Soldiers, Bureau of Granaries, to the Yellow Cabinet. While the Chinese were not concerned with issues of sovereignty, such as the source of political power per se, they were, as a product of traditional political thought, mostly concerned with the functions and responsibilities of government and effectiveness of government in fulfilling its functions and responsibilities, which were many and covered a vast territory. The resulting reality is rule by a number of men or typically government by the literati. Moreover, an interpretation of the basic thesis of Qian Mu concerning his views on traditional dynastic government describes traditional government as generally avoiding rule by autocracy and absolutism until the Northern Sun dynasty (960-1127). This latter governmental avoidance of rule by autocracy and absolutism is attributable to Confucianism except when government is under the influence of an overbearing Emperor or powerful court coterie.

This historically means that a group of persons, such as intellectuals who serve as representatives of a majoritarian interest, usually conducts actual governing and are assumedly representative of well though-out intelligent opinions of the general populace. Traditional culture and its traditional political theory evidence a history of both a sovereignty that is representative of an electorate and indirect democracy. While direct democracy is not in place in modern China or Western countries, indirect democracy is in place in Western countries (or liberal democratic countries), but not in modern China, even though modern

[13] Ch'ien Mu (Qian Mu), Traditional Government in Imperial China: A Critical Analysis app., 121, 142 (Chün-tu Hsüeh & George O. Totten, trans.) (Chinese Univ. of Hong Kong, 1982).

communists evidence rule by groups of persons, such as the CCP and its NPC. In both Chinese antiquity and modern Western countries, the primary concern is selecting the best persons to serve in government. In Western countries, there is an emphasis on popular elections for public office. In Chinese antiquity, public offices that are open to the "general public" through an examination system undertake the same goal pursued by Western countries via elections. Even during the post-Qing period, but before the 1949 founding of modern China, following the enactment of new laws, all citizens enjoyed the right of suffrage, or the right to vote and stand for election.[14] Since 1998, admittedly, one does witness the advent of direct popular vote for local electorate, a county level people's congress, by enactment of the Organic Law of Village Committees of China (*Zhonghua Renmin Gonghegou Cun Min Wei Yuan Hui Zu Zhifa*). However, and demonstrative of the problems of modern Marxism, as a result of the problems of lack a sovereignty that is representative of an electorate, Chinese citizens do not elect candidates to the NPC or National People's Congress Standing Committee (NPCSC). NPC Deputies and NPCSC members retain their legislative seats without challenge from the people. Contrary to Western notions of sovereignty, the CCP retains the power to elect and remove deputies.

For these reasons, modern Marxism and the goal of finalizing its localization are problematic. Hans Kelsen, in *Pure Theory of Law* (*Reine Rechtslehre*, 1934), describes political rights, "as the power to influence the formation of the will of the state; this means: to participate directly or indirectly in the formation of the legal order in which the 'will of the state' expresses itself."[15] For legal positivists, in the tradition of Hans Kelsen, the general norms of the legal order, which are typically statutes, produce this political right. In 1998, by statute, the CCP, through its NPC, introduced the popular vote for local electorates, but denied universal suffrage for its national legislature, the NPC. Kelsen writes, "Participation in legislation that is, the creation of the general legal norms, by those subjected to the norms is the essential element of the democratic form of government, in contrast to autocratic government in which the subjects are excluded from sharing in the formation of the will of the state, and therefore have no political rights." He is referring to the "autocratic police state" (*aristokratischen*) rather than a state of legality, or a *Rechtsstaat* (literally, a law-based state or a constitutional state). Kelsen also observed that a democratic legislature could be effectuated by either direct democracy (or directly by "the people") or indirect democracy. In the former, direct democracy, "the individual has the right to take part in the legislative popular assembly, join in the discussion, and in voting." In the latter, indirect democracy, "the people participate in democracy only indirectly," which is a function exercised "by a parliament elected by the people." In terms of the general norms of modern China's legal order and, especially, legalizing voting rights and other civil and political rights (or the first-generation international human rights), neither direct, nor indirect democracy is forthcoming in the near political future.

In a September 2000 interview, then China president Jiang Zemin, when explaining why the Chinese people are not allowed universal suffrage, said, "The quality of our people is too

---

[14] Liang Shuming, The Theory of Rural Reconstruction, Vol. II, 324-25 (1937). Zhong Hua Ren Min Gong He Gou Cun Min Wei Yuan Hui Zu Zhi Fa (Organic Law of the Villagers Committees of the People's Republic of China), Adopted at the Fifth Session of the Ninth NPC on Nov. 4, 1998.

[15] Hans Kelsen, The Pure Theory of Law, 67-68, 105-107, 138-139 (Max Knight, trans.) (Univ. of California UP, 1967).

low."[16] On February 27, 2007, China's premier Wen Jiabao, in a written response to reform debates appearing in the *People's Daily*, cautions impatient reformers, who urge that political reforms will enhance transition to a market economy, that political liberalization and democracy are a "distant goal." His article is a response to two key articles; the author of one is Zhou Ruijun and the other is Xie Tao. According to Zhou Ruijun, former *People's Daily* editor, greater democracy will defuse tensions over growing gaps between the rich and poor, a gap that will eventually lead to instability. Xie Tao, Remin University vice-president, suggests that China should emulate a Scandivavian-style social-welfare democracy. A problem for greater political liberalization is that Wen Jiabao based his response to these articles and impatient reformers in the language of Marxism, when announcing that China is not yet ready for democracy, even though it remains a distant goal for the "socialism with Chinese characteristics" that the CCP hopes to build. Wen, and quoting Deng Xiaoping, writes that the essence of socialism is to "emancipate and develop productive forces, eliminate exploitation and polarization and eventually realize common prosperity." He announces, "China is and will remain in the primary stage of socialism for a long time," which is an underdeveloped stage characterized by underdeveloped productive forces and a socialist system that is not yet perfect or mature. Wen writes, "We are still far away from advancing out of the primary stages of socialism," and suggest sticking with development guidelines of the primary stage for another 100 years. Wen also adds, "the socialist system is not contradictory to democracy," because "a highly developed democracy and a complete legal system are inherent requirements of the socialist system and an important benchmark of a mature socialist system." Nonetheless, Wen's comments foretell a continuing policy of prioritized economic growth to the exclusion of greater political liberalization or the continuing problem of "poor socialism." Finally, Wen Jiabao writes, "Without sustained rapid growth of the productive forces, it is impossible to finally secure the fairness and social justice that lie at the heart of the socialist system." Since Jiang Zemin's 2000 interview, the social-political environment has not changed.

One source contends that Deng Xiaoping's 18-year reign, as Chinese emperor, is only comparable to that of the Yellow Emperor and founding of the Qin Dynasty. Deng rescued the Communist Dynasty after Mao Zedong's death, while, at the same time, leaving the dynasty in a fragile condition, suggesting that the Communist Dynasty founded by Mao in 1949 has lost the "mandate of heaven," a Confucian moral authority giving it legitimacy, thus, enabling it to rule.[17] For instance, a frailty of the Communist Dynasty is the name, Communist Party, which may be a misnomer because China is not a communist country in any meaningful sense. As for the CCP, the actual principles governing China are not Marxist-Leninist but market-Leninist or capitalist-Leninist. It is the consequence of China pursuing a socialist-political polity, in conjunction with a capitalist-economic policy. Nonetheless, the communists do intend to stay in power. The same source describes a post-Deng China as not governed by socialism, rather by something close to a dictionary definition of fascism. China and its combined forces of free enterprise, state-owned companies and authoritarian political system have more in common with Franco's Spain, South Korea's Chung-hee and Pinochet's Chile than Mao's socialism. In July 1946, Mao, when asked by Huang Yanpei, a scholar,

---

[16] Li YongYan, China ready for democracy in 1940s, not today, May 11, 2004, Asian Times Online. Premier says promoting fairness and social justice is a major task, Feb. 27, 2007, People's Daily. China's Premier Calls Democracy a Distant Goal, Feb. 27, 2007, Washington Post.

[17] Nicholas D. Kristof, The Communist Dynasty Had Its Run. Now What? Feb. 22, 1997, N.Y. Times.

whether he has fought a way to stop the vicious cycle of dynastic change as may pertain to their communist movement, responded, "We've found a way. It's called democracy." However, neither Mao nor Deng, or subsequent leaders to date, have tried real democracy such as a democratically elected legislature.

The problem is the misnomer of "Chinese democracy." From Mao to Wen Jiabao, the concept of democracy employed by the CCP and its leaders remains heavily subject to the influence of Marxist ideology. These leaders, from Mao to Wen, are referring to proletarian democracy rather than Western-style democracy. Karl Marx, in *Critique of the Gotha Program* (*Kritik des Gothaer Programms*, 1875), wrote, "Between the capitalist and Communist society lies the period of change of one into the other. This corresponds to a political transition period in which the state can be nothing else than a revolutionary dictatorship of the proletariat." In translating Marx's intentions regarding "dictatorship of the proletariat" and democracy, there are the insights of Karl Kautsky (1854-1938), an editor of the fourth volume of Karx's *Das Kapital*, whom contends that Marx failed to elucidate the expression because he assumed that the concept of "dictatorship of the proletariat" was understood.[18] Kautsky, in *Social Democracy versus Communism* (*Über Sozialdemokratie und Kommunismus*, 1946), antithetically writes, "He [Marx] used it in a private letter to the executive committee of the Eisenach party, assuming the committee would understand what the dictatorship of the proletariat was without further comment. That this expression in no way signified either repudiation of democracy for absolute power in the state is quite clear from the one fact alone that in the very same letter Marx characterized *the democratic republic* as the form of government in which the class struggle is to be fought out, saying: 'Freedom consists in the transformation of the state from an organ dominant over society into an organ subordinate to society. And today, too, the various existing forms of state are free or not free in the measure in which they circumscribe the freedom of the state.'"

According to Kautsky, or even perhaps Kautsky's Marxism, Karl Marx and Frederick Engels did not find either a democratic republic or democratic parliamentary republic as objectionable. In particular, it was a democratic parliamentary republic that Engels had in mind when writing *A Critique of the Draft Social-Democratic Program of 1891* (*Zur Kritik des sozial-demokratischen Programmentwurfes 1891*).[19] Engels writes, "If one thing is certain it is that our party and the working class can only come to power under the form of a democratic republic. This is even the specific form for the dictatorship of the proletariat, as the Great French Revolution has already shown." Engels had a democratic parliamentary republic in mind, when he adds that under all circumstances the program must include "*the demand for the concentration of all political power in the hands of a representative assembly of the people.*" For those orthodox Marxists and unorthodox Marxists, such as Chinese leaders from Mao Zedong, Jiang Zeming, to Wen Jiabao, continuing to deny the potency of a democratic republic or democratic parliamentary republic, they do so against the natural order (*ordre naturel*) or the laws of nature. By going against the laws of nature, the CCP, since the 1949 consolidation of its power and founding of modern China, continues a paradoxical

---

[18] Karl Marx, Critique of the Gotha Programme, (Peking: Foreign Language Press, 1972). Karl Kautsky, (Ch. 2) Social Democracy versus Communism (David Shub & Joseph Shaplen, trans.) (Rand School Press, 1946) (Shub, David/Shaplen, Joseph, Hrsg. – Verl. der Zwölf, 1948).

[19] Paul Blackledge, Karl Kautsky and Marxist Historiography, Vol. 70, No. 3, Science & Society, 337-359 (July 2006). Frederick Engels, A Critique of the Draft Social-Democratic Program of 1891, In Marx & Engels Collected Works, Vol. 27, Feb. 1890-Apr. 1895.

interrelationship between traditional culture and Marxism, which has been pending without resolution since the 1920s and 1930s.

Jean-Jacques Rousseau (1712-1778), in *The Social Contract* (*Du Contrat Social*, 1762), writes, "'Election by lot,' says Montesquieu, 'is natural to democracy.' I agree." Rousseau, on the qualification of the people to vote, writes, "When election by choice and election by lot are both employed, choice should be used to fill places that call for special skills, such as military commands, and lot for those where common sense, justice and integrity are enough, as in the case of political offices, for in a well constituted state, such qualities are found among all the citizens." Notwithstanding the contributions of John Locke, Thomas Hobbes and other Enlightenment thinkers, the thematic discourses of Jean-Jacques Rousseau in *The Social Contract* best demonstrate the potency of the Enlightenment and its concept of liberty. Contrary to Rousseau's original intentions, his concept of liberty is subject to interpretation as being a positive concept of liberty rather than negative concept. Isiah Berlin, in his famous *Two Concepts of Liberty* (1958) lecture, delineated between the "end of the day" kind of liberty (negative liberty) and "beginning of the day" kind of liberty (positive liberty). The latter, the "beginning of the day" kind of liberty, consist of the pursuit of behavior laid down by a self-chosen rationale principle," rather than negative liberty and its absence of restraint, and being "free to the extent that there are no external hinderances to my pursuit of my own self-chosen ends." Isiah Berlin's categorizations of liberty are directly related to Rousseau's concept of the General Will, and the constraints of positive and negative liberty, or even perhaps being free to do what one "ought to do" or Rousseau's notion of forcing a man to be free. For instance, negative liberty is deeply personal, but positive liberty "is more easily attainable in a group than individually." In terms of positive liberty, the pursuit of freedom becomes a collective venture, "Something *we* do, not something *I* do." Rousseau's *Social Contract* caused negative liberty to become one of - as opposed to the exclusive - means by which liberty is conceivable. In terms of the modern debates concerning totalitarianism, the issues can be expressed in two ways: First, has modern society evolved into a state requiring an election between negative (individual) liberty and positive (collective) liberty? Second, how much negative (individual) liberty must be surrendered in the pursuit of positive (collective) goals?[20]

Classic examples of the destructible General Will are China and its handling of the territories of Macao, a former Portuguese colony, which China resumed sovereignty over on December 20, 1999; Hong Kong, a former British Crown Colony, which China resumed sovereignty over on July 1, 1997; and Taiwan and the opposition led by Taiwanese President Chen Shui-bian against succession and the "one-China policy." Macao, after resumed sovereignty, sits docile under the authority of Beijing. However, Taiwan and many in Hong Kong challenge the status of being a docile satellite of Beijing or even pseudo colony. For Taiwan, succession to the mainland threatens the indestructible General Will and its growth to a state of democratic-elected legislatures. Following succession, Beijing rule poses a threat to legalizing voting rights and other civil and political rights (or the first-generation international human rights). It is a fear exacerbated by the ongoing constitutional crisis in Hong, which has been pending since China resumed sovereignty over Hong Kong in 1997.

[20] Rousseau, Social Contract (1762) 149-57 (Penguin Books, 1968). M. Ulric Killion, China's Amended Constitution: Quest for Liberty and Independent Judicial Review, Wash. U. Global Stud. L. Rev., Vol. 4, No. 1, 43 (2005). Isiah Berlin, Two Concepts of Liberty: An Inaugural Lecture Delivered before the Univ. of Oxford on Oct. 31, 1958. J.S. McClelland, A History of Western Political Thought 262-66 (Routledge, 1996).

Since China resumed sovereignty over Hong Kong, there are two historical events serving as a measure for the state of legality, law-based state, constitutional state or rule of law state, such as the legal traditions of Anglo-American rule of law, German *Rechtsstaat* and French *État de droit*.[21] First, there is the 2002 historical constitutional event, which is the law case of *Ng Siu Tung vs. Director of Immigrations* (Hong Kong's right of abode cases). In Hong Kong, the Court of Final Appeal (CFA) attempted to exercise an assumed power of independent judicial review, but on June 26, 1999, succumbed to another superior authority—the NPCSC in Beijing.[22] Despite a provision of *The Basic Law of the H. K. Spec. Admin. Region of the P.R.C.* (*Zhonghua renmin gongheguo Xianggang tebie xingzhengqu jiben fa*, Basic Law), at Article 84, which allowed the Hong Kong Special Administration Region (HKSAR) to refer to precedents of other common law jurisdictions, the NPCSC and its power of judicial interpretation prevailed.

Second, there is the 2004 historical constitutional event, when the NPCSC again exercised its political, constitutional and interpretational powers over Hong Kong, by adopting, Interpretations of Clause 7 of Annex I and Clause 3 of Annex II to the Basic Law of the Hong Kong Special Administrative Region of the People's Republic of China by the Standing Committee of the National People's Congress. Wu Bangguo, NPCSC chairman and a member of the Standing Committee of the Political Bureau of the Communist Party of China (CPC) Central Committee, during the closing session of the Eighth Meeting of the Tenth NPCSC stated, "the development of the constitutional system in Hong Kong has a bearing on the implementation of the principle of 'one country, two systems' and the Basic Law, relations between the Central Authorities and the Hong Kong SAR, the interests of all Hong Kong people, and the long-term prosperity and stability of Hong Kong." Further, Wu Bangguo stated, "The Central Government has always given top priority to the development of [a] constitutional system in Hong Kong," Wu also said that according to the Constitution of the People's Republic of China (*Zhonghua renmin gongheguo xianfa*, 1982 Constitution) and the Basic Law, "the right to interpret the Basic Law belongs to the NPC Standing Committee." Wu Bangguo said that the current interpretations "have the same power as the Basic Law" and are "necessary and timely . . . to ensure the healthy development of Hong Kong's constitutional system in line with the Basic Law." The two important clauses interpreted, at Clause 7 of Annex I and Clause 3 of Annex II, respectively, relate to the selection of the Chief Executive of the Hong Kong Special Administration Region (SAR), formation of the Legislative Council, and procedures for voting on bills and motions after 2007.[23] These historical events present a pending constitutional crisis in Hong Kong.

---

[21] Ulrich Karpen, Conditions of 'Rechstaat' Efficiency Particularly in Developing and Newly Industrialising Countries, in Fa Zhi (The Rule of Law), (Josef Thesing & Winfried Jung, eds.) (Beijing: Fashi Chubanshe, 2005).

[22] M. Ulric Killion, Post-WTO China and Independent Judicial Review, 26 Hous. J. Int'l L. 507 (2004). Ng Siu Tung v. Dir. of Immigrations, 1 Hong Kong L. Rep. & Dig. 561 (Court of Final Appeal of the Hong Kong Special Administrative Region, Jan. 10, 2002). Ng Siu Tung vs. Director of Immigrations, Court of Final Appeal of the Hong Kong Special Administrative Region, 10 January 2002, FACV Nos. 1-3 of 2001, http://www.hklii.org/hk/eng_jud/HKCFA/2002/20020110_FACV000001_2001.html. The Interpretation by the Standing Comm. of the Nat'l People's Cong. of Arts. 22(4) and 24(2)(3) of the Basic Law of the H.K. Spec. Admin. Region of the P.R.C. (adopted by the Standing Comm. of the 9th Nat'l People's Cong. at its 10th Sess. on June 26, 1999). Basic Law of the H. K. Spec. Admin. Region of the P.R.C., Arts. 82 and 84 (adopted at the 3rd Sess. of the 7th Nat'l People's Cong. on Apr. 4, 1990).

[23] Top Legislature Interprets HK Basic Law, Apr. 6, 2004, People's Daily. Top Legislature Adopts Interpretations of HK Basic Law, Apr. 7, 2004, People's Daily. Interpretations Helpful for Ensuring HK's Prosperity,

As measured by a state of legality, a law-based state, a constitutional state or a rule of law state, Beijing failed miserable in safeguarding established and legalized voting rights, and civil and political freedoms or liberties (or the first-generation international human rights). The constitutional crisis was effectually the destruction of Rousseau's indestructible General Will by the powers of Beijing and its Basic Law, and Beijing's new interpretations that amended the methods for selecting a government head and for forming a CCP-approved legislature rather than a democratic-elected legislature. Taiwan, Taiwanese President Chen Shui-bian and the opposition against succession and the "one-China policy" watch these proceedings and challenges to democracy and democratic-elected legislatures. In terms of the General Will, and the simple act of voting, Rousseau wrote, "The constant will of all the members of the state is the general will; it is through it that they are citizens and free. When a law is proposed in the people's assembly, what is asked of them is not precisely whether they approve of the proposition or reject it, but whether it is in conformity with the general will which is theirs; each by giving his vote gives his opinion on this question, and the counting of votes yields a declaration of the general will." The concepts of the General Will, suffrage and voting, admittedly, are Western conceptions grounded in classical liberalism, and seem foreign to modern China and its government and constitutional practices, including its attempt to finalize the localization of Marxism. For Chinese Marxism, the irony is complete, because traditional culture, and its traditional government, traditional political theory and traditional jurisprudence, evidence vestiges of democratic government. While traditional culture, admittedly, has always contrasted with Western universalism, Marxism has also been in contrast to traditional culture, but, problematically, continues to grow increasingly incongruous with traditional culture and its traditional government, traditional political theory and traditional jurisprudence.

11.3. Liberalism and Legal Positivism

In terms of how best a Chinese neo-liberal regime would blend a distinctively different non-Western culture with Western jurisprudence, two competing Western theories of legal systems -- legal positivism and natural law theory -- produce respective theoretical or moral advantages, or both. One suspects that natural law theory does not provide a proper mechanism for transplanting liberalism, because of its' normative aspects and inclinations to search for a moral and political purpose in analyzing and interpreting legal norms. As for natural law theory, the actions of China's polity and an ontological base in tradition challenges and contradicts Western fundamental principles of justice. China's ontological base in tradition proposes problems for liberalism. For transplanting liberalism, legal positivism proposes a universal theory that is more appealing to a liberal or neo-liberal regime, because legal positivism offers a viewpoint minimizing the concept of community as instrumental in the enforcement of ethics. The collective life of a political community includes its official political acts, such as legislation, adjudication, enforcement and other executive governmental functions. Ronald Dworkin (1989) writes, "The liberal view of

Stability: Top Legislator, Apr. 6, 2004, People's Daily. Chairman Lauds New Moves of Congress, Apr. 7, 2004, China Daily. Joseph Li & Xiao Guo, Basic Law Interpretations 'Timely', Apr. 7, 2004, China Daily. Tonny Chan & Teddy Ng, HK Democracy suffers setback, Dec. 23, 2006, China Daily.

integration I describe takes a limited view of the dimensions of a political community's communal life."[24] A transplant of liberalism via legal positivism to a Confucian society is still problematically contingent on its ability to respond adequately to the unique jurisprudential experiences and needs of a modern Confucian culture. If modern China represents an ontological base in tradition, liberalism fosters new problems and conflicts for China and its political community communal life. Nonetheless, in terms of a Chinese neo-liberal coterie, legal positivism and its universalism is preferably in the construct of a Chinese legal system and constitutionalism.

Legal positivism does have its drawbacks, because it often engenders criticism of being anti-democratic. Ronald M. Dworkin (1989) uses the United States Supreme Court decision of *Bowers vs. Hardwick*, 478 U.S. 186 (1982), to illustrate this contention. In *Bowers vs. Hardwick*, the U.S. Supreme Court upheld a state law, a Georgia law, which made sodomy a crime against constitutional challenge. Dworkin writes, "In *Bowers*, Justice White suggests that the community has a right to use the law to support its vision of ethical decency: it has a right to impose its views about ethics just because it is the majority." The problem of morals and politics, which are inherent conflicts of positivism, serves as an additional source of criticism because mainstream international law positivism, in the tradition of Lassa Oppenheim (1858-1919), has sought to separate law from morals and from politics, many critics dismissed this positivism as amoral, apolitical and atheoretical.[25]

The most current version of legal positivism, without undertaking undertaking a historical journey of legal positivism, from the imperative positivism of John Austin (1790–1859) to the legal realism of Oliver Wendell Holmes, Jr. (1841-1935), are the writings of H.L.A. Herbert Hart and Hans Kelsen (1881-1973) on normative legal positivism or normative positivist analysis of the concept of law. In particular, the concept of conceiving law as a set of social rules is all-important to Hart.[26] On liberalism and legal positivism, Hart writes, "It is not, I think, uncharitable to say that we can see in his argument that he has only half digested the spiritual message of liberalism which he is seeking to convey to the legal profession. For everything that he says is really dependent upon an enormous evaluation of the importance of the bare fact that a rule may be said to be a valid rule of law, as if this, once declared, was conclusive of the final moral question: 'Ought this rule of law to be obeyed?' Surely the truly liberal answer to any sinister use of the slogan 'law is law' or of the distinction between law and morals is 'Very well, but that does not conclude the question. Law is not morality; do not let it supplant morality.'"[27] Hart viewed the separation of law and morals as essential to the meaning of legal positivism. The ideological underpinning of Hart keeps faith with the insistence of the great utilitarians, Jeremy Bentham and John Austin, "on the separation of law as it is and law as it ought to be." In contrast with modern China, a distinguishing feature of this philosophical thought is the fact of origins stemming from intellectual architects of great reform, or utilitarians, addressing legal and social problems in England, at the close of the eighteenth century and beginning of the nineteenth century.

[24] H.L.A. Hart, The Concept of Law, 204 – 205 (Clarendon Press, 1961). H.L.A. Hart, Positivism and the Separation of Law and Morals, Vol. 71, No. 4 Harv. L. Rev. 593, 612-21, (1958). Dworkin, Id.

[25] Benedict Kingsbury, Legal Positivism as Normative Politics: International Society, Balance of Power and Lassa Oppenheim's Positive International Law, Vol. 13, No. 2 E.JIL 1, 45.

[26] John Austin, The Province of Jurisprudence Determined (1832), (Prometheus Books, 2000). Oliver Wendell Holmes, Jr., The Path of the Law, Vol. 10 Harv. L. Rev. 457 – 478 (1897). Hart (1961), Id.

[27] Hart, (1958), Id.

Issues of morality and law are different for China, as opposed to the West, because China is a comparatively monolithic rather than pluralistic society with a strongly entrenched ontological base in tradition. A relatively monolithic society is attributable to China's long and enduring history, which commences with the Huaxia tribe, which appeared in the middle reaches of the Yellow River some three thousand years ago. The Huaxia tribe was the primary tribe of a number of tribes that combined to become the Chinese nation. After the Qin and Han dynasties, this congregation of tribes, the Huaxia tribe, became the Han, a name that still refers to the predominant Chinese ethnic group.[28] It is also within this context, morals and foundational *ethos* are reflective of a systemic and persistent traditional Confucianism. In terms of morality and law, including constitutional *ethos*, assuming modern Chinese *ethos* are reflective of an ontological base in tradition, the issue may simply resolve into whether what is legally wrong, for instance, according to rule of law, is also morally wrong in the sense of traditional Confucianism. The typical intellectual trappings of positivism do not readily dismiss the latter ethical dilemma, because of a distinctive Chinese ontology, as compared to the ontology of Western culture. A simple ethical dilemma grows into a complex ethical dilemma, if not ethical and moral crises, when Western universalism actually demands traditional culture to conform to Western universalism. It is no less a crisis when one demands traditional culture to conform to the Western theorization of Marxism, or the ongoing problem of China's polity attempting to finalize the localization of Marxism.

Hans Kelsen, in *Pure Theory of Law* (*Reine Rechtslehre*, 1934), contrasted ideology to everything that is not natural reality or its description, because positive law must keep itself free from ideology. Kelsen defines ideology as the, "nonobjective presentation of the subject influenced by subjective value judgments and glorifying or disfiguring the subject of cognition." If positive law is perceivable "as normative order in relation to the reality of actual happenings," which ought to conform to it, then positive law may also be subject to label of being an ideology. In this context, ideology differs from the latter characterization, because ideology, and returning to Kelsen's first characterization, is everything that is not natural reality or its description. Kelsen further contrasted positive law to what society deems higher laws. If positive law is perceived in its relation to a higher order, such as those claims of an ideal law or even the right law, and demand that positive law ought to conform with this higher order, such as in relation to natural law or other forms of justice, then positive law, ultimately, presents itself as the ideal law or real law. The latter results in a dilemma leading Kelsen, when speaking to the anti-ideological proclivity of the "Pure Theory," to observe that "a theory of positive law which mixes the latter with natural law or any other type of justice in order to justify or disqualify the positive law much be rejected as ideological." The latter tendency exhibits by presenting positive law as free from an admixture with any ideal law or right law. For Kelsen, the "Pure Theory" seeks the presentation of law as it is, and not as it ought to be, as it searches for the real and possible, rather than the ideal law or right law.

When perceiving the "Pure Theory of the Law" as the true science of law, Hans Kelson did not seek to justify or discredit an existing social order, by serving any political interests via the vehicle of an ideology. As a science of law, "Pure Theory" and its positive law cannot be attributed a higher value than it actually possesses, nor denied validity as a contradiction of

[28] Wang Yanzhong, Chinese Values, Governance, and International Relations: Historical Development and Present Situation, in Changing Values in Asia: Their Impact on Governance and Development 19-26 (Han Sung-Joo, ed., Japan Center for Int'l Exchange, 1999).

an ideal law. For Kelsen, "The postulate to differentiate law and morals, jurisprudence and ethics, means this: from the standpoint of scientific cognition of positive law, its justification by a moral order different from the legal order, is irrelevant, because the task of the science of law is not to approve or disapprove its subject, but to know and describe it. True, legal norms, as prescriptions of what ought to be, constitute values; yet the function of the science of law is not the evaluation of its subject but its value-free description." He further writes, "Thereby the "Pure Theory" places itself in sharpest contrast to traditional jurisprudence which, consciously or unconsciously, sometimes more, sometimes less, has an 'ideological' character in the second meaning of the word." In the latter, he was referring to his second characterization of ideology. Kelsen adds, "Ideology, however, veils reality either by glorifying it with the intent to conserve and defend, it or by misrepresenting it with the intent to attack, to destroy, and to replace it by another." For Kelsen, ideology is rooted in wishing, and not knowing. Kelsen's characterizations or to use his own words, the first and second meanings of ideology are broad and sweeping. His first and second meanings of ideology are so broad that they embrace any written and unwritten laws, or social order, standing outside the province or command of positive law. Kelsen's first and second meanings of ideology are also problematic because of the resulting wide girth for defining what is, or is not, an ideology. In terms of modern China, the CCP, and its one-party CCP rule and self-chosen rationale principle, qualifies as an ideology under Kelsen's conceptualization of an ideology, which should hardly come as a surprise. What poses the greater problem, and moves the simple ethical dilemma from simple dilemma to complex is that traditional Chinese culture, and its traditional jurisprudence, traditional government and traditional political theory, also fits under Kelsen's conceptualization of an ideology.

Hans Kelsen was discussing law and science, and focusing on the problems of the denial of the ought and the law of ideology, when he advanced "Pure Theory" as "a radical realistic theory of law, that is, a theory of legal positivism." For the same reasons, his notions of "Pure Theory" are difficult to use when evaluating law, because by taking law as a science, "Pure Theory" only obligates to grasp the essence of positive law or understand law and do so, by an analysis of its structure. Depending one one's political preferences, it is either a constrictive or expansive concept of legal theory or legal systems. Assuming Chinese traditional culture is representative of the written and unwritten rules serving as a normative guide for Chinese society, the problems are obvious, especially if China's ontological base in traditional culture represents for Chinese society a normative guide, higher law, ideal law or even the real law. As earlier mentioned, as a simple ethical dilemma moves from simple dilemma to complex, an ethical and moral crisis is inevitably produced by the demand that traditional Chinese culture conform to Western universalism, and its Western legal theorizations, including Marxism.

John Austin, in *The Province of Jurisprudence Determined* (1832), observes that a proposition of law was true if it, simply, reported correctly the past commands of a political society.[29] John Austin defined positive law as commands from the government or, simply, a command issued by a sovereign. As for the legitimacy of government or sovereignty, legitimacy is a moral issue, thereby a separate issue. Austin is famous for his command theory of the law and the separability thesis. All of which enhances difficulty of borrowing

[29] John Austin, The Province Of Jurisprudence Determined (1832), (Prometheus Books, 2000). Ronald Dworkin, Laws Empire, (Harv. UP, 1986). Hart (1961), Id.

and transplanting Western rule of law, in a Chinese society bound by a systemic and persistent traditional culture. In the event, a definition for rule of law can be contained within the discipline of normative legal positivism, or perhaps, more accurately, the normative positivist analysis of the concept of law, then rule of law presents itself as a West centric concept of law whose incorporation into non-Western cultures, societies and developing countries poses certain problems. H.L.A. Hart's rejection of John Austin's imperative legal positivism addressed the same problems. Hart, in *Concept of Law* (1961), contends that the true grounds of law lie in the acceptance by the community as a whole of a fundamental master rule, being Hart's rule of recognition. This rule assigns to a particular person or groups the authority to make law. Rules of law are true not just in virtue of commands, but, more importantly, "in virtue of social conventions that represent the community's acceptance of a scheme of rules empowering such people or groups to create valid law." The potential problems are obvious. As observed by Ronald Dworkin (1986), "Many officials of Nazi Germany obeyed Hitler's commands as law, but only out of fear. Does that mean they accepted a rule of recognition entitling him to make law? If so, then the difference between Hart's theory and Austin's becomes elusive, because there would be no difference between a group of people accepting a rule of recognition and simply falling into a self-conscious pattern of obedience out of fear."

In terms of Hans Kelsen's "Pure Theory," positive law and conceptualizing traditional culture as an ideology, the thoughts of F.A. Hayek (Friedrich August von Hayek, 1899-1992), in *Law, Legislation, and Liberty* (1973-79),[30] bears mentioning. Hayek distinguishes made order from grown order, by employing Ancient Greek language to describe these sources of order; namely, *taxis* for a made order, and *kosmos* (cosmos) for a grown order, which also originally meant "a right order in a state or a community." In a quest for spontaneous order, Hayek insisted upon *kosmos*, grown order. However, grown order had to be refined, to a certain extent, by *taxis*, "made" order, thus, allowing for abstract concepts (relations) so long as they are only definable by abstract properties. There are conventional or normative rules that tell us what we ought and ought not to do. There are also rules such as the rules of law that are the "chief instrument whereby we can affect the resulting order." For Hayek, the rules upon which spontaneous order rest need not always be of spontaneous origin, which are *kosmos* (grown order). This is not meant to totally credit "made" order, because as Hayek writes, "Although undoubtedly an order originally formed itself spontaneously because individuals followed rules which had not been deliberately made but had arisen spontaneously, people gradually learned to improve those rules; and it is at least conceivable that the formation of a spontaneous order relies entirely on rules that were deliberately made." Rules of law, mostly, but not all, will be the product of deliberate design, whereas most rules of conduct and morals will be the product of spontaneous growth. The spontaneous order produces a resulting order. However, particular manifestations of rules depend on circumstances that the designers of rules did not know and could not have known, because the particular content of order reflects circumstances known only to persons who obey the rules and apply them to facts only they know. "It will be through the knowledge of these individuals both of the rules and of the particular facts that both will determine the resulting order." For Hayek, the problem is the "complex relationship between values and facts,"

---

[30] Hayek, Vol. I: 33-37, 39-46, 111-112.

blending these values and facts, and the resulting complex social structure "that exist only because the individuals composing them hold certain values."

F.A. Hayek is addressing the problem confronted by social scientists seeking to study complex social structures, which only exist because individuals hold certain values. A problem of the disciples of political science, law and economics, is that they are, actually, social sciences, if not moral sciences, rather than pure sciences, such as engineering, physics and math. Moreover, even pure science does not use observation or experiments in the world, but instead uses only reason and logic in the form of non-specific generalities, providing a foundation in the form of theorems or statements about what is true and what is not, which can be known as certain and true for all time, so long as reason and logic as we understand them remain valid. Richard A. Posner assesses the dangers of positive economics and positive economic theory of law as, simply, the opposite of reductionism, occurring when economic analysts seeking to make simple economic models more complex introduce additional factors such as risk aversion and information costs.[31] The greater complexity enhances difficulty of refutation and substantiation by empirical observation. Hayek made a sharper distinction, however, requiring a higher proof from the sciences and, by doing so, assures us once again of the need for spontaneous order. He made a distinction between the domains of private law and public law (*Staatsrecht*), such as constitutional law. By doing so, Hayek allows space for the development of "made" law in the affairs of organizations, such as governments and their Inter-Governmental Organizations (IGOs), which may serve as a justification for the persistency and evolution of positive law (legal positivism), despite what he deemed the alleged factually false assumptions of constructivist rationalists.

Non-Western developing countries pose distinctively different problems, however, when considering F.A. Hayek's postulations. The scenario of non-Western developing countries does not fit well in Hayek's scheme of things or his discourse concerning taxis, cosmos (*kosmos*), deliberate design and spontaneous order. A problem is that he does not directly address the particularities of non-Western cultures. Even assuming his discourse bears relevancy on the issue of non-Western cultures, it only does so indirectly, because after recognizing distinctive cultural traditions, he relegates them to minimal importance. While noting that some social orders rest on complex systems of rules of conduct even among the animals very low on the evolutionary scale, innate rules (genetically transmitted) and learned rules (culturally transmitted) are given minimal attention. As opposed to a more thorough examination of cultural tradition in terms of non-Western civilizations, he leaves the subject minimized in importance. Hayek writes, "So that new rules may rapidly spread among large groups and, in the case of isolated groups, produce distinct 'cultural traditions.'" Hayek when discussing cultural tradition is addressing distinguishable cultural traits of Japanese macaque monkeys rather than individuals or persons in the sense of man on the higher end of the evolutionary scale. He does briefly return to the subject of culture in an epilogue to *Law, Legislation and Liberty* (1973-79), when he instructs us that yet to be recognized is a present order of society that arose, not by design, but by more prevailing effective institutions in the

[31] M. Ulric Killion (2005) Western Institution Building: The War, Hayek's Cosmos and the WTO, Global Jurist Advances: Vol. 5: No. 1, Article 1, http://www.bepress.com/gj/advances/vol5/iss1/art1. Hayek, Id. Richard F. Crespo, Controversy: Is Economics a Moral Science?, 201-21 Journal of Markets & Morality 1, no. 2 (Center for Economic Personalism: Oct. 1998). Richard A. Posner, Economic Analysis of Law, (Little, Brown & Company, rpt. 1992). Zhang Zhicang, A critique of empiricism in scientific research, Qiushi xuekan, No. 4 (2002).

process of competition. Although remaining critical of constructivist rationalism, or the Cartesian approach, he implicitly recognizes the inherent problem of culture by design. For Hayek, "Culture is neither natural nor artificial, neither genetically transmitted nor rationally designed." However, in this respect, his criticism of the Cartesian approach may be amiss, because a more correct interpretation of the Enlightenment is one emphasizing the distinction separating reason from both culture and tradition.[32]

Although being harshly critical of constructivist rationalism and its attendant factually false assumptions, F.A. Hayek's postulations still bear relevancy in terms of institution building, in non-Western countries. His postulates do so because they both recognize and build on the interrelationship between facts and values, and ultimately, a resulting sort of Hegelian thesis-antithesis synthesis of facts and value to a higher plane or higher synthesis. For Hegel, at any given time an accepted idea or thesis exists, it is soon subject to contradiction by its opposite or antithesis. Out of this conflict of ideas, a synthesis forms, representing a higher form of truth, which becomes a new thesis. The antithesis opposes this new thesis and transforms into a new synthesis and so on and on. In a never-ending chain of ideas, with each one approaching closer to truth, history evolves in an endless process in which all things become gradually "more perfect" by means of conflict-induced change.

In terms of non-Western cultures and institution building or reforms, West centric taxonomies when applied to non-West-specific social, political and legal systems (or institutions), especially economic theory, because of myopic perspectives necessarily limited by abstract theory and assumptions, often calls into question both reliability and practicability of explanation offered by the sciences to explain real life phenomenon. Assuming distinctively non-Western particularities, assumptions employed as descriptors of unconventional economic actors such as non-Western cultures, are often one-dimensional and pallid. Any science void of real world observation and experiments, will neglect the dimensions and dynamics of culture. The latter result is no less dramatic when social sciences and its social scientists ignore the advent of real world observations and experiments. Developing countries transitioning from socialism to capitalism, in terms of an American consensus or Washington consensus,[33] increasingly present issues of an ideology of cultural exceptionalism. The political economy of reforms presents a scenario of uncertain theorems for the West, in its universalistic presumptions of West centric logic and reason rather than recognition of existentialistic non-Western particularities and distinctive ontological bases in tradition.

In terms of tenuous relations between the East and West, China and the West, developing and developed countries, or even liberal and illiberal countries, it is perhaps an issue of an evolution of Western universalism, or a Western universalizing cosmopolitanism, to an *emic* rather than *etic* understanding of Sinicism, Islamism and other non-Western cultures. Linguistic anthropologist Kenneth Pike (1912-2000) coined the neologisms of *emic* and *etic*, and distinguished the two as follows: First, an *emic* "perspective focuses on the intrinsic cultural distinctions that are meaningful to the members of a given society." Second, an *etic* perspective "relies upon the extrinsic concepts and categories that have meaning for scientific

---

[32] Steven D. Smith, Recovering from Enlightenment?, Public Law and Legal Theory Research Paper Series, Research Paper No. 61 (fall 2003), Notre Dame Law School, http://ssrn.com/abstract=449060.

[33] Dickson Eyoh and Richard Sandbrook, Pragmatic Neo-liberalism and Just Development in Africa, Univ. of Toronto, CIS Working Paper 2001-1.

observers."[34] Limiting a West centric perspective is the consequence of only native speakers being truly competent judges of *emic* descriptions, rather than a Western universal perspective, or the *etic* perspective of an outsider searching for universals and generalizations. An inherent benefit of Pike's approach and his intertwined *emic/emit* perspective is the resulting recognition of the forces of culture, native language, politics, economics, appropriate lexicons and other forces. Because the concept of *emic/emit* will insist, "on the relationship of the observer to the data, as against an abstract science in which the observer is somehow eliminated in principle even when this would be impossible in fact." Kenneth Pike sought a greater understanding of particular cultures through the intertwining of *emic* and *emit* perspectives, and not by exclusive reliance on an *emit* perspective. Pike's perceived need for a more generalized background framework as a source of human choice led him to note what he deemed an *etic* structure observable in particular cultures. This "etic universal background pattern and emic culturally specific pattern" are notably intertwined, thus, the *etic* and *emic* are not subject to separate treatment, or "first one, then the other," or as "one outside the mind, the other inside it."

The thoughts of Qian Mu also parallel the ideas of F.A. Hayek and his *kosmos* (cosmos) for a grown order, and Kenneth Pike's intertwined *emic* and *emit* perspective. In addressing the problem of alternative political economic theories that may threaten the very fabric of traditional culture, Qian Mu writes, "Today, we seem to take an experimental attitude toward whatever system we happen to know of. We must remember, however, that if we experiment with a theory or a system which has been initiated by a handful of people or has been practiced merely for a short time in other countries, without establishing confidence among the people, the consequences of such experimentation will be very unpredictable. It is impossible to build up a political system without concern for the traditions of a country. For, if we insist that Chinese history be rewritten and the society overhauled, then we will have confused political systems with revolutions, and shouted 'down with the past!' without paying due respect to historical facts. If this were to happen, we would not be changing government or institutions and reforming society but would be tearing to pieces all of Chinese culture."[35]

A persistent problem concerning issues of the rule of law and constitutionalism for modern China is a Sinic uniqueness or particularism that evolves from China's ontological base in tradition. It is a problem further exasperated by institutional dynamics, because Chinese institutions, such as social, political and legal systems (or institutions), or those institutions comprising Marx's problematic superstructure (*Überbau*), are also reflective of a distinctive Chinese ontology. The latter contention, admittedly, is necessarily contingent on an assumption of both the reality of an ontological base in tradition and the reality of traditional jurisprudence. In terms of ascertaining foundational *ethos* for Chinese institutions and constitutionalism, antithetically, a neo-liberal coterie may argue that concepts of legal borrowing and cultural borrowing present contrary arguments to this idea of traditional Confucianism serving as an ontological base for individuals, society, institutions and

[34] Kenneth L. Pike, Language in Relation to a Unified Theory of the Structure of Human Behavior (The Hague: Mouton and Co., 1967). James Lett, Excerpt from Emic/Etic Distinctions, Encyclopedia of Cultural Anthropology (1996), http://faculty.ircc.cc.fl.us/faculty/jlett/Article%20on%20Emics%20and%20Etics.him. Alan S. Kaye, An interview with Kenneth Pike (Wenner-Gren Foundation for Anthropological Research, Dec. 4, 1993).

[35] Qian Mu, Id.

constitutional *ethos*. Assuming a past of cultural borrowing, or mono-directional cultural exchange, such as from the West to Sinic, an argument based on irredentism is plausible. A proposed neo-liberal coterie may also argue that electing legal positivism, as a legal system, is not contingent on societal morals, nor is the choice of a legal theory contingent on moral considerations.

In addition, a neo-liberal coterie could argue that traditional Confucianism is an unfit source of constitutional *ethos* because, from a Western perspective, it is a concept often deemed somewhat aloft and seemingly notional. Wm. Theodore de Bray writes, "In my view Confucianism was a problematical enterprise from its inception, and, as it responded to the challenges of each age, addressing some perhaps but not others, it had both its successes and its failures. Looked at in this way, the 'good and bad points of Confucianism' actually tend to go together. We get nowhere by conceiving of them as fixed points in a static system. They are to be recognized, if at all, as mirroring each other in a convoluted historical process, as constants and continuities in the midst of discontinuities and difficulties."[36] Some may argue, antithetically, that requisite constitutional *ethos* will emanate from policies in economics, or economic liberalism and its liberal economic policies and theories, because Marxism's emphasis on historical materialism coincides with Confucianism's sensitivity to the particular conditions of society, reinforcing the view of rights as contingent. R. P. Peerenboom observed that some scholars who argue for an expansive theory of human rights based on the commonality *(gongtongxing)* of all people reflect the influence of Marxism in maintaining that rights are a product of the particular historical, economic and material conditions of a society.[37]

Nonetheless, notwithstanding issues of separability thesis and historic excesses and abuses of liberalism or neo-liberalism, an inherent problem of liberalism and legal positivism as pertains to a Chinese ontological base in tradition is lack of a meaningful role assigned to political community communal life in such a legal system. Moreover, even in terms of soft positivism, a minimal assignment of a role to political community communal life, still, does not alleviate the inherent problems of legal positivism. The search for a source of constitutional *ethos* for liberal constitutional reforms must necessarily focus on legal positivism as the only viable legal system. For neo-liberal constitutionalists, legal positivism provides a requisite authoritarian state for implementing Western rule of law,[38] while also allowing for efficient mono-directional cultural exchanges, such as from the West to the East (or Sinic) that are more capable of responding to a Confucian ontology. Comparatively, natural law theory and its denial of the separability thesis, which is essential to legal positivism, poses problems for liberalism or neo-liberalism, especially in terms of constitutional *ethos* being reflective of a Confucian ontology. For these reasons, an ontological Confucianism remains a barrier to mono-directional cultural borrowing when in search of Western constitutional values, while, also, providing the only viable source of genuinely indigenous constitutional *ethos* for Chinese constitutionalism.

---

[36] Philip Soper, Choosing a Legal Theory on Moral Grounds, Vol. 4, Issue 1, Social Philosophy and Policy, (1987), 33 – 48. Wm. Theodore de Bray and & Tu Weiming, (eds.), Confucianism and Human Rights, (Columbia UP, 1988), 255, note 10.

[37] Wm. Theodore de Bray, The Trouble with Confucianism, Tanner Lectures on Human Values, May 1998. R. P. Peerenboom, What's Wrong with Chinese Rights-Towards a Theory of Rights with Chinese Characteristics, 6 Harv. Human Rts. J. 29, 52 (1993).

[38] Hart's Concept of Law Lecture 8, 2000, http://users.ox.ac.uk/~lawf0013/Hart%20Lecture%208%202001.htm. Pierre Manet, An Intellectual History of Liberalism (Princeton UP, 1996).

The same conclusion is no less true as pertains to Marxist political economy and Marxist legal theory or socialist jurisprudence that promotes a socialist market economic system, which requires a socialist market economic legal system. A Marxist legal theory and resulting Marxist legal system or socialist market economic legal system, if measured against Western jurisprudence, would compare only to an extreme form of classical legal positivism, and not modern legal positivism. Chinese Marxist legal theory produced a legal system representing a body of rules laid down and enforced by the CCP and its agents of power or authority, such as the NPC, NPCSC, State Council, Supreme People's Court and other agents. In terms of legal positivism, "Most positivists do not deny that law ought to serve moral ends, the ends of justice, but argue that what law is, is a political instrument, a body of rules manifesting the policies of the legitimately constituted political authorities." When comparing Marxist legal theory, and its attendant dictatorship of the proletariat, to legal positivism, the problem will always be the lack of a body of rules laid down and enforced by a sovereign, a legitimately constituted political authority.[39] It is the problems of value pluralism, positive versus negative liberty, first-generation versus second-generation international human rights, and Rousseau's notion of the indestructible General Will and, "each by giving his vote gives his opinion on this question, and the counting of votes yields a declaration of the general will." By reason of modern Marxism, and continuing struggle for legitimacy of one-party CCP rule and its self-chosen rationale principle, and being an illiberal nation-state or perhaps an illiberal democracy, a Chinese Marxist legal system dictates the extremist positivism in the construct of a legal system, which actually evades the discipline of Western legal positivism, especially modern positivism. A Chinese Marxist legal system, consequently, fares worst than legal positivism in the construct of a legal system and when confronting a systemic and persistent ontological base in tradition.

There also remains the persistent problem of the institutional analysis of a Marxian framework or Marxist political economy, or economic determinism, and basic tenet that the economic base (*Struktur*) of society is the fundamental and exclusive causal influence rather than the superstructure (*Überbau*) and its social, political, legal and religious institutions.[40] A Chinese Marxist legal system when confronting a systemtic and persistent traditional culture and traditional jurisprudence measures up to neither natural law theory and its primordial concern of what law "ought to be," nor modern legal positivism and its retrospective concern with what law "ought to be." In the final analysis, a Chinese Marxist legal system produces, though normally associated with classical positivism, the contagion effects of amoral, apolitical and atheoretical proclivities, because it must, by virtue of an institutional analysis within a Marxian framework, deny the validity of traditional culture or "old" culturalism, including traditional jurisprudence, as the Chinese communist have done so since the 1920s.

[39] Karl Marx, Critique of the Gotha Programme (1875), In Marx/Engels Selected Works, Vol. III, 13-30 (Moscow: Progress Pub, 1970). Fareed Zakaria, The Future of Freedom: Illiberal Democracy at Home and Abroad, (Norton, 2003).

[40] Karl Marx, (preface) A Contribution to the Critique of Political Economy (1859).

11.4. Grotius, Rawls and "Overlapping Consensus"

The issues of transplanting liberal constitutionalism, and a conjectured Chinese neo-liberal coterie, resolves to a question of the ability to integrate Western models and taxonomies with Chinese models and taxonomies, including Chinese institutions such as social, political and legal institutions. Practically speaking, it may simply be a question of whether China will become what Boaventura de Santos describes as "the successful globalization of a given localism."[41] In this context, localism pertains to China's ontological base in tradition. The viability of Western liberalism in modern China is also contingent on liberalism divorcing itself from its historic excesses and abuses, which weighs against its successful transplant in modern China, because China's ontological base in tradition stands as a ubiquitous barrier.

Hugo Grotius's original theory of "overlapping moral consensus" is the "moral consensus" he sought in *De Indis* (*On the Indies*, manuscript, 1604-1505 - pub. 1868 as *De Jure Praedae - On the Law of Prize*) and the *Meletius* (manuscript, 1611 - pub. Leiden, 1988), then later in *On the Laws of War and Peace* (*De jure belli ac pacis libri tres*, 1625). It is a "moral consensus" that addresses the conflict between seventeenth century radical pluralism and the liberal idea of a society that is doctrinally diverse yet politically free and stable, by proposing that the key to realizing this idea is a minimal and "overlapping moral consensus," which is independent of sectarian controversy and invulnerable to skeptical doubt.[42] Grotius's original theory of "overlapping moral consensus" and its subsequent interpretations, such as by John Rawls (1921-2002) and his theory of "overlapping consensus," in *Political Liberalism* (1995), and others, potentially enhances the viability of liberalism and economic liberalism as a transplant in modern China, especially addressing China's ontological base in tradition. Hugo Grotius addressed the issue of resolving religious conflict by reducing religion to ethics, and did so, by leaving religious beliefs diverse, and by further seeking to show Christians of different sects that it was possible. For this reason, many deem Grotius as possibly anticipating John Rawls, by introducing the concept of an "overlapping consensus" of diversity in worldviews based on natural law. It was an "overlapping consensus" that allows liberalism to resolve the problem of pluralism, by drawing on a citizenry's deep convictions, while being at the same time widely received. For Grotius, a critical issue was overcoming conceptual barriers, especially theological barriers, which necessitated the difficult task of obtaining supportive theological opinions. It was an issue of adapting or localizing theological barriers to a Grotian liberal consensus. In comparison, the central ideas of John Rawls, in *Political Liberalism*, are the idea of political liberalism (a form of liberalism not grounded in divisive religions) and the idea of overlapping consensus (the idea that people with different religious conceptions can accept the core of the political

---

[41] Boaventura de Santos, Towards a New Common Sense: Law, Science and Politics in Paradigmatic Transition, 262 (1995).

[42] On the Laws of War and Peace (De jure belli ac pacis libri tres, 1625) (Frank W. Kesley, trans.), Vol. 2, The Classics of International Law, ed. James Brown Scott (Oxford, 1925). Hugo Grotius, De Jure Pradae Commentarius: An Unpublished Work of Hugo Grotius (Lawbook Exchange Ltd., 2003). Hugo Grotius, Meletius, Sive De IIS Quae Inter Christianos Conveniunt Epistola, (G.H.M. Posthumus Meyjes, trans.) (Brill Academic Pub, 1997). Timothy Bipin Samuel Shah, A Horror of Discord: Radical Pluralism and the Invention of Liberalism in the Early Writings of Hugo Grotius, APSA Wildavsky Dissertation Award 2003. Martha C. Nussbaum, Frontiers of Justice: Disabiity, Nationality, Species Membership (Belknap Press, 2006). John Rawls, Political Liberalism (Columbia UP, 1995).

conception). In this context, Rawls stressed that political liberalism concerned his conception of justice and the family of liberal conceptions to which his conception also belonged. In particular, for Rawls, an overlapping consensus "consists of all the reasonable opposing religious, philosophical, and moral doctrines likely to persist over generations and to gain a sizable body of adherents in a more or less just constitutional regime, a regime in which the criterion of justice is that political conception itself." The need for an overlapping consensus arises because those with comprehensive moral views must seek a common ground for reaching consensus about principles of justice.

In terms of the liberalism of John Rawls, the successful localization of liberalism, neo-liberalism, liberal constitutionalism or even neo-liberal constitutionalism, in modern China, is necessarily contingent on a social unity and concord that requires agreement on a general and comprehensive religious, philosophical or moral doctrine. Timothy Samuel Shah summarizes the Rawlsian analysis on liberalism's inherent conflict with diversity and uncommon religious beliefs, as viewing containment of religious pluralism and diversity as necessary to its success. In this respect, Rawls is in agreement with both Hugo Grotius and Rousseau, "that certain religious beliefs stand in the way of liberalism and, whether by direct persuasion or gradual attenuation, have to be overcome 'to clear the way for liberal institutions.'" Rawls's example is neither based on political belief, nor antithetical to liberal ideals, because "it hardly follows from one's believing in the doctrine of eternal damnation that one can be expected to molest, harass, or coerce, or in any way fail to cooperate politically with, those one supposes will be damned."[43] For Rawls, there is a fundamental set of psychological and sociological assumptions defining the relationship between religious belief and political behavior, "according to which some religious beliefs are considered congruent with liberal citizenship, others not." The latter fundamental assumptions, inevitably, produce a conflict, crisis or paradox between tradition and "not uncommon religious belief (damnation)," and liberal citizenship. Shah more clearly states his cases as follows, "Rawls believes that the disappearance or attenuation of some religious beliefs was good and even necessary for liberalism." From Shah's viewpoint, Rawls was anticipating Hugo Grotius's theory of "overlapping consensus" as a creative solution to the liberal problem. The abuse of this creative solution, or Rawlsian analysis, is that its success is, ultimately, contingent on constraining diversity and religious pluralism.

Moreover, the issue of transplanting neo-liberal constitutionalism may turn on definitional meanings. Political liberalism supposes that a reasonable comprehensive doctrine will not reject the essentials of a democratic regime. In a world divorced from the existentiality of Chinese citizenry, arguably, China's ontological base in traditional culture will only survive an inevitable conflict with liberalism if it can be contained within the confines of what Rawls deems the democratic essentials, which are burdens of judgment that displace firm religious faith. Issues of blending liberalism and traditional Confucianism, ultimately, resolve to two issues. Does liberalism's center of gravity, as a set of purely political principles and institutions, formulate and justify itself independent of moral, philosophical and religious doctrines? Is traditional Chinese culture, like Grotius's proposed reduction of *Christian* dogmas to those necessary for ethics, amendable to a reduction to Western *ethos*?

[43] Timothy Samuel Shah, Making the Christian World Safe for Liberalism, In Elliott Abrams, (ed.), Democracy: How Direct? Views from the Founding era and Polling era (Altamira Pr; Oct. 2002).

In terms of traditional Confucianism, Hugo Grotius's original theory of "overlapping moral consensus," and its subsequent interpretations, as a creative solution to the liberal problem may need tweaking or adjusting, by employing Western jurisprudence of historical jurisprudence or historical school rather than jurisprudence in modernity. Contrary to jurisprudence in modernity, especially positivism, for Grotius, the state was a composite of individuals, as oppose to an abstract entity with a personality of its own.[44] A problem of jurisprudence in modernity are legal positivists, disciples of the critical legal studies movement, formalists and even Marxists and their legal theories and socialist jurisprudence, who seemingly do not concern themselves with living creations, and are interested only in the forms of legal relations rather than their content, nor "in the germative powers of the development of law."[45]

Eugen Ehrlich, in *Fundamental Principles of the Sociology of Law* (*Grundlegung der Soziologie des Rechts*, 1913), and quoting Georg Beseler (Carl Georg Christoph Beseler, 1809-1888), in *Popular Law and Juristic Law* (*Volksrecht und Juristenrecht*, 1843), observes, "The people in its totality, or in narrower circles, within whose consciousness popular law lives and has its being, he [Beseler] says, has an immediate intuition of it, 'which grasps the essential elements of everyday life contained in the circumstances and relations of everyday life, and, at the same time, knows the norms that regulate them and applies them.'" Beseler, as a liberal nationalist, opposed the Romanists led by Savigny (Friedrich Carl von Savigny, 1779-1861), while Savigny, in *Of the Vocation of Our Age for Legislation and Jurisprudence* (*Vom Beruf unserer Zeit für Gesetzgebung und Rechtswissenschaft*, 1814: new ed., 1892), strongly opposed an immediate codification of German law. In opposition, Beseler was advocating a people's law based on Germanic principles rather than Romanists jurist law, which would have necessitated a codification of German law. Liberal nationalist such as Beseler, though by 1900 there was an abandonment of the attempt to administer law out of Justinian's books in Germany,[46] oppose the Savigny-led Romanists. Liberal nationalists oppose the Romanists primarily because they would search legal history and jurisprudence as far back as the *Code of Justinian* (*Corpus Juris Civilis*, compiled AD 529 to AD 565) and to later students of Roman law and jurisconsults for guidance in interpreting the development and meaning of German law. For instance, on the European continent, Germanists and legal historians such as Otto Gierke (Otto Friedrich von Gierke, 1841-1921), a renown leader of the German school of legal historians, searched for guidance from the *Code of Justinian* and other sources of Roman law for purpose of interpreting the development and meaning of German law, as he did in his classic *German Law of Association* (*Das Deutshe Genossenschaftsrecht*, 1868-1913).[47]

Nonetheless, and demonstrative of the potential of historical jurisprudence or the historical school, even Herr von Savigny, whom also belongs to the historical school or new historical school (German historical school), recognizes that, "The law grows with the people,

---

[44] Charles S. Edwards, Hugo Grotius: The Miracle of Holland 37 (Nelson-Hall, 1981).

[45] Eugen Ehrlich, Fundamental Principles of the Sociology of Law (China Social Sciences Publishing House, Chengcheng Books, Ltd.: The President and Fellows of Harv. College, 1936). Georg Beseler, Popular Law and Juristic Law (Volksrecht und Juristenrecht) (Leipzig, 1843). Dieter Langewiesche, Liberalism in Germany (Princeton UP, 1999).

[46] Federic William Maitland, English Law and the Renaissance, The Rede Lecture for 1901, 30 (China Social Sciences Publishing House, Chengcheng Books, rpt Cambridge UP 1901, 1999).

[47] Otto von Gierke, Das deutsche Genossenschaftsrecht (German Law of Association), 4 volumes (Berlin 1868, 1873, 1881).

develops with it, and finally dies when the people lose its individuality." What these German legal historians, or perhaps jurists of the Continental common law, recognize is the continuity between the past and present or, simply, legal history, such as the achievement manifest in the *Corpus Juris Civilis*. Eugen Ehrlich wrote, "Accordingly an unbroken chain of oral tradition unites the professors of Constantinople with those of Berytus, the compilers of Justinian's code with each one of the *prudentes* of the days of primitive Rome. It is being understood more and clearly from day to day that this juristic science of the Roman jurist was, at all times, connected by an unbroken continuity with everything that had been accomplished in this sphere in antiquity, was always ready to appropriate the institutions of other peoples, and in its palmy days, which extend into the third century of our era, was able to wield these elements into its system as an organic whole." He is talking of a juristic science of the Continental common law that is heir, predominantly, to the *Corpus Juris Civilis*, which is a "never interrupted, international intellectual activity extending over a period of two thousand years or more."

11.5. Liberalism and Historical Jurisprudence

Kurt Vonnegut (1922-2007) wrote, "We are what we pretend to be, so we must be careful about what we pretend to be." For China, the CCP, and its nationalism and ideologism, in the quest for legitimacy announces they are on the path to finalizing the localization of Marxism, which relegates Chinese rationalism, or more accurately, China's ontological base in tradition and culture to minimum importance. Others recognize the potential of China's ontological base in tradition and culture, and press for modern reforms, especially greater political liberalization, which reveals the fragility of the CCP and its Marxist ideologies. For those recognizing the potential of China's ontological base in tradition, historical jurisprudence or the historical school lends to the viability of its potency.

Historical jurisprudence or the historical school emanates from one of Lord Coke's (Sir Edward Coke, 1552-1634) greatest contributions to English jurisprudence, which is an identification of fundamental law or the "unwritten constitution" with the common law. Harold Berman writes, "Thus Coke's answer to the free monarchists' general theory of government and law was -- no theory at all! He did not deny the validity of King James' version of natural law theory, that law is founded on Reason. Nor did he deny the validity of the King's version of what later came to be called legal positivism, that law is founded on Will, the will of the sovereign. He merely shifted the jurisprudential focus from law in general to English law, and more especially the English common law, which he then defined in historical terms. His answer to James was History, which he saw largely in terms of Tradition and Precedent. He could get away with this just because it was not -- at the time -- a theory, and because English monarchists themselves, and above all King James, continually insisted that the English precedents -- which they interpreted quite differently -- should be respected. For they, too, felt the need for an historical basis for the legitimacy of the monarchy."[48] Lord Coke's groundbreaking non-theory evolves into the jurisprudence of historical jurisprudence. In many cases of his time, Lord Coke asserted the supremacy of the

[48] Richard S. Kay, Preconstitutional Rules, vol. 42, no. 1, Ohio State L. J., 187-207 (1981). Kurt Vonnegut, Mother Night (Dial Press, 1999). Berman, Id.

common law courts. Lord Coke's historicism, implicitly, advances a theory that common law, as a body of principles, concepts, rules and procedures, originates in a remote past, which is, in effect, the fundamental law of the English people (the ancient common law) or the unwritten English Constitution, to which other English law is subordinate.

A critical consequence of Lord Coke's historicism is that it, implicitly, relies on history not only as a check against the arbitrary exercise of power, but also as a guide to determining the limits and channels of political and legal authority. During the first decades of the century, King James proposed, and subsequently enforced, a new legal philosophy or jurisprudence setting forth both a theory of law and government. In this respect, one finds the greatest potential of Lord Coke's model of historicism, because he recognizes pre-constitutional rules and pursues a sort of state-centered or domestic meta-constitutionalism. In this context, pre-constitutional rules or perhaps the substance of unwritten constitutions, serve as a normative guide for how constitutions operate. Further, the rules of this normative guide emanate in a gradual Burkean fashion, reflecting a complex of social factors, especially culture.

Edmund Burke (1729-1797), hailed by many as an anti-rationalist and founder of romantic conservatism, after first supporting the American Revolution (1763-1776 or 1763-Treaty of Paris, 1783) and then though contradictorily attacking the French Revolution (1789–1799), gave up his earlier held belief that it is a matter of expediency for a government to have the support of its people, or to consult the convenience of the people.[49] Edmond Burke supported one revolution, the American Revolution, while opposing another revolution, the French Revolution, on the grounds, though seemingly contradictory, that, "in all disputes between them and their rulers, the presumption is at least upon a par in favour of the people." This contradiction resulted in Burke denying to the French Revolution, his unswerving claim concerning the American Revolution, which is the claim of the people to have a voice in settling discontents with rulers. Edmond Burke, in *Reflections on the Revolution in France* (1790), strongly objected to the overthrow of the French Monarchy and the terrors that ensued, which inspired Tom Paine to write *The Rights of Man* (1791). The dramatic change in Burke manifest in his holding, "that governments are evolved by a long process of adjustments between government and people which should not be violently disturbed." In later years, as Burke moved toward a romantic reverence of history, he viewed the past or history as a source of good sense. As Burke moved toward a reverence of history, he also viewed the constitution of England as its finest creation.

A similar reverence for history and the English constitution can be later found in the writings of Joseph de Maistre (M. Le Comte Joseph de Maistre, 1754-1821), whom observed concerning constitutions, governmental principles and their histories, there are pre-constitutional rules that are analogous to a lowercase usage of a constitution or what is more commonly referred to as fundamental governmental principles. During a nineteenth century, when liberalism dominates, Joseph de Maistre, like Lord Coke (or Edmond Coke), was a theorist promoting conservatism or perhaps even anti-rationalism. What distinguished Joseph de Maistre from Lord Coke was Maistre's emphasis on the importance of religious ideas for the philosophy and politics of conservatism. Joseph de Maistre, when discussing the divine origins of constitutions, in *Essay on the Generative Principle of Political Constitutions*

[49] Edmond Burke, Reflections on the Revolution in France (1790) (Penguin, 1982). J. Bronowski & Bruce Mazlish, The Western Intellectual Tradition from Leonardo to Hegel, 415-–29 (Harper & Row, 1975). Tom Paine, The Rights of Man (1791) (Dover Pub, 1999).

(1810), presented four basic propositions: First, "The fundamental principles of political constitutions exist before all written law. Second, "A constitutional law is, and can only be, the development or sanction of an unwritten pre-existing right." Third, "That which is most essential, most intrinsically constitutional, and truly fundamental, is never written, and could not be, without endangering the state." Fourth, "The weakness and fragility of a constitution are actually in direct proportion to the multiplicity of written constitutional articles." In reference to an earlier British constitution, Joseph de Maistre wrote, "Certainly it has not been made a priori. Never have statesmen gathered together and said: Let us create these powers, balance them in such and such a manner, and so on: No one has though this. The Constitution is the work of circumstances, and the number of circumstances is infinite." Maistre, when further demonstrating his emphasis on religious ideas for the philosophy and politics of conservatism, wrote, "To this general rule, *that no constitution can be made or written, à priori*, we know of but one single exception; that is, the legislation of Moses. This alone was cast, so to speak, like a statue, and written out, even to its minutest details, by a wonderful man, who said, Fiat! without his work ever having need of being corrected, improved, or in any way modified, by himself or others."[50]

The notion "*that no constitution can be made or written, à priori*" bears a special relevancy for Lord Coke's historical school and traditional Chinese jurisprudence. A compelling consequence of Lord Coke's historical jurisprudence or the historical school is that the nature of law, the various sources of law and the purposes of law are definable in terms of the historical experience of the English people. Lord Coke's theory of artificial reasoning identifies, in one of its aspects, with the historical development of national tradition and with the tradition of the English common law. For China and its systemic and persistent traditional culture, the consequences are obvious, because Lord Coke's concept of artificial reasoning is applicable to other types of law, such as canon law, Roman law, natural law and divine law. His concept of artificial reasoning is applicable to other sources of law because in such subject the trained expert, who is the person of learning and experience, is better able to understand its inherent reason, logic, sense and purposes. Lord Coke viewed legislation within the historical context of the precedents of English common law and the historical common law statutes of Parliament, such as the Magna Carta of 1215 (Literally, Latin for Great Charter). For Lord Coke, the great "Magna Carta is such a fellow, that he will have no sovereign." Lord Coke was not an antiquarian viewing the past in static terms, rather he perceived English law as based on immemorial custom or tradition. It was the understanding of Coke that law in this large sense or its legal systems (or institutions), generally, possess both a moral character, which is to do legal justice, and a political character manifesting its purpose is to maintain legal order. Most important, Coke also recognized that law possessed a third character, which is a historic character of preserving and developing the legal traditions of the people whose law it is. Lord Coke's emphasis on the historic character of law required a certain particularism, or particularization, since the universal characteristics of legal morality and legal politics will manifest in quite different ways in different countries and cultures with different legal histories.

---

[50] Neil Walker, Flexibility within a Metaconstitutional Frame: Theoretical Reflections on Flexibility and the future of Europe, In G. de Burca & J. Scott (eds), The EU Constitution: From Uniformity to Flexibility (Oxford: Hart, 2000). J. DeMaistre, Essay on the Generative Principles of Political Contributions, in The Works of Joseph de Maister, 147, 152 (J. Lively ed. 1965). M. Le Comte Joseph de Maistre, Essay on the Generative Principle of Political Constitutions 41-42, 93-95, 129-130 (Little & Brown, 1847).

For China, an ontological base in tradition poses an imposing barrier for invocation of a new polity, such a proposed Chinese neo-liberal coterie and the attempt to finalize the localization of Marxism, especially, in terms of altering its quintessential *ethos*, morals, values and culture. Liberalism and Marxism must successfully traverse the journey of assimilation. In antiquity, during the Han Dynasty, the same was true of Buddhism, though it only experienced a partial success. In terms of the post-Qing era and continuing to the present day, it is also true of an earlier and ongoing struggle to Sinicize or localize Marxism. Indeed, both liberalism and Marxism must necessarily merge with traditional Chinese culture, philosophy, thought, native concepts and language. The latter is necessarily so, because, for China and its cultural and historical experiences, and native concepts and languages, rational institutions are government organizations representing the public interest, which are associated with traditional Confucianism. In modern China, social, political and legal institutions share ontological and traditional-cultural foundational values. Perhaps what Michel Foucault (1926-1984) referred to as the history of the present, ontology of the presents, or critical ontology of ourselves. Foucault even says that critique understood in this sense is the critical attitude itself, because, "it has to be conceived as an attitude, an *ethos*, a philosophical life in which the critique of what we are is at one and the same time the historical analysis of the limits that are imposed on us and an experiment with the possibility of going beyond them."[51]

Qian Mu observed that rational institutions, which are governmental organizations representing public interests, are associated with traditional Confucianism.[52] In the Chinese native language, the nomenclature of "institution," unlike in the West, enjoys an intrinsic traditional Confucian value. The Chinese concept, word (or characters) *zhi du* (or *chih-tu*) translates into the English word of institution. In the West, an institution is an "established practice, law, [or] custom, . . . which is a material and persistent element in the life and culture of an organized social group." However, and distinguishing the Chinese conceptualization of the word (or characters) for institution *zhi du*, it is not as broad or value-free as its English counterpart. In this respect, the value-laden word (or characters) *zhi du* refers to an institution, "which is desirable and possesses an intrinsic value." More accurately, it is an intrinsic traditional culture value-laden concept. In comparison, this intrinsic value-laden conceptualization of the Chinese word (or characters) *zhi du* is the English equivalent of a more elevated and value-laden rational institution. Chinese institutions created to serve the public interests possess this morally elevated characteristic. China's tradition base, or traditional culture and traditional Confucian values, predict foundational morals. As a result, institutions, such as the polity reflect traditional Confucian values in a social, political and legal sense. From consideration of personal relationships (*guan xi*), which are private social networks that operate in situations based on private interactions, to the inner workings of China's polity,[53] in modern China, Confucianism is a persistent and systemic vestige of antiquity. For this reason, and other reasons, China's ontological base in traditional culture and its traditional Confucian values predict foundational *ethos*, morals and values,

---

[51] Kwok-ying Lau, Jan Patočka: Critical Consciousness and Non-Euro-Centric Philosopher of the Phenomenological Movement, Research Centre for Phenomenology and Human Sciences (2002), http://www.o-p-o.net/essays/LauArticle.pdf.

[52]. Ch'ien Mu (Qian Mu), Id.

[53]. George Xuezhi Guo, Guanxi in Chinese Politics (2000) (unpublished dissertation, on file with the Univ. of Virginia), http://millercenter.virginia.edu/resources/print/dissertation_chapters/ 2001/guo%20Chapter.pdf.

consequently, institutions in China are reflexive of traditional Confucian values, or China's ontological base in tradition.

In addition, Lord Coke's historicism, or his groundbreaking non-theory, and perceiving English law as based on immemorial custom or tradition has a special relevancy for China. The historicity of traditional Chinese jurisprudence also bears the trademarks of a law based on immemorial custom and tradition. This is not the same as the borrowing or transplantation by the legislature via enactments of new legal propositions or laws, nor rules of ideology espoused by Marxists, Leninists, communists or socialists in modern China. Rather, in terms of the historicity of traditional Chinese jurisprudence, it is a foundational philosophy grounded in antiquity, with a dominant traditional Confucianism and legalism vying for dominance.[54] More important, notwithstanding the force of modern Marxism, in terms of Chinese antiquity, rights theory has historically been a contingent rights theory, and legal rights have historically been contingent on traditional culture. In this respect, traditional Confucianism is representative of the dominant source and force of both written and unwritten pre-existing rights, and perhaps what has been termed pre-constitutional rules or even meta-constitutional rules (or meta-constitutionalism). All of which serve as a normative guide for how constitutions operate. Lord Coke's historicism based on perceiving English law as based on immemorial custom or tradition, mirrors the circumstances of Chinese antiquity and its traditional culture, including its traditional government, traditional political theory and traditional jurisprudence as historic sources of democracy. According to the thesis of Freed Zakaria, historically, rule of law and a liberal market economy precede both liberal democracy and universal suffrage, because rule of law can only be the result of an evolution of legal systems, and not the starting point.

There are also the seemingly innocuous sources of order that are often overlooked. In terms of earlier rules of order, there is the *Changsha Chu Silk Manuscript* (*Chu Silk Manuscript* or *Chu boshu*) that was first excavated in 1942 from a Chu tomb east of Changsha (Hunan Province).[55] In 1973, a further excavation revealed a silk painting that depicts people praying for wind, alongside pottery and wooden tablets coated with powdered gold. It is a *yinyang*, divinatory art book, which is the only pre-Qin text available of a myth in its complete version. One suspects that archaeological studies have yet to discover many wondrous treasures from antiquity that further substantiate the unwritten rules of order. Problematic in Mainland China, as concerns the potential of new archaeological studies or digs, is the on-going debate whether science will trump tourism, such as the 2007 debate over whether to allow the excavation of one the 28 imperial tombs on the outskirts of China's ancient capital of Xian. According to Zhang Wuchang, University of Hong Kong, the potential "cultural enlightenment from excavating the tomb of Qinshi Huang will surpass the pyramids of Egypt," and, "only by excavating will we find value capable of contributing to society. For instance, Long Daxuan, a Chinese scholar, discusses the influence of local unwritten laws on legal practice, during the late nineteenth century, or late Qing. Based on his

---

[54] M. Ulric Killion, Post-WTO China and Independent Judicial Review, Id. David A. Funk, Traditional Chinese Jurisprudence: Justifying Li and Fa, 17 So. U. L. Rev. 1, 44-45 (1990). Zakaria, Id.

[55] Dong Chuping, Creation Myths of the Ancient Chinese People: A New Discovery, Social Sciences in China (Zhongguo shehui kexue) 62 (spring 2003). Science trumping tourism in China's "Valley of Kings," Mar. 14, 2007, AFP. Long Daxuan, On Local Practice of Law in the Late 19th Century, Xiandai faxue (Modern Law Science), no. 3, 2002. Liu Dake, Dispute Resolution in a Traditional Hakka Village, Minzu yanjiu, No. 6 (2003).

examination of an inscription, being "Perpetual Stipulations and Regulations," which is on a stone tablet from a region in Sichuan Province, Long concluded that it is an invalid argument that unwritten laws stood outside the province of China's legal tradition because customs were not cited in official cases. The intrinsic function and normative aspects of the inscription on the stone tablet, which evidences unwritten laws, demonstrates the irrelevancy of the custom not being cited by government, the interaction between national laws (or Qing laws) and custom (or folk laws), and serves to represent that there were, in antiquity, two different legal standards in the same region of Sichuan Province. No doubt, for the legal historian, "Very often the ability to interpret a picture on an ancient vase would be of much great value."[56]

Harold J. Berman writes, "ever since the early formation of discrete modern Western legal systems in the twelfth century, it had been taken for granted that a legal system has an ongoing character, a capacity for growth over generations and centuries. This was a uniquely Western belief: that a body of law, a system of law, contains, and should contain, a built-in mechanism for organic change and that it survives, and should survive, by development, by growth. The law was thought to be not merely ongoing; it had a history; it constituted a tradition." For this reason, China's legal system, both old and new, must look to its own jurisprudential historicity rather than Western jurisprudence, including Marxist legal theory or socialist jurisprudence. Modern China enjoys its own unique historicity and attendant historical accidents, all of which justifies a China, both old and new, shrouded in a particularism reflexive of its traditional Confucian values, *ethos*, morals, native language, thought system and appropriate lexicons. The answer to China's journey to judicial review lies not in the theories of the Enlightenment Thinkers; it lies in the philosophical underpinnings of its own great thinkers, who contribute to creation of a traditional culture where traditional Confucianism is persistent and systemic. An on-going and ageless struggle of competing Chinese philosophical thought persist in modern China, with their influence offering an often neglected dimension to understanding China's legal system. As observed by Eugen Ehrlich, a primary function of the history of law, though a difficult task, as the founders of the historical school pointed out, "must be to show that the legal propositions and the legal institutions are growing out of the life of the people, out of the social and economic constitution as a whole."

In Chinese antiquity, there was a legal system or institution with a built-in mechanism for organic change that survives, and should survive, "by development, by growth." In antiquity, a socio-econo-legal order was based on a socio-econo-culture-natural history of traditional culture. It is the consequence of traditional Chinese jurisprudence addressing traditional Confucian rules of order, Confucian rules of law, and appropriate norms, *ethos* and morals. For socio-econo-legal order in antiquity, appropriate norms, *ethos* and morals imply the Confucian virtue (*de*) or ethics manifesting filial piety (*xiao shun*), which stems from the concept of humanity (*ren*) and the ethical morality in all human relationships or, more accurately, the hierarchical relationships or society. In antiquity, it is an order based on a traditional Confucian value system and its duty to society first precept, which prioritized society first and above the individual by placing first in the continuum of values, the greater concern of benefiting the state and the kingdom, loyalty to the sovereign and devotion to

---

[56] Ehrlich, Id.

country.[57] The latter forces of society guide the development and evolution of China's legal system or institution.

In antiquity, an earlier development and evolution of law, though seemingly innocuous, occurs when man-made laws replace old customs and rites or natural law (or natural moral law). The latter development and evolution of law has a later Western counterpart in the struggles of classical liberalism, the Age of Reason (Age of the Enlightenment thinkers, 1660-1798) and movement of rational thought, which was the demolition of the old, being the state, society and especially revealed religion, being Christianity. The birth of Western liberalism and its rule of law intertwines with the search, mostly by the Enlightenment thinkers, for an alternative form to replace the political authority of Christianity that when undermined had to be replaced. For early Western liberalism, it is theological-political problem of revealed religion dating back to Christian institutions earlier evolving the concept of a separation of powers, in an earlier struggle between the Papacy and secular rule, such as the Holy Roman Empire. A separation of powers concept further evolves to Machiavelli's *Discourses on the First Decade of Titus Livius* (*Discorsi sopra la prima deca di Tito Livio*, 1513–21) and a constitution comprising the prince, nobility, and the power of the people, with these three powers watching and keeping each other in check, and then to Montesquieu's *The Spirit of Law* (*De l'esprit des lois*, 1748) and separation of the powers of government principle. The latter represent the consequence of an original Enlightenment project emphasizing the distinction separating reason from both culture and tradition. Although the latter examples are not exhaustive, they demonstrate a parallel in the earlier development and evolution of legal systems or institutions and perhaps even parallel an earlier development and evolution in humanism.

A need for new models and institutions of government, eventually, necessitated replacing the authority of the Son of Heaven with the authority of the ruler of the state. Consequently, law as a system or institution would appear and evolve as a built-in mechanism for organic change, while no longer being solely confined to enforcing prescriptions of traditional culture or natural moral law and lending itself to enforcing the standards of man-made laws or the state. A positive law evolved, but left in its evolutionary track a clash between positive law and traditional culture, and its attendant norms, *ethos* and morals, and served as a political expedient for imperialism and centralizing government.[58] What earlier occurs in antiquity, by development and by growth, is traditional Confucianism, and its infusion of law with morals by incorporating the principle of *li*, and legalism, as a harbor for positive law (*fa*), vying for dominance. Admittedly, while what earlier evolved in antiquity constituted new legal institutions, especially the written laws, the new legal institutions problematically focused on safeguarding the powers of government rather than individual rights and privileges or individualized civil individuals. During antiquity, the observance of written laws was imperative and the sought after deterrent effect necessitates laws that were severe. However, the severity of positive law in antiquity does not deny the potential of law in antiquity as a legal system or institution, or as a philosophical form in antiquity, constituting

[57] Tu Keguo, On the Paradox of Social Orientation and Individual Orientation in Confucianism and its Influence, Zhexue yanjiu, no. 1 (2005). Wan Junren, Contrasting Confucian Virtue Ethics and MacIntyre's Aristotelian Virtue Theory, 37, Social Sciences in China (Zhongguo shehui kexue) (summer 2003).

[58] J.J. –L. Duyvedak, The Book of Lord Shang, 47-48 (1928) (Éditions Arthur Probsthain, Londres, 1928, Réimpression par Chinese Materials Center, San Francisco, 1974).

an organic system that could experience a further historical growth and evolutionary development.

China in antiquity did have a legal system, and has had a legal system since antiquity. From the earliest collection of law, from the *Criminal Law of Yu* (*Yu Xing*) (Xia, 2205–1806 B.C.), to *Tang's Six Canons* (*Liudian*) (*Tang Chao*, 618–907 A.D.), and a history of following legal precedents, such as the practices of *tingxingshi* in the Qin Dynasty (221 B.C.-206 B.C.), *jueshibi* in the Han Dynasty (206 B.C.-220 A.D.), *xuyiqianju* in the Tang Dynasty (618 A.D.-907 A.D.) and *yilicongshi* in the Song Dynasty (960 A.D.-1297 A.D.), one observes a legal system or institution in antiquity, an early Chinese consciousness about law and society, especially law's place in society and, most important, a legal system with a built-in mechanism for organic change that survives "by development, by growth."[59] However, the economic determinism of the institutional analysis of a Marxian framework or Marxist political economy, and its tenet that the economic base (*Struktur*) of society is the fundamental and exclusive causal influence rather than the superstructure (*Überbau*), and its social, political, legal and religious institutions, must theoretically deny as matter of necessity, "that a body of law, a system of law, contains, and should contain, a built-in mechanism for organic change and that it survives, and should survive, by development, by growth."

Historical jurisprudence as a legal system presents a challenge for a proposed Chinese neo-liberal coterie, and Marxist political economy and its Marxist legal theory or socialist jurisprudence. For China, liberalism or neo-liberalism, and Western jurisprudence in modernity, may not be the exclusive or best means for integrating both a check against the arbitrary exercise of power and providing for a more independent judiciary in modern China. It is also arguable that with or without the advent of liberalism or neo-liberalism in modern China, historical jurisprudence offers a more viable Western jurisprudence rather than jurisprudence in modernity, which will serve as both a check against the arbitrary exercise of power and provide a jurisprudence allowing for a more independent judiciary. Western universalism, and its attendant theories and models, may not be the exclusive means for promoting a constitutional state or a rule of law state based on traditional jurisprudence, as a system of law with a built-in mechanism for organic change and evolution in modern China. However, a Chinese Marxist legal theory, socialist jurisprudence or modern Marxism does exclusively prohibit the growth of traditional jurisprudence as a system of law with a built-in mechanism for organic change.

Moreover, in terms of scrutinizing Chinese constitutional *ethos*, assuming a neo-liberal coterie recognizes a need for constitutional *ethos*, though Marxist legal theory or socialist jurisprudence must necessarily deny the need, one must necessarily be wary of aquarianism or the trap of a discourse perceiving such *ethos* as if they were motionless, static, compartmentalized, and even predictable.[60] Nonetheless, a discourse in constitutional *ethos* cannot ignore the existentiality of a Chinese citizenry, nor can it proceed in a void divorced from the reality of an ontological base in tradition. The latter is a critical problem of Marxist

[59] Zhongguo Zhengzhi Sixiang Shi, Sui Tang Song Yuen Ming Qing Juan (History of Chinese Politics) (Sui, Tang, Song, Ming, Qing Periods) 59 (Liv Zehua ed. 1996). Nanping Liu, "Legal Precedents" with Chinese Characteristics: Published Cases in the Gazette of the Supreme People's Court, 5 J. Chinese L. 107 (1991).

[60] Paul Freire, The Banking Concept of Education, In Henry Giroux and David Purpel, (eds.), The Hidden Curriculum and Moral Education, (McCutcheon Pub, 1983), 283. William L. Koib, Values Determinism and Abstraction 52, In Barrett, Donald M., (ed.), Values in America, (Notre Dame UP, 1961). Jiang Shigong, Introduction: Legal Transplantation in Contemporary China, Social Sciences in China (Zhongguo shehui kexue) (autumn 2004).

legal theory or socialist jurisprudence, especially, its tenet that the economic base of society is the fundamental and exclusive causal influence rather than the superstructure and its social, political, legal and religious institutions. The issue may simply resolve to one of a purposeful choice, which is reflexive of societal *ethos*, morals and values, for China's polity or citizenry, because a *sine qua non* of a successful resolve of these competing institutions is conflict. Choice is the critical basis of values, because value, ultimately, "implies a code or a standard which has some persistence through time, or, more broadly put, which organizes a system of action." The all-important unit or social good of societal value, "conveniently and in accordance with the received usage, places things, acts, ways of behaving, and goals of action on the approval-disapproval continuum." As observed by Michel Foucault, the functioning of verbal notions by necessity of reality remains contingent on the support of a non-verbal system, or even perhaps Joseph de Maistre's notion of unwritten pre-existing rights, because rule of law can only be the result of an evolution of legal systems, and not the starting point.[61]

11.6. Conclusion

When comparing China's modern Marxism to its ontological base in tradition, the irony is complete because traditional culture, and its traditional government, traditional political theory and traditional jurisprudence, demonstrates vestiges of democratic government. It is equally true that traditional culture, and its traditional government, traditional political theory and traditional jurisprudence, presented a measurable model, though not ideal Western model, of a state of legality, a law-based state, a constitutional state or a rule of law state, such as Anglo-American rule of law, German *Rechtsstaat* and French *État de droit*. The legal and political systems or institutions of old China, though many may disagree, represent those models of governance deserving institutional admiration. While a proposed Chinese neo-liberal coterie and its neo-liberal constitutionalists promote the orthodoxy of Western ideal rule of law and constitutional government, one wonders whether they consider or deny traditional culture, and its traditional government, traditional political theory and traditional jurisprudence, as historic sources of democracy.

[61] Zakaria, Id.

Chapter 12

CONCLUSION: COMPLEMENTARITY OF PARADOXES

12.1. FROM LATE QING TO NEW MILLENNIUM

Since the turn of the nineteenth century, China has struggled with the issues of reform (*gaige*). In Chinese antiquity, issues of reform were distinguishable because reform was primarily a struggle with the historic issue of land reforms (*tudi gaige*), though dynastic China struggled with other issues such as the plight of the peasant farmer and land taxation. During the late Qing (*Qing Chao*, 1636-1911), the focus of reform shifts for a brief and critical historical moment, by focusing on modernizing or Westernizing China rather than land reforms, peasant farmers and land taxation, as Chinese leaders pursued a path of modernization focused on imitating Western capitalist models. The issue of how to modernize or Westernize centered on the debate between reformist policy and revolution. Early leaders advocating modernization or Westernization of China, though not agreeing on a model for reform policy, mostly supported reformist policy. These early reformers ascribed the prosperity and power of Western countries to their constitutional governments, especially parliamentary government, as they explored models without monarchs and models retaining monarchs as heads of states. During the 1890s, reformers such as Kang Youwei, Liang Qichao and others advocated a constitutional monarchy. Subsequently, from 1895 to 1911, there were other reformers such as Sun Yatsen, Song Jiaoren and others that would advocate a democratic republic. These reformers took the road to Western-style politics, because of a shared belief that Western governmental models had most nearly achieved the golden mean (or Confucian Doctrine of the Mean and the Common, *Zhongyong*).

It would not be until the fall of the Qing Dynasty or aftermath of the Chinese revolution (1911) that Chinese intellectuals, especially early Chinese communists, would begin to successfully push forward revolution rather than reformist policy as the preferred method of modernization. Karl Marx and Frederick Engels wrote, "All fixed, fast-frozen relations, with their train of ancient and vulnerable prejudices and opinions are swept away, all new-formed ones become antiquated before they can ossify. All that is solid melts into air, all that is holy is profaned."[1] Following Lenin, Leninism and the Bolshevik Revolution or Red October, the

[1] Karl Marx and Frederick Engels, Selected Works, Vols. I-II, (Foreign Languages Publishing House, 1951), Vol. I, 35. Mao Zedong, Selected Works, Foreign Language Press, 1961, Vol. IV, 413.

force of Marxism, Leninism, communism or socialism, grew in influence. For many Chinese intellectuals, or the early Chinese communists, the Bolshevik Revolution answered the question of whether a backward country could seize state power and commence the pursuit of modernization. As Mao Zedong wrote, "The salvoes of the October Revolution [or Bolshevik Revolution] brought us Marxism-Leninism. The October Revolution helped progressives in China, as throughout the world, to adopt the proletarian world outlook as the instrument for studying a nation's destiny and considering anew their own problems." The 1920s and 1930s witnessed the crystallizing event of the May 30th Movement of 1925, the growing strength of the Chinese communists, the 1921 birth of the Chinese Communist Party (CCP, *Zhongguo Gongchandang*) and preference for revolution rather than reformist policy.

The latter would produce consequences that continue in the new millennium, especially the supplantation of traditional culture (primarily traditional Confucianism), and its traditional government, traditional political theory and traditional jurisprudence, by Marxism, Leninism, communism or socialism, or Mao's socialism. In a post-1949 China and now new millennium, the ideologies, policies, goals and actions of the CCP and its one-party rule dictate modern social order. During the late Qing, and then the 1920s and 1930s, and continuing to the present, a systemic and persistent traditional culture from antiquity would manifest a socio-econo-legal order that continues to be challenged, if not supplanted, by Marxist, Leninist, communist or socialist rule and its economic determinism prescribing rules of order. More accurately, in antiquity, it was social, economic and legal orders primarily based on the socio-econo-culture-natural history of traditional Confucianism, or China's ontological base in tradition. In the new millennium, Chinese society still witnesses the struggle and paradoxical interrelationship between traditional culture or "old" culturalism, and Marxism. Since 2003, the debates in academia and government are centered on the issues of traditional culture in modern China, and the road to a new materialism or dialectic materialism and finalizing the Sinicization or localization of Marxism to the realities of traditional culture and society (*Makesi zhuyi he Zhongguo shiji xiang jiehe*).

In the new millennium, a now firmly entrenched CCP and its one-party rule, in practice, continue to prefer revolution to reform policy, a preference that births during the 1920s and 1930s. Despite burgeoning economic growth and World Trade Organization (WTO) membership, modern China is still a reluctant globalist, multilateralist or neo-liberalist. There is a paradoxical interrelationship between Marxism, and economic liberalism (or neo-liberalism) and its liberal economic institutions, policies and normative norms. China's polity, the CCP, is pursuing a socialist-political polity, in conjunction with a capitalist-economic policy. The latter incongruence of a capitalist-socialist dichotomy may be the greatest and most troubling irony of all, for both Marxists and liberals. The irony is also obvious, because, in part, resource endowments and differing developmental levels (foreign capital and technology, and domestic land and labor) in pursuit of export-based growth, continues to drive post-WTO China's burgeoning economic growth. From 1980 to 2004, China's foreign direct investment (FDI) rose from about $1 billion to $560 billion. Economic liberalism and its liberal economic institutions, including liberal economic policies ranging from assistance in poverty reduction, to sustainable development, also continue to explicitly, or implicitly, drive or enhance China's burgeoning economic growth. Notwithstanding tens of billion dollars in liberal economic foreign aid, China also directly enhanced its economic growth by direct participation in the free market, global market or liberal market economy. International trade in a global market is the product of a Western economic model of capitalism, which experienced profound changes beginning in the 1970s, because of information technology, globalization and financial deregulation. The new global market or liberal market economy is a by-product of classical liberalism, which is, generally, characterized as Western notions of individual liberty, limited government and rule of law, and further, embodying Western values, such as profit, free-market, private property and economic initiative. From the 1920s to the new millennium, and from the early Chinese communists, to the CCP, in practice, there is a continuing preference for revolution rather than reformist policy. A preference for revolution is demonstrated by a continuing reluctance to modernize or Westernize by focusing on imitating Western capitalist models or liberal economic models, and counts as an examples, China pursuing export-based growth rather than import-based growth, and a Chinese model of regionalism (or China's new regionalism, *xin quyu zhuyi*) distinguishable from liberal economic models.

Modern China, or perhaps more accurately, the CCP, is a reluctant globalist, multilateralist or neo-liberalist, for other reasons. In terms of international trade and international relations, external, political economy, or macroeconomic forces affect the CCP and its decision making process. Problematic for the CCP are September 11, 2001 or 9/11, and the economics of terrorism that ensured; geopolitical changes in world politics; pro-democracy movements; War in Iraq; North Korea and nuclear proliferation on the Korean peninsula; Iran and nuclear proliferation; United Nations (UN) Security Council Resolution 1701 (Adopted by the Security Council at its 5511th meeting, on 11 August 2006) and resulting August 14, 2006 cease-fire in the Israel-Lebanon conflict or Israeli-Hezbollah (Hizbollah or Party of God) conflict; and other external forces. China perceives these external, political economy or macroeconomic forces as a threat to internal security, whether true or not, which are threats that affect on-going legal and economic reforms, and greater political liberalization. These external forces serve to substantiate that a primary problem of China and its relations with the West, especially the United States, is the "Western threat," and not the "China threat."

In China's political typology, or its political economy or international relations lexicons, the words (or characters) *xin diguo zhuyi* (neo-imperialist) and *xin zhimin zhuyi* (neo-colonist) are frequently employed, while China focuses on a Western-inspired "China threat" and hails its geopolitical posturing as altruistic. While Wen Jiabao announces, "No one can claim China is practicing neo-colonialism in Africa," in September 2006, both the G-7 group of developed countries and U.S. Treasury Department warn China against overloading developing and least-developed African countries, with "high-priced loans" they cannot avoid to pay. In the real world, and not a CCP-inspired harmonious socialist society and world, China's geopolitical posturing or foreign policy strategies are driven by China's growing dependence on overseas resources and energy supplies, especially oil and natural gas, which are also motivations shaping China's military policy. One source reports, "China relies on relations with rogue regimes because its leaders fear that Western dominance over the international economic order and U.S. control of the sea-lanes will endanger its ability to ensure Chinese citizens' new-found prosperity."[2] In practice, the geopolitical posturing and international relations policies and practices of the reluctant globalist, multilateralist or neo-liberalist are hardly altruistic or humanitarian. China's geopolitical posturing and

[2] Who are the "neo-colonialists" in Africa?, Jun. 26, 2006, People's Daily. Michael M. Phillips, G-7 to Warn China over Costly Loans to Poor Countries, Sept. 15, 2006, WSJ.

international relations policies and practices are, simply, targeting the pursuit of natural resources and influence in the world community. As Karl Marx warned, if confined to a region, communism cannot survive. In order for communism to survive and grow in a relatively backward country, it must take the initiative of expanding its communications with an outside world and actively pursue becoming a world-influencing power in the international community.[3] The ideal of a Marxian utopia or perpetual peace, after the process of Sinicization or localization, though pending finalization, evolved to the ideals of a *xiaokang* and harmonious socialist society, and a harmonious socialist world. Moreover, China and its exercise of soft power are serving as a rallying point against the "Western threat," especially a perceived American hegemony, American empire or even *pax-Americana* (or American peace). It is perhaps a historical consequence of China having dealt with an earlier fear of barbarians, fear of *pax Mongolia* (or Mongol peace); fear of Western powers, especially military powers (Sino-British Opium Wars, 1839–1842 and 1856–1860, and Unequal Treaties (*Bu pingdeng Tiaoyue*); fear of foreigners; fear of desinicization; and now fear of *pax Americana.* All of which results in the CCP being a reluctant globalist, multilateralist or neo-liberalist. While Marxist, Leninist, communist or socialist rule has always presented a paradox for traditional culture, it now presents a paradox for a new dialect vision of world order, which is centered on economic liberalism and driven by liberal economic institutions, such as the International Monetary Fund (IMF), World Bank and the WTO. Assuming finalization is pending, China may now be in the process of attempting to adapt, Sincize or localize Western universalism and its attendant legal and economic theories and models, in the pursuit of the goals of building a *xiaokang* society, and harmonious socialist society and world.

12.2. Positivism, Law and Economics

The circumstances of the CCP being a reluctant globalist, multilateralist or neo-liberalist, while attempting to finalize the localization of Marxism, and perhaps even localize Western universalism and its legal and economic theories and models also hinder much-needed legal and economic reforms. Many recognize the need for legal reforms, in order to sustain economic growth and prosperity. The Asian Development Bank, the World Bank, the WTO and other international bodies, including the CCP, recognize this need to establish sound legal mechanisms. The directional growth and development of Chinese rule of law, independent judicial review and constitutionalism, has national, interregional and international implications that affect the growth and prosperity of both China and the world's economy. The problem for Western experts and authority is that Chinese rule of law remains at one remove from a Western ideal rule of law. China's ontological base in tradition, and its traditional government, traditional political theory and traditional jurisprudence, are still subject to the heavy burden of the influence of Marxism, an influence now lending to a seemingly descriptive rule of law model, or even the anti-thesis of Western ideal rule of law. While the CCP is implementing some improvements to the legal system, China's legal system remains one remove from a constitutional state, where the rule of law restrains the exercise of

[3] Wang Qisheng, "Revolution" and "Counter-Revolution": Interaction among the Three Major Political Parties in China in the 1920s, 79-92 Social Sciences in China, (Zhongguo shehui kexue), (winter 2004).

state power or government power, which is characteristic of Anglo-American jurisprudence, German *Rechtsstaat* and French *État de droit*. In the context of an independent judiciary, the Constitution of the People's Republic of China (*Zhonghua renmin gongheguo xianfa*, 1982 Constitution) lacks positive discursive machinery for judicial review. The 1982 Constitution reveals lack of any real semblance of constitutional authority in its judiciary. Its judicial model subscribes to neither centralized (or concentrated) constitutional review, nor decentralized (or diffused) constitutional review. It also fails to subscribe to models for constitutional review or constitutional courts. The newly established constitutional review body of the Office of Filing and Review of Regulations (*Fagui bei'an shencha shi*) established by the NPCSC in May 2004, and other rules and procedures, including modern juridical practices, did not create the much-needed positive discursive machinery for judicial review. The CCP's proposed mechanism for enhancing judicial review fails to provide the requisite transparency (*toumingdu*), independent judicial review (*duli sifa shencha*) and fairness (*gongping*) needed to protect both economic and non-economic liberty interests, including the rights of citizens, such as civil rights and political freedoms (or the first-generation international human rights).

Notwithstanding issues of Chinese jurisprudence, there are also problems associated with modern juridical practices. Marxist, Leninist, communist or socialist rule created a legal environment that fosters distinctions between law in text (*wenben falv*) and law in action (*xingwei falv*), and rules on paper (*zhi mian gui ze*) and practical rules (*shi jian gui ze*). Juridical practices also encouraged distinctions in constitutionalism (*lixian*, *lixian zhi* or *jianli xianfa*, concepts from the late-Qing, literally, building up the constitution), such as the distinctions between constitutionalism in text and constitutionalism in action. More accurately, in terms of constitutionalism, what actually evolved was a state of extra-constitutionalism in action rather than a law-based state or constitutional state, where the rule of law restrains the exercise of state power or governmental power. Recent laws, regulations and law cases demonstrate that a legal environment where law in action routinely prevails over law in text, and extra-constitutionalism in action routinely prevails over constitutionalism in text, are hardly conducive to promoting a legal system or legal environment conducive to developing positive discursive machinery for judicial review. Modern juridical practices and the legal environment are the direct consequence of a continuing effort to finalize the localization of Marxism. The latter problems directly relate to the consequence of Chinese Marxist legal theory or socialist jurisprudence producing a socialist market legal system or socialist market economic legal system.

In terms of Marxism and institution building, including economic and legal institutions, Marx analyzed the economic structure (*Struktur*) of society, as constituting the genuine basis on which legal and political superstructures (*Überbau*) should erect. A Marxist perspective views the basic structure of society as being economic or material, thus, largely determining the rest of social life. Niklas Luhmann described the social teachings of Marx as reacting to an elemental tenet of modern social development, which constitutes a transition of the primacy of social meaning from politics to economics.[4] Marx viewed the primacy of economics, as he related economics to materialism (or materiality of human needs), as "an ahistorical-anthropological truth and formulates a theory of natural-legal, dialectical and societal development within this framework." Consequently, issues of institution building and

[4] Niklas Luhmann, A Sociological Theory of Law (Transl., Elizabeth King & Martin Albrow, 1985).

transplanting or borrowing Western legal and economic norms are, in part, contingent on an institutional analysis within a Marxian framework or a Marxist political economy rather than a Western conceptualization of political economy. The primary concern of a Marxian framework or Marxist political economy is the subject of the relations of production, as it operates through the vehicle of institutional economics serving as a theoretical system in the analysis of society's institutions, including social, political, legal and economic institutions.[5] The greater problem, in terms of Marxist political economy, is an elemental institutional analysis forthcoming from the basis premises that productive forces determine production relations, economic foundation decides superstructures (or society's institutions and ideas), and a core segment that covers the social division of labor. In terms of liberal economic norms and institution building, Marxist political economy is problematic as a force driving institutional research and analysis, and serving as an explanatory system for institutional phenomena.

A Marxian framework, or Marxist political economy, presents critical issues of modern reforms, including legal and economic reforms. A Marxian framework as the explanatory system for institutional phenomena continues in modern China. Marxist political economy challenges Western political economy ideals, especially liberal economic theories and its normative norms. Marxist political economy equally challenges the task of transplanting Western rule of law, in modern China. Given China's modern political community, modern Chinese communists, and not unlike the communists of the 1920s and 1930s, in practice and in action, still, prefer revolution to reformist policy. All of which are the problematic and evolving paradoxical interrelationships, such as the struggle of Marxism against both traditional culture and Western universalism, which effectively render much-needed legal and economic reforms, including greater political liberalization, increasingly more difficult to implement.

When comparing China's modern social order, or Marxist, Leninist, communist or socialist rule, the irony is complete, because traditional culture, and its traditional government, traditional political theory and traditional jurisprudence, evidenced vestiges of democratic government. It is equally true that traditional Chinese culture, and its traditional government, traditional political theory and traditional jurisprudence, presented a measurable model of a state of legality, law-based state, constitutional state or rule of law state. In terms of legal and economic reforms, and greater political liberalization, Western universalism, and its attendant theories and models, may not be the exclusive means for promoting a constitutional state or rule of law state based on traditional jurisprudence, as a system of law with a built-in mechanism for organic change and evolution in modern China. However, a Chinese Marxist legal theory, or Marxist, Leninist, communist or socialist rule does exclusively prohibit the growth and potential of traditional government, traditional political theory and traditional jurisprudence, as a system of law with a built-in mechanism for organic change and evolution.

The problems of a socialist market economic legal system are many. A primary problem of institutional building, transplanting or borrowing legal and economic systems and normative norms, as relates to a socialist market economic legal system, is a resulting contingency on the institutional analysis of a Marxian framework or Marxist political

[5] Li Shenglong, The Overall Structure of the Institutional Analysis Theory of Marxism, Jingjixue dongtai, no. 5 (2003).

economy. Chinese models of transplanting or borrowing legal norms and legal systems suffer a severe constriction as a consequence of a Marxian framework, which serves as a force driving institutional research and analysis, while also serving as the primordial explanatory system for institutional phenomena. For Marxist political economy, the impetus for development always originates in changing productive forces and relations of productions that satisfy material needs. The latter impetus for development is gravely different from Western theories and models for development and transplanting law and economic systems and normative norms, and challenges the effectiveness of Western theories and models, such as evolutionary theory, cultural theory, utilitarian theory, jurisprudence model, modernization theory and, in part, Ugo Mattei's model, and other models and theories. In the context of China, and ongoing legal and economic reforms, including greater political liberalization, Western liberal economic theory and jurisprudence also possess separable and inherent problems challenging their effectiveness and efficiency, as models for development and transplanting law and economic systems, and their respective normative norms.

There are also the problematic and contagion effects of the amoral, apolitical and atheoretical proclivities of positivism, in both Western liberal economic theory and jurisprudence or the science of law. These issues surround the influence of positivism in both Western liberal economics such as man as "he is" or economics as "it is" and Western jurisprudence or law such as what "law is" or law as "it is." In comparison, there is the worst consequence and paradox of Marxian economic determinism of *Überbau* (superstructure) as "*Struktur* is," which stems from the economic base (*Struktur*) defining and confining the historical growth and evolutionary development of societal institutions and other philosophical forms of the superstructure (*Überbau*). More accurately, a Marxian analysis problematically presents law and economics as "*Struktur* is." In terms of China's ontological base in tradition, there is also the continuing problem of the Neo-Confucianists, who give principle priority over all things and do not attempt to discern between natural and moral norms, or between that by which *x* "is *x*" and that by which *x* "ought to be." In the search for optimal models of legal and economic reform, the problem of positivism is the historic denial of both the potentiality and complementarity of what law and economics "ought to say" or "ought to be."

In terms of the history of economics, or perhaps more accurately, the diachrony of positivism, what followed over the years was the growing influence of positivism, an unintended consequence of Alfred Marshall (1842-1925), though not necessarily of William Stanley Jevons (1835-1882). For Alfred Marshall, economics had always served a moral purpose, and there was not a clear line between science and art. Marshall could not have foreseen this by-product of his personal battle to establish economics as a major separable from other majors, especially, the contagion effects of the amoral, apolitical and atheoretical proclivities of positivism, in both Western liberal economic theory and jurisprudence or the science of law, or more specifically, the discipline of normative legal positivism or normative positivist analysis of the concept of law. In this respect, Western liberal economic theory and jurisprudence, or more accurately, legal positivism, present complementary, and not paradoxical, sources of order. A problem of these complementary sources of order is that in the context of China, they, instead, present issues of paradoxical interrelationships between the competing sources of order of traditional culture and Marxism. In terms of traditional culture, though not for Marxism, Western universalism and its liberal economic theory and jurisprudence present a paradoxical interrelationship, mostly attributable to the influence of positivism in both Western liberal economic theory and jurisprudence. Moreover, both Western universalism, and its attendant liberal economic theories and jurisprudence, especially, normative legal positivism, and Marxism and its Marxist political economy, present paradoxical interrelated sources of order challenging China's ontological base in tradition and its traditional government, traditional political theory and traditional jurisprudence. However, Western universalism, and its legal and economic theories and models, and not Marxism and its Marxist political economy constraints, presents a viable alternative of creating a complementary interrelationship between Western universalism and traditional culture. Western universalism, and its attendant theories and model, and not Marxism and its political economy constraints, still present the genuine option of moving East-West relations from tenuous toward optimality.

It is perhaps an issue of a Western evolution to an *emic*, instead of *etic*, understanding of Sinicism, Islamism and other non-Western cultures. An inherent benefit of a non-West centric perspective is the resulting recognition of the forces of politics and culture, especially, cultural exceptionalism. Kenneth Pike's concept of the *emic/emit* perspective will insist, "on the relationship of the observer to the data, as against an abstract science in which the observer is somehow eliminated in principle even when this would be impossible in fact," as in the case of positivism, including normative legal positivism, and positive economics or the positive economic theory of law. Moreover, it is Western universalism, and its attendant theories and models, and not Marxism and its political economy constraints, still presenting the genuine option of moving East-West relations from tenuous toward optimality, or perhaps being capable of taking full advantages of an *emic/emit* perspective. In addition, it is Western universalism, and not Marxism and its Marxist political economy, which will allow the potential union of universality and particularity, the road to resolving the conflicts of the culture relative, the greater humanity for the greater good (*summon bonum*) for a modern Confucian society, the problematic distinctions between positive and negative liberty, and resolving the dilemma of the essentialization of difference and dubious conclusion of a clash of civilizations, and other positive amenities. Conversely, there are the troubling negative amenities of Marxism and Marxist political economy, such as its essentialization of class struggle and revolution, a paradoxical interrelated source of power that has supplanted and denied traditional culture since the late Qing, and Marxist political economy and its basic tenet that the economic base (*Struktur*) of society is the fundamental and exclusive causal influence rather than the superstructure (*Überbau*).

12.3. Culture, Marxism and Liberalism

The harsh criticism of Jiang Qing, a Chinese scholar, and his idea of reviving *Rujia* (literally, Confucian school) as the core of modern Chinese civilization, including political, cultural and religious institutions of society, fails to recognize the force and influence of traditional culture as both written and unwritten rules governing Chinese society. Most important, Jiang advocates that resort to traditional Confucianism and, implicitly, its notions of humanity and potential union of universality and particularity could solve China's present political and social crises, and the essentialization of difference and dubious conclusion of a clash of civilizations, including the problematic distinctions between positive and negative liberty, and other political and social crises. As observed by Hu Shi, "the problem of China, however multifarious and complicated it may seem at first sight is in reality one of cultural conflict and readjustment." However, and as recognized by Jiang Qing and others, traditional culture has always offered a possible solution to the impasse of cultural conflict. Wm. Theodore De Bary, in a discourse concerning Asian values and human rights, controversially argued that while the traditional Confucian sense of the individual differs from the Western libertarian concept of the individual, traditional Confucianism is not incompatible with Western notions of human rights. Rather, traditional Confucianism enhances human rights and, in this respect, Rousseau's version of liberty presents a savior. In terms of China, "what is amiss in the argument is any consideration of the community as a form of infrastructure that might mediate between individuals and the state, and perform the function of a civil society in protecting the interests of either the individual or people in groups (rather than *en masse*)." By analogy, the "consensual, voluntaristic character of the traditional Confucian ritual ideals," resolves the dilemma of positive liberty versus negative liberty. "Liberty becomes something *we* do, not something *I* do." Thus, traditional Confucian values are potentially reconcilable with Western universalism.[6]

What Jiang Qing and others recognize about the force and influence of traditional Confucianism is the hope that it presents for the future, especially Sinic-West relations. Although traditional Confucianism fell into disfavor during the late Qing, traditional culture now offers hope for the union of the particular and universal, resolving the cultural distinctions between positive and negative liberty and, generally, advancing legal reforms, economics reforms and greater political liberalization. It is a hope that the rebirth of traditional Confucian values bolsters in modern China, a rebirth that the CCP sanctions, if not promotes, albeit for non-Confucianism ends. Indeed, the potential union of the universal and particular may result in an evolution of values resembling Western values, and a rebirth of traditional Confucianism that may represent or birth a new Chinese Renaissance (*Xin Zhongguo De Wenyi Fuxing*) or even the third Chinese Renaissance in Chinese history. As previously mentioned, and gravely distinguishing traditional cultural from Marxism, is that there does exist a historical basis for democracy in China, traceable to a history in traditional government and traditional political theory.

In answer to the question, whether traditional culture, like Hugo Grotius's (1538-1645) proposed reduction of *Christian* dogmas to those necessary for ethics,[7] is amenable to a reduction to Western *ethos*, morals, values, Western universalism, or even liberalism or economic liberalism, it may or may not be amenable. In the context of a "may or may not" answer, there lies a distinct possibility. However, it is probability or possibility for Western universalism and its attendant theories and models, and not Marxism and its Marxist political economy. The primary interrelated paradoxical interrelationships are between traditional culture and Western universalism; Western universalism and Marxism; and, most important, traditional culture and Marxism. The latter, being the paradoxical interrelationship between traditional culture and Marxism, offers the slimmest hope, if any, of resolution, and represents a crisis or paradoxical interrelationship that, historically, has been pending without resolution

[6] M. Ulric Killion, China's Amended Constitution: Quest for Liberty and Independent Judicial Review, Wash U. Global Stud. L. Rev., Vol. 4, No. 1, 43 (2005).

[7] Timothy Samuel Shah, Making the Christian World Safe for Liberalism: From Grotius to Rawls, Timothy Samuel Shah, Making the Christian World Safe for Liberalism: From Grotius to Rawls, Vol. 71, Issue 1, 121-139, The Pol. Qtrly (2000).

since the late Qing. The paradox between traditional culture and Marxism was born of revolution and not reformist policy, and it will undoubtedly take the force of a revolution to resolve this paradox, which may be a technological revolution in the new age that will finally resolve the crisis or paradox of one-party CCP rule and its self-chosen rationale principle and ideology. A failure to guarantee voting rights, suffrage, and other civil and political freedoms (or first-generation international human rights) does not present a measurable model of a state of legality, law-based state, constitutional state or rule of law state, such as Anglo-American rule of law, German *Rechtsstaat* and French *État de droit*. The most obvious conflict and constitutional crisis of such a model of government is that it promotes change by revolution rather than a constitutional model providing for peaceful transitions and changes in government. As Montesquieu said, "Election by lot is natural to democracy."

As observed by Fung Yu-lan (or Feng Youlan) (1895-1990), when discussing the way of decrease (or retreat) and the way of increase (or advance), "If there are two such diametrically opposing patterns of life, it is obvious that there must be two ways of life no less opposing for him who may behold this, and in beholding, govern himself accordingly." Several means or forces can effect Western institution building. Most problematic is the force of hard power, or military power or the threat of military power, which has especially presented a problem for the United States. Many describe the "Bush doctrine" as pursuing a *pax-American* global empire built by forcible means, where empire by consent is not an option. The practical or real alternative for Western countries is what Joseph S. Nye, Jr. earlier phrased, or coined, as soft power, during the early 1990s, which is the soft power that he defined as, "the ability to get what you want by attracting and persuading others to adopt your goals." In this respect, Ugo Mettei's model bears direct relevancy because a problem of the methodology of force is that it frustrates rather than enhances the potential of Ugo Mattei's third model for institution building and transplanting law in intended recipient countries, a model that is fully consensual and is presented, "as diffusion by prestige, focusing on a deliberate process of institutional admiration that leads to the reception of law." The latter model is applicable to an institutional admiration that could equally lead to the reception of Western universalism, and its liberal economic theories and models. A genuine alternative to the methodology of force, however, only births from a genuine understanding and tolerance of Sinicism, Islamism and other non-Western cultures. It is only then that a Western world can engage in effective institution building. A model of institution building that bridges the gap between theory and application, by taking into account a broad range of political economy concerns, ranging from socio-economic concerns to theological-political concerns, including the cosmos (*kosmos*) of these non-Western spheres of humankind. Consequently, Western institution building, regardless of methodology employed, presents a grave responsibility for "all" Western cultures and countries seeking to build, rebuild or reform non-Western cultures and societies.

What Ugo Mattei's model stresses is institutional admiration, which presents problems for Marxism and its Marxist political economy, and essentialization of class struggle and revolution. In terms of a model capable of promoting the requisite institutional admiration, it fails in most respects. Marxism and Marxist political economy have, historically, produced a paradoxical interrelated source of order that has challenged, and supplanted, China's ontological base in tradition. In addition, Marxism and its Marxist political economy could never rise to the level of an institution deserving institutional admiration, because of the state of extra-constitutionalism in practice, and the attended suspension of voting rights, suffrage, and other civil and political freedom (or the first-generation international human rights).

Marxism and its Marxist political economy continues to dictate China's modern social-political environment and hardly qualifies for institutional admiration, especially a CCP struggling for legitimacy, continuing one-party CCP rule and other reasons. Rather, historically, and even during the late Qing, Western universalism, and its models and theories, such as a measurable model of a state of legality, law-based state, constitutional state or rule of law state, and its Western liberal economic theories and models, have produced models of developed and industrialized countries deserving institutional admiration. Models of polities based on the orthodoxy of Marxism, modern Marxism, post Marxism and neo-classical Marxism also do not deserve institutional admiration because of a denial of the wisdom of the unorthodoxy of Kautsky's Marxism, which is Karl Kautsky's (1854-1938) earlier contention, in *Social Democracy versus Communism* (*Über Sozialdemokratie und Kommunismus*, 1946), that neither Karl Marx nor Frederick Engels found a democratic republic or democratic parliamentary republic as objectionable.[8] Moreover, even assuming a Marxist-inspired proletariat democracy embracing a democratic republic or democratic parliamentary republic, it only does so in furtherance of the transition from capitalism to communism, because Karl Marx perceived the necessity of a transitional socialist state such as a dictatorship of the proletariat before the emergence of an ideal society or Marxian utopia. It is traditional culture, and its traditional government, traditional political theory and traditional jurisprudence, serving as historic sources of democracy and deserving institutional admiration, and not Marxism. For these reasons, and others, the paradoxical interrelationship between traditional culture and Western universalism and its theories and models offer the only paradoxical interrelationship that may or not be resolved in the future, or even perhaps the only potential complementarity of these paradoxes or paradoxical interrelationships of sources of order.

The greatest folly of both "old" Marxism (orthodox or classical Marxism) and "new" Marxism (modern, neo-classical or localized Marxism) is the role assigned to the many societal institutions comprising the superstructure, and serving as a primary reason why Marxism will never rise to an institution deserving institutional admiration. In terms of the institutional analysis of a Marxian framework or Marxist political economy, critical components of its economic determinism are the economic base (*Struktur*) of society and the superstructure (*Überbau*), with the latter comprising the socio-economic, legal, political and other institutions of the superstructure. For China, and on-going legal and economic reforms, and the paradoxical interrelationships between competing sources of order, the latter presents problematic phenomenon of the economic base being the fundamental and exclusive causal influence in Marx's materialistic conception of history. For Marx, although the superstructure is an important factor, the economic base is the fundamental and exclusive causal influence.[9] Although some will disagree, the orthodoxy of Marxism maintains that the superstructure, such as the socio-economic, legal and political institutions, is without causal influence. As previously mentioned the worst consequence and paradox of Marxian economic determinism stems from the economic base (*Struktur*) defining and confining the historical growth and evolutionary development of societal institutions and other philosophical forms of the superstructure (*Überbau*).

[8] Karl Kautsky, (Ch. 2) Social Democracy versus Communism (David Shub & Joseph Shaplen, trans.) (Rand School Press, 1946) (Shub, David/Shaplen, Joseph, Hrsg. – Verl. der Zwölf, 1948).

[9] Alex Callinicos, The Revolutionary ideas of Karl Marx (Bookmarks, 1983). Karl Marx, (preface), A Contribution to the Critique of Political Economy (1859).

An elemental problem of Marxian analysis is that the economic base gives rise to the superstructure, thereby presenting the phenomenom of the base conditioning the superstructure, once it comes into existence. A problem is that the economic base conditions the superstructure by limiting its development, which includes limiting the development of constitutionalism, rule of law and independent judicial review; socio-economic and political institutions; and other institutions and philosophical forms of the superstructure. An additional problem for those proponents advocating an increasing role of the superstructure as a causal influence rather than superficial influence is that such advocacy, in essence, renders Marx's materialistic conception of history as a problematic doctrinaire, a false prophecy, false history and failing promise of a future Marxian utopia or perpetual peace. The inevitable consequence, which is good or bad, depending on one's political preference such as rightist or leftist, for China, the CCP and its citizenry is that it renders the attempt to finalize the localization of Marxism to the realities of traditional culture and society (*Makesi zhuyi he Zhongguo shiji xiang jiehe*) as meaningless or, simply, the final reduction of Marxism to a nugatory "ism." Indeed, in the end, we come to discover that for modern legal and economic reforms, including the need for greater political liberalization, and the search for optimal models of reform and moving East-West relations from tenuous toward optimality, the greater issue remains the amenability and complementarity of traditional culture to Western culture and not traditional culture to modern Marxism.

INDEX

A

B

C

D

E

F

H

I

J

K

N

O

P

Q

R

S

T

U

V

W

Y

Z